Derso and Kelen
SENATE SUB-COMMITTEE
NYE
FREE SPEECH
FREE PRESS
MOVIES
WHEELER
RACIAL HATRED
FIGHT FOR FREEDOM RELEASE

Derso and Kelen
FIGHT FOR FREEDOM RELEASE
LINDBERGH
NYE
WHEELER
"I CAN EASILY PROVOKE CIVIL WAR"
HITLER

LAMAR UNIVERSITY-BEAUMONT
0 00 01 00985894

The HAWKS of World War II

The University of North Carolina Press
Chapel Hill

The HAWKS of World War II

by Mark Lincoln Chadwin

Manufactured in the United States of America
Library of Congress Catalog Card Number: 68–15746
Printed by Kingsport Press, Inc., Kingsport, Tenn.

Preface

On June 10, 1940, thirty private citizens printed in newspapers throughout the United States a statement which spoke the unspeakable. They asked that their country, without being directly provoked or attacked, declare war on Germany. This book relates why what they said had not been said publicly before. It suggests why these "Hawks" risked public condemnation and personal attack to agitate for intervention. It describes their struggles with the America Firsters, their relationship with the Roosevelt administration, and the changing tactics they employed in their quest for American belligerency. Finally, it shows that these "Hawks" in fact had little direct influence on the decisions which led the United States into war, but that by counter-balancing the outpourings of the isolationist organizations, they helped free the Roosevelt administration to decide foreign policy issues on their merits rather than because of external pressure.

Some definition of terms is required at the outset. The word "interventionists" will generally be used herein to identify those individuals who during 1940 and 1941 advocated either immediate war or actions that they hoped would eventually lead to belligerency. The term "Hawks," or "Warhawks," will be applied only to that specific group of interventionists who participated in the "Summons to Speak Out" and the Century Group in 1940 and the Fight for Freedom Committee in 1941.

This, therefore, is *not* a history of all of the advocates of American belligerency. It is not a study of the interventionists in the Roosevelt administration or the interventionist press. It is rather the story of a particular group of eminent men who were the most persistent and outspoken partisans of interventionism during 1940 and 1941.

Acknowledgments

It is traditional for an author to acknowledge at the outset his indebtedness to a host of individuals and institutions. These are people and organizations "without whom" (in the stylized cliché of countless Acknowledgments) the following pages could not have been completed. In the instance of *The Hawks of World War II*, this cliché very nearly describes the fact. A great part of this story was recorded only in the memory and personal records of the participants, and their cooperation—as well as that of academic advisors, librarians, friends, and colleagues—was, indeed, indispensable. However, even while acknowledging their generous contribution, the author admits that he, and he alone, is responsible for all errors of fact or failures of judgment.

The author must first thank those hardy individuals who read and criticized the manuscript in various stages of development. William E. Leuchtenburg supervised it as a doctoral dissertation at Columbia University, and his wise advice helped the author to structure his study and come to terms with the English language. Also at Columbia, Robert D. Cross, Henry F. Graff, Roger Hilsman, Jr., and Peter Kenen read the manuscript in its entirety and suggested a number of useful improvements. Among the participants in the events of 1940–41 particular recognition must go to Colonel Francis Pickens Miller, F. H. Peter Cusick, and Herbert Agar. Colonel Miller first introduced me to the story of the Century Group and the Fight For Freedom. He read the first half of the text and arranged to have other former Warhawks cooperate with me. Mr. Cusick's careful reading of the manuscript and patient work with me over a period of several weeks led to significant corrections in the second half of the book. Mr. Agar, despite serious illness, read the entire draft and suggested further helpful changes.

Aside from the above, participants who assisted by letting me see their records or by talking or writing to me about their activities in 1940–41 included Dean G. Acheson, William Agar, Joseph Alsop, Mrs. Ulric Bell, Barry Bingham, Anthony A. Bliss, W. L. Clayton, Benjamin V. Cohen, Lewis W. Douglas, Henry P. Van Dusen, Henry W. Hobson, Ernest M. Hopkins, Katherine Gauss Jackson, Henry R. Luce, Helen Hill Miller, Whitney H. Shepardson, Mrs. Robert E. Sherwood, Robert G. Spivack, Admiral Harold R. Stark, Walter Wanger, and Sir John Wheeler-Bennett.

Among institutional sources of material, recognition should be given to the Princeton University Library, which permitted broad discretion in my use of the Fight For Freedom Papers; also to the libraries of Yale, Harvard, and Columbia Universities; to the New York and White Plains, New York Public Libraries; to Dr. Elizabeth B. Drewry and her fine staff at the Franklin D. Roosevelt Library; to David C. Mearns and his helpful associates in the Manuscript Division of the Library of Congress; and to Dr. William M. Franklin and his knowledgeable colleagues in the Historical Office of the Department of State.

I owe a large debt for their patience and helpfulness to the editorial staff of The University of North Carolina Press and to Miss Caroline H. Farquhar, Mrs. Linda M. Bayer, and Mrs. Martin D. Carmody who helped with the typing and preparation of the manuscript.

These acknowledgments would not be complete without the mention of four special people—W. Averell Harriman, for his great inspiration and his generosity in allowing me the time to complete this work; my parents for their encouragement and support; and my wife, Adrienne, for her sympathetic forebearance of my late hours, preoccupation, and ill-temper.

Contents

	Preface	v
	Acknowledgments	vii
I.	The Shattering of a Dream	3
II.	A Summons to Speak Out	32
III.	Who Were the Warhawks?	43
IV.	The Century Group and Destroyer-Bases	74
V.	Election and Readjustment	109
VI.	Delay and Disappointment	132
VII.	Fighting for Freedom: Organizing	159
VIII.	Fighting for Freedom: Tactics	191
IX.	Fighting for Freedom: Issues	232
X.	An End and a Beginning	263
	Appendix	279
	Bibliography	281
	Index	295

The HAWKS of World War II

I. The Shattering of a Dream

In June, 1940, most Americans were shocked and at least a little frightened by recent European news. A three-week-old German offensive across neutral Belgium and Holland had broken Anglo-French lines, forcing British evacuation at Dunkirk and destroying French will to resist. Earlier, Hitler's armies had overrun Austria and the remnants of Czechoslovakia without meeting armed resistance, shared in the destruction of Poland, and conquered Denmark and Norway after brief battles. For the first time since Napoleon, one man was about to dominate all of Europe.[1]

Americans had followed the European war for nine months through their newspapers and radios, and, according to public opinion polls, the overwhelming majority (seventeen out of twenty in March, 1940) favored Britain and France. They wanted the Allies to win and had expected they would. Before Dunkirk, however, most Americans had viewed the war as

1. Hitler did not actually occupy Sweden, Switzerland, Spain, or Portugal, and his domination over Mussolini's Italy was at this time logistic rather than physical.

though part of an audience at an interesting motion picture. They readily identified the "cowboys" and the "Indians," and their emotions were aroused by the events on the screen. But the outcome, they had been sure, would have no important impact upon their own lives and interests.

The events of May, 1940, shattered this complacency about the war. France was about to surrender; the British chances of victory seemed slim. Now a power avowedly hostile to the principles of self-government and national independence stood on the edge of the Atlantic. Only the British with their fleet stood between the New World and Hitler's Europe. Events had suddenly called into question the isolationist conceptions which had dominated American foreign policy since 1919. The belief that America could live free from political involvement in the affairs of the Old World, an enshrined tenet of American foreign policy for the two decades since Versailles, was now challenged.

American isolationism was a plexus of impulses, traditions, and experiences. Oldest of these was the tradition of "continentalism." To its proponents continentalism meant the development of a North American civilization free from entangling commitments to foreign (European) nations. Washington's Farewell Address of 1797 and Monroe's Doctrine of 1823 were the gospel of the continentalists. Taken together, these two documents seemed to instruct the United States to eschew forever political alliances with the Old World powers and to pursue a policy of non-intervention and neutrality on European matters, in exchange for European non-interference in the New World. As the historian Charles Beard wrote, continentalism "was a positive program for choosing peace or war in the interests of our own destiny and security. . . ."[2] Beard and other continentalists emphasized that their policy had never precluded commercial relations with the outside world, but that it drew the line at *political* entanglements. Nor did continentalism itself imply doctrinaire pacifism. Continentalists like William E. Borah and Hiram W. Johnson were willing to fight to the death in defense of the American mainland—but nothing else.

2. Charles A. Beard, *A Foreign Policy for America* (New York, 1940), p. 18.

Despite imperialistic or internationalistic deviations in the late nineteenth century, such as acquisition of a naval base in Samoa, annexation of Hawaii, participation in a series of limited international conventions and conferences, and retention of Spanish-American War conquests, continentalism had been the dominant American policy for the century since the War of 1812. And there was no question that it had served the country well. Young and weak but possessing great potential wealth, America had the advantage of a century of non-involvement in which to expand across the Continent, decide its sectional dispute, develop a massive industrial base, and mold a national culture. It had been only natural for those who remembered that simple age, free from the complexities and responsibilities of world power status, to want to get back to normal after the Great War.

The national experience in that conflict had reinforced the urge. Wilson and other "idealists" had oversold the American people on the concept that the war was a crusade "to make the world safe for democracy" and to establish a world order based on law and national self-determination.[3] They had rarely mentioned America's emergent commercial and geopolitical self-interest in European affairs. The American people, therefore, had been bitterly disillusioned by the Versailles Treaty's numerous departures from announced American peace terms, and their disillusionment had been sustained through the twenties and thirties by the revisionist histories of Keynes, Millis, and Beard, the publication of diplomatic archives, and Senator Gerald P. Nye's investigations of the munitions industry. These revelations seemed to substantiate the theses that America's allies shared the "war guilt" with her enemies and that United States involvement had not been predicated on self-interest or national honor, but had resulted from financial ties between American financiers and arms manufacturers and the Western powers. They portrayed the Allies' attempts at Versailles to insure their own future security and attain the nationalistic goals agreed upon in secret treaties before American intervention as duplicitous and venal.[4]

3. Selig Adler, *The Isolationist Impulse: Its Twentieth Century Reaction* (New York, 1961), p. 38.

4. See John Maynard Keynes, *The Economic Consequences of The Peace* (New York, 1920); Walter Millis, *Road to War: America 1914–1917* (Boston, 1935). Robert E. Osgood, *Ideals and Self-Interest in America's Foreign Relations* (Chicago, 1953), suggests the terms "Idealists" and

Such interpretations correlated with two older themes in American thought—the belief in American moral superiority and the Populist-Western Progressive myth of an Eastern-British financial conspiracy against the best interests of the country.

The conviction that America was morally superior dated back at least to the Massachusetts Bay Colony. Cotton Mather was only one among many colonials who regarded America as the spiritual leader rather than the follower of the mother country. "Behold, ye European churches," he wrote in 1702, "there are golden candlesticks in the midst of this outer darkness; . . . Consider the light which from the midst of this outer darkness is now being darted over into the other side of the Atlantic Ocean." [5]

Authors and political leaders in every age reiterated it. In his biography of Washington written in 1797, Parson Weems extolled the splendors of the New World. "Where shall we look for Washington, the greatest among men, but in *America?*" he asked. The natural wonders of the continent were, he observed, "so far superior to any thing of the kind in other continents, that we may fairly conclude that great men and great deeds are designed for America." [6] And in his first inaugural address, more than a century later, Woodrow Wilson paid homage to American moral superiority. "Nowhere else in the world," he declared, had noble men and women demonstrated in such a high degree the virtues of sympathy, helpfulness and charity. The American system of government, he added, stands as "a model for those who seek to set liberty upon foundations that will endure. . . ." [7]

In fact, this sense of moral superiority was later used by the Wilson administration to explain American intervention in the Great War. The United States, as the best of nations, had the duty to lead all the nations of the world on the road to a just

---

"Realists" to represent the two often-conflicting traditions derived from the ideas of Woodrow Wilson and Alfred T. Mahan.

5. As quoted in Perry Miller (ed.), *The American Puritans: Their Prose and Poetry* (Garden City, N.Y., 1953), pp. 65–66.

6. As quoted in Daniel Boorstin, *The Americans: The National Experience* (New York, 1965), pp. 343–44.

7. As quoted in August Heckscher (ed.), *The Politics of Woodrow Wilson: Selections from His Speeches and Writings* (New York, 1956), p. 189.

peace and to democracy. However, when Americans learned in 1919 that the rest of the world would not follow, they turned inward to themselves much as the Puritans had done when their image of a theocratic society was rejected by Cromwellian England.

Again and again events of the twenties and thirties reaffirmed America's certainty of her moral strength and everyone else's turpitude. It was in this perspective that most Americans saw French occupation of the Ruhr, continuing Anglo-French colonialism, the ex-Allies' default of their American debts, and their capitulation before Fascist outrages from Ethiopia to Sudetenland. If some on this side of the Atlantic were disconcerted by continued Axis successes at the expense of British and French prestige, others saw it as fitting retribution for Anglo-French misbehavior. In the same vein, most Americans viewed the impotence of the League of Nations and the bankruptcy of collective security in the thirties as proofs of America's correctness in rejecting the League rather than as consequences of U.S. irresponsibility or shortsightedness. Nothing had yet happened to challenge the general assumption that European events could not affect America's security.

Certain vestiges of the Populist protest of the 1890's contributed to opposition to a pro-British foreign policy. The Populists had felt themselves, as Richard Hofstadter has written, "the innocent pastoral victims of a conspiracy hatched" in the countinghouses of New York and London. They were convinced that their crusade for soft money ("free silver") was thwarted by Eastern (often Jewish) and English bankers, and that the availability of credit, railroad rates, and commodity prices were also manipulated by the same distant demons. Although Eastern and foreign financial influence over farmers' livelihoods was a valid grievance at the time, even in the 1890's the idea of close-knit conspiracy was a departure from reality in the direction of the mythological.[8] Nevertheless, this theme was carried forward into the twentieth century by Western Progressives like Robert M. LaFollette, Sr., and George W. Norris, who bitterly opposed American entry into the First World War which they thought

8. Richard Hofstadter, *Age of Reform* (New York, 1955), pp. 60–93.

was instigated by bankers and arms merchants. These antiwar Progressives were subjected to much abuse during that conflict and found vindication in the revisionist literature and the isolationist foreign policy of the twenties and thirties.[9] Although some individuals elsewhere subscribed to the Populist myth of conspiracy, it was most persistent in the rural areas which had been the centers of populism—the Midwest, the Great Plains, and the Rocky Mountains, where it reinforced the sense of security from external threat born of unexposed, interior geography.[10] When President Roosevelt began edging the United States government closer to Britain and France in 1939 and 1940, Gerald P. Nye, Burton K. Wheeler, Ernest Lundeen, Henrik Shipstead, and Jacob Thorkelson—the inheritors of the Western Progressive tradition—cried out in Congress that the country was again about to make the mistake of 1917. On farms across the nation's heartland many listened and agreed.[11]

Pacifist elements in American society also opposed any government action which they thought tended to involve the country in the European war. Many pacifists of 1940 had gone to war willingly in 1917 but had lost their illusions about the grandeur of combat in the slaughtering-pits of Chateau-Thierry and the Argonne Forest. Others had been alienated by the vengeful and unconstructive settlement which followed the armistice.

Pacifism was widespread among the Protestant clergy. The logic of these "holy isolationists," historian Donald Meyer has written, "was a fantasy of agony in the will."[12] Most were appalled at the label "isolationist," for their ancient faith instructed them that all men were brothers under God, and the most progressive theological thought—"the social gospel"—taught them to view morality in terms of collective interest and

9. Samuel Lubell, *Revolt of the Moderates* (New York, 1956) describes their behavior as the "politics of revenge."

10. For the relationship of interior geography to isolationism, see Ray A. Billington, "The Origins of Midwestern Isolationism," *Political Science Quarterly*, LX (March, 1945), 44–64.

11. For instance, see *New York Times*, May 8, 1936 for Nye's denunciation of the Navy bill.

12. Donald B. Meyer, *The Protestant Search for Political Realism* (Berkeley, 1961), p. 399.

responsibility. Yet they recoiled from the thought of United States involvement in the world crisis. In the face of an explicit Nazi commitment to world domination, many clergymen continued to believe that "somewhere there was a conference table" at which all outstanding international issues could be resolved amicably.[13]

Typical of the Protestant pacifists was a group of forty-nine clergymen (including Harry Emerson Fosdick, Adam Clayton Powell, Sr., Roland Bainton, and Sidney Lovett) who pledged themselves on May 5, 1940, to "have no part in any war," asserting that "as an instrument of national policy war settles no issues in the moral realm, is futile in the political, wasteful and suicidal in the economic, and in the religious a denial of God and of the life and teaching of His Son." [14]

Perhaps the most outspoken pacifists in 1940—as in 1968—were college students. They were disillusioned with war's ability to solve problems and preferred to place their faith in man's powers of reason and compromise. They knew that they would man the trenches if America again went to war, and thousands signed the "Oxford pledge" of non-resistance. After the Nazi conquest of Scandinavia in April, 1940, when the government accelerated defense preparations, pacifist demonstrations were held on campuses across the nation. At the University of Chicago marchers carried white crosses symbolic of "Flanders' fields"; at the University of Missouri students displayed signs reading "The Yanks are NOT Coming." In New York City, ten thousand young people demonstrated, and the Columbia University Peace Committee claimed that four-fifths of the student body opposed aid to belligerents by armed force and half were against increases in the United States armed forces.[15]

Several major ethnic groups—Americans of German, Irish, Italian, and Scandinavian descent—also were devoted to a policy of strict neutrality. During the Great War, German-Americans had been singled out for chauvinistic persecution. The German

13. Some, like A. J. Muste, predicted another war would be necessary *after* the one against the Nazis—to prevent the "Sovietizing" of Europe, Asia, and Africa, *ibid.*, p. 314.

14. *New York Times*, May 6, 1940.

15. *Ibid.*, April 20, 1940.

language, German composers and musicians—even German foods—had been proscribed. Afterwards, like the antiwar Progressives, German-Americans felt absolved by the general revulsion from the war. As Samuel Lubell has suggested, German-Americans found in isolationism a reassuring way to assert their Americanism. Their reluctance to fight in 1917, they expected, would be forgotten as they passionately embraced a foreign policy which was at once the majority view and a justification of their earlier position. They feared that another American war against Germany would revive the excesses of 1916–19, once again impeding their efforts to become fully accepted as Americans. As Theodore Hoffman, chairman of the anti-Nazi Steuben Society, said: "Americans of Germanic extraction do not want Communism, Nazism or Fascism and they do not want British imperialism. They want Americanism." Seven hundred thousand strong in the Chicago area, German-Americans were a key factor in making that city the focus of midwestern isolationism. In the 1940 election, they would register their disapproval of the administration's anti-German policy by deserting the Democratic party en masse.[16]

First- and second-generation Americans of German descent, many of whom were proudly aware of their ethnic heritage, were exposed throughout the thirties to the propaganda of self-appointed disseminators of the Nazi line, such as Fritz Kuhn and his *Amerika-Deutsche Volksbund.* The Bundists attempted to convince German-born Americans that they were racially superior to the polyglot Americans and that their first loyalty was to the Fatherland. They sought, generally successfully, to gain control of established German-American organizations, especially in New York City. They established Bund camps as centers for training in the military arts and in Nazi thought, drilled on the streets of Manhattan's Yorkville section, and attacked Jewish passengers on New York subways. Propaganda agencies like the German Library of Information, the Fichte-bund, and Flanders-Hall Publishers—some of which were supported by German government funds—disseminated Nazi propaganda and the writ-

16. William G. Leuchtenburg, *The Perils of Prosperity: 1914–1932* (Chicago, 1958), p. 44; Lubell, *Revolt of the Moderates,* p. 69; Louis L. Gerson, *The Hyphenate in American Politics and Diplomacy* (Lawrence, Kansas, 1964), p. 114; Lubell, *Revolt of the Moderates,* p. 80.

ings of leading American isolationists among Americans of German background. Even with these efforts Kuhn himself never claimed more than 230,000 adherents among the estimated 12,000,000 German-Americans. Yet despite this creditable resistance to Nazi propaganda, most Americans of German descent feared and resisted American involvement in another war against their homeland.[17]

In 1940 many Irish-Americans resisted the growing alignment of the United States beside Great Britain in the struggle against Germany. Approximately fifteen million strong and concentrated in the urban Northeast, they were motivated by a heritage of hatred for the British. For centuries the British had subjugated their homeland and persecuted their religion, and Erin's bitter struggle for independence was still fresh in Irish-American minds. Most disliked Hitler and his strictures on Catholic worship, but they relished England's tribulations as fitting retribution.

When Roosevelt leaned increasingly toward the British in the late 1930's, many Irish Catholics—heretofore a bulwark of Democratic strength—found such movements as Father Charles Coughlin's "Christian Front" more appealing than continued allegiance to the Democrats. Coughlin, in his radio speeches and his weekly, *Social Justice,* insisted that the evils of capitalism and the decay of democracy necessitated a change in the system. He advocated "the Corporate State" as the solution to America's domestic problems and bitterly denounced the "anti-Christian conspiracy" of Jews, Communists, Roosevelt, and the British which was about to entangle America in the war. His anti-Semitic allusions played on the religious distrust and economic rivalry which had long existed between urban Irish and Jew, as well as the conspiratorial legend of the Populists.[18] His Christian Front

17. Evelyn Knobloch, "The Nazi Bund Movement in Metropolitan New York" (Unpublished Master's Essay, Department of History, Columbia University, 1961), p. 65; John Roy Carlson, *Undercover: My Four Years in the Nazi Underground of America* (New York, 1943), pp. 108–31; Wayne S. Cole, *America First: The Battle Against Intervention, 1940–1941* (Madison, Wisconsin, 1953), pp. 118, 122–23.

18. See John Higham, "Antisemitism in the Gilded Age: A Reinterpretation," *Mississippi Valley Historical Review,* XXXXIII (March, 1957); Rudolf Ganz, *Jew and Irish: Historical Group Relations and Immigration* (New York, 1966).

boasted a membership of 300,000, *Social Justice* a circulation of one million.[19]

Although the majority of Irish-Americans rejected the extremism of Coughlin, nearly all agreed with Massachusetts Senator David I. Walsh and Ambassador Joseph P. Kennedy that America had no business "pulling England's chestnuts out of the fire." [20] They remained opposed to United States intervention in the war up to Pearl Harbor.

Italian-Americans also contributed to isolationist and anti-war strength.[21] Italian-American motivation was much like that of German-Americans—they disliked the idea of going to war against their homeland and feared the domestic antagonisms which such a war would arouse. Since Italians were latecomers to America, by 1940 they were not fully articulate politically. Also, they were generally even less attracted to fascism than German-Americans were to nazism. Therefore, they were a vigorous force for isolation only when aroused by what they considered to be defamation of their national character. Roosevelt's allusion to "a stab in the back" when Mussolini invaded France, for instance, drew a host of protests from the Italian-language press and Italian-American leaders. Generally, however, Italian-American opposition to aid to Britain in 1940 and semi-belligerency in 1941 was neither as widespread, intense, nor articulate as that of the German and Irish minorities.[22]

Citizens of Scandinavian descent—many living in the Midwest and rural Pacific Northwest—were the other significant ethnic component of the isolationist coalition of 1940. Influenced by a pacifistic clergy and the tradition of neutralism they had

19. Charles J. Tull, *Father Coughlin and the New Deal* (Syracuse, 1965), pp. 187, 239–47; Lubell, *Revolt of the Moderates*, p. 80; *New York Times*, April 2, 1940.

20. Richard Whalen, *The Founding Father* (New York, 1965), p. 234.

21. Paul P. Diggins, "The Italo-American Anti-Fascist Opposition," *Journal of American History*, LIV (December, 1967), 579, demonstrates both the bravery and the weakness of Italian-American anti-fascism in the prewar period.

22. In 1941 there was relatively heavy Italian-American representation in Fight For Freedom labor activities, but relatively few Germans were involved in FFF work; Adler *The Isolationist Impulse*, p. 266; Gerson, *The Hyphenate in American Politics*, pp. 124–27.

brought with them from Europe, they opposed involvement in foreign disputes. After the Nazi invasions of Denmark and Norway, some Scandinavian-Americans veered away from total non-involvement in favor of policies which they hoped would not involve the United States in war but might lead to liberation of their homelands. Many others, however, remained steadfastly opposed to any increased United Stated commitments abroad.[23]

Some Americans opposed cooperation in the struggle against nazism, not because they believed the United States could be insulated from foreign dangers but because they saw communism as the greater peril. Some Roman Catholic clergy and some businessmen held this view.[24] Since the 1920's the church had taught that "Godless Communism" was Christianity's greatest enemy, with whom co-existence was impossible. Stalin's brutal suppression of Christian worship substantiated this view. On the other hand, the church had been able to achieve at least temporary accommodation with Mussolini and Hitler through the Lateran Accords and the Concordat of 1933. It had found in Spanish fascism a champion against the secularization of that traditional Catholic stronghold. Thus, many American churchmen argued that nazism and fascism, although themselves objectionable, served the useful purpose of protecting not only catholicism but the liberal West from the Red Menace.

Similarly, some businessmen considered Hitler and Mussolini as the inadvertent guardians of free enterprise in the West. They pointed to Italian "corporatism" and the apparent cooperation between German big business and Hitler in reassuring each other that the interests of private industry were secure under these regimes. A few, impressed by Nazi industrial efficiency and economic reconstruction and depressed by American economic problems and Roosevelt's attitude toward business, saw in nazism "the wave of the future" for the whole world. They advo-

23. See, for example, the results of Gallup poll in those states with the highest proportion of Scandinavian-Americans which showed that 95 per cent thought the German attack on Denmark and Sweden unjustified, but 95 per cent also opposed U.S. intervention, *New York Times,* April 28, 1940.

24. The heavy representation of Irish-Americans in the church hierarchy reinforced this tendency.

cated making peace with, or openly embracing, the Fascist revolution.

Most businessmen, however, were either captives of the prevailing isolationism or favored peace for commercial reasons. Although some regarded the accelerating defense mobilization as an opportunity to turn a new profit, most knew that involvement in the war would disrupt or distort their markets, sources of raw materials and labor. Already generally antagonistic to some of the regulatory measures of the New Deal, they feared that "that man in the White House" would institute rigid wartime controls over industry which would in time become permanent.[25]

Political fringe groups on the far left and right exploited isolationism for their own purposes. On the left, members of the American Communist party, followed the dictates of Soviet foreign policy, which found accommodation with nazism expedient in 1940. They declared that a conspiracy between Franklin Roosevelt and "economic royalists of Wall Street" was threatening to take the United States into war on the Allies' side. Before August, 1939, Earl Browder and his comrades had denounced Germany, France, and Britain equally as "imperialist aggressors." Their sudden discovery of Nazi virtue after the signing of the Molotov-Ribbentrop Pact discredited them in the eyes of all but the most gullible fellow travelers.[26]

On the right the Bundists and the Christian Fronters were accompanied by a host of organizations which claimed to be patriotic, anti-Communist, and Christian, and all of which spewed forth racial or religious hate literature. Most were convinced that an interventionist conspiracy existed between Roosevelt, the Communists, and the Jews; and some planned to do something about it. Witnesses before the House Un-American Activities Committee testified that the super-nationalistic pro-Nazi "Silver Shirts" of William Dudley Pelley had been formulating plans since 1934 for a march on Washington to take over the country. "The time has come," Pelley was quoted as saying, "for an American Hitler and a pogrom." Joe McWilliams, who advocated a "revolution against the Jew first, then against Democ-

25. Roland N. Stromberg, "American Business and the Approach of War," *Journal of Economic History,* XIII (1953), pp. 58–78.
26. *New York Times,* June 20, 1940 and May 4, 1940.

racy, then against the Republican and Democratic Parties," led the "Christian Mobilizers." He called for "men to fight for America's destiny and link it with the destiny of Adolf Hitler, the greatest philosopher since the time of Christ." Other organizations advocating or sympathizing with nazism included the Iron Guard, the Ku Klux Klan, the American Crusaders, the American National-Socialist party, the Gray Shirts, the Committee of One Million, American Women Against Communism, and the Boston Sentinels.[27]

In the light of these domestic dissidences, the recent economic tribulations, and (what his political opponents saw as) Roosevelt's propensities for dictatorship, some American leaders opposed American involvement in the war because they doubted the ability of democratic institutions to withstand an extended wartime crisis. As publisher Frank Gannett told the Young Republicans of New York: "If we do get in, everything is gone. We would have a dictatorship more complete than in Italy or Germany or Russia. We would go down to ruin with the rest." [28] Or as Senator Josiah W. Bailey wrote his internationalist friend William Allen White, some Americans were making a comparison between the effectiveness of totalitarianism and democracy. Some were beginning to think that the American system of liberty needed to be further restrained in order to be preserved. If Hitler, Mussolini, and Stalin were able to provide their nations with greater well-being than ours, might America not be tempted to surrender her liberties in her desire for security? "How often lately," Bailey added, "have I heard men say, 'Well, after all, we cannot eat the Constitution.'" [29] Many agreed with Bailey that even with half the world at war, America could and must remain apart, preserving the republican form of government and teaching the rest of the world by her example.

Thus, many strands went into the cord which bound the American public to a non-belligerent attitude in the spring of 1940. The continentalist tradition, the persistence of the conspiracy legend, the pacifist movement, the self-interest of several

27. *Ibid.*, April 3, 1940; Carlson, *Undercover*, pp. 77, 93–96, 151.
28. *New York Times*, April 7, 1940.
29. Bailey to White, July 9, 1940, William Allen White Papers, Library of Congress.

large ethnic minorities, Catholic and business anti-communism, and the propaganda of extremists of the left and right all interacted to resist American commitment to the Anglo-French Allies. Later, in the autumn of 1940 this coalition would find its foremost outlet in the American First Committee.[30]

* * * * * *

The isolationists were opposed by an articulate and organized minority known as internationalists, who long had favored increased United States participation in world affairs and who believed the nation had an interest in the European war. The internationalists' interpretation of history was different from that of the isolationists. They interpreted continentalism not as a rigid, permanent doctrine, but as a pragmatic and changeable expedient which the "founding fathers" had found useful. As internationalist historian Samuel Flagg Bemis wrote in a scholarly article on the meaning of Washington's Farewell Address: "What we have generally construed as a policy of "isolation" we ought really to interpret as a policy of vigilant defense and maintenance of sovereign national independence against foreign meddling in our own most intimate domestic concerns." [31]

Woodrow Wilson was the hero of most internationalists. They viewed America's refusal to join the League of Nations as an evasion of international responsibility and a contributory cause of the current war. In the years after Senatorial rejection of the Treaty, they worked through a number of organizations to educate the American public in Wilsonian internationalism. In 1922 a bipartisan group in New York City founded the League of Nations Non-Partisan Association, the avowed purpose of which was American entry into the League. After failing to convince either political party to put pro-League planks in their 1924 platform, the Association concentrated on securing American membership in the World Court. Its intention was to use Court membership as a steppingstone to League participation. Despite endorsement by Presidents Harding, Coolidge, and Roosevelt,

30. See Chapter V.

31. Samuel Flagg Bemis, "Washington's Farewell Address: A Foreign Policy of Independence," *American Historical Review,* XXXIX (January, 1934), p. 250.

the Court effort failed, and in the late thirties the Association, under the direction of Clark Eichelberger, remained but a vestige of American interest in world organization.[32]

The Council on Foreign Relations, founded in 1921 by a group of New York businessmen, attorneys, and academic and government experts on diplomacy, also helped to sustain the internationalist impulse. Publishing the periodical *Foreign Affairs* as a forum for domestic and foreign leaders on foreign policy and sponsoring study meetings for influential businessmen and foreign affairs professionals, it worked to convert the leadership elite to internationalism. At the same time, the Foreign Policy Association, also with headquarters in New York City, sought to acquaint the public with facts about international economics and politics by means of local study programs and a weekly newsletter to newspaper editors. Other Wilsonians commemorated their hero's ideas through the Bok Peace Award of 1924, a national contest designed to produce a workable peace plan (which later became the American Peace Foundation); the Carnegie Endowment, which underwrote expert studies of the amicable settlement of international problems; and the Woodrow Wilson Foundation (founded by Franklin Roosevelt), which promoted a series of essay contests eulogizing Wilsonian ideals.[33]

During the twenties and thirties these organizations advocated American participation in the League and the World Court, international disarmament, and the peaceful settlement of disputes. They supported economic sanctions against aggression in Manchuria and Ethiopia, advocated cooperation with Britain and France to resist Germany, and opposed the Neutrality Acts as unrealistic and futile. They urged their fellow countrymen to reaffirm the Wilsonian belief that rule of law, principles of democratic self-government, and American conceptions of fair play and morality were universally applicable.[34]

32. Robert A. Divine, *The Reluctant Belligerent: American Entry in World War II* (New York, 1965), p. 11; Adler, *The Isolationist Impulse*, p. 184.

33. Divine, *The Reluctant Belligerant*, pp. 10–12; Adler, *The Isolationist Impulse*, pp. 121–22, 174–200; Foreign Policy Association, *Ten Years of the Foreign Policy Association, 1918–1928* (New York, 1928).

34. Adler, *The Isolationist Impulse*, p. 184.

Many inheritors of an American tradition of imperialistic *realpolitik* also believed the United States had a stake in the current conflict. American imperialism stretched back to at least 1812, but it was in 1890 that Admiral Alfred Thayer Mahan, a naval theorist, supplied a cogent rationale for American expansion overseas. Mahan argued that in the emerging modern world, successful defense of the homeland depended on far-flung possessions which could serve as bases for modern naval power. Among those he influenced were Frank Knox, Grenville Clark, Theodore Roosevelt, and the latter's young cousin Franklin Roosevelt.

Mahan's disciples saw the relations between states largely as a matter of power rather than morality. They were aware that a global community of interest had, in fact, existed between the United States and Great Britain since 1898. They knew that Britain, in order to concentrate on growing problems in Europe and Africa and reinforce her colonial interests in the Far East, had acquiesced in or encouraged the United States to acquire parts of the Spanish Empire, construct the Panama Canal, and enunciate the Open Door policy.[35]

Apart from their moral repugnance to Prussian militarism or nazism, these "realists" believed that control of continental Europe by any one power was contrary to America's national interest. Mahan had shown them that the British fleet had long served as America's Atlantic defender, and they felt that if their fellow citizens understood this they would recognize that British defeat in 1940—as in 1917—would be a national disaster. They understood that in 1940 America had only a one-ocean Navy—in the Pacific, and they knew that technological advances in aerial bombardment and naval and amphibious warfare were making any unprotected expanse of ocean more a highway for attack than a barrier.[36]

35. See A. E. Campbell, *Great Britain and the United States, 1895–1903* (London, 1960), Chaps. III–VII; and Lionel M. Gelber, *The Rise of Anglo-American Friendship: A Study in World Politics, 1889—1906* (London, 1938).

36. Alfred Thayer Mahan, *The Interest of America in Seapower, Present and Future* (Boston, 1897); Knox's editorials in the *Chicago Daily News* through May, 1940; Franklin Roosevelt's message to Congress explaining the destroyer-bases agreement, *New York Times*, September 4, 1940.

Contrary to the disarmament impulse of the more idealistic Wilsonians (many of whom shared the pacifistic idea that the existence of weapons was the cause of wars), most of these realists advocated maintenance of military strength. Under Clark's direction the Military Training Camps Association, a continuation of the preparedness movement of 1916, advocated military training and sponsored annual training camps for its members. Their yearly sojourns at a camping ground near Plattsburg, New York, caused their organization to be dubbed the "Plattsburg movement." Strongly committed to American interdependence with Great Britain, Clark and other "Plattsburgers" sought in June, 1940, to convince the Administration of the need to institute a peacetime draft and send material aid to the stricken Allies.[37]

Willingness to risk participating in the war, like isolationist insistence on neutrality, was often a question of ethnic predilections. Americans of Anglo-Saxon descent and those who emphasized America's British antecedents, feared Britain's downfall.[38] Like the Germans with their Steuben Society or the Italians with their Mazzini Society, Anglo-Saxons and Anglophiles had their own "ethnic" organizations, such as the English-Speaking Union, which since 1918 had celebrated the superior orderliness, lawfulness, and accomplishments of the United States and the British Commonwealth. In 1940 some visionary Anglophiles

37. William L. Langer and S. Everett Gleason, *The Challenge to Isolation* (New York, 1952), pp. 507–8.

38. Anglo-Saxons had been less sensitive than other groups about their ethnic antecedents until the last quarter of the nineteenth century. Then, the increasing presence of imperfectly assimilated (*i.e.*, Anglo-Saxonized) and sometimes radical immigrants from eastern and southern Europe caused many Anglo-Saxons to fear that the cherished virtues of American society and government were in danger of being corrupted by alien influences. Such sentiments were stimulated in part by the writings of Richmond Mayo-Smith and Francis Amasa Walker on population statistics and Madison Grant on the racial superiority of the "Nordic" Anglo-Saxons. These fears were major influences on the growth of the exclusive residential community and private club and the passage of legislation restricting immigration from "undesirable" regions. See Richmond Mayo-Smith, *Emigration and Immigration: A Study in Social Science* (New York, 1904); Francis A. Walker, "Immigration and Degradation," *Forum*, XI (1891); Madison Grant, *The Passing of the Great Race* (New York, 1916); Barbara Solomon, *Ancestors and Immigrants: A Changing New England Tradition* (Cambridge, Mass., 1956), Ch. IV; and John Higham, *Strangers in the Land* (New Brunswick, N.J., 1955).

embraced Clarence Streit's "Union Now" movement. Streit suggested that the English-speaking nations, because of their common legal and cultural heritage, must stand together against the Fascist revolution. He and his followers urged that the United States offer to join with Great Britain as the nucleus of a federal union of fifteen democracies.[39]

Personal identification with England was strongest in the Northeast and Southeast where Anglo-Saxons were most numerous. These were sections whose closest commercial ties were to Britain and whose security rested largely on the benevolence of the Royal Navy. There, too, the social, cultural, and political "establishment" was predominantly Anglo-Saxon in genealogy. England's special relationship to America strategically and historically helped to obscure the fact that Anglo-Saxon Americans' identification with Britain's fate was often as subjective as Irish-Americans' emotional ties to the Emerald Isle or German-Americans' concern for the Fatherland.

Many Americans of Jewish faith also advocated increased assistance to those fighting Hitler. Since their brethren on the Continent were targets of the Nazis' most extreme form of persecution—not merely occasional and "spontaneous" outbursts of anti-Semitism but revilement and decimation as national policy—Jewish-American commitment to the Allies' cause was, understandably, almost complete. The largest community of Jews was in the New York metropolitan area, and their ethnic allegiance (along with the concentration of internationalist organizations in Manhattan) helped make that city the center of pro-Allied sentiment, just as German-American reactions contributed importantly to Chicago's isolationism.[40]

In the spring of 1940 the greater body of internationalists, although privately favoring varying degrees of support for the Allies, spent their energies in providing relief for the victims of totalitarianism in a variety of organizations. A few, such as Eichelberger and Columbia University historian James Shotwell, felt that organization for more positive objectives was necessary. Shortly after the war had begun (at the behest of the President)

39. Clarence K. Streit, *On Freedom and Union Now* (New York, 1940).

40. Gerson, *The Hyphenate in American Politics*, pp. 109–19.

they had asked William Allen White, renowed editor of the Emporia *Gazette* and the symbol of the homespun values of mid-America, to lead an organization dedicated to revision of the Neutrality Act.[41]

By the end of October, 1939, this Nonpartisan Committee for Peace Through Revision of the Neutrality Law had at least skeletal structure in thirty states and the support of such national figures as Henry L. Stimson and Al Smith. With the passage of the "cash-and-carry" amendments in November, the Committee disbanded, but interested participants maintained communications by means of the "Commission to Study the Organization of Peace." For several months this private group discussed the reasons for the failure of the Versailles Treaty and general questions of pacific settlement and international social and economic justice.[42]

The "phony war" provided those who wanted more vigorous action with few crises with which to dramatize America's involvement with events beyond her shores. They could only point to the falsity of Nazi and isolationism claims that Hitler had no designs on the Western hemisphere, quoting back-page news stories about Nazi subversion in Argentina, Uruguay, and Mexico, as well as Yorkville. They commiserated over the admiration of Nazi efficiency and the isolationism expressed in some American military circles; and they hoped aloud that Britain and France would be strong enough to carry the battle without America.[43]

The internationalists were obsessed with the fear that Hitler would conquer the rest of Europe and, with the cooperation or connivance of Moscow, Tokyo, and Rome, dominate Africa and infiltrate South America, thus surrounding the United States. The nation would be cut off from vital raw materials, subverted from within, under continuous aggressive pressure from a concert of foreign enemies who would eventually be

41. See p. 24 for the Neutrality Act.

42. Walter Johnson, *The Battle Against Isolation* (Chicago, 1944), pp. 38–62; Divine, *The Reluctant Belligerent*, p. 68.

43. *New York Times*, March 1, 1940; William Allen White's correspondence for January–April, 1940, White Papers; George F. Creel's speech, San Francisco, May 3, 1940, George F. Creel Papers, Library of Congress.

armed with the sophisticated weaponry of the future—transoceanic bombers, rockets, and nuclear weapons.[44] America, they were convinced, would have little chance to survive as a land of a free society and democratic government.[45]

With the fall of Norway and Denmark, those internationalists who had taken part in the Nonpartisan Committee felt that the time had come for steps to assure an Allied victory. By mid-May, Eichelberger and White, drawing heavily on the Committee mailing list, had organized a nationwide body for all-out aid to Britain and France—the Committee to Defend America by Aiding the Allies. The Committee to Defend America was the major spokesman for pro-Allied sentiment throughout the summer and fall of 1940.[46]

During the next year, many other groups would be formed to educate the public about fascism and isolationism, agitate for greater United States involvement, and reaffirm American faith in democratic principles. There was clergyman L. M. Birkhead's Friends of Democracy which published slashing denunciations of "America First" and photographic evidence of Nazi brutalities. In April, 1941, the theologian Reinhold Niebuhr, a leader of the pacifist movement until Munich, and a number of other former pacifists, social reformers, and liberals would organize the Union for Democratic Action and announce their decision that war against the totalitarians was the best of a number of unhappy alternatives. Judge Ferdinand Pecora formed the Legion for American Unity to rally "foreign-born elements in defense of the U.S. and in opposition to the totalitarian Axis." C. D. Jackson's Council for Democracy served all these bodies as a "service agency," assisting in liaison and organization and compiling scholarly studies on the meaning and application of each principle of the Bill of Rights. In May, 1940, none of these bodies was fully mobilized, and government decisions rested (as they inevi-

44. On May 5, 1940, a front-page article in the *New York Times* told of the isolation of the isotope U-235 and conjectured about its eventual significance.

45. Whitney H. Shepardson's speech, New York, May, 1940, Whitney H. Shepardson Papers, (hereafter WHS MSS), privately held; author's interviews with or letters from Shepardson, Francis P. Miller, Herbert Agar, Henry W. Hobson, William Clayton, Ernest M. Hopkins.

46. Johnson, *The Battle Against Isolation,* pp. 63–64.

tably do) less with the vocalism of pressure groups and more with the elected leaders of the nation.[47]

* * * * * *

Franklin Roosevelt was above all a politician, sensitive to the wishes of his constituency. In 1920 he had gone down to defeat as Democratic vice presidential nominee in an election which most historians believed was decided on the League issue. Through the twenties he remained personally favorable to a foreign policy of international cooperation and collective security. He realized, however, that the American people regarded United States participation in the League as a dead issue, and he adjusted his public views accordingly. As chief exponent of Democratic foreign policy views in 1928, he wrote in *Foreign Affairs* that the Republican foreign policy of commercialism without political responsibility was "negative" and "sterile." But he offered few dramatic alternatives. He defended American intervention in the war, lauded Wilson, and called the League's work "constructive and corrective." He even suggested United States membership in the World Court. But he carefully skirted the issue of American participation in the League or any other transoceanic system of collective security.[48]

Roosevelt's willingness to temper his own ideas on foreign policy to public attitudes and political expediency was most strikingly demonstrated three and a half years later, as he sought the Democratic presidential nomination. Then, in order to allay the suspicions of William Randolph Hearst, the isolationist press lord and Party potentate, he decided not merely to avoid the League issue but rather to put himself on record as opposing United States membership.[49]

47. *New York Times,* April 29, 1941 and May 15, 1941; Council For Democracy brochures, Fight For Freedom Papers (hereafter "FFF MSS"), Firestone Library, Princeton University.

48. Franklin D. Roosevelt, "Our Foreign Policy: A Democratic View," *Foreign Affairs,* VI (July, 1928), p. 573; See also Arthur M. Schlesinger, Jr., *The Age of Roosevelt: The Crisis of the Old Order, 1919–1933* (Boston, 1957); James MacGregor Burns, *Roosevelt: The Lion and the Fox* (New York, 1956); William E. Leuchtenburg, *Franklin D. Roosevelt and the New Deal* (New York, 1963).

49. Schlesinger, *The Age of Roosevelt,* p. 586.

After Roosevelt had attained the presidency, the domestic crisis and continued public isolationism—as well as his own rejection of the League—restricted his actions. Convinced that the United States economy had reached the limits of expansion, he sought to guide domestic adjustment to this fact free from the uncontrollable influences of European economic fluctuations. Thus he torpedoed the International Monetary Conference of 1933 and pursued what was in effect a policy of economic nationalism.[50]

With respect to foreign political matters, the concentration on domestic issues made it necessary until the late thirties to continue the policy of moral pronouncements and military and political non-involvement which Roosevelt had inherited from the Republicans. Thus, with regard to Japan's conquest of Manchuria, Roosevelt and his Secretary of State Cordell Hull pursued the sterile but morally self-justifying Stimson doctrine enunciated by Hoover's secretary of state in 1931.

They responded similarly to the series of European crises agitated by Hitler and Mussolini, denouncing aggression and urging peaceful settlements but also reaffirming United States unwillingness to take part in such settlements. Also, Roosevelt encouraged passage of the Neutrality Act of 1935 (which banned arms shipments to belligerents and travel by United States citizens on belligerent vessels) as a means of preventing the country from being dragged into war over legal technicalities when American national interests were not involved. He did cautiously seek to cooperate with the League when it attempted to apply economic sanctions against Italy, aggressor in Ethiopia. But this effort failed when disclosure of the Hoare-Laval scheme revealed Anglo-French willingness to appease Mussolini.[51]

By October, 1937, the Japanese were again attacking China, and civil war raged in Spain. Hitler, who had denounced the demilitarization clauses of the Versailles Treaty, engaged in massive rearmament, and peremptorily reoccupied the Rhine-

50. Divine makes the interesting point that the public's attitude was less a determined quest for insulation from the rest of the world than a tendency merely to ignore it, *The Reluctant Belligerent,* p. 12; W. Averell Harriman, "Reminiscences," transcribed interviews, privately held.

51. Divine, *The Reluctant Belligerent,* pp. 17–22.

land, was now eyeing Austria and the Sudetenland. Roosevelt was convinced that Americans had to be told that they had a stake in events beyond the hemisphere and that he thought the possibility of war was again threatening the whole world. Fourteen months earlier he had explained American foreign policy as seeking "to isolate ourselves completely from war." Now he suggested vaguely his willingness to take some part in settling the disputes between Europe's democratic and totalitarian states in order to help "quarantine" the contagion of war. However, partly because of the violent reaction of the isolationist *Chicago Tribune* and Hearst papers, and partly because of continued British and French appeasement and his own uncertainty as to how to implement such a quarantine, Roosevelt retreated toward the policy of exhortation.[52]

His popularity and power reduced by the "court-packing" battle, an economic recession, and defeats in the Congressional elections of 1938, Roosevelt met subsequent crises over Austria, the Sudetenland, and Czechoslovakia with eloquent appeals for peaceful settlement and condemnations of aggression. But he offered publicly no meaningful American assistance for either ultimate settlement or resistance. Similarly, when Nazi anti-Semitic excesses outraged many Americans, the President recalled his Ambassador but did not sever relations entirely.[53]

Sensitive to the fact that the American public remained unconcerned about the impact of events abroad on their own security, the President sought quietly to help those resisting aggression and to prepare his own defenses. Shortly after Munich, Roosevelt, assisted by his Secretary of the Treasury, Henry Morganthau, planned the expansion of United States aircraft production. He authorized a loan to Chiang Kai-chek's regime for non-military purposes and secretly empowered Morgenthau to facilitate the inspection and purchase of warplanes from American manufacturers by the French. However, the revelation

52. Franklin D. Roosevelt, *The Public Papers and Addresses of Franklin D. Roosevelt: 1937* (Washington, 1941), p. 406; Dorothy Borg, "Notes on Roosevelt's Quarantine Speech," *Political Science Quarterly*, LXXII (September, 1957), pp. 405–33.

53. Actually, Ambassador Kirk was already in the United States and was instructed not to return to Berlin.

of this arrangement owing to the crash of one such plane with a French official aboard in February, 1939, stirred a hostile congressional reaction. This furor reinforced the impression that the country was still unready to consider that its security was related to that of the western European democracies.[54]

As Hitler threatened Poland in the spring of 1939 and it appeared that the British and French might finally fight, Roosevelt pressed for revision of the Neutrality Law. The Pittman amendment to the Neutrality Act proposed to permit a belligerent to pay cash for arms and transport them out of the country on his own ships ("cash-and-carry"). This would obviously help the European Allies, who had dominant seapower, although in the Pacific it would be a boom to the Japanese. Despite the President's efforts, congressional resistance to what some considered an unneutral commitment delayed passage until November, two months after hostilities began.[55]

While Poland was subjugated and the Pittman amendment passed, the administration pursued a policy of cautious and relatively inactive favoritism for the Allies and the victims of aggression. In September the President had invoked the as yet unrevised Neutrality statutes but had declared, "Even a neutral cannot be asked to close his mind and conscience." In an effort to insulate the hemisphere from war, Under Secretary of State Sumner Welles had achieved passage of the Declaration of Panama at the Pan-American Conference in October. The Declaration erected a neutral zone extending three hundred miles into the Atlantic from the coast of North and South America from which belligerent warships were barred (in theory more than fact). The United States Navy undertook patrol duties in the zone. This favored the Allies by providing a sea area in which "cash-and-carry" ships could be relatively secure from attack.[56]

With its eyes on the German and Italian threat, the government behaved cautiously toward the other two aggressors, Japan and the Soviet Union. Despite the insistence of some foreign affairs experts and strong public willingness (82 per cent

54. John Morton Blum, *From the Morgenthau Diaries: Years of Urgency, 1938–1941* (Boston, 1965), pp. 43–78.
55. Langer and Gleason, *The Challenge to Isolation,* p. 80.
56. *Ibid.,* p. 206.

according to a poll taken in July, 1939) to apply economic sanctions against Japan, the administration refused to embargo oil and scrap iron shipments to Japan on the grounds that this would aggravate relations with the Japanese at a time when the United States had its hands full in Europe. Similarly, Roosevelt hesitated to denounce Soviet attacks on Poland, the three Baltic states, and Finland for fear of driving Stalin permanently into Hitler's camp. Widespread public sympathy for the stubborn Finnish resistance during the "Winter War" evoked only mild government protests to the Soviets and a modest Export-Import Bank credit to the Finns.[57]

During the "phony war" the Allies seemed at least the equals of the Nazis, and no assistance appeared to be needed. A peace mission by Welles to the belligerent capitals in February, 1940, revealed as little willingness to negotiate a peace in the Allied capitals as in Berlin and Rome. However, the fall of Norway, Denmark, the Low Countries, and France in the two months after April 9, 1940, forced the administration to alter its inactive policy. On May 11, Roosevelt warned the country that it was "a false teaching of geography to think that distance itself gives us some form of mystic immunity." South America, he reminded his countrymen, was only four or five hours by air from Africa. A Gallup poll taken in mid-May found that only 55 per cent of the public believed the Allies would win (82 per cent had thought so in September). Similarly, 51 per cent now thought the United States would eventually become involved, while two months earlier only one in three anticipated American involvement.[58]

The possibility of involvement made military preparedness essential. But in the spring of 1940 the United States military establishment remained crippled by the effects of the munitions investigations and the widespread pacifism of the thirties. Roosevelt, expecting trouble, had sought increased appropriations from Congress for military and naval expansion since 1938. He had made some headway with naval rearmament since nationalistic isolationists saw a strong fleet as the best means of

57. Divine, *The Reluctant Belligerent*, pp. 76–82.

58. Langer and Gleason, *The Challenge to Isolation*, pp. 361 ff.; *New York Times*, May 12 and 19, 1940.

defending America without foreign political involvement. A new army, however, ran afoul of the spectre of another American Expeditionary Force. In the spring of 1940, therefore, the United States Army consisted of only 200,000 men, equipped mostly with weapons of World War vintage and almost no modern motorized armor. The Air Corps, never strong, was being rearmed so slowly that in the first three months of 1940 it received delivery of only fifty-seven combat planes. The American Navy was the second largest in the world, but nearly half of its vessels were relics of the Great War. America's defense industries were expanding gradually and haphazardly to meet the demands of British and French "cash-and-carry" orders, but long-range planning for a war economy had been neglected.[59]

With Americans suddenly aware of their interest in Allied survival and their own military weakness, Roosevelt struck again and again from mid-May to mid-June for steps to strengthen the United States and aid the Allies. On May 16 he requested new naval and military appropriations totaling nearly $1.2 billion and a production program for fifty thousand airplanes. Two weeks later he asked a further military appropriation of $1.3 billion to equip a new army and build a two-ocean navy. Fearing for the nation's security and sensing a shift in public attitudes toward defense spending, Congress, although still isolationist in temper, quickly voted the funds.

Roosevelt made dramatic changes in administration personnel and organization. To coordinate industrial mobilization he named a seven-man National Defense Advisory Commission, which brought to Washington a number of top-flight business executives, "dollar-a-year men."[60] He called Republicans Henry

59. Roosevelt, *Public Papers: 1938* (Washington, 1941), p. 1; Samuel Flagg Bemis, *A Diplomatic History of The United States* (4th ed.; New York, 1955), pp. 850–53. After filing its report in November, 1939, the War Resources Board disbanded.

60. The appointment of big business figures to administer industrial mobilization and the promise of opportunities in defense production worked to reassure industrialists. Almost all but the hardcore isolationists, defeatists, and inveterate Roosevelt-haters swung into line behind the National Association of Manufacturers' call on June 23 for all-out defense and national unity. A good number of the remainder were shortly attracted to the American First Committee. See Stromberg, "American Business," *Journal of Economic History; New York Times,* June 23, 1940.

Stimson and Frank Knox to Washington to replace isolationists as secretaries of war and the navy.

Politically the move was a shrewd one, timed to establish a "government of national unity" just before the Republican presidential convention. But Stimson and Knox were also men of long experience, deeply committed to the belief that America's interest lay with the Allies. Only the day before, Stimson had told a Yale University audience that he favored universal military training, opening American shipyards for repair of British ships, and extending massive material assistance and naval protection to the Allies. Knox was a former Rough Rider and Republican vice presidential nominee in 1936. As editor of the only internationalist journal in Chicago, the *Daily News*, Knox had long insisted on naval preparedness and the previous year had championed Neutrality Law revision. As the Blitzkrieg devoured western Europe, his editorials had grown increasingly willing to consider the possibility of American military involvement. Now these proponents of semi-belligerency joined Morgenthau and Secretary of the Interior Harold L. Ickes as advocates in the cabinet of all aid necessary for a British victory. As events gradually showed Britain's inability to achieve that victory, these four became more and more convinced of the need for vigorous "non-belligerent" behavior and, eventually, American intervention.[61]

With the urging of these men, Roosevelt pressed Congress to release current-model American fighter planes to Britain and France on a "cash-and-carry" basis. Still hesitant to publicly tie American interests too closely to those of the Allies, administration officials announced that the release was motivated by their desire to combat-test our new designs and by the fact that British and French orders would provide the capital for the expansion of America's airplane plants. Similarly, when, in response to the pleas of new British Prime Minister Winston Churchill, the War Department released World War I rifles, small arms ammunition,

61. Civilian Production Agency, "Industrial Mobilization in the Defense Period," unpublished manuscript, National Archives; Henry L. Stimson and McGeorge Bundy, *On Active Service in Peace and War* (New York, 1948), p. 319; *Chicago Daily News*, October, 1940 to June, 1940; Blum, *From the Morgenthau Diaries*, p. 251.

and light field pieces for "cash-and-carry" sale to the Allies, officials assured the public that this material was obsolete and of no use to the United States Army. In all, forty-three million dollars worth of such equipment was shipped to Britain in June, 1940, but all was sold on a "cash-and-carry" basis and often through subterfuges like bogus export companies or repurchase and resale by the original American manufacturer.[62]

Such deviousness was necessary because most Americans had not changed their minds about non-involvement in the war and the *desirability* of isolation, even though they were beginning to doubt the possibility of both. Of the four major contenders for the Republican presidential nomination, three—Thomas E. Dewey, Robert A. Taft, and Arthur H. Vandenberg—clung to the isolationist viewpoint (although simultaneously criticizing the Roosevelt administration's failure to provide adequate defense). Only Wendell L. Willkie, who prior to the Republican convention appeared to have little chance to win the nomination, declared his support of "all aid short of war" to the Allies.[63]

By the beginning of June the Gallup Poll reflected the paradoxical public attitude which was to condition Franklin Roosevelt's foreign policy for the next year and a half. According to the pollsters, 65 per cent of Americans felt that if England and France fell, Germany would eventually attack the United States. Five out of every eight expected America eventually to go to war, and three out of four believed we were not giving the Allies enough help. However, only one citizen in fourteen favored a declaration of war on Germany. Thus, there appeared to be a

62. *New York Times,* May 31, 1940; Office of the Secretary of War, "The National Emergency: Part I," unpublished manuscript, pp. C6–C8, Henry L. Stimson Papers, Sterling Library, Yale University; John Bartlett Brebner, *The North Atlantic Triangle: The Interplay of Canada, the United States and Great Britain* (New Haven, 1945) p. 322; Edward R. Stettinius, *Lend-Lease: Weapon for Victory* (New York, 1944), p. 26; Eugene C. Gerhart, *America's Advocate: Robert H. Jackson* (Indianapolis, 1958), p. 213.

63. Oswald G. Villard to White, June 19, 1940, White Papers; Josephus Daniels to Bernard Baruch, November 10, 1940, Josephus Daniels Papers, Library of Congress; Key Pittman's correspondence for June, 1940, Key Pittman Papers, Library of Congress; Charles McNary's correspondence for June, 1940, Charles McNary Papers, Library of Congress; *New York Times,* March 8, 1940 and June 2, 1940.

broad chasm between what a majority of Americans thought *would* eventually happen and what they thought *ought* to be done. Most now recognized that they ought to be concerned in some degree with the outcome in Europe, but they were still unwilling to take any but the most limited steps to influence that outcome.[64]

Although the American public sensed danger in June, 1940, it remained in great part bound by the continentalist, anti-European, and pacifist ideas which had prevailed for two decades. Major ethnic minorities still were torn between old and new allegiances. Many in the American interior continued to believe their civilization safe from any external threat. The danger to America was not yet direct enough or of sufficient duration to convert public opinion from one extreme, isolation, to the other, intervention. Thus it was that by the beginning of June, 1940, no American leader had publicly demanded war.

64. *New York Times,* June 2, 1940 and June 12, 1940.

II. A Summons to Speak Out

On June 2, 1940, Francis and Helen Miller invited a small group of friends to their country home in Fairfax, Virginia, a few miles outside Washington. Miller was an executive of the Council on Foreign Relations. His wife was Washington correspondent for *The Economist* of London and executive director of the National Policy Committee, an organization primarily engaged in compiling and disseminating the differing views of specialists on various issues of public interest. The gathering had been called at the request of Richard F. Cleveland, son of President Grover Cleveland and a Baltimore attorney and National Policy Committee leader, to discuss America's role in the current world crisis. Others present were Stacy May, New York economist; Winfield Riefler, Economic Advisor to the National Emergency Council and a director of the Foreign Policy Association; Mr. and Mrs. Whitney Shepardson (He was the author of the Council on Foreign Relations' annual volume, *The United States in World Affairs.*); Edward P. Warner of the Civil Aeronautics Board; and M. L. Wilson, Department of Agriculture economist.[1]

1. Miller to William L. Langer, February 11, 1952, Frances P. Miller (hereafter FPM MSS) privately held; author's interviews with Miller, Helen Hill Miller, and Whitney Shepardson.

The conversation lasted all day. The guests discussed the recent change in the American attitude toward the war and speculated about the trickle of news beginning to appear in the newspapers concerning the Dunkirk evacuation and Britain's weakness in the face of a German invasion. All agreed that the preservation of the British fleet was crucial to American security. They noted the continuing activity of Nazi agents in this country and the growing number of news stories concerning designs on Greenland, Brazil, and most recently, Uruguay. They agreed that if French possessions in Africa fell into German hands, and if the British fleet were sunk or captured in a Nazi invasion of England, the Western hemisphere would be vulnerable to German subversion and invasion. Such intrusions might come either by a southerly route running from west Africa to the hump of Brazil or by a northerly one with Britain, Iceland, and Greenland as staging points. All were convinced that democracy in North America could not long survive if the totalitarians dominated the rest of the world.

The guests realized to their astonishment that each of them had concluded that America's best course was an immediate declaration of war on Germany. Only by this means could Britain's will to go on fighting be reinforced, and only in this way could American industrial potential be harnessed to the task of defeating nazism without the "peace-time" temptation to do business-as-usual and produce for domestic consumption rather than for war. They were sure that the only way Hitler could now be defeated would be if the full weight of American production and American manpower were thrown into the balance.

What means was available, they wondered, to move America toward a declaration of war? Perhaps they could use the method employed a few days earlier by Shepardson, Miller, and President Henry Wriston of Brown University to secure the appointment of J. Pierrepont Moffat as United States Minister to Canada. This trio had quietly contacted a few of their friends whose judgment they knew President Roosevelt valued, among them editorial writers for the *New York Times* and *Herald Tribune*. They asked these individuals to write editorials or letters to the Chief Executive urging the appointment of "a first-rate man" as the new American Minister to Canada, a country which, as the sole belligerent nation in the Western hemisphere, was of great importance to the United States. They felt their efforts were rewarded when Moffat, an experienced professional diplomat, was named rather than some "deserving" political partisan.

However, the Millers and their guests believed that the question of whether to go to war demanded widespread public consideration. Therefore, instead of employing private persuasion, they decided to act overtly by issuing a dramatic call to war signed by important and influential individuals across the country. Whitney H. Shepardson retired to the study where he drafted what became with only slight revision the published call.

It declared that America now recognized that "Nazi Germany [was] the mortal enemy of our ideals, our institutions and our way of life." If Britain and France were defeated, the United States would, inevitably, have to fight the Nazis alone. In order to prevent this, the Summons urged, "the United States should immediately give official recognition to the fact and logic of the situation—by declaring that a state of war exists between this country and Germany" and should dispatch "all disposable air naval, military and material resources" to the side of our Allies.[2]

While Shepardson was writing, the rest of the guests compiled a list of everyone they knew who had public influence and who might be willing to sign the statement. The list, totaling 127 names, included civic, business, and academic leaders from every region of the country. Francis Miller was asked to solicit the signatures of these individuals. The news release of the statement was scheduled for the Monday morning papers of the following week so that, because of the normal dearth of news over the weekend, it might get front-page coverage.

During the next several days Miller and Shepardson corresponded by wire and telephone, making revisions in the text and deciding on a title. After considering such names as "A Call to the Nation" (ruled out as "too pretentious"), "Action Now," and "A Call to Speak Out," they hit on the phrase "A Summons to Speak Out." Since this title connoted a responsibility to discuss the heretofore "untouchable" subject, it expressed their purpose precisely.[3]

2. "A Summons to Speak Out," mimeograph copy, WHS MSS. For the full text, see Appendix.

3. Unsigned notes attached to "A Summons to Speak Out"; Helen Hill Miller to Shepardson, June 3, 1940, WHS MSS.

Of the 127 individuals solicited 83 responded; 30 said they would sign;[4] 46 others said they would not subscribe to the paragraph favoring a declaration of war but approved other parts of the statement; 6 registered vigorous dissents.[5] It was those 52 who refused to sign and people like them whom the Warhawks tried to convert during the subsequent year and a half. The negative responses which Miller received, therefore, illustrate the kind of resistance interventionism was to meet—from internationalists as well as isolationists.

The few outright anti-interventionists who answered Miller's inquiry molded their responses around three basic arguments: (1) war was immoral and un-Christian; (2) America's interest lay in protecting herself from the fascism at home which war mobilization would bring; and (3) the war was already lost. The first of these arguments was expounded by Clarence Poe, Raleigh, North Carolina, editor of *The Progressive Farmer.* Poe wrote that, although he accepted the necessity of rearmament, he rejected the idea that the only cure for the great evil of war was more war. He was "heart-sickened," he added, by the demand "that America must both acknowledge and accept 'the law of the jungle' as the supreme and inescapable destiny of mankind."[6]

Jonathan Daniels, editor of the *Raleigh News and Observor* and son of Ambassador Josephus Daniels, argued the other two points. Daniels thought that America's duty was "the protection and defense of this hemisphere and perhaps of parts of the East." If the United States entered the war now—too late to effect its outcome—it would lose whatever influence it might have to moderate the peace demands of the victorious Germans.[7]

A few of those willing to consider war against Germany begged off because they thought they did "not feel well enough informed to make a decision of this importance." Some who felt it was America's duty or her interest to defeat Hitler realized that the United States was just not prepared to fight. They believed

4. One other individual, unidentified in the Warhawk's records, responded favorably—but too late to be included in the press release.

5. Three of the dissenters were Robert E. Wood, Clarence Poe, and Jonathan Daniels; the identity of the other three is not recorded, "Memorandum to Those Invited to Sign 'A Summons to Speak Out,'" June 20, 1940, Henry W. Hobson Papers (hereafter HWH MSS), privately held.

6. *Ibid.*

7. *Ibid.*

their country would contribute more by remaining neutral or "semi-belligerent"—at least for a time. Charles M. Spence, a member of the St. Louis study group of the Council on Foreign Relations, expressed this view best. He regarded the defeat of the Allies as an "unspeakable tragedy" and urged "every possible aid short of war." [Nevertheless,] he wrote, "the humiliating and deplorable, but plain, fact is that we are not in a position to defend ourselves, much less give France and Great Britain military assistance." Spence argued that our intervention "would be of only doubtful psychological value to the Allies," and, if they were defeated, would leave the United States in an "extremely perilous" position.[8] His remarks were seconded by Douglas Dow, the Detroit industrialist, who said he would "approve statement recommending non-belligerent status and scrapping of artificial [Neutrality] legislation but believed strongly that the present problem is production, and this can best be met by Knudsen's committee [National Defense Advisory Commission] operating under peacetime law." [9]

Most of the pro-war non-signers pegged their responses to practical considerations of the public's attitude. Will Clayton, Houston cotton millionaire (who was shortly to join the Warhawks), noted that the American people might support Neutrality Act repeal, credits to the Allies, and even recruitment of volunteers in the United States, but they would not yet consider a declaration of war. Several respondents made the telling criticism that the "Summons" itself might work against the very purpose it was supposed to achieve. Louis I. Jaffee of Norfolk, Virginia, wrote: "I think that to urge a declaration of war against Germany now is to court a negative answer that would be in the last degree unfortunate." Chicago's Walter T. Fisher shared this view. "I think [this statement] is unwise from the point of view of your own" objectives, he wrote. "War is not going to be declared next week," he reminded the Warhawks. Since most of the signers of the Summons would be Easterners, it would stir resistance in the Middle West to the interventionists' objectives. The country was now united in its support for rearmament and military preparedness. "Your manifesto," Fisher warned, "will

8. *Ibid.*
9. *Ibid.*

tend to split that unity."[10] Vincent Carroll of St. Louis added, hopefully, "In a week or ten days, perhaps, the thermometer may have risen to the place where the declaration you propose would have the desired results."[11]

Few could know then how little public attitudes toward a war declaration would change in the next year and a half.

The thirty men who agreed with the logic of the "Summons" and felt free to sign were Herbert Agar, editor and Pulitzer Prize winning author from Louisville; Burke Baker of Houston, life insurance executive; John L. Balderston of Beverly Hills, playwright and journalist; Stringfellow Barr of Annapolis, President of St. John's College; J. Douglas Brown, professor of economics at Princeton; Richard Cleveland; James F. Curtis of New York, attorney and former Assistant Secretary of the Treasury; Edwin F. Gay of Pasadena, California, economist and former Dean of the Graduate School of Business Administration at Harvard; Edward T. Gushee of St. Louis, Executive Vice President of the Union Electric Company of Missouri; Marion H. Hedges of Washington, D.C., author and research director; William H. Hessler of Cincinnati, writer on political economics; George Watts Hill of Durham, North Carolina, banker and leader of farmer cooperative marketing organizations; Henry W. Hobson, Episcopal Bishop of Cincinnati; Leroy Hodge of Richmond, economist and author; Calvin Hoover of Durham, economist, author, and editor; Edwin P. Hubble of San Marino, California, astronomer; Frank Kent, columnist of the *Baltimore Sun;* Edward R. Lewis of Chicago, sociologist and historian; George W. Martin, New York attorney; L. Randolph Mason of New York, attorney; Stacy May; Francis Miller; Helen Hill Miller; Walter Millis, editorial writer of the *New York Herald Tribune* and "revisionist" historian of the First World War; George Fort Milton of Chattanooga, newspaper editor and author; Lewis Mumford of Amenia, New York, author; Winfield Riefler; Whitney Shepardson; Admiral William H. Standley of New York, retired Chief of Naval Operations; and William Waller of Nashville, attorney.[12]

10. *Ibid.*
11. *Ibid.*
12. *St. Louis Post-Dispatch,* September 22, 1940.

On Monday, June 10, most of the country's major newspapers carried articles with headlines such as "Declare War on Nazis, Notables Plead; Walter Millis, Author of 'The Road to War,' is One of 30 Urging Action"; or "American War Vote Demanded; Somme is Cited as Our 'Frontier.'"[13] The subsequent story was usually "picked up" from the Associated Press dispatch, which noted that the signers were "speaking as individuals [and] reflected the stand of no organization." The full dispatch ran approximately one column, quoted the greater part of the "Summons," and identified all the signers.[14]

As noted earlier, release of the "Summons" was planned to get prime treatment from editors on a "slow" Monday. What Miller and others could not know was that Mussolini would choose the prior day to attack France—and thereby dominate the headlines. The advance of the *Wehrmacht* to within thirty-five miles of Paris and the public statements by Henry Stimson, Ambassador William C. Bullitt, and General James Harbord favoring "unlimited" material aid to the Allies also attracted much of the editors' attention that day. In several major newspapers a full-page advertisement written and promoted by playwright Robert E. Sherwood appeared; it demanded that the United States "Stop Hitler Now" by giving all-out aid to the Allies. Finally, much newsprint was spent on speculation about what Roosevelt would say in his speech that afternoon in Charlottesville.[15]

Although each of these other events helped arouse interest in the issues with which the "Summons" was concerned, they also detracted editorial and public attention from the "Summons" itself. A sampling of twenty major papers representing various regions reveals that only thirteen carried the story, and only three (Herbert Agar's *Louisville Courier-Journal,* the *Richmond Times Dispatch,* and the *Detroit Free Press*) put it on the front page.[16] Only two of the thirteen (*The Washington Post* and *The*

13. *Detroit Free Press,* June 10, 1940; *New York Times,* June 10, 1940.

14. This dispatch was occasionally followed by one datelined Raleigh, North Carolina, which quoted Daniels' and Poe's refusal to sign.

15. For example, see *New York Times,* June 10, 1940.

16. The twenty papers were the *Boston Globe, The New York Times, New York Herald Tribune, Daily Worker,* Philadelphia *Evening*

New York Times) considered the story interesting enough to get a direct rather than a wire service story, and only one (*St. Louis Post-Dispatch*) thought it worthy of editorial comment. Joseph Pulitzer's paper, staunchly anti-interventionist at this time, commented:

> *The Warhawks Speak*
>
> Hitler's blitzkrieg is doing more than sweep aside Allied resistance; it is also sweeping off their feet certain Americans both at home and abroad with sufficient brains to know better. The war spirit now has surged to the point that 30 men, all of high position in American education, law, letters, and business issue a manifesto urging this country to declare war on Germany at once to defend in France "our ideals, our institutions, and our way of life."
>
> For intellectuals and men of affairs, this is shockingly muddled thinking. Much though American sentiment favors an Allied victory, important though this is to this country's interests, the plain fact remains that we would make a costly and futile blunder by going to war. . . .
>
> The hotheads who issue this demand for war are mostly over military age. Until similar statements from young men who have to do the fighting and dying begin to appear, there will be no reason to fear that the mass of the people are abandoning their determination to keep out. These 30 men have merely lost their balance as a result of the tragic events abroad.[17]

Newspapers as important as the *Los Angeles Times*, the *Boston Globe*, the *New Orleans Times-Picayune*, and the *Chicago Daily News* failed to carry the "Summons" story at all.

The fact that some important journals did not think the "Summons" was newsworthy and that only a very few of those which printed the dispatch thought it merited editorial comment indicates the kind of interest the manifesto stimulated. As one reads the newspapers for the first half of June, 1940, one senses

---

Bulletin, Baltimore Sun, Washington Post, Washington Evening Star, Richmond Times Dispatch, Louisville Courier-Journal, Atlanta Constitution, New Orleans Times-Picayune, St. Louis Post-Dispatch, Emporia Gazette, Cincinnati Enquirer, Chicago Tribune, Chicago Daily News, Detroit *Free Press, San Francisco Examiner, Los Angeles Times.*

17. *Washington Post* and *New York Times,* June 10, 1940, *St. Louis Post-Dispatch,* June 11, 1940.

that the "Summons to Speak Out" was a very small incident amidst the momentous events which began with Dunkirk and ended with French surrender. These great occurrences and the intense analysis to which they were subjected in the news media unquestionably influenced public attitudes more than the "one-shot" statement by a small group of men. Nevertheless, the fact that thirty citizens of accomplishment and reputation were willing to affix their names to a plea for war must have impressed a few *more* readers with the seriousness of the situation and stimulated a few of them to ponder and debate an issue—outright American intervention—which most had tried to avoid considering. Someone, at least, had dared to speak the unspeakable. Although some of the signers may have hoped for more spectacular results, the realists among them knew that this was the most they could expect.[18]

* * * * * *

The Warhawks' efforts might have ended with the "Summons to Speak Out" had it not been for Dr. Henry Pitt Van Dusen, Professor of Systematic Theology at New York's Union Theological Seminary. Dr. Van Dusen was miffed at having been left off the "Summons" list, and he told his friends, the Millers, so when he saw them at a National Policy Committee meeting near the end of the month. He explained that despite his role as seminary teacher, he felt strongly on the subject and had wished the opportunity to express himself. He suggested that they invite one hundred influential private citizens who believed as they did to a weekend conference at some resort—perhaps Hot Springs. After some discussion the trio rejected this idea as too ambitious and cumbersome. They considered, instead, approaching some man of means who was favorable to intervention and who would be willing to act as dinner host to a much smaller gathering. In privacy such a group could deliberate what ought to be done.

Helen Miller disagreed. She argued that once a group of people favoring war organized—even informally—they would be written off by private citizens and public officials as just another

18. Author's interviews with the Millers and Shepardson; author's notes from Henry W. Hobson, February 15, 1965.

pressure group. She thought that such people would have greater impact if—acting strictly as individuals—they made their views known among their own circles of influential friends and in occasional public statements like the "Summons." However, Van Dusen's insistence that the drive for war had to continue uninterrupted until belligerency was attained eventually overcame her arguments.[19]

While plans were made for an initial dinner gathering, Van Dusen took the responsibility for approaching the British Ambassador to Washington, Lord Lothian (Phillip Kerr). With the help of Aubrey Morgan of the British Information Service (the United Kingdom's propaganda outlet) in New York, Van Dusen obtained an appointment at the Embassy on July 4. At that meeting he told Lothian of the group that was about to be formed, and he outlined the conditions upon which they would work to arouse all-out support for Britain. These conditions were "that Britain would undertake under no circumstances to surrender but, in the event of a successful invasion, [would] move the royal family and the government to Canada." Van Dusen said that America must be assured that the Royal Navy would not capitulate but would continue the fight from bases in Canada and elsewhere in the Commonwealth. He then asked how his friends could help Lothian. The Ambassador replied that the British fleet intended to fight to the last ship to prevent an invasion and that the greatest immediate help America could give would be to send some of her over-age destroyers to aid in the defense of the British Isles.[20]

The conversation at an end, Van Dusen returned to New York and reported to the first meeting of the new interventionist group that the British Ambassador intended to cooperate with them. Lothian, who had heretofore been pessimistic about the chances of obtaining destroyers, wrote hopefully to Churchill the next day of "encouraging" new developments in "informed American opinion."[21]

19. Author's interviews with Henry P. Van Dusen and the Millers.

20. Since May 15 Churchill had been privately urging Roosevelt to expedite the sale of U.S. Navy destroyers to Great Britain.

21. Author's interview with Van Dusen; Van Dusen 1940 date book, Henry P. Van Dusen Papers (hereafter HVD MSS), privately held.

Thus, a month after the Warhawks first began to "find" each other, they had published a full declaration of their attitude, begun work on the rudiments of organization, and initiated a working relationship with a foreign government which they regarded as their own and their country's natural ally.

III. Who Were the Warhawks?

At 7:30 on Friday, July 11, 1940, Lewis W. Douglas, President of Mutual Life Insurance Company and former Director of the Budget, gave a dinner for eleven friends and acquaintances at New York's Columbia Club. Five of his guests—Herbert Agar, Bishop Henry Hobson, Francis Miller, Whitney Shepardson, and Admiral William Standley—had signed "A Summons to Speak Out." All who were present shared the belief that the European war was in fact America's war. Since Dunkirk and the fall of France, each had concluded privately that sooner or later American armed intervention would be necessary to prevent world domination by Hitler. Most felt that the United States should declare war immediately to prevent the fall of Great Britain and the surrender to the Nazis of "America's first line of defense"—the British Fleet. But they also knew that what they believed to be America's national *interest* was certainly not its national *desire;* that the overwhelming majority of Americans, though sympathetic to the British, wanted no return to the machine guns, mud, and gas of Chateau-Thierry and the Argonne Forest and no repetition of the "betrayal" of Versailles.

These dozen men were dedicated to changing America's mind.[1]

The twelve who met at the Columbia Club were eventually joined by sixteen others they invited to help them "bring America to her senses." [2] In the ensuing weeks this body came to be known informally as the "Century Group," since many of their weekly gatherings took place at the nearby Century Association, a private club for men of accomplishment in the arts and sciences as well as business and public affairs. As for membership in the Group, "the selection was on the basis of whether he [the prospective member] had brains, and any influence, and believed in what we were doing." The process of joining was strictly informal; as one member later said, "No one plunked down ten dollars and received a membership card." [3] Attendance varied from meeting to meeting, depending on the agenda. Some individuals, while vitally interested in participating in policy decisions, avoided the gatherings at which the mechanics of implementing those decisions were discussed.

Burdened with their belief that America was in immediate danger and that the public was largely unaware of that peril, the Century Group decided to pursue three objectives during the summer and fall of 1940. First, the members intended by public endorsements and personal influence to try to persuade the public to support a policy of "all aid short of war" to Britain. They hoped that such assistance as the sale or loan of fifty to one hundred old American destroyers would help the British to prevent or repulse the German invasion of England, which, they felt certain, was only weeks away.

Second, through a program of news releases, circular letters, and radio addresses, they planned to attack the fallacies they saw in the isolationism which was "the orthodox American dogma." They felt that someone had to take the responsibility for organizing the voice of interventionism to counteract the flow of statements insisting on United States neutrality.

Finally, they proposed to advocate a series of government

1. "Tentative Draft," July 12, 1940; "Meeting at Columbia Club," July 11, 1940, FPM MSS; author's interviews with Francis P. Miller.

2. "Meeting at the Columbia Club," FPM MSS.

3. "Century Group—1940," FPM MSS; author's interviews with Francis P. Miller; *St. Louis Post-Dispatch,* September 22, 1940.

actions, the end result of which would be American involvement in the war. They believed that by shipping food to Britain, by convoying British merchantmen, and by sending units of the United States Navy to "join in the protection of the British Isles and the British Fleet," the government of the United States could gradually "educate" the American people to the necessity of active participation in the war.[4]

* * * * * *

Although the informality of the Century Group dictated that no differentiation be made between "leaders" and "followers," certain individuals contributed more than others. A half dozen men stand out as the key figures in the Century Group during the summer and fall of 1940.

Francis P. Miller, a sponsor of "A Summons to Speak Out" and director of the Group's office, was a leading Southern liberal and internationalist. Born of venerable Presbyterian, Scotch-Irish stock and reared in the Valley of Virginia, young Miller naturally adopted Woodrow Wilson as a hero. After graduation from Washington and Lee, in 1914 he went abroad as an employee of the Young Men's Christian Association and later the World Student Christian Federation in Geneva. In 1917 he saw action with the Field Artillery in France and after the war attended Oxford. Miller, although a layman, was preoccupied with the question of Christianity's place in modern society and government. A Calvinist with a strong sense of communal responsibility, he felt compelled by his religion to take a stand in what he saw as part of the eternal and universal struggle between the forces of good and evil. Looking back on the events of 1940 from the perspective of nearly a quarter of a century, in 1964 he said:

> There are no black and white, of course, in human affairs; the gray predominates usually. But occasionally, as in the case of Hitler, the black wells up. . . . I happen to believe that there are evil forces beyond just evil men. . . . Demonic forces are to me a very real thing. You see it break out sometimes in a group or in a convention, suddenly evil seizes them—a lynching mob in the South.

4. "Meeting at the Columbia Club," FPM MSS.

What makes men go utterly bestial? Why do they want to hang a human being against whom they have nothing? What is this? [5]

In 1930, Miller, then Chairman of the World Student Christian Federation, and his wife Helen Hill had written a book entitled *The Giant of the Western World: America and Europe in a North-Atlantic Civilization.* Some of the ideas expressed in this book indicated the outlook of the interventionists. Twentieth-century technology and commerce, Miller had written, were gradually binding western Europe and North America into one economy and one society. The price of beef in Kansas City affected the cost of living in London, and the cost of steel from Birmingham, England, meant more work or less pay in Birmingham, Alabama. A symphony composed in New York was acclaimed in Berlin and Paris, while a novel written on *la rive gauche* was praised in Boston or Savannah.

Because the destinies of America and Europe were intertwined, Miller asserted, United States intervention in the First World War had been the legitimate behavior of a nation whose interests were affected by the outcome. "The problems of either one of the continents which frame the Western World are problems of common concern," he wrote. For him, therefore, America's isolationism in the 1920's was a temporary aberration which would soon yield to reality, and he enumerated examples of the continuing interdependence of American and European industry and commerce. In all things, he said, the "trend is away from the national to the international." Miller envisioned the common man as the focus of the emerging civilization, his cultural life enriched by the out-pouring of many nations, his needs and tastes satisfied by the products of an international industrial complex both competitive and consumer-oriented. America's "immense power," Miller asserted, "gives us absolute security. It is we who are creating insecurity for the rest of the world. . . . It is we who are invading the markets of our neighbors." [6]

Although the events of the next ten years diminished

5. Author's interview with Francis P. Miller.

6. Francis Miller and Helen Hill, *The Giant of the Western World: America and Europe in a North-Atlantic Civilization* (New York, 1930), pp. 30–35, 140, 257–80, 282–87.

Miller's belief in America's "absolute security," his conviction that America was inextricably bound to the North Atlantic world remained unchanged. His statement that "political entanglement cannot be avoided by verbal incantations" was as true after Dunkirk as it was when Kellogg and Briand signed their pact. Although his admonition about a policy of predatory commercial expansionism was essentially irrelevant in 1940, his insistence that the fate of western Europe was important to America's future was more pertinent than ever. When, in the weeks after Dunkirk, some advocates of preparedness suggested reliance on Western hemisphere solidarity against the threat from Europe, Miller attacked this as a misjudgment. He emphasized instead the special relationship between Great Britain and the United States:

> The Latin American countries do not practice our way of life. There is no basis—political, cultural, economic, geographic or strategic—for a close alliance between the countries of South America and the United States. Further, if we advance them credits or arms there is an excellent chance that these assets will eventually find their way into the hands of the Germans. . . .
>
> The English speaking people, on the other hand, do practice our way of life. The United States Government should be prepared in case of a conquest of the British Isles to draw the remaining free English speaking peoples into a unity adequate to maintain their freedom, to preserve their culture, and to perpetuate their representative forms of government. In any event, the keystone of our foreign policy must be close collaboration with the British Commonwealth of Nations.[7]

In 1940 Miller was organization director for the Council on Foreign Relations, with responsibility for the Council's regional committees. These committees assumed responsibility for analyzing public opinion on foreign affairs and educating their communities in the realities of the world situation. Miller and his wife also were leaders of the National Policy Committee, an organization of private citizens who believed minority blocs and special interest pressure groups asserted too great an influence

7. "Tentative Draft," FPM MSS.

on government policy-making. The Committee organized roundtable discussions on pressing domestic issues and invited experts from industry, government, and university faculties in order to represent a full spectrum of viewpoints. Their findings were then made available to government agencies and interested private citizens. Through the Committee and the Council, Miller had become acquainted with Whitney Shepardson, Herbert Agar, Henry Van Dusen, Allen Dulles, George Watts Hill, Will Clayton, William Standley, and others who contributed to the interventionist cause. Aside from his organizational interests, Miller was active politically—in 1940 he was a Democratic member of the Virginia House of Delegates. This soft-spoken forty-five-year-old-descendant of the Southern aristocracy had the administrative experience, the influential friends, and both the tact and firmness of purpose necessary to fill the position of executive director of the Century Group.

Dr. Henry P. Van Dusen was a close personal friend of Francis and Helen Hill Miller. Born in Philadelphia in 1897, "Pitt" Van Dusen held degrees from Princeton, Edinburgh, and New York's Union Theological Seminary. He had been on the Seminary's faculty since 1926, serving for eight years as Dean of Students. Van Dusen was a Republican, a participant in National Policy Committee meetings, and a member of the Policy Committee of the Committee to Defend America by Aiding the Allies. Because of his student years at Edinburgh and his participation in international Protestant affairs, Van Dusen had influential friends in Britain as well as the United States.

"Pitt" Van Dusen, like Francis Miller, was motivated by an expansive conception of the role of the Christian church in modern life. If the church was, as he had written, "the custodian of the funded values of the past" and responsible for "the continuation of Christ's work in the world," then it was imperative for churchmen to resist the forces which had announced—both by word and deed—their emnity for those values and that work.[8] The dominating impulse on the Union Theological campus during the thirties was involvement in social problems. Clerical students joined picket lines and participated in protest marches

8. Henry P. Van Dusen, "What is the Church? *Journal of Religion*, XVII (October, 1937), pp. 421–22.

—occasionally running afoul of municipal authorities. Van Dusen shared this concern with domestic social conditions, but, toward the end of the decade, his views on foreign policy conflicted increasingly with those of the student body. His belief that the Christian should be prepared to take up arms to defend his faith and his civilization clashed with the pacifism of many of the seminary students who insisted that war was un-Christian whatever its purpose.[9] Van Dusen and other "social gospel" clergymen who favored United States involvement in 1940 did not share the same utopian crusading spirit which had motivated the interventionist clergymen of 1917. They did not seek belligerency as an invigorating and inspiring opportunity but rather accepted it reluctantly as a "negative task," an undesirable obstruction to be overcome before the productive work for social and economic justice could be resumed.

Two events drove Van Dusen to action. First, he was stung by the fact he had not been asked to sign "A Summons to Speak Out." When he read it in the newspapers, he recognized that it said precisely what he wanted the opportunity to say publicly. He believed that the "Summons" alone would not suffice and that it needed to be augmented by a continuing public discussion of the circumstances under which America should go to war. Second, Van Dusen attended a Methodist conference in Chicago on June 27. The subject under discussion was "Christianity as a World Movement." When one speaker on this subject—an eminent clergyman—took the opportunity to make a plea for an American policy of absolute isolation from European affairs, Van Dusen was outraged. He recalled, twenty-five years later, that this more than anything else brought home to him the degree to which the "utter unreality of isolationism" had pervaded American thought. Something *had* to be done. When Van Dusen saw Francis Miller two days later at a National Policy Committee meeting, he proposed a conference of interventionists.[10]

Van Dusen enlisted Henry Luce and Henry Sloane Coffin in the Century Group. He participated in the drafting of major

9. See Morgan P. Noyes, *Henry Sloane Coffin: The Man and his Work* (New York, 1964).
10. Author's interview with Van Dusen.

speeches and memoranda and saw British Ambassador Lothian several times on behalf of the Group. Later, he organized clerical support for aid to Britain and intervention, and directed the Group's campaign against Herbert Hoover's proposal to feed the population of Nazi-controlled Europe.

Lewis W. Douglas was a native of Arizona. Douglas' grandfather had come to the Southwest from England and had made a fortune in copper mining. One of his sons remained a British subject and the other became an American citizen. Lewis, son of the American Douglas, was sent east to Amherst and the Massachusetts Institute of Technology. In 1918 he served as a first lieutenant with the 91st Division in Flanders and the Argonne Forest. Afterwards he taught history at Amherst for a year before devoting his attention to Arizona business and politics. During the 1920's he served as a Democratic congressman and in 1933 accepted an appointment as Roosevelt's Director of the Budget. Douglas ably administered the retrenchment measures of the New Deal's first year. However, when Roosevelt broke up the London Economic Conference and refused to balance the budget if this meant circumscribing federal relief measures, Douglas grew increasingly dissatisfied and finally resigned in August of 1934. He joined the anti-New Deal forces and in 1937 had a hand in the formation of the short-lived "Conservative Coalition," which circulated an anti-Roosevelt tract known as the "Manifesto" among United States Senators.[11]

Now, in 1940, as a leading supporter of Wendell Willkie, the forty-six-year-old Douglas had the ear of the Republican nominee. His efforts in the Willkie camp helped to offset the pressures of Republican isolationists on the candidate during the presidential campaign. Douglas was also the head of the Mutual Life Insurance Company and a member of the Executive Committee of the Committee to Defend America by Aiding the Allies. If Douglas feared that New Deal innovations such as the National Recovery Administration and federal public works threatened (in his own words) "the liberties for which the Anglo-Saxon race has struggled for more than one thousand years," he was even more convinced of the greater danger presented by fascist aggression. In a speech before the United States Chamber of

11. See *New York Times* and *Washington Post,* September, 1937.

Commerce on May 2, he denounced isolationism. "To retreat to the cyclone cellar here," he asserted, "means, ultimately, to establish a totalitarian State at home. . . . This is not merely another European war," he continued. "This is a struggle between two wholly contradictory, two clashing ways of life. We cannot escape the consequences of its outcome." [12]

Having been host to the first Century Group meeting, Douglas became *de facto* chairman of subsequent gatherings. His two most important contributions during the summer of 1940 were establishing close relations between William Allen White's Committee and the Group, and getting Wendell Willkie to promise not to attack Roosevelt's destroyer-bases deal.

Although *Ulric Bell* could not be considered a "leader" of the Century Group in July, 1940, he, like Francis Miller, did put his personal stamp on the movement for intervention. Bell was a hard-drinking newspaperman who had grown with the *Louisville Courier-Journal* from cub reporter in 1910, to city editor, to Washington correspondent. A native of St. Louis, Bell was one of only two men in the Group who had no college training. During the Great War he was a captain in the 83rd Infantry and later Kentucky State Commander of the American Legion. In 1933–34 Bell accompanied Secretary of State Hull to the Montevideo Conference, managing the Secretary's public relations as "press advisor." He remained personally close to Hull and throughout 1941 frequently exchanged information with him or forwarded proposals on behalf of the Warhawks.

During thirty years with the *Courier-Journal,* Bell had imbibed the liberalism, internationalism, and sense of civic duty which motivated that paper's directors—Barry Bingham, Mark Ethridge, and Herbert Agar. Bell's long experience as a reporter had taught him practical lessons about public opinion and politics. The chambers, hearing-rooms, and offices of Washington had been his classrooms. He was, as Francis Miller recalled years later, "weatherwise—he knew the score." [13]

Because of his background, the forty-nine-year-old Bell was "the 'operator' in the Croup; he saw people in Washington;

12. *New York Times,* May 3, 1940.
13. Author's interview with Francis P. Miller; "Biographical Sketch: Ulric Bell," FFF MSS.

he made contacts; he got things done." According to Miller, "He was practical. Herbert Agar was interested in ideas, theories and philosophies, but Ulric reduced these to concrete agenda of things that had to be done, and he got them done." Bell knew "all the newspapermen and put them in touch with the Group."[14] His friendship with Steve Early and General Edwin M. "Pa" Watson of the White House staff was also useful to the Warhawks.

In October, 1940, when Francis Miller returned to his work at the Council on Foreign Relations, Ulric Bell left Washington and went to New York to direct the Century Group's office. There he made the day-to-day policy decisions, arranged the Group's dinner meetings, and organized the campaign of public letters and speeches which the Warhawks sponsored. When the formal organization for intervention, the Fight For Freedom Committee, superceded the Group in April, 1941, he became its Executive Chairman.

If Bell was to be a "leading actor" in the interventionist drama, then *Ward Cheney* was the production's "angel." At first the Group's expenses were divided evenly among the members, but as its work expanded this system became too great a burden for the less affluent individuals. Cheney's contributions eventually covered half of the Group's expenditures, which during the first two months totaled a modest $3,500. The main expenses incurred were rent of the small office, postage, telephone and telegraph charges, and the salaries of Francis Miller and one or two office workers.

Cheney was forty-one years old, a Protestant, and a Connecticut resident. He headed Cheney Brothers, a large manufacturer of silk fabric, and was an alumnus of and a heavy contributor to Yale University. A lifelong Republican, in 1940 Cheney became so certain that the Democratic administration was the surest vehicle for an "all-out" policy that he crossed party lines to vote for Roosevelt. Cheney believed that America's future lay with Britain and that his countrymen must resist the forces of oppression which, he was convinced, would soon threaten America directly. Basically a private person, whose interests tended to

14. Author's interview with Francis P. Miller.

the arts and literature, he considered himself an inept speaker. Although he rarely missed a Group meeting, he tended to listen rather than talk. His strength lay in his quiet willingness to sustain his strong convictions with his personal fortune.

The piercing eyes of *Herbert Agar* revealed the intellect and determination which lay within. Born in 1897 in New Rochelle, New York, of Catholic parents, he received degrees from Columbia and Princeton. He served as an ordinary seaman in the Navy during the Great War and later worked as London correspondent for the *Louisville Courier-Journal.* After migrating to Louisville, he rose swiftly to become editor of the *Courier-Journal.* As such he was an influential advocate of Franklin Roosevelt and the New Deal. He was also an outstanding figure in the Southern literary renaissance which included Robert Penn Warren, William Faulkner, Tennessee Williams, and Thomas Wolfe. At the age of forty-one he won the Pulitzer Prize in history for *The People's Choice: from Washington to Harding.* A lively survey of the presidency, *The People's Choice* concluded that America's leadership had been, with few exceptions, in the hands of incompetent and inexperienced mediocrities for the past century. According to Agar, the golden age of American politics had ended in 1829, when an intelligent, principled, and well-bred elite had been supplanted by Jacksonian democracy.

A versatile writer on art, literature, and poetry, as well as history and current affairs, Agar sensed deeply America's cultural ties to England. As Francis Miller recalls: "Herbert was our Old Testament prophet. He was our conscience, our goad, our stimulator. . . . He was brilliant intellectually and morally very convincing. When he spoke to you . . . you felt that Mount Sinai itself had spoken, that these were the Commandments, and it had to be done.[15]

As a liberal, Agar was revolted by Nazi persecution of Jews, Catholics, and all other dissenters. He had criticized the Third Reich in his editorials since the early thirties. After Dunkirk he believed that the evil did not threaten Europe alone. In the summer of 1940 he joined with Helen Hill Miller to write, ". . . The people and politicians of the United States are next in

15. *Ibid.*

line. . . . The United States has this peculiar distinction: in all the world, when her turn comes, there will be no friend remaining, no hope of outside aid."[16] Like so many of the Warhawks, he was sure that time was working against them. It was necessary, he felt, to strike before the enemy attacked us in a time and place of his own choosing: "We are late, very late, but in 1940 we still have time. We shall not have time in 1942."[17] Agar, a signer of "A Summons to Speak Out," saw the President at least twice in the summer of 1940 on behalf of the Group and later was a leading speaker and policy-maker for the Fight For Freedom.

* * * * * *

Each of the twenty-two other Warhawks contributed significantly to the Group or its successor, the Fight For Freedom. Some lent the weight of impressive reputations, others volunteered their voices or their pens. Some assumed responsibility for specific campaigns by the Century Group, others rose to leadership in the Fight For Freedom. A few took little interest in the Group discussions but on some specific occasion rendered irreplaceable assistance to the interventionist cause. Most numerous among the Group members were columnists-news commentators and businessmen. Aside from Ulric Bell, the columnists and news commentators included: Geoffrey Parsons, Major George Fielding Eliot, John L. Balderston, Joseph Alsop, and Elmer Davis.

By 1940 *Geoffrey Parsons* had been chief editorial writer of the *New York Herald Tribune* for sixteen years. Born on Long Island in 1879 and educated at Columbia University, he had worked for the *New York Evening Sun* before joining the *Herald Tribune*. In his spare time he wrote literary essays and poetry. As a staunch Republican writing for a Republican newspaper, he had penned columns critical of Roosevelt's domestic and foreign policy since 1933. After Munich, however, the editorials of the *Herald Tribune*, like the warnings of the President, placed increasing emphasis on the "unpleasant truth" that America's future was bound up with the fate of western Europe. After the

16. Helen Hill and Herbert Agar, *Beyond German Victory* (New York, 1940), pp. 4–5.
17. *Ibid.*, p. 8.

Bishop Henry W. Hobson

Herbert Agar

Francis P. Miller

F. H. Peter Cusick

THE BERLIN BULLIES

"Fats" Goering | "Spider" Goebbels | "Lefty" Laval | "Snoops" Himmler | "Heel" Hitler | "Stool" Quisling | "Dip" Darlan | "Rats" Ribbentrop | "Batboy" Konoye | Pinch-H Lindbe

YOU DON'T WANT THIS TEAM TO WIN —

Whether you're yelling for the Yanks or Whether you're rooting for the Dodgers

HELP BEAT THE BERLIN "BULLIES"

DON'T wait for the last half of the ninth inning to support the U.S.A. — because Schicklgruber's saps won't tolerate baseball games or football or basketball or anything else that smacks of good sportsmanship or fair play.

Sports fans are pretty independent people. There's something sacred about the right to call a player a "bum" or to dub a rookie "Stinky". We've got to protect those rights — or one fair day we'll wake up to find one of the Gestapo Gunmen sitting behind us saying that we can't call the Umpire a "thief" or that we can't even cheer our team.

Now's the time for a little national unity, boys. The World Series is a lot of fun — because we are free men. Our team — Roosevelt, Willkie and the rest — they all like ball games. They're decent people like you and me.

But can you imagine Adolf "The Punk" Schicklgruber enjoying a game?

No — and that's just the difference. Americans like to have fun. But Hitler and his bloodthirsty team want to destroy our world.

We can't take chances. Let's get in there pitching! Now is the time!

BEAT THE HELL OUT OF HITLER

Join the:
FIGHT FOR FREEDOM
1270 Sixth Avenue
New York City

Republican convention of 1940, Parsons drafted the foreign affairs section of Wendell Willkie's acceptance speech.

Although *George Fielding Eliot* was born in Brooklyn in 1894, he was educated in Australia. He served with Australian forces in the Dardanelles and on the Western Front and, after the war, with the Royal Canadian Mounted Police. Later he was a Major in the United States Army Intelligence Reserve and an accountant in Kansas City. From the beginning of hostilities he was naval correspondent on the *New York Herald Tribune* and military analyst for C.B.S. By the time of Munich, Eliot was urging America to arm in order to deter potential aggressors. He remained confident, however, that there was "no reason for assuming that if general European war occurs we shall necessarily be drawn into it." He was sure that British and French naval power would be ample to protect American commerce.[18] By the summer of 1940, with the French out of the war, a Nazi invasion fleet assembling in Channel ports, and the *Luftwaffe* nesting in fields from Bergen to Bordeaux, the balance of power in the North Atlantic had shifted; and Eliot, now living in New York, was not alone among the experts making stunned reappraisals.

A journalist by trade, *John Balderston* of Beverly Hills was best known in 1940 for his dramas and screenplays. Born in Philadelphia in 1889, he had attended Columbia University briefly before becoming a war correspondent in 1915. As a McClure Syndicate writer, his emotional articles were partial to Great Britain. In 1917 he became director of information in Great Britain and Ireland for the United States Committee on Public Information. From 1923 to 1931 he worked for the *New York World* as its London correspondent, in his spare time writing a well-received novel and play, *Berkeley Square*. As a screen-writer in the thirties, his credits included "Lives of A Bengal Lancer," "Last of the Mohicans," and "The Prisoner of Zenda." After spending so much time on the Continent and in Britain, Balderston understood the ties which bound America's life, thought, and culture to western Europe's. In August and

18. George Fielding Eliot, *The Ramparts We Watch* (New York, 1938), pp. 348–49.

September, 1940, he directed the pro-British "William Allen White News Service" in Washington.

Harvard-educated *Joseph Alsop* was thirty years old, the youngest member of the Group. Despite his youth, this Connecticut-born Episcopalian had already co-authored two political best-sellers, *The 168 Days* (with Turner Catledge), relating the story of Roosevelt's duel with the Supreme Court, and *Men Around the President* (with Robert Kintner). In mid-1940 he and his fellow columnist, Kintner, published *An American White Paper,* which described America's place in the world crisis. Because of his contact with men of power and influence in the Capital, Alsop was valuable to the Group as a source of information and as a means of reaching "the people who counted." Impatient for involvement in the battle against the Axis, he left the Group at the end of the summer and, after a short stint in the Navy, joined the American Volunteer Group—the "Flying Tigers"—in China.[19]

Elmer Davis was the only native midwesterner to participate in the gatherings. Born in 1890 in the town of Aurora, Indiana, just across the Ohio River from Kentucky, Davis had grown to manhood in his native state. He attended Oxford's Queen's College on a Rhodes Scholarship. During and after the First World War he was on the staff of the *New York Times.* In 1940 Davis was a highly respected radio news commentator. He had a dry sense of humor and a gift for expressing his thoughts pithily; and his C.B.S. broadcasts from Washington made him a celebrity in every home that had a radio. Although his native Midwest was the most isolationist section of the country, Davis embraced the internationalism and Anglophilism prevalent among the Eastern Establishment.

Six Group members came from the world of trade and commerce. Aside from Lewis Douglas and Ward Cheney, these included Will Clayton, Whitney Shepardson, James Warburg, and George Watts Hill.

Will Clayton was born in Mississippi in 1880; he had no college education. His personal success story was written in the books of the Houston firm of Anderson, Clayton and Company,

19. Author's interview with Joseph Alsop.

which Clayton had founded at the age of twenty-four and which grew to be the largest cotton brokerage house in the world. During the First World War this Democrat had been a member of the committee on cotton distribution of the War Industries Board, and since 1938 he had directed the Houston regional study committee on the Council on Foreign Relations. In 1940 he was a vice president of the Export-Import Bank.

A native of Worcester, Massachusetts, *Whitney H. Shepardson* held degrees from Colgate and Harvard and had been a Rhodes Scholar at Oxford. A Republican and a Baptist, Shepardson had been involved in international affairs first as an attorney, then as a member of the United States Commission to Negotiate the Peace at Versailles, and later as an international investor and executive. In 1940 this forty-nine year old New Yorker's main business interest was International Railways of Central America. Since 1934 he had been co-author of the annual Council on Foreign Relations volume, *The United States in World Affairs,* as well as treasurer and a director of the Council. Shepardson was one of eight in the Group who had signed "A Summons to Speak Out," and it was he who drafted that document.

James P. Warburg was one of only two foreign-born members of the Group. Born in Hamburg in 1896 of Jewish parents, he was brought to the United States as an infant. A graduate of Harvard and an officer of the naval Flying Corps during the World War, Warburg, like Shepardson, pursued simultaneous careers in commerce and letters. By 1940 he had published nine volumes ranging in subject from politics to the manufacture of leather goods. Warburg's relationship with President Roosevelt was based on mutual respect and exasperation. As a leading Democratic banker, Warburg had been brought into the administration in 1933 by Raymond Moley. His pleasure at Roosevelt's first efforts of retrenchment was replaced by disappointment and distaste for the deficit financing and monetary experimentation which followed. In 1935 and 1936 he published two small books denouncing Roosevelt's "orgy of wild spending" and predilection for "dictatorship." However, he found Landon so unpalatable that by election day he had returned to the Democratic side. In the late thirties, as Hitler gained in strength and ambition from the appeasement of France and Britain, Warburg became convinced that the "only hope of averting a second World War lay in a much stronger policy." By the summer of 1940 it seemed clear to him that the American people could no longer hope to avoid war, if they wished to live in a world not totally hostile to the democratic way.[20]

George Watts Hill, a Presbyterian and a Democrat, was a leading citizen of Durham, North Carolina. Born in New York in 1901, he was educated at Chapel Hill and admitted to the North Carolina bar in 1924. Seven years later he was a director of Durham's Erwin Cotton Mills. In 1940 he was president of a local bank and leader of cooperative marketing and farmer organizations. Hill participated in the work of the National Policy Committee's southern affiliate and was a signer of "A Summons to Speak Out."

Three eminent attorneys—each of whom had vast experience in international relations and government service and two of whom were destined for greater things—participated in Group meetings. They were Frank L. Polk, Dean G. Acheson, and Allen W. Dulles.

Sixty-eight-year-old *Frank L. Polk* was the oldest member of the Group. Twenty years before, he had been the man burdened with conducting America's foreign affairs at the moment the United States Senate was rejecting the Versailles Treaty. From July to December, 1919, while President Wilson lay paralyzed in Washington, Polk, as Acting Secretary of State, had been the head of the American delegation in Paris. There he had witnessed the first harmful effects of America's renunciation of international responsibility. After that experience the Yale alumnus had returned to the city of his birth, New York, and had been engaged in private law practice.[21]

Dean G. Acheson had law offices in New York and Washington. After having graduated from Groton, where, like Franklin Roosevelt, he had absorbed Headmaster Endicott Peabody's preachments of Christian duty and *noblesse oblige,* Acheson had attended Yale College and Harvard Law School. An ardent Bull

20. Arthur M. Schlesinger, Jr., *The Age of Roosevelt: The Politics of Upheaval* (Boston, 1960), p. 634; James P. Warburg, *The Long Road Home* (Garden City, N.Y., 1964), p. 179.

21. Frank L. Polk Papers, Sterling Library, Yale University.

Mooser in 1912 when he was nineteen, Acheson had served in the Navy and had then become private secretary to Justice Louis D. Brandeis. During two decades as a practicing attorney, this Connecticut-born Episcopalian had represented clients as varied as the House of Morgan and the Soviet Union. He had served as Franklin Roosevelt's Under Secretary of the Treasury until the President forced his resignation in October, 1933, in a dispute over gold-buying. Acheson, however, had retained Roosevelt's respect and, despite his distaste for some of Roosevelt's fiscal measures, he remained in the Democratic party. As early as November, 1939, Acheson argued that America's foreign policy should have two aspects, one "prophylactic," designed to protect our interests and security, and the other "therapeutic," directed at solving the problems underlying the current global unrest. By protecting our interests he did not mean continentalism; as he told undergraduates at Yale's Davenport College, "Nothing seems to me more foolish than a policy designed to assure that if we must fight, the fighting shall be done on our own territory." [22]

New York attorney *Allen W. Dulles* came from a family steeped in foreign affairs. This forty-seven year old son of a New York Presbyterian minister counted among his relatives two secretaries of state and a minister to Great Britain.[23] As a young diplomat in Switzerland in 1918, Dulles had been one of the first to suggest the organization of a group of scholars to study the problems of postwar Europe, which an American peace conference delegation would have to face. This idea evolved into the "Inquiry" which (despite the shortcomings of the Versailles Treaty) was the first effort by American diplomacy to achieve expertise on the problems of eastern Europe and the Balkans. Dulles himself had served with the American Commission to Negotiate the Peace and had remained in the State Department

22. Dean G. Acheson, *Morning and Noon: A Memoir* (Boston, 1965), pp. 267–75.

23. Dulles' earliest recorded policy position had been decidedly anti-British. While still in grammer school, he had been fascinated by the discussions of the Boer War he had heard between his grandfather, John Watson Foster (Benjamin Harrison's Secretary of State) and his uncle, Robert Lansing (subsequently Wilson's Secretary of State). Young Dulles penned an essay supporting the Boers which his grandfather had published privately. See John Robinson Beal, *John Foster Dulles: A Biography* (New York, 1957), pp. 34–35.

into the twenties, first as Chief of the Near Eastern Division and later as American representative at the various disarmament and arms traffic conferences. As early as 1935 Dulles and Hamilton Fish Armstrong had published an examination of American neutrality legislation, which posed the question, "Can We Be Neutral?" By September, 1939, with Poland in flames, Dulles was certain that "no neutrality legislation can give us the advantages of an isolation which does not in fact exist, and those who preach the contrary are not . . . the realists they call themselves."[24] Ten months later, Dulles was an avowed interventionist.

Three educators—James B. Conant, Ernest M. Hopkins, and William Agar—attended Century dinner meetings.

James Bryant Conant was born in Dorchester, Massachusetts in 1893. As an undergraduate and graduate student at Harvard he had excelled in chemistry and, after receiving his doctorate, had become an instructor there in 1916. His war service was as an officer in the Sanitary Corps and the Chemical Warfare Service. When he returned to Cambridge he advanced to professor and then chairman of the Chemistry Department, finally becoming President of Harvard University in 1933. A nominal Republican, Conant, unlike most of the Group, was more a Germanophile than an Anglophile, and his horror at what the Nazis were doing to Germany played a large part in his hatred of Hitler. At the same time that Conant was active in the Century Group, he was also a leading spokesman for the Committee to Defend America. Later, although the President enlisted him in the scientific aspects of the preparedness program, Conant agreed to be a sponsor of the Fight For Freedom.

Ernest M. Hopkins had been President of Dartmouth College since 1916. A native of New Hampshire, a Republican, and a Baptist, he was an alumnus of the school he directed. During the Great War he had been Assistant to Secretary of War Newton Baker, his work focusing on the War Labor Policies Board. In this capacity he had known young Franklin Roosevelt, who, as Assistant Secretary of the Navy, had been Secretary Josephus Daniels' representative on the Board. Like Acheson,

24. Allen W. Dulles and Hamilton Fish Armstrong, *Can America Stay Neutral?* (New York, 1939), pp. 153–54; also, see their *Can America Be Neutral?* (New York, 1935).

Warburg, and other conservatives in the group, the sixty-three year old Hopkins disliked some of the Roosevelt administration's new departures in domestic policy. He feared that "initiative, courage, hardihood, frugality, and aspiration for self-betterment" were being penalized by some New Deal legislation. He saw increasing government intervention in the lives of the people as "inducing a deterioration in our national character to a point little short of self-destruction."[25] Hopkins and the other anti-New Dealers feared the eventual results of surrendering economic freedom and private liberty to the federal government in this time of national crisis, but they were convinced that the external danger was great enough to justify such a surrender. Most remained frankly pessimistic about the reassertion of traditional rights when the peril was passed. For the anti-New Deal interventionists, a world governed by Roosevelt was unpleasant to contemplate, but a world dominated by Hitler was unthinkable. In 1941 Hopkins became a frequent speaker for the Fight For Freedom.

William Agar, Herbert Agar's older brother, was a geologist and school principal. A Democrat, he held a doctorate from Princeton University. He was twenty when the Great War began, and he served first with the French Service Sanitaire des Etats Unis and later as a pilot in the United States Army Air Service. Afterwards he taught geology at Yale and at Columbia, before becoming Headmaster of the Newman School in Lakewood, New Jersey. Dr. Agar served the Group as a specialist on Catholic affairs and later was a full-time member of the staff of the Fight For Freedom.

Henry Van Dusen enlisted two other clergymen in the Century Group—*Henry Sloane Coffin* and Henry W. Hobson. As president of the Union Theological Seminary, Dr. Coffin was Dr. Van Dusen's superior. A Republican and a native New Yorker, Coffin had earned degrees from both Yale and Edinburgh—one of seven members of the Group to be educated in part in Great Britain. He had served as pastor of two New York churches before becoming president of the Seminary in 1926 at the age of

25. Arthur M. Schlesinger, Jr., *The Age of Roosevelt: The Coming of the New Deal* (Boston, 1958), p. 476.

forty-nine. Dr. Coffin was the author of several books on religion and morality the general theme of which was the necessity for Christian involvement in public issues. Believing that Christians had to participate actively in the struggle against the totalitarians for the future of modern man and having confronted nazism during a trip to Germany a few years earlier, Dr. Coffin engaged in the work of the Century Group from its inception.[26]

Bishop Henry W. Hobson was born in 1891 and reared in Denver, Colorado. However, like the overwhelming majority of the other Group members, he had received an Eastern education, first at Yale and then at the Episcopal Theological School in Cambridge, Massachusetts. A major in the 89th Division of the A.E.F., he was wounded twice and gassed once. After the war he served in churches in Connecticut and Ohio before being named Bishop of Cincinnati. A Democrat, Hobson was an eager signer of the "Summons." In the spring of 1941 he was chosen Chairman of the Fight For Freedom. Hobson was outspoken in his criticism of what he called "the lie of isolationism." No one, he told a New York congregation, "hates war more than I do. I have seen its horror and its waste. But," he insisted, "there are evils worse than war:"

> There are values in life which are of such supreme importance for man's whole well-being that they are not just worth sympathy, not just material backing, not just moral indignation which spends itself in lofty words—but worth dying for. As a Christian I cannot find these values in any program which would substitute a spirit of patriotic isolationism and selfish appeasement for the truth that as children of God we, 'members one of another,' have a world-wide responsibility for the well-being and rights of man. . . .
>
> To march under the banner of 'America First,' if that slogan means that we of America adopt the isolationist and appeasement position of 'Save ourselves no matter what happens to the other fellow,' is to be guilty of that lie that denies the very nature of life which God has bestowed upon us.[27]

26. Noyes, *Henry Sloane Coffin.*

27. Henry W. Hobson, "The Lie of Isolation: A Sermon Preached in St. Bartholomew's Church in the City of New York on Sunday morning, December 1, 1940," HWH MSS; Hobson and Coffin were among the signers of the statement "America's Responsibility in the Present Crisis,"

There were two publishers in the Century Group, *Henry R. Luce* and Harold Guinzburg. Luce, the Republican publisher of *Time, Life,* and *Fortune* magazines, was born in Shantung province, China, in 1898, the son of an American missionary. After spending his boyhood in China, he had returned to America to attend Hotchkiss and Yale. Subsequently, he studied at Oxford and served as a Second Lieutenant in the United States Field Artillery. After the war he came to New York and made his fortune by creating a popular, entertaining news magazine. His father's missionary zeal was not much diluted in Henry Luce—only redirected into publishing and world affairs. "America is responsible," he declared in 1941, "to herself as well as to history for the world environment in which she lives." America's mission was too great for her to live "like an infinitely mightier Switzerland discreetly and dangerously in the midst of enemies." The twentieth century was not to be the era of the totalitarians, he intoned, but would be instead "the first great American Century." [28] In May, 1940, Luce returned to the United States from a tour of Britain and France. Shocked by what he had seen, he urged Americans to set aside their political differences so that they would have the strength of unity when they "take their stand at Armageddon."

Despite his propensity for florid phrases, Luce's hard-boiled criticisms of papers drafted by the Group focused attention on obtaining specific benefits for the United States from any "deal" with the British. Although he was certain that America would eventually have to fight, he believed that until his country had rearmed it served its own and Britain's interest best by remaining a non-belligerent supplier of arms and food. Thus, in the summer of 1940, he functioned as a moderating counterbalance to those in the Group who demanded immediate hostilities.

Harold Guinzburg, a Jewish native of New York, was the president of Viking Press. Guinzburg held a Bachelor of Arts degree from Harvard. Like Henry Luce, he had become a suc-

---

issued in May, 1940, by Van Dusen, which declared that the U.S. had compelling practical and moral reasons for "lending . . . support" to the Allies, HWH MSS.

28. Henry R. Luce, "The American Century," reprint from *Life* magazine, February 17, 1941, p. 7.

cessful publisher while still in his twenties, founding Viking Press in 1925. Although an infrequent speaker, he attended Group meetings regularly and published some of the writings of other interventionists. During 1941 Guinzburg was consulted on day-to-day policy by Bell and Peter Cusick at Fight For Freedom headquarters.

Broadway and Hollywood were also represented in interventionist councils, the former by three-time Pulitzer Prize winner *Robert E. Sherwood* and the latter by motion picture producer Walter Wanger. Sherwood, born in New Rochelle in 1896, had left Harvard to join a regiment of the Canadian Black Watch in 1917, and had returned to America an ardent pacifist. But Nazi use of force had nullified the concept of non-violence. As Sherwood watched the disappearance of half a dozen "pacifistic" and "neutral" nations and the organized persecution of the "non-violent" Jewish race, he came to realize that force could only be defeated by force. Throughout the winter of 1939–40 this New York Democrat had been active in the work of war relief organizations and in May became a member of the Policy Committee of William Allen White's organization. His Broadway hit, "There Shall Be No Night"—which won the Pulitzer Prize for drama in 1941, was a eulogy to Finland's heroic resistance to aggression. In June, 1940, Sherwood published a full-page advertisement in major newspapers across the country on behalf of the Committee to Defend America. In uncompromising tones the advertisement urged America to "Stop Hitler Now" by sending aid to the Allies and asked readers to write to Washington demanding immediate action. In the fall President Roosevelt—impressed by the newspaper appeal—asked Sherwood to collaborate with Harry Hopkins and Samuel Rosenman in writing his campaign speeches; thereafter Sherwood was a regular visitor at the White House.[29]

Walter Wanger, a Jew, was born in San Francisco in 1894 and educated at Dartmouth, Heidelberg, and Oxford. Despite a reputation for "extravaganzas," Wanger believed strongly that the movies could be a potent instrument for educating and informing the public. As a young man of twenty-four, he had

29. Robert E. Sherwood, *Roosevelt and Hopkins: An Intimate History* (New York, 1948), pp. 11–13, 127–34; Walter Johnson, *The Battle Against Isolation* (Chicago, 1944), pp. 85–88.

been an attache to the American peace mission at Versailles and had for a time considered a career in diplomacy. On his return to the United States, however, he became general manager of the fledgling Paramount Studios. His interventionist attitude was representative of the strong pro-Allied sentiment which prevailed in the film industry. He served the cause of intervention as a fund-raiser, organizer, and speaker.[30]

Only one Group member had devoted his life to military service—*Admiral William H. Standley.* From 1933 to 1937 Standley had been Chief of Naval Operations. In retirement he resided in New York where he participated in the regional study committee of the Council on Foreign Relations and wrote articles on questions of naval strategy and preparedness. He was especially aware of American naval weakness in the Atlantic. Born in 1872 in California, Standley was an Episcopalion, an Annapolis graduate, and a signer of "A Summons to Speak Out." He had seen action in both the Spanish-American War and the First World War and had been a member of the American delegation to the futile London Disarmament Conference of 1934. During 1940 his speeches and articles in favor of vigorous American action were directed not only at the public, but at his fellow officers, too many of whom, the Warhawks suspected, held isolationist views.[31] He later became United States Ambassador to Moscow.

* * * * * *

What, then, were the composite characteristics of the twenty-eight men of the Century Group?

Eighteen of the twenty-eight had been born in the Northeast, and in 1940, twenty-one lived in that region, mostly in and around New York City. Three others had first seen light in the South, and five resided there in 1940. Three had been born in the central expanse of America, which was traditionally said to be insulated from the impact of foreign affairs, and only two (Hobson and Douglas) lived there in 1940. It is interesting to note that the geographic distribution of the Policy Committee of

30. Walter Wanger to author, December 24, 1964.

31. See William H. Standley and Arthur A. Ageton, *Admiral Ambassador to Russia* (Chicago, 1955).

White's organization was similar, with twenty-one of twenty-eight from the Northeast and only four from the central states. A comparison with America First's nine executive leaders, however, reveals the expected contrast—all were from the Midwest, seven of them residents of Chicago.[32]

The Group's members' average age was forty-nine. They were thus old enough to have achieved prominence and maturity, yet young enough to act vigorously in support of their beliefs. Of those of military age in 1917, all but three (two of them clergymen) had been in some form of military or government service. As a group, therefore, they understood what going to war implied. Those in the Group who were veterans looked back upon their wartime contribution with a sense of pride in duty done. Although some saw a new war as a last—but inevitable—resort, a few looked forward to it as a revitalizing and purifying national mission.

Thirteen of the Group were identifiable as Democrats and nine as Republicans. However, on domestic issues, those who were clearly conservative outnumbered the liberals more than two to one.[33] Like White's Committee and unlike the America First Committee, which became a vehicle for some political opponents of Roosevelt, the Century Group, although meeting during the height of the 1940 campaign, maintained a generally non-partisan tone. As one participant later proudly declared: "So seldom in American life do you see leading Republicans and Democrats working together during the Presidential campaign. . . . We were both [*sic*] working for our respective candidates, but we came together once a week at the Century Club, leaving all rancor behind, to talk about national interests." [34]

Since political influence had been one criterion for membership, it followed naturally that the Group had access to the leaders of both the administration and the opposition. If Acheson, Agar, and Sherwood could gain a hearing at the White

32. Wayne S. Cole, *America First: The Battle Against Intervention, 1940–1941* (Madison, Wisconsin, 1953), pp. 14–19; Johnson, *The Battle Against Isolation,* p. 246.

33. For example, liberals: Miller, Van Dusen, Herbert Agar and Guinzburg; conservatives: Douglas, Cheney, Parsons, Eliot, Clayton, Polk, Acheson, Dulles, Hopkins, and Luce.

34. Author's interview with Francis P. Miller.

House, then Parsons, Douglas, and Dulles had the confidence of Willkie. The Warhawks also had friends in Congress (including such dissimilar individuals as Carter Glass and Claude Pepper). More important for the moment were their representatives in the Republican nominee's camp and in the administration—the two focal points of foreign policy in a presidential election year.[35]

If the high political standing of the Group's members gained them a hearing in the councils of power, then their vocational backgrounds contributed to the effectiveness of their appeals to the public. The America First Committee leaders were overwhelmingly (seven of nine) involved in business; and the Policy Committee of the Committee to Defend America was a balanced body, including religious, organizational, educational, business, labor, and cultural representatives.[36] The Century Group membership, however, was concentrated in the communications media. Eleven of the Group (Herbert Agar, Alsop, Balderston, Bell, Davis, Eliot, Guinzburg, Luce, Parsons, Sherwood, and Warburg) devoted most of their time to some form of writing, editing, or publishing. Eleven others (William Agar, Coffin, Conant, Douglas, Dulles, Hobson, Hopkins, Miller, Shepardson, Standley, and Van Dusen) wrote books or articles in their spare time or as an adjunct to their professional endeavors. Wanger's movies were a powerful if indirect influence on public attitudes, while Davis' broadcasts were an immediate channel for getting facts and opinions before a nation of radio listeners.

The heavy concentration in the cosmopolitan worlds of journalism, publishing, and theater certainly contributed to the Group's success. Being conversant with many other people engaged in the same kind of work, Group members always knew

35. The America First leaders appear to have had more "contacts" in Congress than the Century Group. The Warhawks did not begin to emphasize their relations with Congressmen until the Lend-Lease debate (February, 1941) and the beginning of the Fight For Freedom. For the relationship between America First Committee and the "like-minded minority," see citations for Senators C. Wayland Brooks, Bennett Champ Clark, Rush Holt, Hiram Johnson, Robert M. La Follette, Gerald P. Nye, Robert H. Reynolds, Henrik Shipstead, Robert A. Taft, and Burton K. Wheeler, as well as those for Congressmen Stephen A. Day, Hamilton Fish, Clare Hoffman, Robert Hutchins, Karl Mundt, Jacob Thorkelson, and Charles W. Tobey in Cole, *America First,* pp. 281–305.

36. *Ibid.,* pp. 14–19; Johnson, *The Battle Against Isolation,* p. 246.

someone they could count on if they wanted an editorial or a column written, a speech drafted, or a news release publicized.

The presence in the Group of five international businessmen or financiers (Douglas, Clayton, Shepardson, Warburg, and Cheney) seemed to support the isolationist contention, popularized by Senator Nye's investigation, that Wall Streeters were willing to send American boys abroad to die to protect their foreign investments. However, so crude a relationship between these individuals' economic interests and their foreign policy views did not in fact exist. Cheney, whose chief overseas trading partners were in France and Japan, stood to lose as much as he might gain from any war boom; and the Japanese were also among Clayton's best customers for raw cotton.[37] Shepardson's interests were primarily in Latin America, not Europe. Douglas and Warburg would suffer financially if Britain fell, but Douglas (who had fought in the Argonne) and Warburg (who had been a naval flier during the Great War) could hardly be accused of sending others abroad to fight their battles. It would be fairer and more realistic to say that, as international businessmen, these individuals emphasized the relationship between America's well-being and the free flow of commerce across the Atlantic. They were especially concerned over their country's access to markets and raw resources in the British Commonwealth, the European nations, and their overseas colonies. They feared that German victory over Britain and subsequent control of the seas would deny the United States vital materials needed for her own defense.

One characteristic of the Group as a whole which heightened and focused their internationalism was the overseas experience of its members. Much more than the America First leaders and even more than the leaders of the Committee to Defend America, members of the Century Group were personally acquainted with Great Britain and the Continent. At least twenty-five of the twenty-eight had had significant personal experience

37. Although the Rome-Berlin-Tokyo relationship was not formally acknowledged until the signing of the Tripartite Pact in September, the interdependence of the three powers' ambitions had been demonstrated by events since Ethiopia and by the interlocking nature of the Rome-Berlin Axis and the Anti-Comintern Pact.

abroad—often in England. Miller, Van Dusen, Davis, Coffin, and Wanger had studied at British universities. Balderston and Herbert Agar had been London correspondents for American newspapers. Eliot and Sherwood had served in the armed forces of the Commonwealth. Nearly everyone in the Group had visited the British Isles and the Continent more than once, either on vacation or business.

This is not to say that these men worked for war merely because they knew more about Europe than other Americans. However, their lives bore witness to the growing interdependence among nations and even continents, nurtured by improvements in communication and transportation. Each man had a personal knowledge, respect, and, perhaps, love for people and places, enterprises, and cultures across the Atlantic. They were highly aware of happenings overseas and were accustomed to considering European—especially British—events and problems as part of their own lives.[38]

It is important in attempting to understand why *these men* decided to speak out for war *so early* to recognize that almost all the men of the Century Group were members of the Eastern Establishment. Sociologists tell us that an "establishment" is that body of business, cultural, intellectual, and political leaders who are the authoritative bearers of their society's values. They are not merely momentary leaders or celebrities but are the sustainers of "respectable" tradition and are recognized as such by society as a whole.[39] In 1940 the Establishment on the Eastern Seaboard was "dominated by an old stock upper class whose members were . . . still overwhelmingly white, Anglo-Saxon, and Protestant in origins and convictions" and were generally internationalists. The members of this elite were identifiable by their positions of leadership in all respectable fields of endeavor, as well as by their family backgrounds, education at Eastern prestige prep schools and universities, and membership in discriminating men's clubs.[40]

38. Of the original Group Luce was probably the only one who was truly an "Asia-ist."

39. See, for example, E. Digby Baltzell, *The Protestant Establishment: Aristocracy and Caste in America* (New York, 1964), pp. 7–10.

40. *Ibid.*, pp. xi, 226–59. Also suggestive on the Eastern Establishment are Richard Rovere, *The American Establishment and Other Reports,*

All the Century Group's members were white, and twenty-two of twenty-eight were Protestant. With the exception of Guinzburg, Warburg and Wanger, every name regularly on the dinner lists had an unquestionable Anglo-Saxon ring. Each man was preeminent in a respected field of endeavor, and over half of them were celebrated national figures. This chapter's biographical sketches have suggested the old-stock background of most of the Group and have documented the high proportion of Harvard, Yale, and Princeton graduates among them. The fact that the Century Group took its name from the exclusive club where they often met demonstrates the Warhawks' unquestioned social acceptability. Most of the Catholics and Jews in the Group, men like William and Herbert Agar and Warburg, were undoubtedly Anglo-Saxon in "convictions," behavior, and education if not in origins and were, therefore, assimilable into the Establishment.

The Anglo-Saxonism of the Group was at least one reason why these men wanted war during the summer of 1940 and why they were so outspoken. Although others recognized the cultural and strategie ties between Britain and America, as "ethnics" the Warhawks had a stronger sense of the interdependence between the two greatest Anglo-Saxon countries.[41] Like Irish-Americans or German-Americans, they saw America's national interest—to some degree at least—from the perspective of their own mother country. And this personal identification with England impelled them to speak out in a way that a reasoned appreciation of United States geopolitical interests alone might not have.

Their position in American society also encouraged or even demanded outspokenness. As members of the Establishment, as old-stock leaders whose Americanism was self-evident, they were freer to advocate radical solutions to America's international dilemma than more recent immigrants. Isolationists could easily demonstrate the subjectivity of a Polish-American or Jewish-American who declared for war—they were, after all, unassimilated foreigners with foreign loyalties. But this was harder to do with a Miller, Hobson, or Standley. A decade before Alger Hiss and Joe McCarthy, popular faith in the disinterested

Opinions and Speculations (New York, 1946); and M. Evans, *The Liberal Establishment* (New York, 1965).

41. See footnote 38, Chapter I.

patriotism of WASP members of the Establishment was infrequently questioned. Although they never discussed it among themselves, the Warhawks sensed that their "American-ness" freed them to advocate a policy which, out of other mouths, might have been branded "unAmerican." [42]

Since nearly all the men in the Group were members of the Establishment, as bearers of traditional values they undoubtedly felt a special responsibility to speak their minds, however much this brought them into conflict with the majority. On so critical an issue as national security, they saw it as their duty as leaders to risk temporary alienation from their society in order to save it. In some of the Warhawks, deep religious convictions contributed to the willingness to sacrifice time and risk reputations in an unpopular cause.

Whether they were liberals who hated fascism's destruction of civil liberties and self-government, or conservatives who feared the totalitarians' destruction of personal independence and private property, the Group, as Establishment members, felt that the traditional values of their society (values of which they were *ex officio* the sustainers and bearers) were being threatened by the Fascists. In the face of an ideological and moral threat as well as a military one, they understood it to be their duty to arouse the nation. Thus, in this way as well, the Group's self-identification as part of the American elite contributed to its willingness to work for intervention in the summer of 1940.

In the final analysis Anglophilism, Establishment membership, and international experience remain only partial explanations of why these men worked for war so early. After all, other men of similar background either opposed United States involvement entirely or believed non-military measures would suffice to protect America and even save Britain. Of greater

42. Author's interview with Francis P. Miller; Right-wing "revisionists" may have grounds to accuse the Warhawks of a "conspiracy" to involve the United States in war but certainly not of a "liberal conspiracy" to get the United States into a war in the "interests of the Soviet Union." The original members of the Group were predominantly conservative, not liberal; and the Warhawks made their decision for war at a time when the Molotov-Ribbentrop Pact was very much in effect and when it seemed possible that war against Germany might also lead to war with Russia.

weight in the Group members' decision to become Warhawks was their reasoned appraisal of the world political realities.

The United States, their analysis began, had a one-ocean navy and a problem to face in the Pacific. If Britain fell and with it her fleet, South America, always politically unstable and already infiltrated by Nazi agents and German "commercial" ventures, would be indefensible against Hitler. After Dunkirk these men were convinced that it was a delusion to believe that Britain, if given sufficient supplies, could overcome the combined might of Germany and Italy. Britain was first in line and we were next. Hitler, they felt certain, could not rest while a prospering democracy defied his ideology and control across an ever-narrowing ocean.[43]

To keep Britain fighting and to rearm the United States, they reasoned, would require massive and immediate industrial mobilization in which the special interests of labor, capital, and consumer must be subjugated to the needs of national defense. From what they knew of human nature, many in the Group were convinced that the American people would not make such a self-sacrificing commitment until the situation was one of total national emergency—a state of war. Thus, they believed all-out war was a necessary precondition to an effective defense effort and to adequate aid to the British.[44]

If they concentrated in their own councils on the practical, concrete questions of the day, the Warhawks never forgot that America's "national interest includes economic, financial, territorial and defense interests, but is not limited to these." The American people would probably not fight out of strict self-interest, they realized, unless attacked directly. But, they asserted, "There are other interests for which the United States will fight":

> They have to do in general with our faith in the American way of life. In its idealized social version this way of life stems from the Ser-

43. "Tentative Draft," FPM MSS.

44. The history of the industrial mobilization effort during the next eighteen months supports this view, Civilian Production Agency, "Industrial Mobilization in the Defense Period," unpublished manuscript, National Archives.

mon on the Mount and the French Revolution. Even the lowest levels of American society are rarely free from the camaraderie of the egalitarian or the touch of mercy of the humanitarian. In its political and legal version this way of life is deeply rooted in English soil. It includes the representative form of government, the liberties and obligations of the Bill of Rights and a relatively free system of production and trade.

We went to war hoping to make the world safe for this way of life in 1917 and we will go to war again hoping to make at least our continent safe for it. This is our paramount national interest.[45]

The Warhawks felt that cold analyses of world politics—no matter how valid and necessary these might be—would not rouse public support for their cause. They believed that only through appeals to a sense of America's ideals and her historic mission (which they felt so strongly themselves) could the American people be rallied to battle.

45. "Tentative Draft," FPM MSS.

IV. The Century Group and Destroyer-Bases

The work for intervention began in July, 1940. Influential private citizens of pro-war attitudes held organized weekly or bi-weekly meetings in New York to decide on ways to stimulate all possible assistance to Great Britain and eventually to take America to war. At these gatherings the Warhawks assigned to themselves specific responsibilities for influencing other national leaders to speak or act for aid and intervention. Although this intervention movement continued until Pearl Harbor, its concrete accomplishments of the summer of 1940 were its most significant. Operating as liaison between the British Embassy and the American press and between Wendell Willkie and Franklin Roosevelt, the Group made important—perhaps indispensable—contributions to the consummation of the Destroyer-Bases Agreement. Although its propaganda thereafter helped to stimulate support for other government actions, never again did the Warhawks contribute so directly to the making of history.

At the July 11 meeting at the Columbia Club, the Warhawks began their work. At that gathering, several individuals accepted specific assignments. Henry Coffin and Henry Luce went to Washington to see Secretaries Hull and Stimson (and, they hoped, President Roosevelt) to urge expanded assistance to the British, especially the approval of Churchill's request for the sale or loan of destroyers. Francis Miller took a leave of absence from the Council on Foreign Relations and began organizing a small office to coordinate the Group's activities. Lewis Douglas agreed to pursue the question of all-out aid to Britain with William Allen White's Committee and with Wendell Willkie. Douglas and Whitney Shepardson drafted a memorandum of the "common conclusions" reached at the initial meeting. Henry Van Dusen volunteered to explore new ways to present Britain's case to the American people. The rest of the members were asked to use their own judgment in choosing means of "awakening America to the danger" and furthering interventionism.[1]

The Douglas-Shepardson memorandum stated the conclusions of the guests: that the current threats "to the American way of life and to the interests of the United States in Europe, Latin America, and the Far East all resulted from the power of Nazi Germany"; "that the survival of the British Commonwealth of Nations . . . free of German control, is an important factor in the preservation of the American way of life"; "that the survival of the British fleet is a factor of critical importance in the defense of the United States and its interests"; that the United States had "only a few weeks more" in which to act to protect her interests; "that the United States *should* act"; and "that our action should be open and not furtive." To this much all had agreed.[2]

Douglas and Shepardson went further, however, by proposing six specific actions, drawn partly from Van Dusen's discussion with Lothian: (1) American ships should be sent to evacuate British children; (2) the United States should convoy food to England; (3) credit should be extended to Great Britain for any purpose; (4) munitions exports to Britain should be expedited; (5) American naval vessels and aircraft should support the Royal Navy and help defend the British Isles; and (6)

1. "Meeting at Columbia Club," draft, July 11, 1940, WHS MSS; examples of members acting independently included Hobson to Willkie, August 9, 1940, and Hobson to Robert A. Taft, August 7, 1940, HWH MSS; also, Acheson's letter to the *New York Times,* August 11, 1940. The best published account of the destroyer-bases agreement is Philip L. Goodhart, *Fifty Ships That Saved The World* (Garden City, N.Y., 1965).

2. "Meeting at Columbia Club," FPM MSS.

in return, the British government should guarantee that if Great Britain fell, the Royal Navy would not surrender but would disperse to the United States and to the Commonwealth nations and continue the fight. This program, the memorandum concluded, would best be brought about by a treaty between the two governments, duly ratified by the United States Senate.[3]

Henry Luce disapproved of these six points. He argued that only the initial, general conclusions had received the approval of all. Luce was not prepared to take steps which he felt meant immediate armed clashes with Germany in the Atlantic. As he wrote Miller: ". . . Whereas I would agree that definite and even considerable *risks* of war should be taken—openly and with the full knowledge and consent of the people—I am not willing that definite acts of war be taken at this time. There is a great deal still to be done which is not a definite act of war—repeal of the Neutrality Act, for example."[4] In the period between July 11 and July 25, the date set for the next gathering, Shepardson, Miller, and Douglas discussed Luce's objections and decided to cut out the point about United States air and naval units participating in the defense of Britain.[5] But it was too late to prevent the circulation of mimeographed copies of the memorandum among the Group members and friendly newspaper editors and publishers.[6]

Within a week of the Columbia Club dinner, Francis Miller had secured the modest office which was to serve as the Group's clearing house, a two-room suite in the Albee Building on 42nd Street off Fifth Avenue. The interventionists saw a favorable portent in the number of the suite, 2940. Hitler had sworn the Third Reich would rule for a thousand years, they noted, but their cause, and not his, would survive to the year 2940. By coincidence the suite adjoining the Group office was occupied by the German Fellowship Forum, directed by Friedrich Auhagen. The Forum was a Nazi front disseminating pro-

3. *Ibid.*
4. Luce to Francis P. Miller, July 29, 1940, WHS MSS.
5. Francis P. Miller to Shepardson, July 30, 1940, WHS MSS.
6. Clayton to Eugene Meyer, July 13, 1940, WHS MSS; this memorandum was also apparently circulated among sympathetic individuals at the Democratic National Convention in Chicago, Clayton to Douglas, July 15, 1940, WHS MSS.

Hitler propaganda and a gathering place for German agents. During the next half year, Miller and his successor in Room 2940, Ulric Bell, were able to assist the Federal Bureau of Investigation by providing information as to the goings-on next door. Auhagen, when apprehended, testified to the activities of many agents of the German government in this country, and J. Edgar Hoover wrote a personal note of thanks to Room 2940.[7]

The operation of the office was limited in scope. Miller and a staff of two or three secretaries coordinated the efforts of the Group. Members met or telephoned to discuss some point of policy or some new issue or event. Miller made arrangements for subsequent dinner meetings, wiring out-of-town members as to time and place. Mimeographed copies of the meeting memoranda as well as speeches, columns, and editorials by Group members or other internationalists were dispatched to journalists and influential public figures on a private mailing list.

Most of those on the list were known to Miller or his wife because of their interest in the work of the regional foreign relations groups or the National Policy Committee. They included Ralph McGill of the Atlanta *Constitution*, W. W. Waymack of the Des Moines *Register and Tribune,* Barry Bingham of the *Louisville Courier-Journal,* Walter Millis, Dorothy Thompson, and Ernest K. Lindley of the *New York Herald Tribune,* Anne O'Hare McCormick and Hanson Baldwin of *The New York Times,* William Hessler of the *Cincinnati Enquirer,* George Fort Milton of *The Evening Tribune* of Chattanooga, and Donald Sterling of the Portland, Oregon *Journal.* Most of these journalists remained on the mailing lists of the Warhawks through the next year and a half, giving news coverage and editorial expression to interventionism, as well as providing information about changes of public opinion in confidential letters to the New York office. In 1941 some, like Dorothy Thompson and Barry Bingham, were willing to stump the country on behalf of the Fight For Freedom. For the moment, however, their contribution consisted of giving widespread public exposure to the copy which flowed out of Miller's office.[8]

7. Hoover to Bell, November 25, 1940, FFF MSS.

8. Author's interview with Francis P. Miller; "List of Newspapers," May 29, 1940, FPM MSS.

The "private" propaganda campaign of Room 2940 was based on the premise that time was too short to make a successful direct assault on the isolationists in Congress who were obstructing aid to Britain. The things that had to be done could not wait upon the election. The Warhawks were certain (as were nearly all observers) that by election day the Germans would already have launched an invasion of the British Isles. Instead, through their relations with leaders of the press in all sections of the country, the Group sought to condition public thinking to the immediate necessity of "all aid to Britain." To convert the Congress and the public to interventionism would take months if not years. Now the main consideration was to help keep Britain going.[9]

Lewis Douglas had been given two tasks to perform—one rather easy, the second more challenging. As a member of the Policy Committee of the Committee to Defend America by Aiding the Allies, he was to establish liaison between that nationwide organization and the Century Group "for the purpose of pressing on it the necessity of continuing a vigorous educational program in respect of the vital importance of the British fleet to our defense."[10] This was the beginning of a period of close cooperation between the Warhawks and the William Allen White Committee. During the following months Clark Eichelberger, director of the national headquarters of the Committee to Defend America, attended several Century Group meetings, and George Field, executive secretary of the New York chapter, also maintained close contact. Under White's leadership the Committee took the view that the British fleet was "our first line of defense," and agitated for the sale of destroyers to Britain.[11]

On July 23, the Committee to Defend America announced a four-point program calling for the sale of United States destroyers through private companies to the British, evacuation of

9. Author's interview with Francis P. Miller and Shepardson.

10. "Meeting at Columbia Club," draft, WHS MSS.

11. White was invited to the meeting of July 25, 1940, but was unable to make the trip from Kansas, White to F. P. Miller, July 25, 1940, FFF MSS. He received a memorandum of that meeting's proceedings and of July 11, 1940, WAW MSS. White's attitude is illustrated in White to C. H. Crandon, August 27, 1940; White to Eichelberger, June 11, 1940, and August 15, 1940; and White to Roosevelt, June 10, 1940, WAW MSS.

British children on American ships, agricultural credits for Britain, and an embargo on oil shipments to Fascist Spain. From July 30 to August 1, White's Committee ran advertisements in five major eastern and midwestern papers declaring, "Between Us and Hitler Stands the British Fleet!" It urged readers to write Washington to request sale of over-age destroyers to Great Britain. A chart showed the unequal comparison between friendly and hostile naval forces if the British fleet sank or surrendered. Later on in August the Committee to Defend America sponsored radio speeches by retired Admirals Harry C. Yarnell, Yates Sterling, Jr., Ambassador William C. Bullitt (recently returned from France), and White himself. These speeches emphasized United States dependence on British naval power and appealed for release of destroyers. Rallies in Chicago and in Estes Park, Colorado, also attracted nationwide attention.[12]

Through the work of its six hundred local chapters, as well as newspaper ads and radio addresses, the Committee to Defend America provided direct publicity for aid to Britain, while the Century Group worked covertly. Unlike the Warhawks, White hesitated to get too far ahead of public opinion and often found the Warhawks' positions too extreme. He refused to commit his organization to a peacetime draft, for example, while the Group arranged a radio address by Colonel William J. Donovan in favor of selective service. Furthermore, White clung to a genuine belief that assistance in supplies and munitions would be sufficient, a view the Century people deemed unrealistic.[13]

Douglas' second task was to present the Group's idea of a destroyer transfer to the Republican presidential candidate, Wendell Willkie, "with a view to persuading him, should the present Administration agree to the project, at least to refrain from attacking it in the political campaign and at the most to support it."[14] Willkie was convinced of the short-sightedness of isolationism and aware of the probability of America's eventual participation in the war, and his pre-convention statements on

12. Walter Johnson, *The Battle Against Isolation* (Chicago, 1944) pp. 84–122.

13. *Ibid.*, p. 92.

14. "Meeting at Columbia Club," draft, WHS MSS.

foreign affairs stood in clear opposition to the isolationism expressed by the other Republican contenders. Some observers viewed Willkie's victory in Philadelphia as the triumph of internationalism over isolationism in the G.O.P. But Willkie was now leader of the whole party, not just the internationalist wing. He had to consider the sensibilities of all segments of the Republican party, including isolationists like Gerald Nye, Karl Mundt, Hamilton Fish, Dewey Short, and his running mate, Charles McNary.

Douglas, as a leader of the conservative anti-Roosevelt Democrats, did have entrée to the counsels of the Republican candidate; but his arguments for outspoken advocacy of all-out aid fell before the political fact that such a stand would cost Willkie the support of the party regulars, most of whom were isolationists. Furthermore, as a "latter-day" Republican whose relatively recent adherence to the Democratic party made some regulars uneasy, Willkie had to be careful not to appear too much in harmony with Democratic foreign policy, regardless of his personal feelings.[15] Temporarily, at least, Willkie restricted his foreign policy utterances to general statements of an internationalist tone and to attacks on the inadequacy of the Democratic administration's defense preparedness.

The second dinner meeting of the Warhawks took place at the Century Club on Thursday, July 25. Several signers of the "Summons to Speak Out" who had not been present on July 11—Richard Cleveland, George Watts Hill, and William Waller—were present. Several important figures from the news media—including Alsop, Davis and Parsons—were invited, as were James Rowland Angell and Charles Seymour, past and current Presidents of Yale University, and Grenville Clark of the "Plattsburg Movement."[16]

Coffin and Luce described their talk with Secretary Hull. Hull had listened sympathetically to their proposals for transferring American destroyers to the British, but his reply had been

15. In 1932 Willkie had supported Albert Ritchie for the Democratic presidential nomination.

16. This was also the first group meeting attended by Cheney, Polk, Sherwood, Wriston, and Wanger; "List of Invitations," July 25, 1940, FFF MSS.

discouraging. He had emphasized the legal barriers and political dangers involved in such action. Luce probably also told the Group of his conversation with President Roosevelt about destroyers. The President, like the Secretary of State, had stressed the difficulties of taking such action only two months before he was "up" for an unprecedented third term and in the face of congressional isolationism.[17]

Standley and Shepardson dwelled on strategic considerations. They emphasized the fact that "the weakest and most vulnerable sector in the American defense line is the North Atlantic." They stated that if Germany were to gain control of that area before America had built her projected two-ocean navy, "the United States could be invaded from the Atlantic. . . . In order to remove the risk of invasion the Government should take any steps necessary to prevent German control of the North Atlantic. The most certain preventive," they decided, "is the continued existence of the British fleet. And the fate of the British fleet will be settled by the battle for the control of the North Atlantic which is about to begin on the shores of England, Scotland and Ireland."[18]

Following this general analysis Joseph Alsop presented a report on "the present British military, naval and aviation situation" based on conversations he had had with Lord Lothian, British military attachés and intelligence officials, Secretaries Hull, Stimson, and Knox, and American intelligence officers.[19]

Alsop had been enlisted in the Warhawks' work in a meeting in the suite of the *Louisville Courier-Journal* during the Democratic convention. Here Herbert Agar, Ulric Bell, and Barry Bingham had asked him to obtain from both British and American sources in Washington as much data as he could pertaining to the situation of the British, their material needs, and their chances of repelling the imminent Nazi invasion. Alsop was willing to assist, provided any projected propaganda campaign for specific assistance to the British had the approval of United States authorities. He had, in fact, already been ap-

17. Luce to author, February 1, 1965.
18. "Notes on Conversation," pencilled by F. P. Miller, July 25, 1940, WHS MSS.
19. "Memorandum of Meeting," July 25, 1940, FPM MSS.

proached by John Foster, counselor to the British Embassy, on the subject of publicizing Britain's need for destroyers. But he refused to cooperate without the administration's approval. Now, with the assent of Secretaries Hull, Stimson, and Knox, he proceeded to interview members of the British mission in the Capitol and officers of the American intelligence establishments.[20]

American and British air experts differed sharply, Alsop told his listeners, over the question of whether the Royal Air Force would succumb to the *Luftwaffe*. The British saw the odds against defeat in the air at "six to one," while their American counterparts considered them "even." The British were confident that the technical superiority of their aircraft and the ability of the Royal Air Force pilots would enable them to withstand an all-out German assault. However, American intelligence men believed that the Royal Air Force would "be driven from southern bases within seven days at the beginning of 'all-out' attack and forced to retire to new base[s] leaving southern industrial England unprotected from the air." "England is now beginning to feel the strain of the shortage of pilots," Alsop added, and the United States "could be of tremendous assitance to Britain by allowing [American] pilots to join British forces." [21]

"The Naval situation," Alsop observed, "is more desperate than anyone realizes." Having publicly admitted the loss of twenty-seven destroyers, and with over fifty destroyers in shipyards for repairs, the "British now have less than 100 destroyers available for active service . . . for convoy, necessary sea patrol, Mediterranean patrol. They had 450 in 1917 for [a] smaller job." The rate of loss through the "Germans' mine drive on destroyers is such that they may drive the English Navy out of the straits of Dover, and therefor[e] be able to storm across the Channel." "Unless the British are given *immediate* additional destroyers," he contended, "odds are absolutely against defending the British Isles." [22]

Focusing on the American side of the Atlantic, Alsop noted that the "United States has more destroyers than all the rest of the navies of the world put together," including 140

20. Author's interview with Alsop.
21. "Memorandum of Meeting," July 25, 1940, FPM MSS.
22. *Ibid.*

recommissioned "four-stackers" of the First World War. These were being used to train crews on naval patrol in the Atlantic and "can easily be spared for more serious duties. High United States naval ranks heartily approve transfer of [a] minimum of fifty destroyers to Britain immediately," he said, although "lower ranks" oppose it. Alsop put forth the suggestion that these vessels might be transferred to the Canadian Navy. In this way they would remain in the Western Atlantic for hemisphere defense, but would free other Canadian vessels for action around the British Isles.[23]

He noted that a law passed in 1917 (forbidding the sale of armed vessels to belligerents) and the Walsh rider to the naval bill of June, 1940 (forbidding the sale of "surplus military material" under most circumstances) apparently rendered such a transfer illegal. He saw three ways to circumvent these statutes. The most obvious was legislative action—repeal of the obstructions—but that, he declared, was "absolutely closed due to the bullheadedness of Messrs. Vandenberg, Nye, and Wheeler, etc." His second suggestion was a "legal opinion obtained through legal shenanigans . . ." by which he meant stretching the statutes to suit the needs of the moment. The third and most attractive method was to "get Roosevelt and Willkie to act jointly." If both were to express the opinion that a destroyer transfer was in the national interest, he argued, the American people would accept it even though it was technically illegal: "The situation is hopeless unless Mr. Roosevelt and Mr. Willkie realize their responsibility and act together. It would be a popular move. Secretary Hull states [that a] Roosevelt and Willkie agreement on foreign policy and [such a] statement would bring all questions of foreign policy out of politics. Secretary Stimson also agrees."[24]

In later years Alsop recalled that Secretary Knox—convinced of the inevitability of American involvement—had been most enthusiastically in favor of a destroyer transfer. Knox had sent Alsop to see Chief of Naval Operations Admiral Harold R. Stark and Director of Naval Intelligence Admiral Walter S.

23. *Ibid.*
24. *Ibid.*

Anderson. Stark at first had been reluctant to part with any of the destroyers and had emphasized the legal barrier which had been created by the Walsh amendment, Section 14(a) of the Naval Expansion Act of June, 1940. Since this section required that the Chief of Naval Operations certify that any "surplus" vessels being disposed of were "not essential to the defense of the United States," it placed the burden of the decision about releasing the destroyers on Admiral Stark, something he found rather uncomfortable. Stark had doubts about the constitutionality of the amendment, since it placed him, a subordinate, in a position to overrule the Commander-in-Chief. However, he had insisted to Alsop that, regardless of his desire to help the British, he could not declare the destroyers "surplus" only a few months after he had testified to the Congress that they ought to be refitted and recommissioned.[25] Alsop asked Stark if he would approve the transfer if the objections of the Walsh rider could be met, and the Admiral reluctantly agreed.

Alsop's interview with the Director of Naval Intelligence was even less encouraging. Admiral Anderson was convinced that Britain was going down, and he desired to conserve American strength for the defense of our own shores rather than risk vessels in a lost cause. The journalist came away with the impression that only the civilian heads of the armed forces—Knox and Stimson—and a very few far-sighted officers like General Marshall grasped the necessity for immediate aid to Britain. The rest either clung to the misconceptions of isolationism and neutrality or were quick to concede Britain's defeat.[26]

In the discussion which followed Alsop's report, attention centered on the over-age destroyers. As Francis Miller wrote in the memorandum of the meeting, "So strong was the feeling that the United States should take this action in self-defense, that there was little discussion concerning the consideration to be asked in return for taking such a step." Henry Luce, however,

25. Admiral Stark recalls that he used the same argument successfully in a telephone conversation with the President, during which Roosevelt also strongly urged that Stark simply declare the destroyers "surplus"; author's interview with Harold R. Stark, April 14, 1967.

26. Author's interview with Alsop.

insisted that any transaction involving destroyers should be in the form of a *quid pro quo.* Someone, probably Van Dusen, suggested that the United States should ask in return for "some guarantee that the British fleets should neither be scuttled nor surrendered, but, in case of a successful German invasion of England, should operate thereafter from Canadian and/or American bases."

Luce felt that even this would not be sufficient, since such a guarantee would have no binding force on future British governments. In the event of total defeat, a "Quisling" or Vichy-like regime might barter the British fleet for a milder peace settlement. Instead, he thought, "these destroyers should be offered to Britain in exchange for immediate naval and air concessions in British possessions in the Western Hemisphere." Such bases would improve our Atlantic strength, thereby rendering some destroyers on Atlantic patrol "non-essential" to national security.[27]

"It was generally agreed," Miller's memorandum continued, "that the time was too short for a Congressional debate on the proposed program, and that effective action could only be taken in time by the President, in cooperation with United States naval officials. Consequently—individuals in whom the President believes should see him, and urge him to take action on the reasonable assumption that Mr. Willkie would go along with him."[28] Again Henry Luce had some reservations. It would not do, he told Francis Miller after the Meeting, to give Roosevelt the impression that his action was to be dependent upon Willkie's cooperation, for if Willkie refused to make a joint statement, then the President might do nothing.[29]

Miller's memorandum listed four other "practical steps" to be taken by the Group. These included "a radio program of education to be launched immediately . . . the group to cooperate fully with William Allen White's Committee, and the Committee with the group . . . a newsletter to be prepared by three or four outstanding special writers," and "moral backing and

27. "Memorandum of Meeting," July 25, 1940, FPM MSS.
28. *Ibid.*
29. Francis P. Miller to Shepardson, July 30, 1940, WHS MSS.

practical support for the Committee for the Release of Ships for European Children." [30] Another paper, apparently drafted by the Group as a whole, stated succinctly the logic for a destroyer transfer. In shortened form, it read:

> The most valuable sector in the American defense line is the North Atlantic.
>
> If Germany wins control of the North Atlantic, the period prior to the completion of our own two-ocean navy will be a period of acute danger for us. During that period the United States could be invaded from the Atlantic.
>
> In order to remove the risk of invasion, Government should take all possible steps to prevent German control of the North Atlantic.
>
> The most certain preventive (until our two-ocean navy is built) is the continued existence of the British fleet.
>
> The British chances of success are at present doubtful; but responsible British officials believe that they could successfully withstand invasion if they had one hundred more destroyers.[31]

On August 1, Herbert Agar, Ward Cheney, and Clark Eichelberger went to the White House to see the President. They showed him the two memoranda of July 25 and urged the release of ships to evacuate British children. They asked for and received his approval of their "radio program of education." Specifically, Roosevelt said that a radio address by General Pershing, commander of the American Expeditionary Force in the First World War and the nation's most revered military figure, would be helpful. These matters aside, the conversation focused on the necessity of a destroyer transfer and the practical means of accomplishing it. The visitors told Roosevelt that William Allen White and Lewis Douglas were ready to act as liaison between the White House and Willkie, and Roosevelt apparently raised no objection to this suggestion.[32]

Roosevelt's generally non-committal responses and his

30. "Memorandum of Meeting," July 25, 1940, FPM MSS.

31. "Notes on Aid to Britain," July 25, 1940, HWH MSS.

32. Stetson Conn and Byron Fairchild, *The Framework of Hemisphere Defense* (Washington, 1960), p. 53; J. R. M. Butler, *Lord Lothian* (London, 1960), p. 292; William L. Langer and S. Everett Gleason, *The Challenge to Isolation, 1937–1940* (New York, 1952), p. 749.

DETECTIVE DIVISION
CIRCULAR NO. 1
AUGUST, 1941

POLICE DEPARTMENT
FIGHT FOR FREEDOM

CLASSIFICATION

WANTED FOR MURDER

ADOLF SCHICKLGRUBER
Alias Hitler

Wanted for MURDER; ARSON; GRAND LARCENY; POSSESSION OF FIRE-ARMS; PIRACY; TREACHERY; RELIGIOUS PERSECUTION.

DESCRIPTION—Age, 52 in 1941; height, five feet, seven inches; weight, 150-165; hair, black, shaggy locks hangs over forehead; eyes, black, have demented gaze; complexion, sallow; football mustache, eleven hairs on each side; foppish dresser, but has marked devotion to brown shirts and an old trench-coat.

PARTICULARS—This man has tendency to become hysterical on slight provocation, has been known to throw himself on floor and gnaw rugs; guttural voice apt to rise to shrill tones when excited or thwarted. He has delusions, particularly about his place in history and his powers over vast numbers of people. He is sadistic, malicious, bombastic, vengeful, mystical, maniacal, addicted to public hysteria on "race purity;" suffers from dreams of persecution. He is a congenital liar. He has worked at only one known trade — house painting.

RECORD—He has served one term in prison, and has a police record of inciting to riot in various cities.

SHOOT ON SIGHT! This man is dangerous, will attack without warning; he is always surrounded by armed thugs and expert gunmen.

REWARD! If captured, dead or alive, the reward will be freedom for the entire world and peace for all nations.

Right Hand: 1. Thumb 2. Index 3. Middle 4. Ring 5. Little

Left Hand: 6. Thumb 7. Index 8. Middle 9. Ring 10. Little

NOTIFY
FIGHT FOR FREEDOM, INC.
1270 SIXTH AVENUE, NEW YORK CITY TEL. CIRCLE 6-4250

STOP 'EM OVER THERE
NOW
—And
You'll Keep 'em Away
from Here
Join the Fight for Freedom Committee Now

lack of enthusiasm for a destroyer exchange disappointed his three callers. They left with the impression that the President was inordinately fearful that a destroyer sale might hurt his chances for re-election—especially if Willkie refused to endorse such a transaction. White, in commenting on Roosevelt's hesitancy, declared that since his renomination, the President appeared to have "lost his cud." [33] Nevertheless, his Committee and the Century Group immediately embarked on the program of broadcasts and newsletters (and, in the instance of the Committee to Defend America, advertisements and rallies) intended to condition public opinion to the idea of a destroyer deal and, thereby, "make it politically possible for Roosevelt to act." [34]

Actually, ever since Churchill first asked for destroyers on May 15, Roosevelt had privately favored sending them; but he was convinced that existing statutes, legal opinions, and the political situation prevented it. The Walsh amendment, little more than a month old, was intended to prevent just such a transaction. Another seemingly insurmountable obstacle was Attorney General Jackson's June opinion that the sale of motor torpedo boats then being constructed was "absolutely illegal." A 1917 law prohibited the sale of "any vessel built as a vessel of war with any intent or under any agreement that such vessel shall be delivered to a belligerent nation." This law seemed as applicable to the destroyers as it was to torpedo boats. Lastly, Roosevelt was troubled by the political capital isolationist Republicans would make of such a "giveaway" at a time when the United States was unprepared to defend itself. In the light of rising public hysteria about America's defenselessness and the country's residual isolationism, he feared a destroyer deal might cost him re-election.[35]

Nevertheless, on the day after the Agar-Cheney-Eichelberger visit, the President and his advisors took the first steps leading to a destroyer transfer. At the cabinet meeting that afternoon, a discussion took place which was similar to the one at

33. Langer and Gleason, *The Challenge to Isolation,* p. 749.
34. Author's interview with Francis P. Miller.
35. John Morton Blum, *From the Morgenthau Diaries: Years of Urgency, 1938–1941* (Boston, 1965), p. 102; Langer and Gleason, *The Challenge to Isolation,* p. 745.

the Century Club a week earlier. This debate, Secretary Stimson noted in his diary, was "one of the most serious and important . . . that I have ever had in a Cabinet meeting."[36] Secretary Knox began by describing his recent talks with Lord Lothian, in which the British Ambassador had re-emphasized Britain's urgent need for destroyers. Knox—supported by Stimson and Ickes—proposed that Britain be allowed to sell some Western hemisphere possessions to the United States in exchange for fifty or sixty destroyers.[37] Secretary Hull objected to a *purchase* as a violation of the Havana agreement he had just concluded relating to the non-transfer of hemispheric territory, and he suggested the alternative of *leasing* the territory in question.[38]

There was general agreement around the table that Britain should be aided, but all recognized that Congress would not pass the necessary legislation for release of the destroyers without "an iron clad guarantee" from Britain about her fleet and a *quid pro quo* involving Commonwealth bases in the Atlantic. The President decided to seek "diplomatic" solutions to both the foreign and domestic aspects of the problem. Hull and Welles would seek assurances from Britain about what would happen to the Royal Navy in the event of defeat. At the same time White, Douglas, and others would try to persuade Willkie to influence Republican congressmen to support legislation releasing the destroyers. Unlike the Century Group, the White House still considered congressional action permitting the sale of the destroyers worth a try.[39]

After the meeting the President received a letter from Ickes. If the British went down, the Secretary wrote, the American people would want to know why the destroyers had not been

36. Henry L. Stimson diary, entry of August 2, 1940, Stimson Papers.

37. Elliott Roosevelt (ed.), *F.D.R.: His Personal Letters* (New York: 1950), pp. 1050–1.

38. Conn and Fairchild, *The Framework of Hemisphere Defense,* p. 54.

39. Harold L. Ickes, *The Secret Diary of Harold L. Ickes: The Lowering Clouds, 1939–1941* (New York, 1954), pp. 292–93; Elliott Roosevelt (ed.), *F.D.R.*, pp. 1050–53. Many isolationists had a long-standing interest in obtaining American bases in British Caribbean islands. They suggested that such bases could serve as repayment of Britain's defaulted World War I debts.

sent to their aid. He declared, "It seems to me that we Americans are like the householder who refused to lend or sell his fire extinguisher to help put out the fire in the house that is next door, although that house is all ablaze and the wind is blowing from that direction." Ickes endorsed a legal memorandum from Benjamin V. Cohen, counsel to the National Power Policy Committee and White House confidant. Cohen, writing at the suggestion of Alsop and John Foster, arrived by somewhat strained logic at the conclusion that the President, under his constitutional responsibility as Commander-in-Chief, already had the legal authority to release the destroyers. Therefore, no enabling legislation from Congress was necessary. Roosevelt, however, wished to exhaust other methods before resorting to what Alsop had called "legal shenanigans."[40]

Later that evening the President spoke by telephone to White who was in Estes Park, Colorado, for the Committee to Defend America rally, not far from where Willkie was vacationing. He asked the Kansan to go ahead with efforts to persuade Willkie to act jointly with him on the question of destroyers. White said he would call the White House as soon as he had spoken to the Republican nominee. In his efforts to convince Willkie, he was joined by Douglas (who had left New York for Colorado shortly after the Century meeting) and Russell Davenport, a former managing editor of *Fortune* magazine and a founder of the "Willkie for President" movement.[41]

Simultaneous with their efforts to get Roosevelt and Willkie to cooperate on destroyers, the Century Group proceeded with its "radio program of education." General John J. Pershing was the Group's first speaker. Two of Francis Miller's friends from the Council on Foreign Relations, Walter Mallory and Frank Altschul, had approached Miller shortly before the July 25 dinner meeting with the idea of an address by Pershing on the need for a destroyer transfer and military draft legislation. There

40. Elliott Roosevelt (ed.) *F.D.R.*, p. 1053; Langer and Gleason, *The Challenge to Isolation*, p. 746; Ickes, *The Secret Diary of Harold L. Ickes*, pp. 288–94, author's conversation with Benjamin V. Cohen, February 5, 1968.

41. Elliott Roosevelt (ed.) *F.D.R.*, p. 1051. Davenport reported to the White House through Archibald MacLeish, the poet and Librarian of Congress; MacLeish to author, December 6, 1965.

was one man, a long-time friend of the General's by the name of George Christiancy, who could persuade the ill and aging soldier to speak, they told Miller. On Monday, July 29, Mallory and Miller met Christiancy for lunch at the Yale Club of New York and obtained his cooperation. Furthermore, General James Harbord, formerly Pershing's Chief of Staff, was persuaded to call the General (who lived in Washington) to obtain an appointment for Christiancy. The telephone conversation had its amusing aspects since both of the retired warriors were hard of hearing, but the desired arrangements were made, and Miller and Christiancy flew to Washington. Before emplaning Miller arranged to have Herbert Agar and columnist Walter Lippmann come to Pershing's hotel to write the General's speech.[42]

In Washington all went well. Christiancy had a favorable talk with Pershing in his suite in the Ritz-Carlton. Then Herbert Agar, who had been at the White House earlier that day, relayed the President's "request" that the General speak to the country. That sealed the matter. Pershing declared it was his responsibility to address the nation, regardless of his doctor's warning about impairing his health. When Agar and Lippmann completed their draft, Pershing suggested only minor changes. In the meantime Joseph Alsop obtained radio time for the broadcast.[43]

On Sunday evening, August 4, Pershing delivered his address "Security of the Americas" as the central presentation of a Mutual Broadcasting System program on the international situation. The General declared "that all the things we hold most dear are gravely threatened," and "that no war was ever prevented by hiding the danger and by arguing that the danger does not exist." "More than half the world," he asserted, "is ruled by men who despise the American idea and have sworn to destroy it. . . ."[44] Pershing advocated top priority for the program of rearmament and with it "the establishment of the principle of universal selective service."

42. F. P. Miller to Mallory, August 1, 1940, WHS MSS; Christiancy to F. P. Miller, telegram, July 31, 1940; Mallory to Christiancy, July 26, 1940, FFF MSS; author's interview with Francis P. Miller.

43. F. P. Miller to Christiancy, August 29, 1940, FFF MSS; F. P. Miller to Alsop, August 5, 1940, WHS MSS; author's interview with Francis P. Miller; Herbert Agar to the author, January 30, 1968.

44. *New York Herald Tribune,* August 5, 1940.

He continued: "I am telling you tonight, because it is my duty to warn you before it is too late, that the British Navy needs destroyers and small craft to convoy merchant ships, to escort its warships, and hunt submarines, and to repel invasion." He mentioned the United States' "immense reserve of destroyers" and asked that America "safeguard her freedom and security by making available . . . at least fifty of the over-age destroyers. If the destroyers helped save the British fleet, they may save us from the danger and hardship of another war."

Pershing concluded with an inspirational invocation. The war now being fought was

> a revolution against the values which we have cherished, and which we wish our children to cherish in the future. It is a revolution that denies the dignity of men, and which banishes the hope of brotherhood and comradeship on earth.
>
> . . . It must be faced with daring and devotion. . . . We must reaffirm our noble tradition. We must make ourselves so strong that the tradition we live by shall not perish from the earth.[45]

Pershing's effort was the first major public discussion of the destroyer issue, and it commanded nationwide attention. The *New York Times* headline read: "Pershing Warns U.S. to Aid Britain by Sending 50 Destroyers Now"; and most editors across the country relegated accounts of Colonel Lindbergh's address to Chicago isolationists to less prominent space. The *New York Herald Tribune's* front-page picture of Cordell Hull congratulating Pershing after his broadcast seemed to demonstrate administration approval of his proposal. Pershing himself received over seven hundred letters, telegrams, and postcards; and the favorable responses outnumbered the unfavorable nearly four to one. Many who wrote him declared they were sending copies of their letters to Roosevelt, Hull, and Knox.[46]

45. *Ibid.*

46. Circular telegram, Francis P. Miller to Century Group members, August 5, 1940, FFF MSS, asked them to have friends wire Administration officials *à propos* Pershing's speech; Letters in John J. Pershing Papers, Library of Congress, were favorable to his speech by a count of 584 to 154; *New York Times*, August 5, 1940; *New York Herald Tribune*, August 5, 1940.

Six days later, on Saturday, August 10, Admiral Standley, a signer of the "Summons" and an active participant in Century meetings, delivered a nationwide radio address drafted with Joseph Alsop's assistance. Standley opened by quoting from the "Summons to Speak Out" and reiterated his desire for an immediate declaration of war. He then addressed himself to the matter of American sea power. In words similar to those of the July 25 memoranda Standley noted that until the United States completed its two-ocean navy its sea power in the Atlantic would consist primarily of the British fleet. The Admiral painted a grim image of the economic isolation which would confront America if the Nazis conquered England, neutralized or captured the Royal Navy, and controlled the high seas. He added that in the narrow Channel waters only small craft—destroyers and torpedo boats—would be effective against an invasion armada.

"At the very least," Standley asserted, "Congress should declare a national emergency and give the Commander-in-Chief of our armed forces full powers, including whatever disposition of our army, navy and air force is called for by the public interest. Am I advocating war? Call it what you like. If what we are doing now is Peace, then words don't mean what they meant when I went to school." He insisted the naval strategy demanded dispatch of the destroyers. "Warships are not built," he asserted, "to be hoarded in little packets away from the main theatre of action but for use. . . . Use them for the purpose for which they were built and maintained—to keep the enemy from our shores." [47]

Again the following week the Group induced an eminent military leader to speak to the nation. This time the speaker was Colonel William J. Donovan, Medal of Honor winner and former commander of New York's "Fighting 69th." Of Irish ancestry, Donovan spoke with special influence to Irish-Americans, many of whom were particularly chary of being drawn into "bloody England's" war. As a former Republican candidate for governor of New York, Donovan could also appeal to many who were hostile to the New Deal President. The fact-finding mission to

47. "Address by Admiral William H. Standley over C.B.S.," August 10, 1940, HWH MSS.

Britain he had just completed equipped him with special knowledge of the current crisis.[48]

Donovan focused his attention on the Burke-Wadsworth Selective Service bill, which was currently before Congress. He acknowledged that it was possible that Hitler meant America no harm and that preparedness and a peacetime draft were unnecessary. "But let us weigh against this," he suggested, "the price of unpreparedness in the face of a threat which turns out to have been a real threat. We have seen other nations pay that cost—the nations of Europe that have fallen. . . ." Unpreparedness now, he insisted, would be a gamble with the freedom of future generations, a gamble the current generation had no right to make.[49]

Drawing on his World War I experiences, Donovan recalled that American boys had been sent to France untrained and had suffered excessive casualties when first exposed to combat. This risk must not be taken again. The government owed the soldier "a fair chance for his life." He insisted that "natural leadership" and "primitive military skills" would not do in modern warfare, where highly coordinated movements of mechanized units and sophisticated weapons were employed. A volunteer system, he was certain, would not work in total war. The American people must have the protection of universal selective service, no matter how distasteful peacetime conscription might be. Still, in the end he held out, as had Pershing, the hope that America might yet avoid complete participation: "But while it is absolutely true that if you want to fight, you've got to be strong, it is equally true in this world of today that if you want peace, you've got to be stronger still—and it is because I am for peace that I am for conscription."[50] Although Donovan did not espouse the Warhawks' belief that American entry into the war was inevitable, his assistance was welcomed in dealing with the immediate problem of rallying support for "mobilization" measures and educating the public to current international realities.

48. Francis P. Miller to Sterling Fisher, August 15, 1940, WIIS MSS.

49. "Address of Colonel William Donovan," August 17, 1940, FPM MSS.

50. *Ibid.*

In addition to the speeches by eminent Americans, the Group enlisted a number of Britons to present their case directly to the American public, in disregard of supposed United States neutrality. Henry Van Dusen arranged through Ambassador Lothian for trans-Atlantic broadcasts by English clergymen—Catholic as well as Anglican—to be carried over nationwide hookups on four successive Sundays beginning August 4. With the cooperation of Lothian, he also initiated a program which brought representatives of various segments of British society—the Church, labor, women, educators, the left wing, Roman Catholics—to the United States for speaking tours. However much these speakers denied that they wanted the United States to come into the war, the purpose of these presentations was to stimulate sympathy for Britain and support for all-out aid and intervention.[51]

Meanwhile, in Colorado Springs, Douglas, White, and Davenport were pursuing matters with the vacationing Republican nominee. In the week immediately following the Century meeting of July 25, Willkie apparently gave these envoys reason to hope that he would agree to cooperate with Roosevelt on the destroyer release, for their communications to their eastern friends were optimistic. In arriving at a decision, however, Willkie apparently conferred with Arthur Krock, columnist for *The New York Times,* an opponent of the Roosevelt administration and one of the most cogent of isolationists.[52] Shortly afterwards a news story and a Krock column on "the matter of certain envoys to Colorado Springs" appeared in the *Times.* The news article, quoting an "authenticated report," mentioned Davenport's efforts and declared that Archibald MacLeish, the poet and Librarian of Congress, had asked Davenport to put the matter before Willkie. The article said that Willkie's response was that "to make such a promise [of silence or support] . . . was virtually to urge the action on the President. He was not in any position to do so as he was not sufficiently familiar with the background." The information necessary to make such a decision was available only to the President, and Willkie did not wish to

51. Van Dusen to Lothian, August 9, 1940, HVD MSS; author's interview with Van Dusen.

52. Author's interviews with Van Dusen, Francis P. Miller.

prejudice the freedom of legislative action of Republican members of Congress with respect to releasing destroyers. His general position of "all aid short of war" was publicly known, but he could not be expected to assume responsibility for specific aspects of the administration's policy.[53]

Krock's column included much of the same material but added that "the high military command of the Navy Department opposes the transfer of these vessels, and this opposition has increased since the Act of Havana." [54] Referring to the Walsh amendment, Krock asserted that the "recent appropriation bill" made the consent of Congress necessary before the release of "any vessel in or built for" the United States Navy. Although he noted that there were rumors circulating that Willkie would not attack a destroyer transfer if it were consummated, Krock thought Roosevelt's behavior during 1933 established a precedent for Willkie's refusal to cooperate. Had Roosevelt, he asked, cooperated with Hoover in the critical months between Roosevelt's election and inauguration? He had not.[55]

The consequences of Krock's column were (to quote Francis Miller) "pernicious" to the cause of the Group. Other commentators, like General Hugh Johnson and Virginius Dabney, echoed Krock's interpretation of the Navy Department's attitude. As for Willkie, although he had not expressed his decision openly, it was apparent to the Group that he was turning away from them, and they believed Krock was to blame. Miller wrote to Henry Coffin on August 6, ". . . Sinister have been the meanderings of Arthur Krock's mind. He has really done us dirt." [56]

53. *New York Times,* August 2, 1940.

54. The Pan-American states at the Havana Conference in the last week of July decided to establish collective trusteeship over colonies in this hemisphere whose mother country had been occupied. As the prime naval power of the New World, the U.S. Navy, therefore, had to expect expanded responsibilities involving these colonies.

55. *New York Times,* August 1, 1940.

56. F. P. Miller to Coffin, August 6, 1940, WHS MSS; F. P. Miller to Shepardson, August 7, 1940, FFF MSS; White called Roosevelt on August 6, 1940, to assure him that Willkie would make a favorable statement. As late as August 8, 1940, he told Stimson that Willkie's speech was "highly satisfactory," Stimson diary, entry of August 12, 1940, Stimson Papers.

All uncertainty seemed eliminated on August 9, when Willkie issued a prepared statement in which he reserved "unhampered right of public discussion." In phraseology that closely paralleled the recent writings of Krock, he said his

> . . . general views on the foreign policy and vital interests of the United States in the present international situation are well known, having been stated by me publicly several times.
>
> . . . I do not think it appropriate for me to enter into advance commitments and understandings.
>
> The Chief Executive and Congress must bear their appropriate responsibilities, and the candidate for the President of the United States should reserve to himself an unhampered right of public discussion.[57]

Willkie also alluded to Roosevelt's actions in 1933 as precedent for his own behavior. Despite the candidate's pronouncement, Douglas continued to urge Willkie, in personal meetings and long-distance telephone conversations, not to attack a destroyer transfer if Roosevelt completed it.

* * * * * *

When Secretary of State Hull proposed an exchange of destroyers for Caribbean bases and a guarantee concerning the Royal Navy, British officials, although still keenly interested in destroyers, reacted coolly. Churchill opposed as injurious to British morale any public discussion or statement about the disposition of the fleet in the event of defeat.

He felt that the British public would not stand for the *sale* of part of the Empire; perhaps long-term *leases* could be arranged. Even this *quid pro quo* gave him second thoughts because (as he later wrote), "There was, of course, no comparison between the intrinsic value of these antiquated and inefficient craft and the immense permanent strategic security afforded the United States by the enjoyment of the island bases." [58]

On Sunday, August 4, after discussing the British position with Lord Lothian, Hull left Washington for White Sulphur

57. *New York Times*, August 10, 1940.

58. Winston S. Churchill, *The Second World War: Their Finest Hour* (Boston, 1949), pp. 402–3.

Springs, West Virginia, for a vacation. Before departing he called Roosevelt at Hyde Park. In their telephone conversation the two men agreed that there were two serious objections to taking a bill authorizing release of the destroyers before Congress—the danger of stirring up isolationist antagonism, and the inevitable delay before action would be taken. With this, Hull departed, leaving the diplomatic negotiations in the hands of Sumner Welles.[59]

On August 11, *The New York Times* printed a letter by Dean Acheson, and his law partners, Charles Burlingham, Thomas Thacher, and George Rublee. All four were legal advisors to past Democratic and Republican administrations. Acheson's letter made the same point as Ben Cohen's earlier memorandum, namely that the United States Code and the Act of 1917 could be construed in such a way as to permit the sale of destroyers to Britain. This was not surprising because it had been originally drafted by Cohen at the suggestion of Supreme Court Justic Felix Frankfurter.[60] It argued that these statutes and international law prevented only the sending out of *vessels built specifically for the purpose of entering belligerent service.* Since the old destroyers had not originally been constructed with such intent, it was permissible to sell them to Britain. This unsolicited and unofficial legal opinion suggested the way to avoid a congressional battle for new legislation, and its logic was quickly appropriated by administration officials.[61]

59. Cordell Hull, *The Memoirs of Cordell Hull* (New York, 1948), pp. 832–33. Van Dusen also saw Lothian that day to inform him of what Pershing was going to say in his radio address.

60. Frankfurter reportedly thought that Acheson's signing of this letter might help bring about *rapproachement* between this most useful man and the President. Acheson and Cohen selected Thacher and Burlingham as signers partly because neither could be regarded as Roosevelt men. Thacher was a Republican and Burlingham, although a Democrat, had been an outspoken opponent of Roosevelt's court-packing plan. Rublee, the fourth signer, had served both the Wilson and Hoover administrations and had been head of the Intergovernmental Committee which attempted to aid refugees from Nazi Germany during the late thirties. John Foster Dulles also had been considered but was never approached, possibly because his clients included several important German firms; author's conversation with Cohen.

61. *New York Times,* August 11, 1940; Benjamin V. Cohen to Marguerite Le Hand, August 12, 1940, President's Secretary's File "Destroyer Bases," Roosevelt Papers; author's conversation with Acheson.

In a cabinet meeting on August 16, the legal question was discussed and, as Secretary Stimson noted, Attorney General Jackson "grasped the point that the consent of Congress is not necessary and made a very good statement." Stimson was sure the letter of his four friends had been instrumental.[62] The following day, in a letter to Knox, Jackson addressed himself to the specific obstacles in the Walsh amendment, Section 14(a) of the Act of June, 1940. "It is my opinion," he stated, "that the Chief of Naval Operations may, and should, certify under section 14(a) that such destroyers are not essential to the defense of the United States if in his judgment the exchange of such destroyers for strategic naval and air bases will strengthen rather than impair the total defense of the United States."[63]

The Acheson letter and Jackson's opinion constituted perversions of the original intent of Section 14(a). Chairman David I. Walsh of the Senate Naval Affairs Committee had written this amendment specifically to prevent the transfer of government property (such as destroyers) to foreign hands. Because of this it had received the support of isolationists in Congress.

The Anglo-American negotiations, carried on largely through telegrams between Roosevelt and Churchill, progressed gradually. Disagreement centered around the number of destroyers or other materiel—flying boats, torpedo boats, and small arms—involved. Under the pressure of imminent invasion the British were unwilling to haggle too long, and on August 15 Churchill signaled his willingness to accept the American terms as to materiel.[64]

On two points, however, agreement came less readily—a fleet guarantee and a *quid pro quo.* For political reasons the Americans believed both were necessary. Roosevelt felt that he had to be able to go to the American people with a hard-driven "horse trade" as well as a definite British promise about dispersing the fleet in the event of disaster. Churchill knew that any objective observer could see that he would be getting the poorer

62. Stimson diary, entry of August 16, 1940, Stimson Papers.

63. Attorney General to Secretary of the Navy, August 17, 1940, President's Secretary's File "Destroyer-Bases," Roosevelt Papers.

64. Churchill, *Their Finest Hour,* pp. 406–7.

end of any *quid pro quo* involving destroyers-for-bases, and he feared to undermine growing British confidence by public mention of the possibility of defeat. He felt that his June 4 speech had been sufficient "guarantee."[65] At that time, three days after Dunkirk, he had declared: "We shall never surrender, and even if, which I do not for a moment believe, this island or a large part of it were subjugated and starving, then our Empire beyond the seas, armed and guarded by the British Fleet, will carry on the struggle until, in God's good time, the New World, with all its power and might, steps forth to the rescue and liberation of the Old."[66]

On August 15 he relented to a degree and wrote Lothian that, "As regards an assurance about the British Fleet, I am, of course, ready to reiterate . . . what I told Parliament on June 4."[67]

Despite the fact that agreement had not been reached on a *quid pro quo*, Roosevelt believed events had progressed enough by August 16 to tell a press conference that the United States government was holding conversations with Great Britain regarding the acquisition of naval and air bases in the Western hemisphere. He referred vaguely to the fact that the United States would give Britain something in return, but he emphasized that the negotiations for bases were in no way connected with the question of destroyers. Then he boarded a train for upstate New York where he was to meet Canadian Prime Minister MacKenzie King and conclude the Ogdensburg Agreement, a plan for the joint defense of North America.[68]

While official Washington hummed with the activity of defense preparedness and destroyer negotiations, unofficial Washington was also hard at work. The Group felt the need for a continuous flow of "hard" information on the British situation both for its own enlightenment and for dissemination to friends among the editors, columnists, and radio commentators. Therefore, in the interim between Joseph Alsop's inquiries in July and

65. *Ibid.*
66. *Ibid.*, p. 400.
67. *Ibid.*, p. 406.
68. *New York Times*, August 18, 1040; Mark L. Chadwin, "The Destroyer-Bases Agreement of 1940" (Unpublished Masters Essay, Columbia University, 1962), Chap. IV.

the establishment of the "William Allen White News Service" by John Balderston in the last ten days of August, Helen Miller was asked to be the Group's "Washington correspondent." She was selected in part because she was not a member of the all-male Century Group and might therefore be less likely to arouse isolationists' suspicions, and in part because she had known the British Ambassador some years before.[69]

Although Alsop had obtained approval of American authorities before his discussions with British officials, Mrs. Miller apparently did not. She and Henry Van Dusen, by cooperating with the British Ambassador on political matters and by disseminating British propaganda, were in fact acting in the interests of a foreign power to involve their own country in a war. Although they were convinced that their actions were in the national interest, technically they could have been prosecuted for failing to register as agents of a foreign power and for violations of the Logan Act.[70] Given the administration's strongly pro-British policy and the President's approval of the Century Group's "radio program of education," such prosecution was most unlikely.

Mrs. Miller went to the British Embassy several times during the first two weeks in August. Each time she transmitted the inquiries of the Group as to Britain's military shortages. Her questions elicited from the British Ambassador a "Confidential Memorandum on Needs of Great Britain" in which he mentioned first the "implements of war" Britain desired most: "1. Destroyers and motor torpedo boats; 2. Aeroplanes; 3. Rifles, machine guns and 75mm. field guns." Then he enumerated the legislative and political assistance Britain hoped for, including repeal of the Neutrality Act or those provisions which barred Americans from entering the service of a belligerent, prohibited American vessels

69. Author's interview with Helen Hill Miller.

70. The text of the Logan Act (U.S. Code Title 18, Sec. 953) reads: "Any citizen of the United States, . . . who, without authority of the United States, directly or indirectly commences or carries on any correspondence or intercourse with any foreign government or any officer or agent thereof, with intent to influence the measures or conduct of any foreign government or of any officer or agent thereof, in relation to any disputes or controversies with the United States, or to defeat the measures of the United States, shall be fined not more than $5,000 or imprisoned not more than three years, or both."

from entering the combat zones around Allied ports, and outlawed the extension of short- and long-term credit to a belligerent. Lothian asked for the "adoption of a status of non-belligerency instead of formal neutrality." This, he wrote, would "not imply any military action" but would give "great moral encouragement to Great Britain." Non-belligerency, Lothian hoped, would lead to "repeal of Neutrality Act and Acts such as the Act of 1917 which at present prevents the sale of any warships to Great Britain." All of Lothian's "needs" which were not quickly acted upon by the Roosevelt administration were incorporated in the program of the Century Group or, subsequently, the Fight For Freedom.[71]

The Group recognized that the use of the question-and-answer method of gathering information and the limited mailing operation of Room 2940 were stop-gap measures, sufficient only until a propaganda service could be organized in Washington. The idea of such a service was jointly developed with the Committee to Defend America. Eichelberger participated in the Century meetings on the ninth and fifteenth in which the Washington agency was organized and John Balderston selected to direct it. Because of the preponderance of experienced publicists in the Century Group, the White Committee was willing to leave responsibility for the news service largely in its hands. White himself was so confident that the two organizations were of one mind on the subject of aid to Britain that he agreed to lend the agency his own influential name—thus it was called the "William Allen White News Service." [72]

On August 22, the first day of the service, both Miller and White sent out letters of introduction and explanation, Miller to his "2940" mailing list and White to his many friends in the newspaper business around the country. White declared, "This will not be a propaganda service, yet it will consist of news, fresh news we hope, bearing on issues in which we are interested and, of course, will bear on the causes we are trying to further. Mr. John L. Balderston . . . will write the daily or semi- or tri-weekly

71. "Confidential Memorandum on Needs of Great Britain," initialed "P.K.," FPM MSS.

72. "For Consideration," August 15, 1940, FPM MSS; author's interview with Francis P. Miller.

news story or private bulletin from our Washington office and they will be sent out after I have read and okayed them. . . ."[73]

Balderston's first issue printed much of the material Alsop had privately disclosed on July 25 regarding British naval losses and the scarcity of destroyers both on the high seas and in the Channel. Subsequent dispatches told of the surplus materiel the United States had sold to the British earlier in the summer and described a slight but insufficient improvement in British destroyer strength. On September 2, the day before Roosevelt announced the completion of the destroyer-bases agreement, Balderston gave the reasons for the negotiations having been delayed and again emphasized that sending destroyers was the most important assistance we could give England.

Shortly after the destroyer-bases agreement, the news service became embroiled in a controversy (to be dealt with in the next chapter), and with Balderston's departure from Washington it folded in early October. However, by providing some grist for editorial mills across the country, the service assisted in preparing the public to accept the destroyer-bases agreement and in awakening people to America's peril.[74]

On August 17, while the Group was relaying British Embassy information to the internationalist press and Roosevelt was at Ogdensburg, Wendell Willkie delivered his acceptance speech for the Republican presidential nomination. Willkie criticized Roosevelt for having "dabbled in inflammatory statements and manufactured panics" and for having "meddled in the affairs of Europe," and even for having "unscrupulously encouraged other countries to hope for more than we are able to give." But with respect to an agreement on destroyers and bases, Willkie hinted that he might go along with measures designed to reinforce the British fleet. "We must admit," he said,

> that the loss of the British fleet would greatly weaken our defense. That is because the British fleet has for years controlled the Atlantic, leaving us free to concentrate in the Pacific. If the British fleet were

73. Form letters from White and Miller, August 22, 1940, FPM MSS.

74. William Allen White News Service letters of August 24, August 28, August 30, September 3, and September 4, 1940, FPM MSS.

lost or captured, the Atlantic might be dominated by Germany, a power hostile to our way of life, controlling in that event most of the ships and shipbuilding facilities of Europe. This would be a calamity for us. We might be exposed to attack on the Atlantic. Our defense would be weakened until we could build a navy and air force strong enough to defend both coasts.[75]

Warhawk Geoffrey Parsons had in fact drafted this section of Willkie's address. Since Parsons' *Herald Tribune* editorials were much more belligerent, it is apparent that he was not trying to enunciate his own or the Group's views through Willkie's mouth but was expressing the candidate's non-committal position. Republican isolationism and his candidate's need to retain freedom to maneuver in subsequent campaigning constrained Parsons to write ambiguously.[76]

On August 18 Prime Minister MacKenzie King and President Roosevelt left Ogdensburg. During the two days they had spent together watching United States Army maneuvers and discussing the world situation, the destroyer-bases issue had been raised, and the Prime Minister had been quick to give his active and complete support to such a venture. From Canada's viewpoint as a belligerent, almost anything that brought Britain and the United States closer together was reassuring. Roosevelt told the Canadian leader he would consult with him on matters concerning any bases (such as Newfoundland) in which Canada had immediate interests, and King apparently offered air base facilities for American use in Canada apart from those being offered in Empire possessions by the London government. Upon returning to Ottawa, King was so optimistic that he wired Churchill to begin sending over crews to man the destroyers.[77]

Good news awaited Roosevelt's return to Washington. In

75. *New York Times*, August 18, 1940.

76. Parsons' son saw Willkie shortly after the speech and took him to task for advocating Roosevelt's foreign policy while attacking Roosevelt for implementing that policy. Willkie replied, "That's funny, your own father wrote that part of my speech."; as told to author by Geoffrey Parsons, Jr., November 9, 1965.

77. Nancy Hooker (ed.), *The Moffat Papers* (Cambridge, Mass., 1956), pp. 326–29; Henry L. Stimson and McGeorge Bundy, *On Active Service in Peace and War* (New York, 1948), pp. 358–59; Conn and Fairchild, *The Framework of Hemisphere Defense*, p. 372.

his absence Attorney General Jackson had convinced General Marshall and Admiral Stark that they could in good conscience certify that prospective bases would be of greater value to the national defense than the destroyers. Furthermore, the results of two public opinion polls completed over the weekend were encouraging. In one instance 61 per cent favored selling fifty destroyers to England; in the other 62 per cent approved such a transaction. In light of the fact that only 53 per cent had favored giving more help to England on July 18, it is probable that the agitation of the White Committee and the speeches and editorials instigated by the Century Group helped accelerate this change in public attitude.[78]

British resistance to a *quid pro quo,* however, still remained, diminished now by Churchill's willingness to repeat his June 4 statement. Nevertheless, Churchill was sufficiently confident of success by August 20 to announce to the House of Commons, "His Majesty's Government is entirely willing to accord defense facilities to the United States on a ninety-nine year leasehold basis, and we feel that our interests no less than theirs . . . will be served thereby." He made no mention, however, of destroyers, a fleet guarantee, or a *quid pro quo.*[79]

In his cable to Roosevelt the next day, Churchill stated, "I had not contemplated anything in the nature of a contract, bargain or sale between us. . . . People will contrast on each side what is given and received," he continued. "The money value of the armaments would be computed and set against the facilities and some would think one thing about it and some another." He still asked that the transfer of destroyers "be entirely a separate spontaneous act" with no connection to the base leases. Futile telephone calls, meetings, and memoranda were exchanged between President and Prime Minister, Ambassador and Secretary without solving the dilemma. It appeared the matter might founder on the issue of a *quid pro quo.*[80]

78. "Gallup and Fortune Polls," *Public Opinion Quarterly,* IV, 4 (December, 1940), 713.

79. Churchill, *Their Finest Hour,* p. 408.

80. Conn and Fairchild, *The Framework of Hemisphere Defense,* p. 58; Churchill, *Their Finest Hour,* p. 410; Eugene C. Gerhart, *America's Advocate: Robert H. Jackson* (Indianapolis, 1958), p. 217.

The break came on Monday, August 26, when Green L. Hackworth, legal advisor to the State Department, proposed that the island bases be divided into two groups, one to be exchanged for the destroyers, fulfilling Roosevelt's desire for a *quid pro quo,* the other to be freely given by Britain, satisfying Churchill's desire for a "spontaneous gift." In five more days an exchange of notes relating to destroyers and bases and an *aide-memoire* alluding to Churchill's June 4 statement on the Fleet had been written and approved by both governments. Thus, by the end of August the diplomatic negotiations had been completed.[81]

On August 30 Ulric Bell, Ward Cheney, Francis Miller, and Herbert Agar met Archibald MacLeish at Washington's Hay-Adams House, across the street from the White House. MacLeish, through Russell Davenport, was still serving as one of the informal lines of communication between the President and the Willkie camp. Now the five men gathered to hear the final word on the candidate's attitude on destroyers. They (apparently) received two telephone calls—one from Lew Douglas, who was vacationing in Sun Valley, and one from Davenport, who was with Willkie. The gist of both messages was the same —the Republican candidate had just promised that he would not attack a destroyer deal. The five were overjoyed. Bell sped the message to the White House. Roosevelt, despite his decision to complete the negotiations, had remained apprehensive about the political consequences of a destroyer transfer. Bell's news was most reassuring.[82]

On Tuesday morning, September 3, President Roosevelt announced the news of the destroyer-bases agreement to the nation. Speaking to the White House press corps gathered aboard the presidential train returning from a tour of ordnance plants, Roosevelt compared the transaction to the Louisiana Purchase (in which an ancestor of his had participated). He suggested that, like President Jefferson, he was forced to act without

81. Hull, *Memoirs,* pp. 837–38; F. D. Roosevelt, *Public Papers: 1940,* pp. 392–93.

82. Douglas telephone conversation with author, January 8, 1965; Francis P. Miller telephone conversations with author, August 13, 1965, and May 18, 1967; MacLeish to author, December 6, 1965; Herbert Agar to author, January 30, 1968. The surviving participants are uncertain as to the exact number of calls.

consulting Congress before the opportunity to act evaporated. He explained with "folksy" simplicity that the agreement was a mutually beneficial horse-trade rather than an act of American charity or a step toward belligerency.[83]

The isolationists in Congress and elsewhere reacted sharply to the announcement. Senator Nye called Roosevelt's circumvention of Congress "a dictatorial step." Senator Homer Bone said, "It is a tragic mistake to deprive ourselves of some of the most valuable ships in our Navy. It is obvious they cannot be obsolete ships here and be effective units on the other side." Representative Harold Knutson of Minnesota proclaimed, "The whole world is gone crazy"; and Congressman Paul W. Shafer of Michigan lamented, "There is no longer any need for Congress." Representative George Tinkham of Massachusetts warned, "This is the first long step toward war." Of Roosevelt, Tinkham added, "There is no difference between his action from either Hitler, Mussolini or Stalin." [84]

Despite these outcries, newspaper comment across the nation as generally favorable. The *Philadelphia Record* called the agreement "this master stroke of combined good will and good business," and even Colonel McCormick's *Chicago Tribune* hailed the acquisition of bases as "A Triumph!" However, many felt that "the action is wisely taken, the means extremely regrettable." As the *Cleveland Plain Dealer* expressed it, "Frankly, we would like it better if some degree of cooperation on the part of Congress had been sought." [85] The Group's program of press releases, news letters, and radio addresses was, no doubt, in part responsible for such widespread acceptance.

In a tone of moderate criticism, Wendell Willkie told a crowd in Rushville, Indiana: "The country will undoubtedly approve. . . . It is regrettable, however, that the President did not deem it necessary in connection with this proposal to secure the approval of Congress or permit public discussion prior to adoption. The people have a right to know of such important commitments prior to and not after being made." [86] Although

83. F. D. Roosevelt, *Public Papers: 1940,* pp. 376–91.
84. *New York Times,* September 4, 1940.
85. As quoted in *New York Times,* September 5, 1940.
86. *New York Times,* September 4, 1940.

some in the Group may have hoped for a more completely favorable statement, under the circumstances most were satisfied or even delighted by Willkie's relative restraint.[87]

For the members of the Group one job was done. They were certain that they had hastened the completion of the destroyer-bases agreement, and there is no question but that they had. They had made a limited but important contribution to the stimulation of favorable public opinion through the radio speeches, especially Pershing's, and the pro-British propaganda they circulated to columnists and editorial writers. Their contributions to the "private" aspects of the destroyer-bases arrangement were even more significant. The President and the Secretaries of State, War, and the Navy may well have been encouraged to act by their confidential talks with respected friends like Agar, Cheney, Coffin, and Luce. Unquestionably Dean Acheson's letter to the *New York Times,* helped clear away the legal obstacles to a destroyer transfer. And Lewis Douglas, together with White and Davenport, must be credited with convincing Willkie to eschew a politically expedient attack on the destroyer sale. If Willkie had listened to Republican isolationists and denounced the release of needed naval vessels in July or August, it is possible that Roosevelt might have delayed the completion of negotiations until after the election.

At the time, the speedy dispatch of destroyers to England *seemed* much more important than in fact it was. By the time any sizeable number of these vessels had reached the British Isles, Hitler had postponed the invasion they were intended to help repel. They did serve—effectively, considering their age—on less dramatic but necessary North Atlantic convoy duty until newly constructed escort vessels replaced them in 1942 and 1943. The destroyer deal's greatest significance lay in its impact on British morale and on United States status relative to the war. About to undergo the aerial pounding of the autumn of 1940, Britons took heart from the fact that America seemed to be rallying to their side. The sale of a number of war vessels by the *government* of a country at peace to the *government* of a country

87. Francis P. Miller to Allen Dulles, September 6, 1940, FFF MSS. Late in the campaign, when Willkie sensed he was losing ground, he attacked the deal in several speeches.

at war, regardless of official disclaimers, was—according to international law—a step in the direction of belligerency.[88] The Warhawks, of course, were pleased with both of these results.

88. See the three comments on the destroyer transfer in *American Journal of International Law*, XXIV (October, 1940), 669–97, by Edwin Borchard, Herbert W. Briggs, and Quincy Wright.

V. Election and Readjustment

In the early autumn of 1940, Francis Miller explained the Group's function as "getting certain things done which individual members of the Group could help get done in their personal capacities. We [do] not," he added, "conceive of ourselves as having the function of initiating a broad program of education among the American people."[1] Yet, by the time Miller wrote these words in October, the Century Group had already begun to place less emphasis on private endeavors to achieve specific government actions and more upon a "program of education"—on propaganda.

This change was partly the result of the Warhawks' deliberations about the Group's future function. It also represented their response to the appearance of a dynamic organization—America First—whose purposes were antagonistic to their own. This new body's vigorous campaign to keep America out of war and discredit interventionism forced the Group to defend itself and react to its opponents' positions and proposals. No longer

1. Francis P. Miller to C. D. Jackson, October 9, 1940, FFF MSS.

were the Warhawks able anonymously to facilitate pro-British, interventionist actions free from organized public criticism. Lastly, but probably most importantly, their role changed because their relationship with the White House changed. With the Group "exposed" and with election day approaching, the President reduced his ties with the Warhawks. Widespread anti-interventionism made identification with them a political liability. The Group was perturbed by what they saw as Roosevelt's unstatesmanlike reluctance to render any dramatic new assistance to Britain before the election. They regarded his hesitancy to declare a national emergency and his public reassurance of "no foreign war" as defaults of leadership. Since the President would not lead public opinion in the proper direction, the Warhawks convinced themselves that *they* must try to do so. At the least they hoped to help counter-balance the effect of isolationist propaganda on public attitudes and official decisions.

At a dinner meeting on September 5, 1940, attended by nineteen interventionists, Lewis Douglas and Herbert Agar led a discussion of the future usefulness of the Century Group. They reviewed the unfinished program of July 11—convoys to evacuate English children, extension of credit to Britain, and deployment of American naval vessels to protect the British Isles. They mentioned the new British needs which John Balderston had just described in a News Service release—torpedo boats, flying boats, flying fortresses, tanks, rifles, Norden bombsights, and training fields in the United States for Commonwealth pilots. They pondered longer-term questions of supply—the financial crisis Britain would soon face in paying for arms purchases in the United States and her need for larger allocations of American munitions production.

After some deliberation the Group resolved to postpone its decision on whether to continue its efforts and appointed two committees to explore possible future fields of endeavor. One, chaired by Allen Dulles, was to examine the possibilities for better coordination of American and British production "to determine whether our group is a suitable group to do anything about it." The other, led by Herbert Agar, was to study methods for awakening "the American people to the meaning for them of this world revolution."[2] The report of Agar's committee hardly left the decision in question. "The people are ready to believe the truth," it declared. "Who will tell it? We could change the tide of history in two or three months."[3]

In meetings at the Century Club on September 13 and 19, the Group decided to continue the work indefinitely. Therefore, its members began immediately to address themselves to new challenges—Herbert Hoover's plan to feed captive Europe and General Robert E. Wood's America First Committee. From the subsequent trend of the Warhawks' efforts, it is apparent that they considered "awakening the American people" the primary task.[4]

To further this awakening the Group asked certain individuals to be responsible for specific segments of the public—William Agar for Roman Catholics, Bishop Hobson and Dr. Van Dusen for Protestants, Will Clayton for big business, Dr. Van Dusen for students, and Presidents Hopkins and Wriston for college presidents. It also enlisted Katherine Gauss Jackson, daughter of Dean Christian Gauss of Princeton, and Helen Everitt, New York magazine writer and executive, to attend to women's organizations and magazines.[5] Although it was not until October 17 that Whitney Shepardson prepared a formal statement of the "future function of the Group," Herbert Agar enunciated the direction in which the Warhawks were moving a month earlier when he asked Helen Everitt to establish liaison between the Warhawks and national women's magazines. The Group, he declared, was motivated in part by dissatisfaction with the way the politicians were running the campaign. "These leaders" are afraid to speak out, Agar wrote, "because every honest word may

2. "Notice," September 6, 1940, WHS MSS; Francis P. Miller to Dulles, September 6, 1940; Francis P. Miller to Herbert Agar, September 6, 1940, FFF MSS.

3. "Subcommittees Report to Meeting at Century Club," September 13, 1940, Ulric Bell Papers (hereafter UB MSS), privately held.

4. Herbert Agar to Helen Everitt, September 15, 1940; Francis P. Miller to Herbert Agar *et al.*, September 10, 1940, FFF MSS; "Dinner List, Century Club," September 19, 1940, WHS MSS.

5. "For Consideration" and "Dinner List," October 3, 1940; FFF MSS.

lose the votes of some angry, noisy minority. . . . Since our leaders appear to insist on a 'public demand' before they are willing to lead, we believe we must do everything in our power to create such a demand." [6]

He outlined the plans agreed upon in the meetings on September 12. First, Miller and Bell would expand the work of the New York office. Their job would be "to think of things for the rest" of the Warhawks to do—including exerting "personal pressure on men and institutions." Second, William Agar would work full time "to organize throughout the country a Catholic presentation of our story. We do not expect to win the Catholic Church, which as you know is the steadiest and strongest force for appeasement in the country," he commented. "But we do expect to divide it, and thus weaken its effectiveness, by giving to the Catholics who are on our side permission to believe that appeasement is by no means a united Church policy." Third, Kay Jackson would work half time at Room 2940 doing a similar job with women's organizations. Fourth, a man would be recruited to "do the same job in labor circles."

Agar added that these plans covered only a "two or three month period." "After that, with luck, a larger and far more powerful organization may be ready to take over our work." [7]

Activity would still center upon reaching the people who influenced the public, rather than upon direct solicitation of grass-roots support. The Group would expand this effort, however, and focus on those individuals who "made opinion" in specific segments of the population. Agar's letter and Shepardson's later report on "future functions" showed that the Warhawks still considered the Group only a temporary expedient. Shepardson expected that the Committee to Defend America or the Council for Democracy would gradually absorb its work. Agar, however, may already have realized that a separate organization having the ultimate goal of belligerency would be necessary.[8]

6. H. Agar to Everitt, September 15, 1940, FFF MSS.

7. *Ibid.*

8. "Report of Committee on Future Function of the Group," October 15, 1940, FPM MSS.

Unlike the campaign of the summer, the Warhawks' fall and winter plans were not cleared beforehand in Washington. In October and November, Roosevelt and Hull, faced with winning an election, were irritated by "those zealots" who were demanding that they move farther and faster than they felt their national constituency desired to go. Group members visited the White House only rarely now, and when they did it was usually on other business than foreign affairs.[9]

The Group existed on a month-to-month basis until the founding of the Fight For Freedom. Ward Cheney accepted much of the financial burden of maintaining an office and paying mailing and printing expenses. Because the Group still sought to keep its work confidential and unpublicized, it decided it could not undertake a semi-public appeal for funds—which would have necessitated increasing the number at the dinner meetings.

The informality of the Group meant that changes in personnel were continuous and easy. Some of the original members, like Allen Dulles and Frank Polk, apparently felt that the Group had served its purpose by facilitating the destroyer-bases agreement, and they drifted away. Others—Whitney Shepardson, Geoffrey Parsons, and Elmer Davis—thought their usefulness as objective analysts of foreign affairs would be impaired by continued association with a "pressure group." Joseph Alsop, who disliked committee work, and Henry Luce, who clashed with the Group over food for occupied Europe, also departed. Dean Acheson, who attended meetings infrequently but participated in the drafting of several Warhawk statements, became Assistant Secretary of State for Economic Affairs in February, 1941, and dropped out entirely. Though he did not leave the Group, Francis Miller handed over operation of Room 2940 to Ulric Bell and returned to his work at the Council on Foreign Relations. Robert Sherwood, who was being drawn increasingly into speech-writing for the President, no longer attended the meetings, but his wife, Madeline, soon began to assist Bell in the Group's office. Sherwood remained an important link between the Warhawks and the White House during the following year.

9. William L. Langer and S. Everett Gleason, *The Undeclared War* (New York, 1953), pp. 200–205.

In most instances departure from the Group did not mean an end to the work for intervention. Most ex-members continued to pursue the same aims in their private capacities that their former associates sought collectively, and friends who continued to attend meetings kept them abreast of happenings within the Group.[10]

New additions in the fall included the historian Henry Pringle, who took an increasingly active role in drafting the Group's literature; the columnist Robert S. Allen, who replaced Alsop as the Warhawks' "ears" in Washington; and Maury Maverick, the liberal former congressman and mayor of San Antonio. Ulric Bell was elevated to a position of new leadership when he was placed in charge of Room 2940. Later on in the winter, Conyers Read, University of Pennsylvania history professor; Michael Williams, former editor of the liberal Catholic magazine, *Commonweal;* and F. H. Peter Cusick, New York advertising executive and close advisor of Wendell Willkie, began to attend the dinners regularly. Cusick soon joined Bell in the work at Room 2940. Taken all together, the personnel changes of the fall and winter of 1940 altered the makeup of the Group distinctly (but unintentionally) in the Democratic and liberal direction. With the deepening involvement of Lewis Douglas in the Committee to Defend America and the departure of Acheson, Dulles, Shepardson, Parsons, and Luce, leadership fell increasingly to the liberals—to Bell, the Agars, Cusick, and Van Dusen.[11]

New organizations concerned with aid to Britain or intervention were springing up across the country in the winter of 1940–41. Some of these, such as Katherine Jackson's Women's Committee for Action and its adjunct, the Student Defenders of Democracy, were in fact created by the Century Group, in cooperation with the Council for Democracy and the White Committee. They were part of the Group's plan to appeal to leaders of specific segments of the public. Others, such as the Friends of Democracy, the Council of National Morale, the Kentucky League for British Victory, and the "Buy a Bit of a

10. "Notice," signed by Francis P. Miller, October 23, 1940, FPM MSS; see dinner lists, September, 1940, to February, 1941, FFF MSS.

11. *Ibid.*

Fighter Plane" movement, were organized by individuals who were not members but whose similar goals and activities brought about varying degrees of communication.[12]

"Exposure" of the Century Group's activities came in late September, 1940. On the twenty-sixth, Senator Rush D. Holt, embittered by recent political defeat, assailed the pro-British pressure groups on the floor of the Senate. Together with Bennett Champ Clark, Gerald P. Nye, Burton K. Wheeler, Henrik Shipstead, John Danaher, and David I. Walsh, he denounced the activities of the White Committee, the Group, and Balderston's News Service. The Senators characterized them as agencies of the British government and part of "a conspiracy to involve America in the war." They based their charges primarily on an article written for the *St. Louis Post-Dispatch* by Charles Ross.[13]

The article itself was an objective study of the behind-the-scenes activities which preceded the destroyer transfer and of the structure and method of the White Committee and the "Miller Group." In writing the piece Ross had requested the assistance of his long-time acquaintance Whitney Shepardson, and Shepardson had obtained permission for Ross to visit Room 2940 and see any records he wanted to see. Both Shepardson and Miller had hoped that a full disclosure of the Group's activities by a competent and objective reporter would forestall future attempts at "sensational revelations" by isolationists.[14]

Ross told the story of the News Service, including the misunderstanding between White and Balderston over the September 4 newsletter. That dispatch had listed the "further needs" of the British—torpedo boats, flying boats, flying fortresses, Norden bombsights, and training fields in the United States for Commonwealth pilots. As Ross reported it, White at first had approved this newsletter, but after its circulation he realized that it could be construed to commit his organization to support all of

12. W. E. Wheeler to Bell, December 21, 1940; Francis P. Miller to C. D. Jackson, October 9, 1940; material about "Council on National Morale," FFF MSS.

13. U.S. *Congressional Record*, 76th Cong., 3d Sess., 1940, Part 11, pp. 12646–56; *St. Louis Post-Dispatch*, September 22, 1940.

14. *St. Louis Post-Dispatch*, September 22, 1940; author's interviews with Shepardson and Francis P. Miller.

the "further needs." He therefore disavowed it, and the dispute which ensued hastened the News Service's demise.[15]

Despite the fact that the *Post-Dispatch's* isolationist editors burdened Ross' straightforward description with sensational headlines and captions, the Warhawks were generally satisfied with the results. Francis Miller, for one, thought the article "such a superb job of reporting that we can well afford to rest our case upon the facts as he gave them." [16]

The Senators, however, pounced upon the Ross article as proof of a British conspiracy. Holt declared that Balderston "had just returned" from England and that "Mr. Balderston was brought back here to create war propaganda. . . . It is a known fact among those who have studied it," he boldly asserted, "that John L. Balderston is not interested in preserving America but is directly under the British Ministry of Information." Holt then read excerpts from *Who's Who,* noting that Balderston "was in a propaganda agency in the World War . . ." and that of his two home addresses "he thinks more of his English home and puts it in advance of his American home in *Who's Who.*" The Senator and his colleagues then proceeded to dissect the News Service bulletin of September 4, referring to it as "Balderston's demands." Holt mentioned also that after the dispute with White, Balderston departed, discredited, for the West Coast.[17]

Unable to sue Holt for slander because of congressional immunity, Balderston replied with a twenty-three page memorandum to newspaper editors entitled, "The William Allen White Committee News Service and a Little 'Smear Campaign' in the Senate." He addressed himself to each of the isolationists' accusations and insinuations. He denounced as "a deliberate lie" the charge that he was an agent of the British Ministry of Information. In issuing the newsletters he was acting, he said, as an American citizen in what he considered the best interests of his country. Furthermore, he was paying all of his own expenses

15. *St. Louis Post-Dispatch,* September 22, 1940, WAW News Service, September 4, 1940, FPM MSS; Walter Johnson, *The Battle Against Isolation* (Chicago, 1944), pp. 119–21.

16. Francis P. Miller to Charles Edmundson, October 23, 1940, FFF MSS.

17. U.S. *Congressional Record,* 76th Cong., 3d Sess., 1940, Part 11, pp. 12646–56.

except telephone and telegraph charges, accepting no remuneration whatever for his full-time efforts.[18]

He had not retreated under fire to California after the September 4 misunderstanding, Balderston insisted, but had returned to the Coast to attend to his personal finances after having worked "for exactly the time I told the White Committee before I started that I could afford to work." He had not, he responded, "just recently returned from Britain." He had not been there since the beginning of the war, more than a year earlier. He *had* been in "a propaganda agency during the First World War," but, he noted, Senator Holt,

> . . . while speaking was reading to himself in *Who's Who* the words: "Director of Information, Great Britain and Ireland, for U.S. Government Committee of Public Information, 1917–19." Those words were under his eyes, but the words he uttered for permanent embalmment in the *Congressional Record* were, "He was in a propaganda agency." The inference this man desired to convey is now plain to anybody: "A propaganda agency—abroad, so presumably foreign." [19]

Balderston explained that he put his London address into *Who's Who* because the production of his plays had required his frequent stays in that city but added that he was not ashamed of his love for London, where he had spent so much time, both as an agent of the United States government and a correspondent for American newspapers.[20]

He said that his press release did not represent itself as "Demands," nor even as a policy statement of the White Committee but as a report of information about British needs to American editors. "They were a news story," he declared. He also mentioned that most of the material enumerated in the letter of September 4 was supposed to have been part of the destroyer-bases agreement but had been left out through the inadvertent error of American officials, and that the Committee to Defend America, after momentary confusion, had adopted most of the "Demands" as part of its program. Characterizing Holt's harangue

18. Available in FPM MSS and FFF MSS.

19. John L. Balderston, "The William Allen White News Service and a Little 'Smear Campaign' in the Senate," FFF MSS.

20. *Ibid.*

as a typical "Copperhead smear tactic," Balderston charged that the Senator might well be contributing ". . . materially to the defeat and downfall of his country [by working] to prevent military and economic action by us on a decisive front, at a time when but for him and his co-workers Hitler could have been stopped away from our shores while we still had one powerful friend left in this miserable world." [21]

The Ross article and the Balderston-Holt controversy focused public attention on a heretofore covert operation. They also marked the first instance when isolationists' actions placed the Warhawks on the defensive. Hereafter, they would be increasingly involved in direct public debate with individuals of opposite views. More and more the Group would find itself responding publicly to its opponents' positions and proposals rather than operating confidentially to initiate and facilitate the events *behind* the headlines.[22]

While Balderston clashed with Senate isolationists, the other Warhawks prepared for battle against the new nationwide organization for isolation, the America First Committee. Originally the creation of R. Douglas Stuart, Jr., the son of the first vice-president of Quaker Oats Company and a Yale law student, the Committee had grown from campus to nationwide proportions during the summer. Stuart enlisted the assistance of General Robert E. Wood, chairman of the board at Sears, Roebuck and Company; Hanford MacNider, Iowa manufacturer and former national commander of the American Legion; Jay Hormel, president of Hormel Meat Packing Company; and Philip LaFollette, former governor of Wisconsin.[23] On September 4 these men announced the birth of their organization. The America First "Principles" declared:

1. The United States must build an impregnable defense for America.

2. No foreign power, nor group of powers, can successfully attack a *prepared* America.

21. *Ibid.*

22. Holt repeated the exercise on December 16, 1940, focusing his attention on the Century Group and its friends in the interventionist press; U.S. *Congressional Record,* 76th Cong., 3rd Sess., 1940, Part 12, pp. 13916–21.

23. Wayne S. Cole, *America First: The Battle Against Intervention, 1940–1941* (Madison, Wisconsin, 1953), pp. 10–16.

3. American democracy can be preserved only by keeping out of the European war.

4. "Aid short of war" weakens national defense at home and threatens to involve America in war abroad.[24]

At the outset the America First Committee was successful in attracting influential personalities to its National Committee. Its membership included Chester B. Bowles, William Benton, Avery Brundage, William Castle, Mrs. Bennett Champ Clark, Henry Ford, Lillian Gish, Colonel Charles A. Lindbergh, Alice Roosevelt Longworth, Frank Lowden, Mrs. John P. Marquand, George Peek, Amos Pinchot, Edward Rickenbacker, Mrs. Burton K. Wheeler, and Robert Young.[25]

Under the direction of an executive committee operating from Chicago (the center of isolationism, much as New York was the focus of interventionism), local chapters were formed in most major cities in the country, and nationwide auxiliaries began organizing young people, women, and Negroes. During the ensuing fifteen months the Committee supported an arms embargo, a negotiated peace, and a referendum on declaring war. It opposed Lend-Lease, occupation of the Atlantic islands and Iceland, convoying materiel to Britain, extension of the draft, shooting-on-sight, and revision of the Neutrality Act. Although the America First Committee endorsed the maintenance of adequate defenses, according to its foremost historian it "at no time made a concerted drive for the accomplishment of that end." Those Americans who had been isolationists in the spring of 1940 and had not altered their views (see Chapter I) and those who now saw war against Hitler as a hopeless and impossible task rallied to the side of America First.[26]

The America First movement reached its apex during the debate over Lend-Lease when its members flooded Congress with anti-Lend-Lease mail far out of proportion to public attitudes as reflected by the public opinion polls. However, as America moved closer to war because of the sinkings and confrontations in the Atlantic during the summer and fall of 1941, support for America First diminished. The inept organizational direction of the Committee's inexperienced national leaders and the public

24. *Ibid.*, p. 15.
25. *Ibid.*, pp. 20–23.
26. *Ibid.*, pp. 24–31.

blunders of America First speakers, especially Colonel Lindbergh, accelerated its decline.[27]

Late in 1941 the America Firsters' lack of discrimination in accepting members and financial support exposed them to charges that they were being manipulated by Axis agents. The arrest and conviction of two of their speakers, Laura Ingalls and Ralph Townsend, for failure to register as agents of foreign powers substantiated these allegations. The gradual polarization of unsavory elements in American society—including the Communist American Peace Mobilization (prior to the German invasion of the Soviet Union), the Ku Klux Klan, William Dudley Pelley's Silver Shirts, Joe McWilliams' American Destiny party, and Father Coughlin's Christian Front—around America First and the too-frequent failure of its national leaders to disavow such support, provided interventionists with much material useful in discrediting organized isolationism.[28]

In the fall and winter of 1940 the Century Group scrutinized the America First Committee's activities, even though it had neither the finances nor organization to challenge the isolationists at the grass-roots level. For the moment they left this to the William Allen White organization, whose efforts were hampered by conflicts of policy and personality on the national level. However, at least one individual connected with the Group did some spadework on the America Firsters, compiling several reports on their personnel, background, policy, and probable behavior.[29] Prior to the founding of the Fight For Freedom the Warhawks limited their counteraction to reprinting and distributing written material and recruiting capable speakers who could "match" reputations with the leading isolationist spokesmen.[30] Thus a radio speech by Mrs. Irving Berlin, arranged by

27. *Ibid.*, pp. 24–25.

28. *Ibid.*, pp. 24–25, Chaps. VII, VIII; John Roy Carlson, *Undercover: My Four Years in the Nazi Underground of America* (New York, 1943), pp. 240–60.

29. "Detailed Report on America First Committee," November 27, 1940; "Report on Interview with William Castle," unsigned, November 19, 1940, FFF MSS. "Current Activities on [*sic*] America First," December 5, 1940, UB MSS.

30. One reprint considered most effective was Herbert Agar, "The Lotus Eaters of 1940," *Louisville Courier-Journal*, November 17, 1940, FFF MSS.

the Group, served to "neutralize" an earlier broadcast by Anne Morrow Lindbergh. "The Nazis had disguised old-fashioned tyranny to look like something new," Mrs. Berlin declared. "They have touched the heart of a poet like Mrs. Lindbergh. In this war Mrs. Lindbergh would have us believe that there is a conflict—not between good and evil—but between the old and the new. She is even wrong about which is the old. A man has led his people out to conquer. There is nothing new about that."[31] Similarly, the Warhawks chose James Warburg to respond to businessmen like Ambassador Kennedy, General Wood, and Graeme Howard, who were preaching accommodation with "the new wave of the future." Warburg reminded businessmen of some facts of recent history: "The German steel magnate, Thyssen, and other large German industrialists and bankers supplied much of the money which enabled the Nazi party to come into power. They thought they could control or 'come to terms' with Hitler. Some of Mr. Thyssen's friends are today taking orders from Hitler; some are in concentration camps; some are dead. . . ."[32]

In addition, Room 2940 reprinted and circulated to its mailing list of journalists and civic leaders editorials and articles advocating United States involvement, or illustrating the Nazi threat to the Western hemisphere. A *Louisville Courier-Journal* article by Ulric Bell described Nazi efforts to control newsreels about Europe shown in American theaters. A Friends of Democracy brochure which the Group distributed characterized the America First Committee as a "Nazi Transmission Belt." It documented Nazi approval of the America First Committee and indicated a number of similarities between the statements of that Committee and the outpourings of the German propaganda ministry.[33]

In February Room 2940 reprinted an article by Warburg which excoriated as "a particular present day lie" the America

31. "American Forum of the Air—Mrs. Irving Berlin," January 5, 1941, FFF MSS.

32. James P. Warburg, "No Covenant with Tyranny," December 19, 1940, FFF MSS.

33. "By Ulric Bell," September 30, 1940; Francis P. Miller, "Note," September 28, 1940; Friends of Democracy, "The American First Committee—The Nazi Transmission Belt," FFF MSS.

First claim that " '88 per cent of the American people, as shown by the Gallup poll, do not want war and they are being pushed around by the 12 per cent who do want war.' " The article noted that the very same poll which the isolationists were quoting also revealed that "68 per cent of the American people were in favor of helping Britain go on fighting *even at the risk of war,*" and that only 9 per cent favored a negotiated peace.[34] Citing of such survey statistics became a familiar part of the interventionist-isolationist debate. In February, 1941, the Group circulated the findings of a poll taken by Elmo Roper of constituents of isolationist Congressman Hamilton Fish, showing that Fish's views "on U.S. foreign policy are not shared by his constituents, a majority of whom agree with President Roosevelt's ideas regarding aid to Britain." [35]

To meet the various arguments against aid to Britain and United States involvement, the Group arranged a series of pamphlets discussing particular aspects of the current crisis. The series was entitled "America in a World at War" and was published by Farrar & Rinehart at irregular intervals through 1941. Among the titles were Henry Pringle's "Why? A Question-Answer Discussion of Preparedness, Aid to Britain, Food Blockade, Appeasement, Pan-American Friendship, etc."; James Truslow Adams' "An American Looks at the British Empire"; William Agar's "Where Do Catholics Stand?"; Helen Hill Miller's "America's Maginot Line"; and James Warburg's "The Isolationist Illusion and World Peace." [36]

In the meantime, the Women's Committee for Action, an informal adjunct to the Group, sought to neutralize the strong attraction which pacifism and non-involvement had for American mothers and wives. The Committee was comprised largely of professional women and performed on a smaller scale among women's clubs and youth organizations the same functions that the Century Group performed among men. At women's gather-

34. James P. Warburg, "The Isolationist Illusion," February 19, 1941, FFF MSS.

35. Elmo Roper, "Summary of a Study of Certain Aspects of Thought among Residents of the 26th Congressional District of New York," February, 1941, FFF MSS.

36. Copies of each are available in FFF MSS.

ings and student meetings, they attacked "the illusory and temporary peace" that isolationism offered. They argued that more of America's husbands and sons would have to die if America waited to fight on her own soil instead of meeting the threat abroad, and they advocated increased aid to Britain, continuance of the food blockade of Europe, and universal military training for American men. They began organizing college youths favorable to aid and intervention into the "Student Defenders of Democracy." On college campuses they encountered the powerful, simplistic appeal of America Firsters, who stressed that it was *young* men who would have to fight and die in any war that their elders began. The Women's Committee and the Student Defenders used a combination of exhortation and reason in their efforts to convince young people of the necessity of such sacrifice.[37]

The speed with which America armed for battle depended largely on the cooperation of the leaders of big business, yet in the autumn of 1940 such industrialists as Graeme Howard, Henry Ford, Edward Ryerson, and Thomas Hammond were outspoken in their isolationism. The businessmen in the Group, therefore, concentrated on convincing undecided businessmen of the necessity of America's participation.[38] Lewis Douglas went to the National Association of Manufacturers meeting to declare:

> Should these forces of organized violence gain a part of their objective—sweep the British fleet from the seas and dismember the British Empire . . . we will then, in fact . . . be the most vulnerable of nations. . . .
>
> We would then be desperately alone in the world, confronted by powers aimed at recasting the civilization of the world, controlling all of two Continents, a part of a third, holding under their dictation all the raw materials necessary, not only to subsistence but to the successful enforcement of their will, operating industrial facilities with a capacity greater than ours, shipbuilding facilities many times in excess of our productive possibilities, manned by what one might almost call conscript labor. And all of it—raw materials, industries,

37. "For Consideration," October 3, 1940; "For Consideration," October 17, 1940; "Report," October 23, 1940, FFF MSS.

38. Francis P. Miller to Bell, November 7, 1940, FFF MSS.

shipyards, airplane factories—all of it—controlled by a State and its allies whose purposes are world power—world revolution.[39]

Ward Cheney and James Warburg exerted pressure on influential businessmen with internationalist views to speak out on the current crisis at private parties or public meetings. After the elections Wendell Willkie attended several Group meetings and agreed not only to approach his many supporters in business but also to address an internationalist rally in Chicago. Will Clayton, Charles E. Wilson of General Motors, and financier Thomas Lamont were asked "to talk to various business groups in their own communities . . . as they undoubtedly will be respected in their locale." Mark Ethridge, Vice President and General Manager of the *Louisville Courier-Journal,* and close associate of Bell and Herbert Agar, told the Retail Merchants Association of Louisville that German businessmen had acquiesced and assisted in Hitler's rise to power and that British businessmen had also deluded themselves that they could appease and trade with Hitler. "Anybody," he bluntly asserted, "who thinks we can trade with a Hitlerized continent except on Hitler's terms and by his methods is either a plain fool or an ignoramus." [40]

One America First industrialist singled out for special denunciation was Henry Ford. Ford was not only an isolationist. In the 1920's his *Dearborn Independent* had been a fountainhead of anti-Semitism, and until recently he had been an unbending foe of unionism. Thus he was vulnerable to attack on domestic as well as foreign policy issues. The interventionists struck at him each time he declared his isolationism or his opposition to industrial mobilization. A reprint distributed by Room 2940 of a *PM* article by Kenneth Crawford declared of him:

. . . Henry Ford went to Delphi and became the American oracle. He had a run-in with New York bankers and declared them a bad lot. He said some of them were Jews and therefore that Jews were a bad

39. "Remarks of Lewis W. Douglas at the Meeting of the National Association of Manufacturers," December 13, 1940, FFF MSS.

40. "Dinner Meeting," November 11, 1940; Cusick to Herbert Agar, Memorandum, January 31, 1941; Mark Ethridge, "The Economic Consequences of a Hitler Victory," undated, FFF MSS.

lot. Knowing nothing about it, he pronounced history bunk. As a nation we took all this nonsense more or less seriously. . . . We didn't say what we knew: that Henry Ford is a profoundly ignorant man who makes mistakes when he influences public thinking on any subject beyond the mechanics of motor car manufacture.[41]

Herbert Agar also jabbed sharply: "Henry Ford is a symbol of the American failure. . . . In foreign policy he stands for ignorant American idealism, as in the peace ship, plus ignorant American isolationism. In domestic policy he stands for the failure to accept social responsibility which has made American individualism a term of reproach. Again he is not a fascist in a literal sense; he is a fascist only in that he represents one of the main reasons for fascism."[42]

Like Ford, the American ambassador to London, Boston businessman Joseph P. Kennedy, drew special attention from the Group. During the thirties Kennedy had become especially intimate with the British leaders who conducted the appeasement policy and had shared their views respecting "accommodation" of the New Germany. He believed that Britain's shaky finances could not support the strain of rearmament and prolonged warfare, and he was horrified by the thought that American boys—his own sons, perhaps—would be called on "to pull England's chestnuts out of the fire." The ideas of Kennedy and his British friends clashed with those of Winston Churchill, who was futilely insisting on the need to resist Nazi aggression. After Churchill became Prime Minister, Roosevelt relegated Kennedy to the status of a diplomatic figurehead. Anglo-American relations were carried on by direct telephone conversations and telegrams between President and Prime Minister, and by special envoys like William Donovan and Harry Hopkins. While Donovan and Hopkins brought home optimistic reports on Britain's chances of survival, Kennedy's dispatches prophesied Britain's speedy demise. He was undiplomatically free in expressing his opinions, telling a *Boston Globe* reporter that "Democracy is

41. Kenneth Crawford, "The Model T Put Wheels on Progress, but Henry Ford Stopped Rolling," *PM*, December 31, 1940, FFF MSS.

42. H. Agar, "Who Are the Appeasers," *The Nation*, March 22, 1941, FFF MSS.

finished in England, [and] it may be here." He argued that Britain should sue for peace and that the United States should arm itself, but avoid any act which might involve it in the war. In October, 1940, amid persistent rumors that his work in England was at an end, Kennedy came home to campaign for Roosevelt.[43]

Kennedy told Americans there were no valid reasons for them to get into the war. He warned that our involvement might force us to adopt the very totalitarian methods we sought to resist. American promises of aid, he insisted, were encouraging Britain to continue a fight to which she was not equal, and the materiel we were sending abroad was weakening our own defenses. In the last days of the presidential campaign, when Roosevelt himself was telling an uncertain electorate, "Your boys are not going to be sent into any foreign wars," Kennedy's assistance was not repudiated but welcomed by the White House.[44]

After the election Kennedy visited the West Coast and privately lectured leaders of the movie industry. Group members Balderston and Wanger recorded that he insisted that the production of anti-Nazi films should stop because America would soon have to make its peace with Hitler and do business with Germany. Noting that many in the movie industry were Jewish, he allegedly suggested that they learn by the experiences of their European brethren and become more circumspect in their behavior so as not to invite similar retribution.[45]

The Warhawks were outraged by Balderston's reports of Kennedy's activities on the West Coast and decided on "an open demand upon the President—a demand sponsored by forty or fifty outstanding people, many his staunchest supporters—that Kennedy be repudiated as an official spokesman for the United States in any capacity." The Group persuaded people like President William Green of the American Federation of Labor, Presi-

43. Richard Whalen, *The Founding Father* (New York, 1965), pp. 245–320, 338–45.

44. *Ibid.*, pp. 321–48.

45. Balderston to Bell, November 27, 1940; "Small Dinner Meeting, Century Club," November 22, 1940, FFF MSS; Whalen, *The Founding Father*, pp. 346–48.

dent Frank Graham of the University of North Carolina, and journalists Samuel Grafton, Ralph Ingersoll, and Dorothy Thompson to sign the draft letter to the President.[46]

The letter was to be sent to the White House on December 2. It postulated that "a total emergency confronts the nation" and "that we can no longer carry on . . . in the tempo of normalcy—if we are to escape the evil fate which already has befallen half the world." It continued:

> Your Ambassador, Mr. Kennedy, has left unrepudiated and in fact has reiterated the view that the fight for democracy in Europe is a hopeless one and that this country can only prepare to accept the inevitable outcome. When he came home from England his intimate friends even then knew that he was in effect the enemy of the democratic way of life. . . . Now by indisputable evidence, his voice leads the brazen chorus of those who would shout down every policy you bespeak. . . .
>
> . . . Your administration still harbors this most deadly and effective appeaser in our land—effective because the country realizes he is eminently distinguished in that he helped you to win the election, that he is your Ambassador and that he is still a member of your administration. . . . Therefore, we beg of you as friends, and many of us as your partisans, to deprive this man of any official status.[47]

Announcement of Kennedy's resignation appeared in the morning papers of the second, making delivery of the letter unnecessary. The Group believed itself responsible for the resignation, and the memorandum of the following dinner meeting claimed that word of the forthcoming letter precipitated the Ambassador's departure. However, Kennedy's resignation had actually been submitted on November 6, and the impending public letter may have served only to force an earlier disclosure of that fact.[48]

Although Kennedy was out of government service, the Group kept him under surveillance. As Ulric Bell wrote William

46. "Small Dinner Meeting, Century Club," November 22, 1940; form letter by Bell, November 29, 1940, FFF MSS.

47. Herbert Agar *et al.* to Roosevelt, telegram, undated, FFF MSS.

48. *New York Times*, December 2, 1940; "Luncheon, Century Club," December 9, 1940, FFF MSS.

Green, "Kennedy's resignation does not remove him as a menace to the institution[s] of the United States. . . . The trouble is he *was* Ambassador and that gives his words weight with many people.[49]

A leading isolationist in education and an individual around whom much campus pacifism polarized was Dr. Robert M. Hutchins, President of the University of Chicago. In late January, Hutchins told a radio audience that America was not morally and spiritually strong enough to go to war. He declared: ". . . We are morally and intellectually unprepared to execute the moral mission to which the President calls us. . . . If we would change the face of the earth, we must first change our own hearts. . . . The American people require a moral regeneration. We are turning aside from the true path of freedom because it is easier to blame Hitler for our troubles than to fight for democracy at home" [50]

Warned of Hutchins' impact on college students by Dorothy Overlock of the Student Defenders of Democracy, the Warhawks counter-attacked vigorously.[51] Serving as moderator of a radio symposium of young people organized to respond to Hutchins, Maury Maverick accused him of retiring "into the ivory tower" and "closing his eyes to the nature of the struggle." The Warhawks circulated an editorial of the *Chicago Times* which said, "If [his] theory of perfection were carried to a logical end, the doctrine of Christianity would never have spread beyond the person of Christ himself." [52] Barry Bingham, President of the *Louisville Courier-Journal,* characterized "Dr. Hutchins' denial of the capacity of America to accept the militant Christian way" as a "bitter condemnation of his native land. . . . If we accept his advocacy of the coward's course, if we draw in and resolve on inaction . . . we predetermine our spiritual ruin." [53]

49. Bell to Green, December 12, 1940, FFF MSS.

50. Robert M. Hutchins, speech in New York City, February 15, 1941, *Vital Speeches of the Day,* VII (March, 1941), 9.

51. Agnes Reynolds to Dorothy Overlock, January 26, 1941, UB MSS. Miss Overlock later married Ulric Bell.

52. "A Clash of Assumptions," *Chicago Times,* January 26, 1941, FFF MSS.

53. Bell to Bingham, telegram, January 29, 1941. Bingham's speech was apparently written by someone in the Group and was telegraphed to

The Warhawk attacks on Ford, Kennedy, and Hutchins exemplified the change in the Group's role. Instead of manipulating from backstage as in the summer, its members were responding increasingly to the isolationists in direct, personal terms. The need to arouse emotions for their minority cause was compelling them to simplify and even brutalize the facts about their antagonists. Was Joseph Kennedy "the enemy of the democratic way of life?" Was Robert Hutchins, self-sacrificing defender of civil liberties, a "coward" as Barry Bingham implied? Probably not, but propagandizing demands simplicity of statement and clear delineation of good and evil—and the Century Group had already largely changed from covert lobbyist to public advocate of the interventionist cause.

* * * * * *

The President's behavior in the two months between the destroyer-bases agreement and election day excited little enthusiasm among the Warhawks. The record of rearmament was uneven. Coastal defenses along the Atlantic were dramatically improved, but the Army-Navy Priorities Board reported in October that the goal of a fully equipped one-and-a-half-million-men army by April, 1942, could not be reached with existing production rates. The seven-headed National Defense Advisory Commission, adrift in a sea of interagency rivalries and unclear responsibilities, provided uncertain leadership, and Roosevelt resisted suggestions that a declaration of national emergency would effectively galvanize industry. Plans for stockpiles of strategic materials had not gotten beyond the talking stage. Secretary Morgenthau argued that Axis assets should be frozen, but Secretary Hull opposed freezing assets as too provocative; for the moment the President agreed with Hull.[54]

Most importantly in the estimate of the Warhawks, three

---

him by Bell. Despite the effort to neutralize the effect of Hutchins' address, liberal Warhawks recognized that the educator had made at least one valid point—that America lagged in the pursuit of democracy at home. When the Fight For Freedom was organized, it pledged itself not only to strive for military victory abroad, but also to seek expanded justice and opportunity at home.

54. Langer and Gleason, *The Undeclared War*, pp. 215–25; Civilian Production Agency, "Industrial Mobilization in the Defense Period," unpublished manuscript, National Archives.

times during the campaign the President explicitly disavowed intervention. On September 11 he told a Teamsters convention that he rejected the efforts of "those who seek to play upon the fears of the American people," an implied slap at the interventionists. He reaffirmed the Democratic platform plank: "We will not participate in foreign wars, and we will not send our army, naval or air forces to fight in foreign lands outside of the Americas except in case of attack."[55] Although his Columbus Day address in Dayton, Ohio, affirmed, "We will continue to help those who resist aggression and now hold the aggressors far from our shores," eleven days later he insisted that there was "no secret treaty, no secret obligation, no secret understanding . . . with any other Government . . . to involve this nation in any war or for any other purpose."[56]

In his last major campaign speech, to the "Boston Irish" on October 30, Roosevelt reaffirmed his opposition to intervention. At the insistence of Morgenthau he announced his willingness to let the British purchase 12,000 additional aircraft from American manufacturers—on the grounds that British orders would stimulate expansion of United States production capacity. However, he climaxed his address with words his listeners wanted much more to hear: "And while I am talking to you mothers and fathers I give you one more assurance. I have said this before, but I shall say it again and again and again: Your boys are not going to be sent into any foreign wars. They are going into training to form a force so strong that, by its very existence, it will keep the threat of war far away from our shores. The purpose of our defense is defense."[57] The Warhawks, although well aware of the pressures generated by a political campaign, were disappointed.[58] In light of Roosevelt's widening lead over his opponent as reflected in the polls, they believed that such explicit campaign promises tied his hands unnecessarily.

If Roosevelt's performance had been less than satisfactory in the eyes of the Group, Willkie's had been worse. When the

55. *New York Times,* September 12, 1940.
56. *Ibid.,* October 13 and 24, 1940.
57. *Ibid.,* October 31, 1940.
58. For example, see draft statement signed "W.H.S." (Whitney H. Shepardson) in UB MSS.

polls in September showed Roosevelt pulling away, Willkie sought votes desperately. He pledged on the one hand to do anything to save Britain and on the other to keep the United States out of war above all else. He warned his listeners that re-election of Roosevelt meant war and even made a belated attack on the destroyer deal. Because of Willkie's fluctuations and the continued isolationism of his party (including his running mate Charles McNary), and because many of the Warhawks had long been Democrats, the Group overwhelmingly supported Roosevelt.[59] Even a lifelong Republican like Ward Cheney, convinced that interventionism had a better future under Roosevelt than under Willkie, jumped party lines to vote for FDR. Most of the Warhawks understood the President's recent utterances to be tactical political necessities. They hoped that after re-election he would lead public opinion in the direction they believed it had to go.

One of the few personal encounters any of the Group had with the chief executive during this period reinforced this expectation. James Warburg, who had made his peace with Roosevelt, saw him briefly on October 18 and came away with the "impression that, with the election out of the way, he [Roosevelt] would welcome the maximum interventionist pressure." Therefore, the Warhawks welcomed Roosevelt's victory on November 5.[60] Although some wondered how fast he could move in the light of his recent explicit promises, most of the Warhawks hoped that the tempo of events—so fast from June to September—would once again quicken. Now, perhaps, the unfinished work of the summer—American financial credits and naval support for Great Britain, and all-out mobilization at home—could be completed.

59. The greater persistence of isolationism in the Republican party was reflected in the Congressional votes on the Pittman Amendment, various defense appropriations, and the Selective Service bill.

60. James P. Warburg, *The Long Road Home* (Garden City, N.Y., 1964), p. 184; *New York Times*, November 6, 1940.

VI. Delay and Disappointment

During the four months from election day to early March, the Warhawks were disappointed by what they viewed as Roosevelt's persistent slowness and indecisiveness. They were not only disenchanted with the administration's failure to lead the nation more vigorously, but also with hesitancy of their chief ally, the Committee to Defend America, to push the President harder. They found themselves still very much on the defensive—*opposing* food for occupied Europe, *opposing* supplies for Vichy, *opposing* a negotiated peace. Handicapped in part by the lack of nationwide organization, they were largely unable to seize the initiative for the things they wanted accomplished—convoy of British merchantmen, naval and air support for the British, and, of course, an American declaration of war. With the important exception of Land-Lease, their expectation that the impetus for intervention would increase after election was not fulfilled. To meet the organizational shortcomings of what had by now changed from a confidential manipulative operation to a propaganda and public pressure group, the Warhawks seriously considered transforming the Century Group into a nationwide grass-roots organization for all-out aid and intervention.

Immediately after election day the Century Group cooperated with other internationalist organizations and pro-Democracy groups in a "National Unity" drive, designed to salve the wounds of partisanship and stimulate bipartisan support for Roosevelt's pre-campaign foreign policy. In New York the night after the election, Alf Landon, the 1936 Republican presidential candidate, and Robert Jackson, Roosevelt's Attorney General, spoke for internationalism and aid to Britain from the same stage in Carnegie Hall. The *Courier-Journal* sponsored a similar bipartisan rally in Louisville. The greatest single contribution to the national solidarity campaign, the Warhawks felt, was made by Wendell Willkie. On November 11 (although vowing "loyal opposition" on domestic issues) he pledged himself "to work for the unity of our people in the completion of the defense effort, in sending aid to Britain, and in insistence upon the removal of antagonisms in America." The Warhawks saw Willkie as a particularly influential addition to their cause, and Willkie, who admired many of the men in the Group, cooperated increasingly with them. At the suggestion of Harold Guinzburg, he prepared to take a "fact-finding" trip to Britain as a means of getting the 'Blitz' story across to the American people." Someone in the Group, probably Bell or Herbert Agar, then proposed to the White House that Willkie be sent as personal representative of the President. Roosevelt readily agreed.[1]

As part of the Unity drive the Century Group informally surveyed the country to see what measures public opinion would support. Immediately after the election Ulric Bell sent questionnaires to Group members and sympathizers all over the country designed to ascertain how the election had affected regional attitudes on national unity and on aid to Britain, relief for Europe, and Axis propaganda in this country. Typical responses from such individuals as Maury Maverick in Texas, Ernest Hopkins in New Hampshire, Bishop Hobson in Ohio, William Allen

1. "Outline for Dinner Meeting," November 11, 1940, FFF MSS; *New York Times*, November 7 and 12, 1940; author's interview with F. H. Peter Cusick.

White in Kansas, and W. W. Waymack in Iowa affirmed that the campaign had not exacerbated differences of opinions on foreign affairs and that the American people actually favored more extensive aid to Britain and stricter control of Axis agents.[2]

Despite Warhawk expectations that the President would begin the job of galvanizing public opinion immediately after elections as he had in May and June, 1940, Roosevelt made no significant utterances on foreign policy between election day and Christmas. Instead, for three weeks he chose to let the inadequate mobilization machinery in Washington run itself and listened without making decisions to debates in the cabinet on creation of a propaganda agency, an oil embargo of Japan, aid to China, and extension of financial credits to Britian. On December 3 he departed for a two-week cruise of the Caribbean aboard the cruiser *Tuscaloosa*.[3]

Meanwhile, the Century Group involved itself in a variety of controversies and usually found itself in a defensive or at best counter-offensive position. The most important of these engagements involved the Hoover food plan. Former President Herbert Hoover's plan to feed the civilian populations of occupied Europe was perhaps the most complicated moral issue the Warhawks ever faced. Hoover believed that the situation was essentially the same as in 1914 when he had directed the distribution of food to civilians in occupied Belgium. He knew that people were starving and felt that America, in keeping with her humanitarian traditions, should feed them. To do this the United States government would have to persuade the British to relax their blockade and convince the Germans not to remove the American supplies or continue to denude occupied areas. Since the food shipments would be of a non-military nature, Hoover argued, they could not be construed as contributing to the Nazi war effort.

2. "Questionnaire" from Bell, undated; Maverick to Bell, November 7, 1940; White to Bell, November 8, 1940; Hopkins to Bell, November 12, 1940; Hobson to Bell, November 9, 1940; Waymack to Bell, November 12, 1940 FFF MSS.

3. William L. Langer and S. Everett Gleason, *The Undeclared War* (New York, 1953), pp. 215–44. Unknown to the public or the Group, Roosevelt decided to seek Lend-Lease legislation while on his cruise.

Hoover first disclosed his food plan on August 11. The Germans met his proposal first with silence, then evasion. The British responded on September 15 with outright refusal. Thereafter, Hoover and his "National Committee on Food for the Five Small Democracies"[4] directed their attention to stimulating public demand for State Department pressure on the British to relax the blockade. Until Pearl Harbor the former President campaigned for European relief with radio addresses, newspaper advertisements, magazine articles, public statements signed by influential citizens, and in private meetings with State Department and British Embassy officials. At times he amended his proposals to include provisions that Germany return all supplies she had already sequestered, or that the commodities be purchased not with American funds but with the frozen assets of the European countries, or that thirty million dollars worth of American farm surpluses be purchased and held ready for shipment pending German and British agreement on the ground rules. However, his basic intention of supplying food to that part of Europe occupied by the Nazis remained fixed.[5]

Most of the Warhawks saw the Hoover plan as insidious because it appealed to Americans' humanitarianism while actually helping Hitler.[6] As Lewis Douglas declared, "Our hearts indeed go out to the men, women and children on whose lives have fallen the cruel blows of the invading hosts." But, he asked, "what reliance can we place on any promise given by the forces of organized violence . . . whose hands have violated all the firm rules by which men have held each other in mutual respect in the past?" Douglas declared it was not possible to send economic assistance to "occupied and 'unoccupied' France without easing

4. Denmark, Norway, Belgium, Luxemburg, and The Netherlands.

5. *New York Times,* August 11, 1940, September 15, 1940, November 16, 1940, December 8, 1940; Langer and Gleason, *The Undeclared War,* p. 378, Walter Johnson, *The Battle Against Isolation* (Chicago, 1944), pp. 169–70.

6. Henry Luce believed that aiding war victims was so important that he broke with the Group. James Conant considered it inappropriate for a college president to oppose the plan, and John Balderston thought the entire matter was too unimportant to concern the Group; Bell to Bingham, March 29, 1941; Conant to Francis P. Miller, September 27, 1940; Balderston to Bell, November 11, 1940, FFF MSS.

in one way or another the economic pressure which is one of the world's best hopes of downing Hitlerism." [7]

Robert Sherwood debated the issue with Dr. Clarence E. Pickett of the American Friends Service Committee before the Foreign Policy Association. Sherwood reminded the audience: ". . . The blockade is operating on both sides. . . . Hitler is doing his best to starve Britain and Ireland with his submarines and long-range bombers. Yet I have never heard Mr. Herbert Hoover suggest that we might ask Hitler to relax his blockade so that we could send food and other non-military supplies to Britain." [8] Herbert Bayard Swope challenged Hoover's assertion that situations in 1914 and 1940 were similar: "There is no analogy between today and 1914. Then, the German war machine overran Belgium and France, but peoples in the occupied zones were left untouched. Only for a brief time, at the very end of the war, were the Belgians pressed into service. But now, every man, woman and child is part of the Nazi war machine. They have become helots, compelled to work for German triumph." [9]

The material circulated by Room 2940 on the Hoover plan took two separate approaches to the issue. In a documented study Dr. Van Dusen addressed himself to a number of "factual statements by Mr. Hoover and certain members of his Committee" which Van Dusen found "in some instances quite untrue." He presented statistics which contested Hoover's assertions that the little democracies in normal times imported 30 to 60 per cent of their food supplies, that "no large stocks of food are carried in these countries," and that German sequestration of their indigenous food supplies was not substantial. He challenged Hoover Committee statements that the current conditions were "precisely the same" as those of the last war, and that none of the

7. 'By Lewis W. Douglas," October 20, 1940; Douglas to Francis P. Miller, September 28, 1940, FFF MSS.

8. "Speech by Robert E. Sherwood at Luncheon of Foreign Policy Association," December 7, 1940, FFF MSS; *New York Times*, December 8, 1940.

9. Herbert Bayard Swope, "Shall the United States Feed the Conquered Nations of Europe?" American Forum (radio) October 20, 1940, FFF MSS.

supplies sent for Belgian relief in that war had been taken by the Germans.[10]

Taking a different approach, William Agar sounded an almost metaphysical appeal in a letter to the Catholic magazine *America,* in which he discussed the moral and religious questions involved in the food controversy. He admitted that the Christian had a duty to give charity to the needy, but he insisted that if we gave succor in this instance there was no certainty that "God will not reward our charity by allowing Hitler to conquer us." "Such blind faith," he added, "overlooks the fact that such an action on our part will strengthen the avowed enemy of Christianity. . . . The fact we must face is this. Hitler intends to exterminate Christianity. His Nazi Era is designed to supplant the Christian Era, and our Christian consciences cannot dictate to us that we should assist him."[11] Hobson, Coffin, and Van Dusen penned similar articles or speeches addressed to Protestant public opinion.

Although the Group publicly supported British insistence upon a total blockade, some of the churchmen—Van Dusen, Coffin, and occasional dinner guest Henry St. George Tucker—tried to persuade Lothian to soften the harshest aspects of the blockade. The denial of medicines, vitamins, and powdered milk to the children of occupied Europe, they felt, was going too far. Not only did they believe it was inhumane; they were also certain that many more Americans were appalled by British rigidity on this particular point than by prohibition of supplies for adults.[12]

In mid-September Van Dusen asked Lothian if he could again come to the Embassy to see him. Since Lothian had other business in New York he suggested instead that he would be glad to have dinner with Van Dusen and a few of his associates in Manhattan. At the ensuing meeting Van Dusen, Coffin,

10. Henry P. Van Dusen, "The European Food Problem and the Hoover Proposals"; "Mr. Hoover and the Facts," FFF MSS.

11. William Agar, "To the Editors," October 18, 1940; William Agar to Bishops, form letter, March 28, 1941, FFF MSS.

12. Van Dusen to Lothian, September 11, 1940, HVD MSS; author's interview with Van Dusen.

Tucker, and two other (unidentified) Group members insisted that an absolutely rigid blockade was a mistake and argued that Britain was impairing her image in the eyes of Americans by appearing to starve innocent children. Lothian presented his government's view that any food sent to Europe would become an asset of the German war machine. Even if the Nazis guaranteed delivery of the provisions to those for whom they were intended, he insisted, their history of broken guarantees would make such assurances meaningless. He did say, however, that the matter was still under discussion in the British government and that he would bring it up when he returned to England for consultations.[13]

The Century people refused to let the question drop. When Hoover renewed his attacks on the British blockade shortly after the November elections, Coffin, Tucker, and Van Dusen wrote to Lothian, now in London. Again they urged a "more positive policy" for "the safeguarding from actual starvation of children." They suggested that the British offer to permit the passage of minimal provisions which would be distributed in occupied Europe under the supervision of the Surgeon General's Corps of the United States Army. If the Germans refused to allow such supervision, at least the British would have demonstrated their willingness to help. In a letter of November 12, Van Dusen emphasized that what was needed above all was a definite statement of British policy one way or the other, accompanied by an explanation of their reasoning. He stressed the fact that the Group would continue in its full support of the total blockade, "if in the considered judgment of your Government that is the only safe possibility." [14]

On November 26 he wrote again. This letter not only demonstrated that the Group was reconciled to continuation of the total blockade, but it also illustrated the close cooperation between the Group and Lothian. In it Van Dusen asked Lothian to delay issuing any statement defending the total blockade until after two releases on the blockade now being circulated for

13. *Ibid.*

14. Coffin and Henry St. George Tucker to Lothian, telegram, undated; Van Dusen to Lothian, November 12, 1940, and November 22, 1940, HVD MSS.

signatures by the Group could be published. Furthermore, he appended a draft statement he had written for the British Ambassador. Lothian's statement did not appear for two weeks, and when it did, it closely paralleled Van Dusen's draft.

The relationship between the British diplomat and the American clergyman was terminated a few days later by Lothian's sudden illness and death; but the Warhawks continued to maintain close contact with the British. Van Dusen, for example, spent the New Year's holiday in Ottawa with the Earl of Athlone, Governor General of Canada.[15] More significantly, Bell and Cusick continued and expanded their relationship with Aubrey Morgan and John Wheeler-Bennett of the British Information Service, talking with them by telephone once or twice a week. On several occasions during the following year, Bell and Cusick were even asked to be present at the BIS office in Rockefeller Center while the British agents received confidential telephone messages from officials in London about which they wanted the Warhawks immediately informed.[16]

The contest between Hoover's committee and the Group to attract the public's attention and support often became a race to see which side could "line up" the most prestigious advocates. If Hoover arranged a statement by European refugees who favored food shipments, the Warhawks publicized the opposition of the Norwegian, Dutch, and Czech governments-in-exile to Hoover's scheme. The former President received the support of the Relief Committee of the Northern Baptist Convention and the General Council of the Presbyterian Church; clergymen Coffin, Van Dusen, and Hobson then solicited the signatures of well-known religious leaders for a dissenting communique. If a number of educators and intellectuals announced their support for Hoover's charitable proposals, Sherwood or Herbert Agar arranged for other writers and teachers to respond by expressing their belief that the British blockade, however harsh, was necessary to America's interests and the eventual liberation of Eu-

15. Van Dusen to Lothian, November 26, 1940, and December 11, 1940; Van Dusen appointment book for 1940, HVD MSS; *New York Times;* December 11, 1940.

16. Author's interview with Cusick; "British Information Service" file in FFF MSS.

rope.[17] The first Group declaration appeared on October 6; although expressing deep sympathy for the civilian populations of Europe, it asserted:

> Unless the British Government gives its free consent, uncoerced by any external pressure, it is our reluctant but considered judgment that the American people should have no part in the scheme. It may well be that the issue is between restraining the natural impulse to relieve privation, and giving a measure of immediate relief, the effect of which will be to make the status of slavery more tolerable. Between the agony of empty stomachs for a time on one part of the world and the agony of stricken souls in every part of the world there can be but one choice.[18]

The signers were Carrie Chapman Catt, John W. Davis, Harold W. Dodds, William Green, Carlton J. H. Hayes, Umphrey Lee, A. Lawrence Lowell, James G. Patton, Reverend William Scarlett, Robert E. Speer, Herbert B. Swope, and Mary E. Woolley, as well as Group members Henry St. George Tucker, Henry Coffin, and James Conant.[19]

The Warhawks were shocked and angered when Hoover's committee nullified this pronouncement by issuing a news release alleging that most of the signers would be willing to compromise if a solution could be found to the problem of insuring food distribution—a deliberate distortion. Bell and Miller circulated among newspaper editors stinging letters from Coffin and Green to Hoover refuting this charge.[20] Subsequently

17. For example, see *New York Times,* Decembr 11, 1940; "Open Letter to Dr. Hendrik Willem Van Loon," undated, FFF MSS; *New York Times,* December 8, 1940, December 25, 1940; Hobson to Rev. Samuel McCrea Calvert, November 13, 1940, FFF MSS.

18. "Statement Regarding Food for Europe," October 6, 1940, FFF MSS.

19. The non-members were, respectively, the women's suffrage leader, the 1924 Democratic nominee for the presidency, the president of Princeton University, the president of the A.F.L., professor of history at Columbia University, the president of Southern Methodist University, the former president of Harvard University, the president of the National Farmers Union, the Episcopal Bishop of Missouri, professor of education at New York University, the journalist and foreign affairs specialist, and the former president of Mount Holyoke College.

20. Green to H. Hoover, telegram, undated; "Note to Editors" from F. P. Miller and Bell, October 13, 1940, FFF MSS.

Hoover's committee characterized the signers of the statement as having succumbed "to an emotional hate where they are losing all sense of decency." Bishop Hobson came to their defense in an article entitled "Food or Freedom." [21] The Episcopalian leader set forth his main objections to the Hoover plan in two sentences: "First, I am convinced that in the long run it would cause more rather than less suffering. Second, I am convinced that at best the plan would prolong the war, and at worst do much to assure a totalitarian victory." [22] The Group organized public statements similar to that of October 6 periodically during the following six months. In some instances the signers were Catholic laymen or clergy; in others they were university students, eminent women, or well-known educators and writers.[23]

The Century Group felt that its efforts were at least partly responsible for changes in public attitudes, as reflected in the polls, and for the administration's perseverance in support of the British blockade. In September one in every three Americans believed food should be sent to occupied Europe. Two months later less than one in five still held that opinion.[24] At no time did the American government adopt the Hoover plan of relief or put serious pressure on the British to relax their blockade of occupied Europe.[25]

However, a concurrent Warhawk campaign to keep all supplies from Vichy France failed. The Group insisted that "appeasement everywhere else in the world has been a dismal failure," that Marshal Pétain was a puppet of the Nazis, and that supplies to unoccupied France would either indirectly or directly assist the Axis. Their campaign of public statements and magazine articles disregarded the subtle maneuvers by which American diplomats were attempting to keep Vichy from voluntary alignment with the Axis or outright conquest by the *Wehr-*

21. Henry W. Hobson, "Food or Freedom," December 1, 1940, FFF MSS.

22. *Ibid.*

23. Mrs. Henry G. Leach, *et al.*, "Statement," December 8, 1940; Carlton J. H. Hayes, *et al.*, "Statement," November 22, 1940; American Student Defense League release, December 5, 1940, FFF MSS.

24. Hadley Cantril (ed.), *Public Opinion, 1935–1946* (Princeton, 1951), p. 1103.

25. Langer and Gleason, *The Undeclared War*, p. 378.

macht.[26] As in the later effort to have the United States withdraw its diplomatic recognition of Vichy, the Warhawks were motivated by the belief that a clear division between the forces of good and evil was necessary. They insisted that Vichy had already chosen sides by supplying such military material as parachute silk and aluminum ore to the Nazis. Despite several telegraphic appeals to Secretary of State Hull organized by his acquaintances in the Group and a public declaration by a group of writers—including Sherwood, Pringle, Mumford, Philip Wylie, Marc Connolly, Van Wyck Brooks, and Maxwell Anderson—this campaign failed. The State Department, convinced that Vichy's neutrality could be "purchased" for a pittance, dispatched two grain ships to Marseilles by the end of April, 1941, and subsequently permitted the American Red Cross to distribute milk and medical supplies in unoccupied France.[27]

When the Group protested the sailing of the grain ships to Hull, he replied stiffly to Ulric Bell that this action was taken only after the British government had "been satisfied that the assurances given by France will adequately safeguard the distribution of the foodstuffs so that no part of it or the equivalent will leave the unoccupied zone." Bell, recognizing that his relationship to the Secretary was more important to the Warhawks than this one issue, responded with a long personal letter which began "Dear Judge." After pointing out that he and his interventionist friends had no "desire to be presumptuous or arbitrary," he went on to suggest that pacifist and isolationist elements in the United States might gain momentum from such "compromises" and that American aid to Vichy might "disillusion" the British about the effectiveness of their blockade. He closed by reiterating that Hull could count on him as a "devoted friend and follower." This letter, of course, had no demonstrable effect on policy but probably did smooth the Secretary's ruffled sensibilities.[28]

26. Group telegram to Cordell Hull, March 19, 1941; George Rublee tried to convince the Group that some provisioning of Vichy France would not be unwise, Rublee to Bell, March 21, 1941, FFF MSS. See also William L. Langer, *Our Vichy Gamble* (New York, 1947).

27. Group news releases, October 27, 1940, and March 22, 1941, Langer and Gleason, *The Undeclared War,* p. 378.

28. Hull to Bell, March 24, 1941; Bell to Hull, March 29, 1941, UB MSS.

The food controversy showed that a close relationship between the British officials and the Century Group endured after the destroyer-bases agreement. It also demonstrated a continuing concurrence between some of the policies of the administration and the Warhawks. On this count, however, too much should not be claimed for the Group. Roosevelt apparently made up his mind in the summer to resist the feeding plan—before the Group ever took up the issue, and he was willing to ignore entirely its protestations respecting Vichy.[29]

Other examples of the essentially responsive nature of the Group's activities in the fall and winter were the "peace offensive" and the "death tag" story. Stimulated by Hitler's inability to put an end to British resistance, the suffering of civilians in blockaded, occupied Europe, and the desire to keep America out of the war, Senator Wheeler and General Wood discussed a "negotiated peace" in December. Implying that the British fought on primarily in the hope of American entry, Wood said, "If America would state definitely that it would not enter the war it is probable there would be a negotiated peace next spring." Wood and most America Firsters were quick to state their preference for a British victory (however impossible) to either a Nazi conquest or a negotiated peace. Colonel Lindbergh, however, declared that he preferred a negotiated peace to a *British* victory, since a complete victory by either side would "result in prostration of Europe such as we have never seen."[30]

To the Warhawks a negotiated peace at this point would have been no peace at all. Rather, it would have been a cease-fire during which the Germans could reorganize before lungeing out to overpower Britain with the full productive might of western Europe. In the "peace offensive" the Warhawks detected a sinister motive. Wrote Major Eliot:

> Once let there be a negotiated peace and no one can doubt that American rearmament will be fatally handicapped. The wishful think-

29. Harold L. Ickes, *The Secret Diary of Harold L. Ickes: The Lowering Clouds, 1939–1941* (New York, 1954), p. 275.

30. Copy of Robert E. Wood to Horace Bowker, December 19, 1940, FFF MSS; Wayne S. Cole, *America First: The Battle Against Intervention, 1940–1941* (Madison, Wisc., 1953), p. 39.

ers will overrun the land. We shall be smeared from head to foot with the poisonous honey of German promises and German assurances of good-will. Our industries will turn once more from swords to plowshares.

But meanwhile Germany at home will be consolidating her position. . . . In a year or two an immensely stronger Germany, and one far more formidably established in every part of the world, will be ready to resume the onward march to the world conquest which will remain the German goal. . . .

It is for such a German victory, whether they know it or not, that those Americans who now talk of a negotiated peace are working. . . .[31]

Others in the Group—Bell, Herbert Agar, Warburg, Douglas, and Miller—reiterated in their own editorials and speeches the thought that circumstances would never be better for resisting Hitler. Once again their attitude was similar to, if more militant than, the President's. In his "Arsenal of Democracy" speech in late December and his State of the Union message in January, Roosevelt, too, insisted that negotiations were out of the question and that "enduring peace cannot be bought at the cost of other people's freedom." Although these words did not suggest that Roosevelt shared the Group's desire for immediate hostilities, they did seem to commit the United States not merely to assistance for Britain but to liberation of Europe as well.[32] In fact, the Warhawks communicated frequently and unobtrusively by telephone with the White House on this issue. Peter Cusick recalls that Sherwood, Early, Lowell Mellett, and David K. Niles, all of Roosevelt's staff, actively encouraged and even instigated some of the Group's efforts to counter the "peace offensive."[33]

The "death-tag" story involved a similar Group response to an antagonistic thrust. In January the Scripps-Howard newspapers, which, unlike the isolationist McCormick, Hearst, and Patterson dailies, had followed a moderate editorial policy, published a sensational article headlined, "ARMY ORDERS 4,500,000 SPECIAL TAGS FOR IDENTIFYING WAR DEAD." The text described the

31. "Major Eliot Warns Peace Party in U.S. It's Playing Hitler's Game," *New York Herald Tribune*, December 27, 1940, FFF MSS.

32. *New York Times*, December 30, 1940, and January 7, 1941.

33. Author's interview with Cusick.

letting of contracts for the manufacture of dog tags and suggested that the tags were evidence that the administration was planning a new American Expeditionary Force.[34]

The Century Group was appalled by what they considered damaging "yellow journalism." They wrote an open letter to Roy Howard and arranged to have it signed by outstanding pro-administration publishers and writers including Sherwood, Williams, Birkhead, Cass Canfield, John Farrar, Dorothy Thompson, Alexander Sachs, Rex Stout, and George S. Kaufman. It declared that the "death tag spread" was either "stupid journalism or an attempt to undermine the defense program" and that it "was a deliberate distortion of the truth to give your millions of readers the impression that the routine preparation of these medical tags indicate[s] the early dispatch of an expeditionary force." Disregarding the fact that many interventionists were convinced that American armies would be necessary to liberate Europe, the letter rhetorically asked publisher Roy Howard, "Have you information . . . that any place exists to which an army could be sent?"[35]

The "death tag" episode was typical of the numerous minor controversies in which the Group involved itself increasingly as it abandoned its confidential and largely manipulative endeavors of the summer of 1940. Thereafter, a considerable proportion of the Warhawk effort was expended in random responses to new isolationist accusations or proposals. Even after interventionism again seized the initiative (and was meeting gradual success on the issues of lend-lease, convoying, occupation of Atlantic islands, and shooting on sight), the need to defend itself from public attacks and to refute new positions of America First persisted.

Even when the Warhawks were not forced to the defensive, the new role they were taking by directly entering the competition for public support dictated the nature of their utterances. Now they took special care to tailor their words to the predilections of the particular audiences they addressed. For instance, when Francis Miller addressed the Daughters of the

34. *New York World-Telegram,* January 29, 1941.
35. Sherwood *et al.* to Roy Howard, February 14, 1941, FFF MSS.

American Revolution, a genteel, chauvinistic group which opposed many New Deal reforms, he declared:

> In Hitler and his Nazis the Beast has thrown off its human mask and has taken possession of man. The Beast we thought we had driven back to the jungles has emerged and enslaved the souls of millions.
>
> . . . .
>
> This is no ordinary war. This is no balance of power struggle. This is the supreme and ultimate conflict of a thousand years. The Beast has met the man. Hitler has met Mason and Washington and Madison.
>
> . . . .
>
> As America enters upon this conflict with Hitler she resumes again her pioneer role. She becomes once more the champion of free men. She re-discovers her appointed destiny.
>
> . . . .
>
> For twenty years we have been longing for a job—longing for a task worthy of our heritage and of our faith. We became unhappy and distraught because we did not know what to do next. Now we have found our job.[36]

What would appeal to the D.A.R. more than a crusade against the bestial in which America "resumed again her pioneer role"? Even though Miller himself supported most of the New Deal and was unquestionably a liberal, he was willing to play to his listeners' antipathies by implying in his last paragraph that the endeavors of recent years had been unworthy of the national heritage. Like others in the Group, Miller was politically experienced and understood the necessity to bend or temper some of his views to rally support on the paramount issues. As he himself had observed in an earlier memorandum, coolly rational analyses of the national self-interest could carry public opinion only part of the way. Inspiration and emotional exhortation, he was convinced, must finish the job.

One of the few areas in which the Group did seize the initiative was Roman Catholic—especially Irish Catholic—public opinion. Herbert Agar had voiced the thought of many of the

36. "Address of the Honorable Francis Pickens Miller before the William Byrd Chapter of the Daughters of the American Revolution," Montpelier, Virginia, September 17, 1940, FPM MSS.

Warhawks when he had said that the Catholic church was "the strongest and steadiest force for appeasement in the country." [37] This was owing in part to the Nazis' success in convincing some churchmen that nazism served Christianity by shielding the West from the Bolshevik East. Furthermore, a large and influential proportion of American Catholics were of Irish ancestry and thus susceptible to anti-British propaganda. Anglophobic propaganda, spiced with anti-Semitism and anti-Rooseveltism, was dispensed by a small but noisy segment of the Catholic clergy led by Father Coughlin and Father Edward Lodge Curran.[38] Even other, less demagogic leaders of Irish Catholic opinion, John T. Flynn of the New York City Board of Education and Ambassador Kennedy, occasionally twisted the lion's tail.

Because they felt that the need was greatest in this segment of society, the Warhawks—led in this work by Professor William Agar—appealed specifically to Catholic opinion. Thus Agar and professors Carlton Hayes and Ross Hoffman, attorney William Carr, and Chancellor James Byrne of New York University circulated among leading Catholics letters and petitions on the Hoover food plan, aid to Great Britain, and national unity. Most of these statements stressed the thesis that "Hitler intends to exterminate Christianity, and his Nazi era is designed to supplant the Christian era." Under such circumstances, the declarations usually continued, actions (such as assisting Great Britain or withholding humanitarian aid from the victims of war) which would be unthinkable under other circumstances become not only permissible but imperative. The signers were Roman Catholics of all vocations, usually headed by a dozen or more priests. Among the most frequent and eminent clergymen to sign were Archbishop Joseph Schrembs of Cleveland, Bishop Robert E. Lucey of Amarillo, and Bishop Edwin V. O'Hara of Kansas City. Agar also peppered Catholic periodicals, especially *Commonweal* and *America,* with articles by Professor Hayes, Michael Williams, and himself.[39]

37. Herbert Agar to Everitt, September 14, 1940, FFF MSS.
38. Cole, *America First,* pp. 131–54.
39. Form letter from Emmet, Byrne, and William Agar, January 23, 1941; form letter from William Agar, October 14, 1940; Group news releases,

In November, 1940, when Winston Churchill asked American officials to persuade the Irish government to permit British forces to operate from bases in southern and western Ireland, the Century Group tried to help. The rate of sinkings had risen alarmingly, and Churchill knew he could provide Atlantic convoys with additional naval and air cover from bases in Ireland.[40] When word of Churchill's request reached William Agar, he obtained the cooperation of Chancellor Byrne and Christopher Emmet in soliciting the signatures of Irish-Americans for an open letter to Irish Prime Minister Eamon de Valera. The letter pleaded with Ireland to open her ports to the British fleet as "America is preparing to do herself." It continued: "It may seem strange for Irishmen to say it, but only if England survives can Eire be free. It took Ireland centuries of bitter struggle to win her liberty, and her unity is now only a matter of time—unless Hitler wins. But Ireland will lose all she has won, and more, by a Nazi victory. . . . While England may have tried to impose her brand of Christianity on Catholic Ireland, the Nazis are the declared enemies of Christianity itself.[41] Room 2940 also circulated an illustrated pamphlet asking Irish-Americans to agitate for such bases and quoting Popes Pius XI and Pius XII on the evils of nazism.

Diplomatic overtures to Ireland, however, came to nothing. When Secretary of State Hull mentioned the bases to the Irish Minister to Washington, the Minister not only rebuffed the proposal but also warned that the "tactless" attempt of private citizens to bring Irish-American pressure to bear on the Irish government could adversely affect relations between the two countries. Thus, in one of the few instances in the fall when it seized the initiative and sought to influence diplomatic events

---

October 25, 1940, November 6, 1940, and November 25, 1940, FFF MSS. Not all who were asked to sign consented. Playwright Eugene O'Neill was among those who refused. He claimed America had no right to ask Ireland to do what America herself would not do—become a belligerent subject to aerial and naval attack; O'Neill to William Agar, undated, FFF MSS.

40. Langer and Gleason, *The Undeclared War*, p. 232.

41. "Open Letter to Eamon de Valera," undated; covering letter from Emmet, Byrne, and William Agar, January 23, 1941, FFF MSS.

concurrently with administration action, the Century Group failed completely.[42]

* * * * * *

Since President Roosevelt made no major statement on foreign policy during the seven weeks between election day and Christmas, when the Group learned that he would speak to the nation on December 29, they were determined to do what they could to evoke from him the strongest possible statement. James Conant and Lewis Douglas drafted a telegram to the President which was quietly circulated for signature among a number of public figures known to the President, including Grenville Clark, David Dubinsky, Marshall Field, E. Roland Harriman, Robert S. Millikan, Walter Millis, Charles Seymour, and Edward Weeks. When 170 prominent figures had signed, it was sent without publicity to the White House. In it Conant and Douglas mentioned America's ". . . too prevalent indifference and apathy toward what is happening in the world. . . . If, before 1938 ignorance and lethargy and disbelief brought many European democracies to their grave and led the United Kingdom to the thin edge of disaster, so ignorance and lethargy and disbelief here are blinding us to our own peril." The signers asked Roosevelt ". . . to clarify once more but perhaps in greater detail, the nature of the conflict which threatens . . . and to make it the settled policy of this country to do everything that may be necessary to insure the defeat of the Axis powers, and thus to encourage here and everywhere resistance to the plausible but fatal arguments of appeasement.[43]

As a trial balloon, two days before his speech, Roosevelt made this telegram public, but as one historian of the period observed, "the balloon descended without recording any remarkable variations in the political climate.[44]

The "Arsenal of Democracy" speech Roosevelt gave—

42. "What are We Catholics Going to Do?" FFF MSS; Langer and Gleason, *The Undeclared War*, p. 236.

43. Douglas and Conant to Roosevelt, telegrams, December 27, 1940; form telegram, December 23, 1940, FFF MSS.

44. Langer and Gleason, *The Undeclared War*, p. 246–47.

written in part by Robert Sherwood—did sound a new tone. Declaring that the gulf between democracy and totalitarianism could not be bridged, Roosevelt characterized a negotiated peace as a false hope. America need not fear attack while Britain controlled the Atlantic, he said, but she "could not rest easy if the Axis powers were our neighbors there." In order to pursue the necessary policy of all material aid to Britain, production for domestic use had to be sacrificed and the notion of business-as-usual discarded. "We must have more ships, more guns, more planes—more of everything," he stated. The President insisted that the British wanted only material from America and that his administration had no intention of sending an expeditionary force. "You can, therefore, nail any talk about sending armies to Europe as a deliberate untruth," he asserted.[45]

Public response was overwhelmingly favorable. The President's Press Secretary, Steve Early, said that telegrams of approval outnumbered opposing ones one hundred to one. The Group followed up its message to Roosevelt with an "open letter to Congress" (drafted by Acheson, Conant, and Warburg) on the day after the President's speech. The letter affirmed America's willingness to take the risks necessary to resist tyranny and aggression and urged the legislators "to act fearlessly and swiftly, so that our country may continue to be free."[46]

Encouraged by the public response, Roosevelt, in his State of the Union Address on January 6, reiterated our "full support" of those resisting aggression and "determination that the democratic cause shall prevail." He even indicated lofty war aims for America by declaring:

> In the future days, which we seek to make secure, we look forward to a world founded upon four essential human freedoms.
>
> The first is freedom of speech and expression—everywhere in the world.
>
> The second is freedom of every person to worship God in his own way—everywhere in the world.
>
> The third is freedom from want—which, translated into world

45. *New York Times*, December 30, 1940.
46. Langer and Gleason, *The Undeclared War*, p. 249; "An Open Letter to Congress," December 30, 1940, FFF MSS.

terms, means economic understandings which will secure to every nation a healthy peacetime life for its inhabitants—everywhere in the world.

The fourth is freedom from fear—which, translated into world terms, means a world-wide reduction of armaments to such a point and in such a thorough fashion that no nation will be in a position to commit an act of physical aggression against any neighbor—anywhere in the world.[47]

Four days later he sent the Lend-Lease bill, designed to assist Britain in financing the war, to Congress.

The Conant-Douglas letter had little effect either on the drafting of Roosevelt's two addresses or on the planning for Lend-Lease. Both the speeches and the bill embodied positions often taken by the Century Group, but they were products of Roosevelt himself and of interventionists in government (Sherwood, Morgenthau, Samuel Roseman, Harry Hopkins), not the Century Group.[48] At best the Conant-Douglas letter helped set the stage—"warm up" the audience, as it were—for the "Arsenal of Democracy" address.

Stimulating support for the Lend-Lease bill was the last major project of the Warhawks prior to the formation of the Fight For Freedom. The bill authorized the President to "sell, transfer, exchange, lease, lend or otherwise dispose of" any defense article to "any country whose defense the President deems vital to the defense of the United States." It also provided for the repair of any defense article (including ships) belonging to such a country and the sharing with it of "defense information." It was designed to meet Britain's monetary crisis, the result of her extensive arms purchases in the United States.

The Century Group was eager to take up the cause of Lend-Lease. Since autumn it had denounced as self-deceiving Americans' pride in their "aid to Britain." One article they circulated said America had not *given* any aid to Britain. All she had done was "*sell* planes, *sell* guns, *sell* ships to Britain."[49] The

47. Langer and Gleason, *The Undeclared War*, p. 253.
48. *Ibid.*, pp. 213–46.
49. James S. Pope, "American Hearts and Order Books Open for England," reprint from *Louisvile Courier-Journal*, November 29, 1940, FFF MSS.

isolationists, on the other hand, loosed a barrage of criticism. The *Chicago Tribune* denounced H.R. 1776 as a bill "to destroy the Republic." Senator Wheeler labeled it "a triple-A foreign policy; it will plough under every fourth American boy." When Senator Nye declared it a White House conspiracy to make Roosevelt a dictator, other Republicans echoed his views. To prevent a purely partisan lineup over the bill, Wendell Willkie, Representative James Wadsworth, and Senator Warren Austin rallied a few Republican legislators to its side.[50]

While committee hearings and floor debate went on in the House of Representatives, the Century people cooperated with the White House and the bill's legislative managers. After talking with someone close to Roosevelt—possibly Sherwood—Ulric Bell told the Group on January 9, "The President wants aid from the outside on the Lend-Lease plan because party lines are apt to be formed against him and his plan, which is bound to cause delay in passing the bill."[51] The Group asked the Women's Committee for Action to conduct intensive appeals for letters to Congressmen and Senators from their constituents. The women also organized themselves into an active lobby (to combat the efforts of the Coughlinite "Mothers of the U.S.A."), sending people to Washington to see legislators and sit in the galleries when the bill reached the floor. Members of the Century Group succeeded in convincing ten governors, including Democrats Herbert H. Lehman of New York and James H. Price of Virginia and Republican Harold E. Stassen of Minnesota, to take strong positions in favor of the bill while it was being debated in the House. On the advice of Secretary of State Hull and Secretary of Commerce Jesse Jones, Will Clayton went to St. Louis (his former home) and Lewis Douglas visited Chicago and Minneapolis to stimulate enthusiasm among the industrialists for Lend-Lease. The usual flood of mimeographed reprints went out from Group headquarters. By January 24 Ulric Bell was sanguine about the prospects for passage in the House and satisfied with the flow of favorable

50. Only 24 Republicans (out of 159) in the House and 10 (out of 27) in the Senate voted for Lend-Lease. Langer and Gleason, *The Undeclared War*, pp. 258–59, 276, 283.

51. "Dinner Meeting," January 9, 1941, FFF MSS.

mail to Capitol Hill. On February 8 his confidence was justified when the House passed the bill, with some amendments, 260 to 165.[52]

The real battle over Lend-Lease came in the Senate. First, as in the House, administration officials pleaded their case before the Foreign Affairs Committee, which included administration critics D. Worth Clark, Guy Gillette, Robert M. LaFollette, and Gerald P. Nye. Next a series of opponents of the bill spoke—General Wood, Colonel McCormick of the *Chicago Tribune*, historian Charles A. Beard, T. J. Watson of the Chamber of Commerce, and Joseph Curran of the National Maritime Union. Finally, testifying on behalf of the legislation came Mayor Fiorello La Guardia, former Ambassador James W. Gerrard, President Conant, and Wendell Willkie. Willkie, who had been in England as Roosevelt's special envoy, returned especially for the hearings.[53]

While the proceedings droned on in the Capitol committee rooms, the Century Group relaxed its efforts to arouse public opinion, convinced that victory was close at hand. William Agar circulated a petition on Lend-Lease among Catholic religious leaders, and he and Beatrice (Mrs. George S.) Kaufman drafted speeches supporting the bill for Mrs. Berlin, Maury Maverick, Governor Lehman, and Judge Wayne Bayless. But most of the Warhawks were concentrating on other issues—the Hoover food plan, the draft of a manifesto demanding an end to diplomatic relations with the Axis, and the idea of a new nationwide organization for intervention.[54]

In the last week of February, however, Ulric Bell sounded an alarm. The floor debate in the Senate was over a week old and

52. "Report on Women's Activities of the Bell Group," January 23, 1941; "Sending Spokesmen to Key Cities to Talk to Key Businessmen," unsigned memorandum, February 6, 1941; circular memorandum from Bell, January 24, 1941; Langer and Gleason, *The Undeclared War*, p. 276.

53. Langer and Gleason, *The Undeclared War*, p. 277–83.

54. Form letter from William Agar, January 31, 1941; William Agar's draft of speech for Maverick, February 4, 1941; speech material marked "Sent to Governor Lehman"; draft of speech for Wayne W. Bayless, January 16, 1941; draft of speech for Ellen Berlin, February 6, 1941, FFF MSS.

showed no signs of abating. It was giving the isolationists a platform, and they were exploiting it. Robert Reynolds of North Carolina denounced supplying Britain's "millionaires" with funds out of the pocket of the "one-gallused, overall-clad farmer or laborer." Burton Wheeler charged that the bill's chief supporters were the same "international bankers" who had involved America in the last "European catastrophe." When Bell noticed that Gallup poll statistics indicated a decline in support for the bill from 58 to 55 per cent, he moved to mobilize his forces. "There is every reason to believe that a very great danger lies in these factors," he told Group members. "The Gallup Poll itself will be utilized as a psychological spring-board by the forces led by Senator Wheeler." Bell feared that by protracting the debate the opposition might turn the tide. There is "no great militancy being shown by those favoring it," he said, "and its opponents are being allowed to indulge in time-killing tactics." He blamed the procrastination in part on "official pussyfooting" and the fact that "some administrationists are still dealing with the bill as something which is a way out rather than a frontal means of resisting Hitler."[55]

In replying to the attacks from isolationists, Bell cast aspersions on the integrity of some opponents. He denounced the National Committee to Uphold Constitutional Government, which opposed Lend-Lease as dictatorial: "Its familiar cry is against 'unlimited one-man rule here'—familiar because only last Sunday Mussolini described the United States as 'a political and financial oligarchy dominated by Jewry through a very personal dictatorship.'" Although in this instance there was no factual basis for drawing such a conclusion, Bell, for propaganda purposes, tried to identify these opponents with Mussolini and anti-Semitism.[56]

Again petitions flowed to Congress, this time from "young Americans under thirty-five," urging "full support to the forces fighting Nazism today." "None of us is famous," the message

55. Langer and Gleason, *The Undeclared War*, p. 281; memorandum from Bell, February 27, 1941, FFF MSS.

57. Bell to Norman Vincent Peale, February 20, 1941, and covering note from Bell, February 24, 1941, FFF MSS.

declared; "we represent no organization, we are simply those 'common people' whom the risks of such action would affect most surely."[57] Bell saw to it of course, that this appeal and others like it received good press coverage.

Dorothy Thompson, close ally of the Group, repeatedly attacked the isolationists. In her March 7 column she charged them with using the congressional debate as "a rostrum from which to agitate the country, confuse and disrupt the foreign policy of the United States." She also accused Senator Rufus Holman "of picking up, almost verbally Hitler's . . . cry that opposition to him is all a Jewish plot."[58] The same night she told a nationwide radio audience that America was not divided on the real issues, since the polls showed that more than two out of every three Americans felt helping Britain was more important than keeping out of the war. The following afternoon, Mrs. Dwight Morrow spoke over the radio for Lend-Lease, and Ulric Bell sent a memorandum to Douglas, Sherwood, and Grenville Clark reminding them that they had an appointment with Willkie on the eleventh to discuss what "further militant part" he should play if "the Senate filibuster materialized."[59]

However, further action proved unnecessary. At the very time Bell was writing, the Senate was voting sixty to thirty-one in favor of Lend-Lease.

During the Lend-Lease fight the cooperative relationship which had existed between the Group and the White House during the destroyer-bases negotiations was renewed. Once more the Group was not merely moving along parallel lines with (and ahead of) the administration. It was coordinating its efforts with the President's desires, even though those desires were expressed only through intermediaries and even though some members were privately critical of Roosevelt's continued unwillingness to force the issues. In general, the Warhawks did not regain their

57. "Youth Petition to Congress," February 26, 1941, FFF MSS.

58. Dorothy Thompson, "On the Record," *New York Herald Tribune*, March 7, 1941.

59. "Dorothy Thompson Speech," March 7, 1941; memorandum from Bell, March 6, 1941; Bell to Douglas, Sherwood, and Clark, March 8, 1941, FFF MSS.

role of the prior summer as discreet intermediaries and manipulators of individuals in the very top rank of the administration and the opposition. Rather, the Group served as the clearinghouse for petitions, letters, statements, and speeches—the same task with which it had concerned itself since the fall.

The debate over Lend-Lease further revealed to the Century Group its inadequacies as a pressure group. The Warhawks' lack of grass-roots organization and broad-based financial support limited their effectiveness. The smallness and geographic concentration of the Group, although advantageous in arriving at policy decisions, meant that beyond the New York area its work was only fragmentary. Also, many in the Group were convinced that public discussion was focused too much on immediate issues such as the Hoover plan or Lend-Lease, Irish bases or "death tags" and not enough on the over-all implications of the world crisis for America. Men like Francis Miller, George Watts Hill, and Herbert Agar felt that they themselves had wandered from their original and overriding purpose—active and total American participation in the war against the Axis.

During the fall and winter some in the Group had hoped that one of the organizations with which they cooperated might evolve into an "all-out" movement for intervention. Such a body, they anticipated, would adapt the viewpoint of the Group for use on a direct, nationwide basis and thereby absorb the functions and personnel of the Group itself. This had not happened. The Committee to Defend America, with whom the Century people worked most closely, had 750 chapters throughout the country, but it was divided internally over whether to continue to support "all aid short of war" or declare for American intervention. While some members of the Committee—especially in the New York chapter—shared the Century Group's desire to move toward belligerency, others, including Chairman White, resisted repeal of the Neutrality Law and the Johnson Act. White refused to use such comparatively mild phrases as "non-belligerency" to describe his Committee's policy objectives and vetoed its involvement in the food plan controversy. Like his friend President Roosevelt, White was determined not to get ahead of public opinion and acknowledged that the Century Group's identification with his Committee caused him "headaches." He felt increasingly embarrassed by the Century Group's positions—or at least by his own inability to keep up with them.[60] As he wrote Eichelberger on December 3: "I am worried all the time about the Century Club crowd. They are probably more nearly right than I am. They are young men and of course are impatient with my leadership; . . . I realize that probably my leadership is crippled by my slow judgement, by my desire to keep fairly abreast of public sentiment and not to get out too far in front. That has been a life technique and I cannot readjust my years to a new technique. . . ."[61]

Although the Committee to Defend America's policy grew gradually more aggressive after White's resignation at the end of 1940, it did not "catch up" with the position of the Warhawks until the summer of 1941. And after White left, it never regained the organizational effectiveness it had shown during the destroyer-bases period.

Other organizations seemed no better equipped to serve the Warhawks' purpose. The Council for Democracy answered only part of the need as the Warhawks saw it. The Council expressed its motivating beliefs in lofty moral terms, and its studies of the freedoms guaranteed under the Bill of Rights were erudite. But it did not adopt a militant program for "all-out" war, and it lacked grass-roots organization. The Women's Committee for Action and the Student Defenders of Democracy had demonstrated greater ability to make direct appeals for public support and they shared the Century Group's interventionism. But by their makeup neither could become the core of a national organization, although both might serve such a core as valuable satellites. Another cooperating body, Dr. L. M. Birkhead's Friends of Democracy, did understand the need to gain attention by using the dramatic or sensational, but it had not enunciated definite goals for war or peace.[62] Furthermore, the rumored establish-

60. Johnson, *The Battle Against Isolation,* pp. 171–200; "Dinner Meeting," February 20, 1941, FFF MSS; William Allen White's correspondence with Clark Eichelberger, December, 1940, White Papers.

61. Johnson, *The Battle Against Isolation,* p. 176.

62. There is voluminous literature and correspondence from all of these bodies and other, regional or special interest groups in FFF files from the winter of 1940–41 which documents the Group's scrutiny of their work.

ment of a federal propaganda agency, similar to the Committee of Public Information of World War I, had not materialized.[63]

In early 1941 liberal Protestant church leaders—among them Century leaders Coffin, Hobson, Van Dusen, and Miller—filled one gap in the pro-Democracy line by sponsoring and contributing to a new "journal of Christian opinion," *Christianity and Crisis*, edited by Reinhold Niebuhr. By means of this periodical they hoped to awaken the concern of the church leaders and the church-going public to the world crisis overtaking them. The militant magazine was intended to neutralize Christian pacifism. But even this, they realized, would have a decisive effect on only a small part of the American public.

Despite the Warhawks' hopes, no dynamic national propaganda organization dedicated to an "all-out" policy appeared during the winter of 1940–41. And the administration was still providing what they regarded as inadequate leadership. Therefore, the members of the Century Group reached the conclusion that they themselves had to undertake the task of creating a nationwide grass-roots movement which would convert a majority of Americans to interventionism.[64]

63. Ickes, *Secret Diary,* p. 403.

64. W. E. Wheeler to Bell, January 25, 1941; Bell to Humphrey Cobb, April 1, 1941; Francis P. Miller to R. E. Danielson, October 24, 1940, FFF MSS.

VII. Fighting for Freedom: Organizing

Through the fall and winter of 1940 some Century Group members and their interventionist acquaintances reflected on the need for a nationwide interventionist organization. The Warhawks grew increasingly aware of the unsuitability of the other pro-democracy groups for the purposes of interventionism. They were as dissatisfied after the election as before it with the progress Roosevelt was making in moving the nation toward war. Therefore, by mid-February they decided to begin erecting a national committee which would vigorously campaign for "all-out" policy. Working through this new entity, the Fight For Freedom Committee, the Warhawks sought to demonstrate that every geographic section and every social segment of America would support war.

The germinal idea of the Fight For Freedom had been under discussion since the early fall. In September William T. Couch, director of the University of North Carolina Press and a local Committee to Defend America leader, wrote Francis Miller: "I do not believe the job that needs to be done can be done until two problems are solved: one, proper leadership; two, regional organization with statewide committees." He declared that, for those who favored intervention, "the program of aid 'short of war' cannot be defended except perhaps as a temporary measure."[1]

When neither the White Committee nor any other organization seemed to match his fervor, Couch, in cooperation with George Watts Hill, reorganized his followers as the North Carolina Committee to Defend America Now.[2] However, he recognized that such a geographically limited effort was an unsatisfactory substitute for a national interventionist movement. In mid-February he wrote again, this time to Clark Eichelberger, Executive Director of the Committee to Defend America by Aiding the Allies and sometime guest at the Century dinners.

Couch declared that one of the greatest obstacles to his work was public "complacency and inertia." "Too many people from England and too many sympathizers in this country are expressing too much confidence that Britain will win. When people who share this feeling are asked to form a Committee," he lamented," their feeling is, 'Why should we take any trouble? Britain is going to win and we need not bother ourselves.'" The opposition in Congress was aware of this tendency, Couch asserted, and was "betting on a reversal of the trend of public opinion . . . within the next two or three months."[3]

Couch suggested to Eichelberger that the Committee to Defend America by Aiding the Allies formulate a policy statement "embodying an extensive program relating not merely to giving aid to Britain adequate to winning the war but also a program for winning the peace after the war." He advocated that all the pro-British and interventionist bodies "arrange dramatic programs" which would "arouse mass interest" and "change the present attitude toward agitation." Most people considered agitation "out of style" and "somewhat ridiculous." "If [the interventionist] cause were not to be lost," Couch concluded, programs were needed that would "shock people out of their complacency. . . ."[4]

Another individual who made an early contribution to the

1. Couch to Francis P. Miller, September 11, 1940, FFF MSS.

2. Hill to "Leaders Throughout the Southern States," December 27, 1940, FFF MSS.

3. Couch to Eichelberger, February 13, 1941, FFF MSS.

4. *Ibid.*

concept of the Fight For Freedom was Dr. Van Dusen. In October, 1940, he saw the need for ". . . a formidable body of outstanding citizens, well distributed geographically, to bond themselves together as guardians of post-election national unity. . . . The proposed large body of citizens . . . would serve firm notice on the incoming administration and all concerned that the country no longer could tolerate bickering and dissension and would constitute itself a sort of committee of national safety." [5]

This idea received the active support of Ulric Bell and Will Clayton. Others in the Group, such as Francis Miller and Herbert Agar, although interested in this plan, believed it did not go far enough. Convinced that Britain was fighting America's war, they argued that any new organization must pose what they saw as the paramount question: Could Americans afford to let others fight their battles for them? By the time of the dinner meeting on January 9, the matter of nationwide organization was no longer speculative. At that meeting Lewis Douglas was asked to report on the "proposal for formal organization and the forming of public sentiment on neighborhood unit lines." [6]

That same evening Francis Miller asked the Group to prepare a "statement on the Fight For Freedom." This was apparently the first time this phrase was used in a significant manner in Group gatherings. By "the Fight For Freedom" Miller meant a declaration by the Warhawks on America's war aims (defeat of anti-Christian, aggressive totalitarianism) and America's goals for peace (a worldwide society of justice through law and equal opportunity).[7]

By the end of January James Warburg had drafted this Fight For Freedom Declaration. It stated that the proper goal of American statesmanship

> . . . is not to keep America out of the war but to keep the war, in its military phase, out of America. . . . It is the American idea that

5. As quoted in Bell to Herbert Agar, October 19, 1940, FFF MSS.

6. *Ibid.*; "Dinner Meeting Agenda, Century Club," January 9, 1941; author's interview with Francis P. Miller.

7. "Outline of Dinner Meeting, Century Club," January 9, 1941, FFF MSS. Possibly in preparation for enlarged operations, the Group moved from the suite in the Albee Building to larger quarters in the R.K.O. Building in Rockefeller Center, "Removal Notice," January 15, 1941, FFF MSS.

life should be lived in such a way as to give everyone a fair chance, that brotherhood can be made real in this world, that democracy is a code of conduct as well as a political system. Hitler's war is a world-challenge to this way of life. . . .

. . . .

We must use our full strength to beat the Axis. We who sign this statement cannot know where and when that strength would best be used. But we know it must be used in whatever way will beat Hitler fastest. For this great end we must be ready if necessary to use our merchant and our naval vessels, our money and our factories, our airplanes and our men.[8]

Although originally intended simply as another dramatic public statement in the nature of "A Summons to Speak Out," this draft evolved into the inaugural declaration of the new organization.

After the January 9 meeting the idea of a nationwide organization hung fire for more than a month, until February 13, when John Farrar, publisher of the Warhawks' pamphlet series, mentioned his hope for "a coordinating group who could function as a directing body for the various committees who are active in Aid-to-Great Britain and democracies. There are so many of them," he noted, "and they seem to duplicate efforts and not to be particularly compatible." He proposed that the leaders of the various organizations begin holding weekly dinner or luncheon meetings, so that they could coordinate concurrent programs and avoid duplication and conflict. This suggestion was easily implemented by expanding the Century Group invitation lists to include leaders of other bodies, like former Senator Ernest W. Gibson (Committee to Defend America), L. M. Birkhead (Friends of Democracy), Raymond Gram Swing (Council for Democracy), and Lewis Mumford (American Friends of German Freedom).[9]

The delay of several weeks probably resulted from the assurances Douglas and Herbert Bayard Swope had given at the

8. "Proposed Manifesto as Revised at Dinner Group Meeting," January 30, 1941, FFF MSS.

9. There was apparently no discussion of a new organization at the February 6 meeting; see "Dinner Meeting Agenda, Rockefeller Center Club" February 6, 1941, FFF MSS. It is mentioned again in "Outline of Dinner Meeting, Rockefeller Center Club," February 13, 1941, FFF MSS.

January 9 meeting about the policy of the Committee to Defend America under Gibson's new leadership. Interventionists in the Committee, especially some members of the New York City chapter, were optimistic that White's moderation would now be replaced by a willingness to agitate for steps approaching belligerency. Douglas' elevation to the chairmanship of the Committee to Defend America policy committee reinforced this hope.[10] According to Douglas, the CDA now favored "whatever is needed to insure the defeat of the Axis," a definite step beyond the policy of "all aid short of war." He had assured the gathering that dissension within the Committee was being reduced. Apparently the Century Group delayed its own discussions about forming a new committee in order to see whether the Committee to Defend America would enunciate more radical policies and effectively stimulate popular support for them.[11]

By late February, however, the more militant Warhawks decided to press ahead with formation of the new organization.[12] Perhaps the inability of the Gibson Committee to affect appreciably the speed of congressional action on Lend-Lease influenced the Group's decision. Possibly they believed that the Committee to Defend America's moderate, all-aid-short-of-war wing remained too great a drag on the organization as a whole. Whatever the reason, a radical draft statement was presented to the dinner meeting on February 27. It asserted that

> . . . the war in Europe, Asia and Africa is one war. It involves our destiny as well as it involves the destiny of Britain, Greece or China.
>
> It is our war. Our freedom is at stake. Let us not shrink from fighting for it ourselves. Let us not use the British, Greek or Chinese as if they were mercenaries to fight our battle.
>
> It will serve no purpose to make ourselves the arsenal and the larder of democracy, if the arms and food we produce do not reach their destination.

10. *New York Times,* January 10, 1941.

11. "Outline of Dinner Meeting, Century Club," January 9, 1941, FFF MSS.

12. The closest thing to documentation of this appears in Bell to Cobb, April 1, 1941, FFF MSS. Here he denies the new movement connection to other bodies and admits "we do say that the answer is war." He also declares, "This new body will have to leave some of the timid ones behind."

> It is our responsibility to keep the sea lanes open. Our Navy with its air force is a formidable weapon. Together with the British Navy it can control the seas, and control of the seas will win the war. We must not shrink from using it. . . . We must use it now or we may never have a chance to use it.[13]

For the first time since "A Summons to Speak Out," the Warhawks found the time right for saying publicly and without qualification exactly what they intended.

Since the new Committee was to be broadly based, the guest lists for the dinner meetings lengthened. Most assiduously cultivated was the attendance and support of Wendell Willkie, who was kept constantly informed of the Fight For Freedom plans by Peter Cusick. Other new additions were Dr. Conyers Read, Professor of English History, who was to lead an active chapter in Philadelphia, and Wayne Johnson, former general counsel to the Internal Revenue Service, who would become the organization's treasurer.[14]

The founders of the new movement desired leadership of the most unimpeachable moral and patriotic character. To serve as Honorary Chairman, the Group wanted Carter Glass, aging chairman of the Senate Finance Committee, a standard-bearer of conservative fiscal policy and an exponent of a vigorous, internationalistic foreign policy. But Glass had never before allowed any agitation group to use his name. Francis Miller, a fellow Virginia Democrat, was delegated to approach him, and to the surprise of many the Senator consented to serve—stipulating only that demands on his time be kept to an absolute minimum.[15]

Glass's decision was a mixed blessing for the Fight For Freedom. His belligerent statements on the floor of the Senate and his impeccably conservative reputation were probably beneficial, but his views on civil rights antagonized some potential

13. "The Fight For Freedom Committee, at the Princeton Club," February 27, 1941, FFF MSS. Note that the title now includes the word "committee," illustrating the transition from a single declaration to something more permanent.

14. Bell to Willkie, telegram, March 3, 1941; Bell to Willkie, March 8, 1941; "Outline of Dinner Meeting, Rockefeller Center Club," February 13, 1941, FFF MSS.

15. Bell to Francis P. Miller, March 26, 1941; Rixey Smith (Glass's secretary) to Bell, undated, FFF MSS.

Negro members. On at least one occasion he intervened (through his secretary) to prevent leaders of a FFF youth group from committing their organization against the poll tax by threatening "the unpleasant notoriety of losing your honorary chairman."[16]

With Glass as titular head, the Warhawks sought an active spokesman to serve as Chairman of the new organization, and they seized upon Bishop Henry W. Hobson. Hobson had been a devoted worker for destroyer-bases and a signer of the "Summons." In the debate over Hoover's food plan, he had demonstrated an understanding of the harsh choices which faced men of morality and faith in the current crisis. He was youthful and vigorous. Furthermore, as a church leader his word would have moral influence, and as a World War hero his patriotism was unchallengeable. Hobson found acceptance of the chairmanship a problem of conscience, and he laid down some preconditions. On March 14 he wrote Bell:

> My chief concern is that as a Bishop in the Christian Church I have a supreme allegiance to a way of life, and a course which takes precedence over other loyalties—such as allegiance to country. There might be a conflict between Christian duty and national interest [,] and I would have to put the former first. As chairman of a committee seeking to arouse our country to the dangers involved in the present world revolution [,] I would as a Christian be forced to insist that the program concern itself not only with national safety but with the larger issue of freedom for all men throughout the world. A situation might develop in which national safety would seem to lead along one road, while a loyalty to the rights of all mankind would call for sacrifice even of national safety. I must support the latter because I am convinced that the survival of the way of freedom, which is God's gift to all men, can come only as there are those willing to be 'done to death' . . . for a cause which is eternal. . . .[17]

Hobson's concern with "the larger issue of freedom for all men throughout the world" coincided with the ideas of Miller, the Agars, Van Dusen, and Warburg about the "larger struggle" of which World War II was only a part, and this concern condi-

16. Rixey Smith to Bell, December 3, 1941, UB MSS.
17. Hobson to Bell, March 14, 1941, FFF MSS.

tioned both the principles and the tactics of the Fight For Freedom. On March 20, fifteen of the Group members met, accepted Hobson's reservations, and elected him Chairman of the new organization.[18]

The Fight For Freedom was not formally inaugurated for another month. This was part because of the Group's desire to focus maximum attention on the issue of relief for Vichy France, which was reaching a climax.[19] The Warhawks spent the interval laying a solid groundwork in membership. They sent copies of the Fight For Freedom Declaration, accompanied by requests for signatures, to leading private citizens who might be willing to "take the all-out line." Although New Yorkers tended to dominate the lists of signers, the Committee worked to get "high quality" names with great geographic spread. When some potential signers criticized the February 27 draft as being "too extreme" or "subject to willful misrepresentation," the organizers circulated several "toned-down" redrafts. (These, of course, disappointed some uncompromising Warhawks.) As late as April 17, only two days before Hobson's opening address, a new draft was wired to those whose support was especially desired.[20] This final statement began: "Hitler cannot allow our goods to get to Britain; if he does he will be beaten. We cannot allow our goods to be sunk in the Atlantic; if we do, we shall be beaten. The problem is simple, and the answer is a willingness to do whatever is necessary to insure a Hitler defeat. This means accepting the fact that we are at war, whether declared or undeclared. Regardless of what we do, Hitler will attack us when he feels it is to his advantage." The United States had recognized the peril of Axis victory, the declaration continued, and had abandoned neutrality to the point of making itself "an arsenal and larder of the forces of democracy." Now, the American people must realize

18. Francis P. Miller to Bell, March 17, 1941; Bell to Francis P. Miller, March 26, 1941; "Dinner Meeting, Century Club," March 20, 1941, FFF MSS.

19. "Outline of Dinner Meeting, Rockefeller Center Club," March 13, 1941; Bell to Grenville Clark, March 18, 1941, FFF MSS.

20. Bell to Conant, April 15, 1941; "List of Those Receiving Letter of April 1"; "Fight For Freedom List," April 1, 1941; "List of Signers," April 28, 1941; circular telegram from Bell and Hobson, April 17, 1941, FFF MSS.

that there was no moral or realistic way to avoid armed combat. The United States still remained "in the immoral and craven position of asking others to make the supreme sacrifice for this victory which we recognize as essential to us. Once the United States accepts the fact that we are at war we shall at last find a peace within ourselves which can never come as long as we seek safety at the cost of others' sacrifices." [21]

On Saturday, April 19, the 166th anniversary of the Battle of Lexington, Bishop Hobson addressed a nationwide radio audience. "We believe," he stated,

> first, that freedom is worth fighting for. Second, that for us to say that Hitler's defeat is essential to insure man's freedom is a cowardly and immoral position unless we are willing to face the dangers and sacrifices others are suffering in this struggle for freedom. Third, that it is dishonest to engage in a wholesale material support of those fighting to defeat the dictator aggressors, who seek to enslave man, without facing and admitting the fact that we are in this war. Fourth, that unless we act *now*, with a recognition of the fact that we are at war and a readiness to do whatever is necessary to make certain Hitler's defeat, we shall lose the present war.[22]

Directing his attention to the moral problem which war posed to men of religion, Hobson argued that only force could prevent the triumph of evil when the leader of that evil "had made himself impervious to the action of God's Spirit." Against Hitler and his followers any appeal "on a spiritual basis [would be] ineffective." Thus, force was the only remaining course.[23]

Then turning his attention to the new organization, he affirmed that "the Fight For Freedom Committee has no political affiliation, no connection with any group or special interest in society." Its members would be individuals from all regions, all segments of society and all walks of life. They would be united by a desire to "meet the present crisis with reality, courage, honesty, and a loyalty to those ideals upon which the future existence of our nation depends." They believed that "the present

21. *New York Times*, April 20, 1941.

22. Henry W. Hobson, "Fight For Freedom Address," April 19, 1941, as reproduced in "Our Enemy is Hitler," brochure, FFF MSS.

23. *Ibid.*

world conflict is an irreconcilable struggle between dictatorship and freedom, and that if dictatorship wins . . . there will be little hope for freedom anywhere." [24]

The following day Peter Cusick issued a Fight For Freedom press release—the first of hundreds—listing some of the sponsors of the Fight For Freedom. By early June, the list was complete, and it was impressive. It bore the names of the presidents of Harvard, William and Mary, North Carolina, Mount Holyoke, Smith, Bowdoin, Brooklyn, and St. John's, as well as professors and headmasters of many other institutions. The clergymen who signed included bishops of the Episcopal, Catholic, and Methodist faiths. Labor was represented by seven international executives including Frank L. Rosenblum, Executive Vice President of the CIO, and A. Philip Randolph of the Brotherhood of Sleeping Car Porters. Among the authors and playwrights who were sponsors were Louis Adamic, Maxwell Anderson, Edna Ferber, George S. Kaufman, Moss Hart, Russell Crouse, Marquis James, Lewis Mumford, Rex Stout, Van Wyck Brooks, Dorothy Parker, and Edna St. Vincent Millay. The stage and screen were represented by Ethel Barrymore, Edward Arnold, Melvyn Douglas, Helen Gahagan, Peggy Conklin, Dorothy Stickney, Pedro de Cordoba, Ralph Morgan, Douglas Fairbanks, Janet Beecher, and Henry Hull. From the news media and publishing field came Cass Canfield, Jay Franklin Carter, Robert S. Allen, John Farrar, Nicholas Roosevelt, Freda Kirchwey, Walter Millis, and Lowell Thomas. Sponsors from the bar and the business world included Grenville Clark, C. M. Gile, James Speyer, Lloyd Paul Stryker, Roger Lapham, General John O'Ryan, and James Gerard. Among the government officials who sponsored the organization were Congressman E. Harold Cluett, New York City Councilman Stanley Isaacs, Judges Dorothy Kenyon and Edward S. Jouett, and presidential advisors and emissaries Donovan, Conant, and Standley.[25]

Three days after Hobson's address, the dinner Group, enlarged to thirty-one, met as an *ad hoc* policy committee of the Fight For Freedom. After an opening statement by Hobson, the

24. *Ibid.*
25. "List of More Important Sponsors of Fight For Freedom, Incorporated, as of June 9, 1941," FFF MSS.

gathering nominated an Executive Committee composed mostly of Century Group members living near New York City and therefore able to meet on short notice. On this Committee were Bell (the Chairman), Cheney, Guinzburg, Read, Warburg, Hobson, Herbert Agar, Dulles, Miller, Van Dusen, Mrs. Jackson, Johnson, Dorothy Overlock of Student Defenders of Democracy, the Chicago businessman Marshall Field, and the New York restaurateur Mac Kriendler. The diners appointed a Finance Committee to assist Johnson in raising money, and they decided to use the limited funds currently available to finance some newspaper advertisements on crucial issues for publication primarily in New York and Washington papers. The suggestion of an immediate campaign for a declaration of war was set aside, at least until the Committee had a stronger base. "First," said Pierre Jay, "we must set the stage." [26]

To "set the stage" meant two things: (1) to erect the structure of an organization with a popular following strong enough to make such a demand meaningful, and (2) to condition the American public to the idea that the war against Hitler was unavoidably their war. The process of developing an organization—creating both local chapters and national divisions concerned with special interest groups—continued until Pearl Harbor.

The organizational structure of the Fight For Freedom Committee was similar to its two contemporaries, the Committee to Defend America by Aiding the Allies and the America First Committee. At the top were the titular and largely inactive Honorary Chairman, and the Chairman, who was the active spokesman and public leader. Because of his clerical duties Chairman Hobson operated from his own home base in Cincinnati rather than from national headquarters in New York's Rock-

26. "Dinner Meeting, Century Club," and "Agenda of Informal Meeting of Fight For Freedom Committee, Century Club," April 22, 1941, FFF MSS. For some weeks after the founding of the FFF the "dinner group" continued to function, bringing leaders of other pro-democracy bodies together with the FFF leadership. In practice, the news media treatment of the Fight For Freedom blurred the distinction between the early "stage-setting" and the later campaign for a war declaration. The new organization was described from the outset by most newspapers as advocating a declaration of war.

efeller Center. Three men directed the operation of that office. Ulric Bell as Chairman of the Executive Committee was the prime policy-maker as well as the individual responsible for co-ordinating the efforts of the national leaders and keeping in close touch with the administration. Peter Cusick, the Executive Secretary, was in charge of publicity and day-to-day policy as well as management of the office. He also traveled extensively, organizing local chapters. Wayne Johnson directed the Committee's finances, over-seeing both solicitation and dispensing of funds, as well as attending to any legal problems which arose. By May 8 the work had expanded to the point where the responsibilities for correspondence, speakers, publicity, the labor movement, Catholics, and local organization each were delegated to a different individual. The Committee also hired a professional organizer to oversee initial organization in certain important cities—Minneapolis, St. Louis, Cincinnati, and Kansas City—but found this arrangement unproductive and ended it after three weeks.[27]

As a separate entity from the Executive Committee (whose membership was drawn mostly from New York area residents), a Policy Committee was named which included eminent members of the Fight For Freedom from all over the country. They were generally people whose other responsibilities or distance from New York precluded their attending weekly meetings or working at national headquarters. The Committee consisted of Mrs. Calvin Coolidge (a Vice-Chairman of the Fight For Freedom); Herbert Agar; Burke Baker; Laird Bell, attorney and president of the Chicago Council on Foreign Relations; attorney Henry B. Cabot; Mary Ellen Chase, professor of English literature at Smith College; Grenville Clark; James B. Conant; William J. Donovan; Melvyn Douglas; Allen Dulles; Marshall Field; Richard M. Griffith; Harold Guinzburg; J. B. S. Hardman, labor theoretician; Pierre Jay; Henry Goddard Leach, author; Dorothy Overlock; Clarence B. Randall, vice president of Inland Steel Corporation; Conyers Read; Spyros Skouras, motion picture executive; Dan Tobin, president of the Teamsters; Henry Van

27. "Executive Committee Meeting," May 8, 1941, FFF MSS; author's interview with Cusick.

Dusen; Sinclair Weeks, Boston financier and manufacturer; and Walter White, Ohio truck and bus manufacturer.[28]

The title *Policy* Committee was largely a misnomer. This group was really a "committee of influentials" intended to give the FFF weighty respectability. Although almost all of the members of this Policy Committee did participate actively in some aspect of the Fight For Freedom—as speakers, organizers of city-wide chapters, solicitors of signatures, or fund-raisers—most decisions on policy arose too rapidly to permit the gathering of the Policy Committee from all corners of the country. Only on one or two questions of supreme importance (such as the decision to demand an immediate declaration of war in the autumn of 1941) were the members of the Policy Committee polled for their opinions.

While the Executive Committee was establishing the Fight For Freedom national headquarters in New York, the work of organizing local chapters went ahead throughout the country. By the time the professional organizers submitted their final report a month after the Fight For Freedom began, 273 chapters were in various stages of organization. The Fight For Freedom eventually had chapters in sixty-five major cities, mostly in the regions along the Atlantic, Pacific, and Gulf coasts, but also in Denver, Colorado Springs, Chicago, Kansas City, St. Louis, Cincinnati, and Akron. In nine states—all in the Northeast and South—it had statewide organizations. By December, there would be 372 local FFF committees ranging in size from a half-dozen individuals in small towns of the Midwest and Rocky Mountains to thousands of members in the eastern cities of New York, Philadelphia, Baltimore, and Washington.[29]

In important cities the national headquarters handpicked the leaders of the local chapter from interventionists known to the Executive Committee. In smaller towns, apparently anyone of good character who volunteered his services could form a

28. "Organization Meeting of the Board of Directors of the Fight For Freedom, Incorporated," May 22, 1941, FFF MSS.

29. "Final Report on Organization Department, Opened May 1—Closed May 22"; George Havell to FFF Speakers, December 12, 1941, FFF MSS.

Fight For Freedom chapter.[30] The national headquarters distributed to such individuals twelve pages of mimeographed directions on how to organize a committee and what to do once established. These were largely common-sense admonitions to keep members of subversive groups out, get clergymen, young people, and ethnic minorities (especially those from occupied countries) in, and seek the support of local newspapers, radio stations, and civic organizations. The emphasis was on the use of local services, local literature, and local celebrities to "sway the hometown folks." Supplementary circulars on picketing, collecting petition signatures, and conducting rallies followed the original instructions; and, after Hitler invaded the Soviet Union, the national leaders also passed the word to resist infiltration by Communists and to avoid cooperation with "fronts." [31]

Aside from organized chapters, the Fight For Freedom established so-called "Main Street" connections in over 650 towns in the forty-eight states. "Main Street" meant that the town newspaper agreed to accept the weekly "clipsheets" that national headquarters sent out. These sheets included news articles about the British war effort, the resistance movements in occupied Europe, and the activities of the Fight For Freedom, as well as interventionist editorials and cartoons. These items—like regular wire service stories—were intended to be used intact as space-fillers or by the editor who was too hard-pressed or too lazy to write his own copy.[32]

In practice Bell, Cusick, and others at FFF headquarters established personal relations with several hundred editors and publishers all over the United States. When the Warhawks needed to express a policy viewpoint quickly or test attitudes in different parts of the country, they could call dozens of friendly newspapermen by telephone. This careful cultivation of journalists was a natural result of the Warhawks' belief "in the immense impact of the written word." [33]

30. "Plan of Organization for Local Fight For Freedom Committees," FFF MSS.

31. *Ibid.*, "Volunter Activities"; "What to Do Once Organized"; "Memo to All Editors" from A. Liddon Graham, undated, FFF MSS.

32. "Questionnaire Record," June 17, 1941; "Special Questionnaire Survey" forms, FFF MSS.

33. Author's interview with Cusick.

Some of the local organizational work of the Fight For Freedom consisted either of absorbing local interventionist groups or of merging with other nationwide bodies. The Hill-Couch Committee in North Carolina merged with the new organization, as did an Indianapolis group, the Indiana Defense Committee.[34] Frequently an entire chapter of the Committee to Defend America—more willing to declare openly for participation in the war than were their leaders—came over intact. A report written for the leaders of the Committee to Defend America testified to the fact that while the Fight For Freedom was gaining momentum throughout the spring and summer of 1941, the CDA was losing it. This document declared that two hundred Committee to Defend America chapters had applied for Fight For Freedom charters, and it posed three alternatives: the CDA could continue gradually losing support to the Fight For Freedom; it could disband and throw its strength with the newer organization; or it could merge with the Fight for Freedom in "a unified propaganda organization." [35]

By June 11, the New York City chapters—the largest in both organizations—were negotiating a merger.[36] However, amalgamation even on the chapter level was slowed by the older organization's "emotional loyalty and esprit de corps built up in the cause of more than a year of hard fighting." Its members feared total absorption which, apparently, some Fight For Freedom leaders were advocating. As one Committee to Defend America official wrote, a merger of the New York City chapters of the two groups would "force the National Committee to Defend America to a more belligerent position and perhaps lead to an eventual merger of the national organizations. Such a national merger," he observed, ". . . would require a good deal of painful purging in the National Committee to Defend America, unless Fight For Freedom were to be slowed down. . . ." Apparently both sides realized that amalgamation at the national

34. Bell to Cusick, Graham, Havell, memorandum, June 5, 1941, FFF MSS.

35. "Memorandum from Irwin Jaffe," May 1, 1941, copy in FFF MSS.

36. Committee to Defend America news release, June 2, 1941; Herbert B. Swope, Jr., to Hugh Moore, June 11, 1941, FFF MSS.

level was unattainable and that "local mergers throughout the country were the only practical solution." [37]

Although the two National Committees continued to exchange information and attempted to coordinate their programs, friction was considerable. Both were fighting for financial support from the same sources. Most Fight For Freedom people privately condemned the Committee to Defend America's "pointless" continuation. Also, Bell and Clark Eichelberger of the Committee to Defend America were personally incompatible. Every two or three weeks a luncheon would be arranged to make "peace" between the two men, but a new rift would inevitably occur shortly thereafter.[38]

On August 15 Ulric Bell sent a letter to New York area members announcing the "New York Fight For Freedom Committee to Defend America." [39] Integration of the New York chapters entailed the fusion of a number of Fight For Freedom people onto the older group's structure. Frank Kingdon, Herbert Swope, George Gordon Battle, George Field, and Arthur Goldsmith, all of the Committee to Defend America, remained as Chairman, Vice Chairman, Secretary, and Treasurer of the chapter, and their office staff continued intact. However, William Agar, Ward Cheney, Ulric Bell, and Burgess Meredith of the Fight For Freedom also became officers. Both national organizations contributed $300 per month to the combined chapter to supplement its fund-raising activities.[40]

At the moment of merger the chapter issued a statement calling for complete mobilization of the resources of the United States to ensure "the final destruction of Nazi tyranny," and urging all-out American participation in the war.[41] Unity between the FFF and the Committee to Defend America on an "all-out" policy came more easily in New York than elsewhere

37. Committee to Defend America unsigned letter to William Agar, July 31, 1941; Emmet to Bell, July 31, 1941; "Executive Committee Luncheon," August 25, 1941; Bell to James Gould, December 3, 1941; Harrison Eudy to Bell, May 10, June 24, September 30, 1941, FFF MSS.

38. Author's interview with Cusick.

39. "Dear Member," from Bell, August 15, 1941, FFF MSS.

40. *Ibid.;* "Concerning FFF-CDA Relationship," November 24, 1941; William Agar to Bell, memorandum, undated; Field to Frank Kingdon *et al.*, memorandum, August 8, 1941, FFF MSS.

41. "Dear Member," August 15, 1941, FFF MSS.

because the New York CDA chapter had been consistently more militant than its national leadership—and at times seemed nearly divorced from it. Herbert Bayard Swope, for instance, had been a frequent participant in Century Group meetings since the summer of 1940, and the New York chapter's insistence on more extreme measures had contributed to William Allen White's resignation as National Chairman at the end of 1940. Similar mergers in major cities occurred in Denver in June and New Orleans in July. In smaller communities CDA chapters willing to embrace belligerency frequently would apply for an FFF charter directly to the Rockefeller Center headquarters before the problem of a local rival (and the resulting difficulties of amalgamation) arose.[42]

Although the two Committees were unable to merge at the top, by the fall of 1941 their national campaigns and policy statements were nearly identical—differing only in degree of aggressiveness and timing. Following the FFF's lead, in May the Committee to Defend America advocated the repair of British war vessels in American shipyards, an embargo on Japan, and—if necessary—the convoying of Lend-Lease shipments to Britain. In July it supported aid to Russia and "clearing the Atlantic" of Axis warships by using the United States Navy. From the middle of the summer on, the national CDA, now under Eichelberger's chairmanship, insisted that war was inevitable and United States entry should be speeded up. However, it never demanded an immediate declaration of hostilities. The Committee to Defend America's "follow-the-leader" pattern spurred Bell to comment repeatedly: "Those guys are stealing our stuff again—and they wouldn't do it when I asked them to do it." [43]

In the instances where two local chapters merged, the Fight For Freedom factions appear to have dominated decisions

42. See "CDAAA Chapters" file, FFF MSS; *Denver Post*, June 22, 1941; *New Orleans Times-Picayune*, September 25, 1941.

43. Eichelberger to "The Chapters," August 9, 1941 (on Russia); CDA news release, July 24, 1941 (On Atlantic war), September 17, 1941 (on diplomatic ties); "Mr. Congressman—Don't Hamstring America" (on Selective Service); CDA news letter, September 26, 1941 (on Neutrality Act); CDA news release, October 18, 1941, FFF MSS; Walter Johnson, *The Battle Against Isolation* (Chicago, 1944), pp. 210, 218; author's interview with Cusick.

on policy and tactics. The militant, dramatic, and often vitriolic tone of the newer group overwhelmed the more temperate posture heretofore associated with the Committee to Defend America, and for "FFF-CDA" chapters, outright interventionism became an announced aim rather than an embarrassment.[44]

While the number of local chapters expanded during the eight months from April to December, national-level committees, divisions, and adjuncts were established to deal with special problems—finances and speakers—or to appeal to special interest groups, among them labor, Negroes, and foreign language minorities. As the number of new chapters decreased in the fall, the Fight For Freedom placed increasing emphasis on the formation of these "focused" appendages.

Finances were the responsibility of Wayne Johnson and his committee, and Johnson himself gave the Fight For Freedom its first $1,500 at one of the formative meetings in March. According to its records, the national Fight For Freedom spent $275,000 during its nine-month existence, but the account books do not tell the whole story. Peter Cusick recalls that the Fight For Freedom received and spent closer to one million dollars and that many of the larger contributions were often earmarked for specific uses such as the placement of a particular advertisement. In addition, some interventionists contributed the services of their employees and themselves, or picked up the tab for various meetings or luncheons.[45]

More than three quarters of the Fight For Freedom income was spent on printing, mailing, newspaper advertising, and a "colossal" telephone bill. The telephone, Cusick recalls, was the principal means of communicating with local chapter heads, interventionist newspaper editors, and friends in the Congress and White House, "especially when things had to be done quickly." Little money from the national treasury was spent on local projects. Local chapters were expected to raise their own funds and be entirely self-supporting. However, chapters in cer-

44. See "New York FFF-CDAAA" files, FFF MSS.

45. "Report on Examination of Cash Receipts and Disbursements for the Period November 1, 1941 to January 15, 1942," FFF MSS. Hereafter cited as "Report on Examination." Also, author's interview with Cusick.

tain key areas—Chicago, Cincinnati, and Harlem—were deemed so important that the New York office did provide some financial assistance.[46]

No one got rich working for the Fight For Freedom. Peter Cusick, as Executive Secretary, received the top salary of $150 per week, while the men in charge of the divisions and bureaus (labor, publicity, speakers, etc.) received salaries of $50 and $75. Thirty-five other full- and part-time office workers (who provided direction and continuity for the efforts of a volunteer force of nearly two hundred) completed the payroll.[47]

Johnson had some early problems with finances. He retained a professional fund-raising firm but found after a short time that it was accomplishing little. Eventually, the increase in contributions which accompanied the growth in membership underwrote increasing expenditures, and when final accounting was made after Pearl Harbor, the Fight For Freedom had a surplus of nearly $30,000.[48]

Among the Committee's largest contributors—those who gave $10,000 or more—were Lucius Littauer, Republican former Congressman and philanthropist, Mrs. David K. Bruce, and Laurence D. Rockefeller. Rockefeller also saw to it that an "arrangement" was made regarding the Fight For Freedom's rent after it moved to Rockefeller Center and that the expenses the Committee incurred at the Rockefeller Center Club were met. In the fall of 1941 a second request to the Rockefeller family for a substantial cash donation received a novel reply. John D. Rockefeller informed the Committee that he would be willing to contribute heavily if the Warhawks could show him they were effective in changing the public's attitude toward belligerency. If the Committee could push the pro-war figure in the Gallup Poll up to 25 per cent, he told them, he would contribute another $10,000. The poll figures reached 21 per cent but climbed no higher, and the Committee never got the money.[49]

Heavy donors to the Fight For Freedom included movie

46. "Report on Examination," FFF MSS.
47. Payroll Book of Fight For Freedom, Inc.; "Salaried Employees," address list, December 10, 1941; "Report on Examination," FFF MSS.
48. "Report on Examination."
49. As told by Cusick.

magnates Darryl Zanuck, Jack and Harry Warner; also Mrs. Harry Payne Whitney, the sculptress; Mr. and Mrs. Marshall Field; Dr. and Mrs. Max Ascoli (he was dean of the graduate faculties at the New School for Social Research); and Mr. and Mrs. Frank T. Altschul. According to the Committee's records, it received five hundred donations of between $100 and $10,000.[50] Most of the donors were identifiable as members of the Eastern Establishment or the Jewish faith. These large contributions accounted for well over half the Fight For Freedom's funds. Many of these donations resulted from the efforts of the affluent men on the Finance Committee, who solicited their acquaintances through personal letters or at intimate fund-raising dinners in New York City.[51]

One of the most effective of these fund-raisers was Mac Kriendler, owner of the exclusive restaurant "21." Kriendler picked up the tab for dozens of affairs at which Beatrice Kaufman, Madeline Sherwood, Harold Guinzburg, and others solicited financial support from wealthy interventionists. For a time it was difficult to get a good table at "21" without being a contributor to the Committee. Barry Bingham, publisher of the *Louisville Courier-Journal,* also contributed in a special way by continuing to pay salaries and expenses of Ulric Bell and Herbert Agar, despite the fact that they were spending nearly all of their time working for the Fight For Freedom.

At the same time that the Warhawks obtained these weighty donations, they also received thousands of smaller contributions (some as small as a nickel). These, together with the proceeds from sales of pins, stickers, and tickets to the "Fun to Be Free" shows comprised the balance of the national organization's income.

Although the financial condition of the Committee only gradually became satisfactory, the work of George Havell's speakers bureau progressed quickly. As early as the first week in

50. "Record of Large Contributors," October 30, 1941, FFF MSS.

51. *Ibid.*, "List of Acceptances, Douglas Miller Luncheon at India House," October 20, 1941; Wayne Johnson to John W. Cutler, April 30, 1941; unsigned, undated memorandum to Herbert Agar listing Jules S. Bach, Harry Payne Bingham, Cornelius N. Bliss, and J. P. Morgan as "the names you have selected for solicitation"; FFF MSS.

June, national radio networks carried Fight For Freedom speakers two or three times a week. Individuals of national reputation spoke on regional hook-ups or addressed important meetings at least a half-dozen times a week—frequently under joint FFF-CDA sponsorship. Herbert Agar, a dynamic speaker, bore the brunt of the national speaking assignments, making six major addresses in May and June alone. The other members of the Executive Committee also spoke frequently, often on one or two days' notice. Wendell Willkie, mystery writer Rex Stout, and essayist-columnist Alexander Woollcott were among the most popular Fight For Freedom speakers. Others who on several occasions spoke under Fight For Freedom auspices were James Conant, Lewis Mumford, William Donovan, Carl Sandburg, Dorothy Parker, Dan Tobin, Harold Ickes, Sergeant Alvin York, Burgess Meredith, CBS news correspondent Edmond Taylor, and Maury Maverick.[52]

The Fight For Freedom schedule of major speakers was supplemented in the spring and fall by scores of street corner or village green rallies at which interventionists of local repute displayed their oratorical talents. In places where isolationists were well organized—as in New York City's Yorkville section—these affairs sometimes degenerated into shouting matches and fisticuffs. However, the interventionists themselves distributed instructions on how to organize picket lines and heckle at America First rallies.[53]

52. See the series of memoranda entitled "Schedule of Speaking Engagements" for each chronological period of the FFF's existence; also "Outstanding Engagements Prior to August 9, 1941," and form memorandum by Bell, June 13, 1941, FFF MSS. Relating to Willkie's assistance, see Havell to Burke Miller, May 22, 1941, FFF MSS.

53. Twice in June FFF rallies in New York City were disrupted by Bundist youths or members of the American Nazi party who heckled, slapped, and spat upon participants. Police protection came too late. The Fight For Freedom counter-attacked after the two June incidents with a meeting on the sidewalk outside of Joe McWilliams' American Nazi headquarters in the Yorkville section of New York. This time police protection was adequate, and no serious interruptions occurred. The newspapers referred to the frequent verbal clashes between interventionist and isolationist groups in mid-town Manhattan as "The Battle of Fifth Avenue."

Also, within a month after its inception, the Fight For Freedom was making inquiries of Mayor La Guardia as to the whereabouts of America First meetings for which police permits had been issued, for the purpose of

The Fight For Freedom Speaker's Bureau not only arranged air time, auditorium rental, transportation, and accommodations for its speakers; it also issued literature suggesting to neophytes what should be said and how. In some instances this material consisted of pages of answers to hostile questions the speaker might be asked from the audience, such as, "Hitler has never challenged or attacked us; why should we interfere with him?" or "Why help Europe in her imperialistic wars?" Some memoranda suggested source books from which material for speeches might be obtained, while others detailed the specific points the Committee wanted emphasized.[54]

The Speakers Bureau—working in cooperation with the Committee to Defend America—did succeed in putting the interventionist case before a greater portion of the American public than any other division, adjunct, or campaign of the Fight For Freedom. Almost every other day, some interventionist speaker reached a nationwide radio audience in an address, an interview, or a debate. The personal appearances of Willkie, Ickes, Donovan, and occasionally Mrs. Roosevelt at major interventionist rallies stimulated local interest and support. Regardless of whether one was an isolationist, an interventionist, or an "undecided," if he owned a radio in 1941 he could hardly have avoided hearing what the Warhawks had to say.

Of the special interest appeals of the Fight For Freedom, the most extensive and most successful was the appeal to labor. At its first meeting the Executive Committee decided that the approval of organized labor would be assured (1) by supporting the unions' right to bargain collectively, (2) by emphasizing the

---

"peacefully distributing handbills to the audiences so that they may read the other side of the controversy." A memorandum was prepared for Ulric Bell defining the laws on picketing in various states, and volunteers from the Student Defenders, other youth groups, and women's auxiliaries began picketing and handbill distribution at isolationist meetings. FFF news release, July 11, 1941; reprint of ad, *New York Times*, June 22, 1941; affidavits of Merle Miller, Mrs. Alis Skelly, T. James Tumulty, September 3–5, 1941; Abe Rosenfield to Jacob Potofsky, June 23, 1941; FFF news release, June 14, 1941; Rosa M. Chayes to Fiorello La Guardia, May 20, 1941; C. D. Randall to Bell, memorandum, May 22, 1941; FFF news release, May 23, 1941, FFF MSS.

54. "Questions and Answers for Speakers," June 6 and 19, 1941; "Suggestions for Speakers," FFF MSS.

Fight For Freedom's solidarity with labor's greatest benefactor, Franklin D. Roosevelt, and (3) by obtaining the support of Dan Tobin of the Teamsters, whom they described as the "most influential labor leader" in the country. On the recommendation of David K. Niles of the White House staff and Isador Lubin, the Commissioner of Labor Statistics, Abe Rosenfield was recruited to organize the Committee's labor division.[55]

The Fight For Freedom took a dramatic if questionable stance in favor of collective bargaining in late May. On May 23, Rear Admiral Emory S. Land, Chairman of the Maritime Commission, told the Senate Defense Committee that a strike of 1,700 AFL and CIO machinists in the San Francisco Bay shipyards had been "instigated undoubtedly by selfish and subversive influences which must be eliminated in this instance and whenever in the future they show their face. There are no limits in my belief," he added, "to what should be done to bring about a cessation of that strike." He suggested shooting those who interfered with defense work.[56]

Ulric Bell immediately sent Land a telegram challenging his "explosive and ill-considered statements." Bell defended labor's right to strike and insisted that delays in production could be overcome "by a spirit of mutual understanding and intelligent use of appropriate machinery for the settlement of disputes."[57] Land responded with a telegram to Bell explaining his harsh words. The strike was illegal under existing statutes, he wrote, and only 1,700 out of a labor force of 17,000 had gone out. Most union leaders condemned the walkout as the work of subversives and malcontents, and the president of the AFL Metropolitan Trades Union himself had led his men through the picket lines. Bell, Land concluded, had "no proper conception of the facts in the case."[58]

At this juncture, Peter Cusick recalls, Bell realized the shakiness of his position and cabled two California FFF leaders,

55. "Notes Taken by Mr. William Agar at Executive Committee Meeting of the Fight For Freedom Committee," May 8, 1941, FFF MSS; author's interview with Cusick.

56. *New York Times,* May 24, 1941.

57. FFF news release, May 24, 1941, FFF MSS.

58. Emory S. Land to Bell, telegram, May 29, 1941, Official File 4431, Roosevelt Papers; FFF news release, June 11, 1941, FFF MSS.

attorney Bartley Crum and *San Francisco Chronicle* publisher Paul C. Smith. Crum, who was also an attorney for Harry Bridges, head of the West Coast longshoremen's union, reached Bridges and got him to help arrange an end to the strike.[59] Although Bell probably jumped over hastily to the support of the San Francisco strikers, the position he took in this dispute helped to establish the Fight For Freedom's reputation as a friend of labor.

Tobin's membership was the result of persistent efforts by Fight For Freedom labor division head Abe Rosenfield, Wayne Johnson, and Harold Ickes. Rosenfield apparently tried first in late April, without success. By the first week in May, no other major union official had joined the Fight For Freedom, and Ulric Bell asked Secretary Ickes to try his luck with Tobin. Ickes recorded in his diary that "Tobin said he did not know much about the organization but that he would consider joining it if I thought he ought to." Ickes told him it would be a good idea and that he himself would join if he were not a government official. Shortly afterward, Wayne Johnson also approached Tobin, and, at last, the Teamster leader consented—not only to become a member but also to tell his reasons for joining to a nationwide radio audience.[60]

With the Land episode labor leaders began joining the Fight For Freedom and signing the Committee's public statements and pledges "of full support to the President in implementing his foreign policy." On June 11, ninety-eight AFL and CIO leaders from the Middle and Far West issued a statement through the Fight For Freedom praising Roosevelt's recent proclamation of an unlimited national emergency and announcing their own determination to resist the encroachment of totalitarianism. The labor leaders asserted their willingness "to accept the inevitable conclusions of the militantly democratic and antifascist policy which you proclaimed as yours . . ." implying that

59. Author's interview with Cusick.

60. Harold L. Ickes, *The Secret Diary of Harold L. Ickes: The Lowering Clouds, 1939–1941* (New York, 1954), p. 507; Wayne Johnson to Bell, May 29, 1941; Francis P. Miller to Bell, March 7, 1941; Labor News Service, June 28, 1941, FFF MSS. Also see editions of Labor News Service, June to December, 1941 in FFF MSS.

they were ready to go to war, if necessary. Two weeks later, Tobin's speech accelerated the movement of labor leaders into the interventionist camp. Thereafter, labor leaders of national repute participated in every major campaign, rally, and radio program which the Fight For Freedom undertook.

A main link between the Fight For Freedom and union locals was the "Labor News Service," a clipsheet the national headquarters sent weekly to shop stewards and union newspaper editors across the nation. It announced recent enlistments by labor leaders or entire locals in the Fight For Freedom and criticized "labor's enemies" or "obstructionists." Thus the sheet attacked Governor Eugene Talmadge for his approval of a Klan flogging of six CIO workers, denounced the Smith "right-to-work" bill passed by the House of Representatives in December, 1940, and assailed the American First Committee for its "genuine anti-labor bias" in refusing to hire union stagehands for a meeting in a Seattle theater. At the same time the Labor News Service extolled the pro-labor sentiments of such Fight For Freedom figures as Wendell Willkie and Bishop Hobson and repeatedly mentioned the work of labor leaders Tobin, Randolph, Frank Grillo (of the United Rubber Workers of America), and Sidney Hillman (of the Office of Production Management) on behalf of the Fight for Freedom.[61]

In regard to overseas events, the publication identified labor's friends and enemies and respectively praised or excoriated them. Relying heavily on materials supplied by the British Information Service, it sought to reassure American workers that they would not lose the gains their unions had made during the thirties by showing that the British labor movement was not losing its earlier social advances. The articles occasionally included biographies of Labor party leaders, detailing their heroism and total commitment to beating Hitler. The News Service described in sharp contrast the subjugation of Nazi-controlled labor on the Continent. Some of these stories praised the brave efforts at sabotage by workers in the occupied countries; others portrayed the horrid living and working conditions, not only in the conquered countries but in Germany as well.[62]

61. Labor News Service, June to December, 1941 in FFF MSS.
62. *Ibid.*

The Labor Division was the most successful of all the segmented appeals of the Fight For Freedom. By the beginning of July, seven national or international union executives were sponsors of the Fight For Freedom, and by October at least 21 executives and 1,600 shop stewards were participating in the Labor Division's Neutrality repeal campaign.[63] The Warhawks found it relatively easy to arrange impressive lists of labor leaders to support each of their intermediate proposals as well as their ultimate goal. By contrast, America First, partly because it was a bitter opponent of Roosevelt, organized labor's protector, and partly because of its domination by big-business personalities, attracted little labor support. Only two major labor figures—Kathryn Lewis, daughter of the United Mine Workers leader, and William L. Hutcheson, vice president of the American Federation of Labor—joined America First. An America First attempt to set up a labor division met with total failure, and only a handful of locals, mostly from the Chicago area, endorsed America First principles.[64]

A similar though less extensive "special" appeal to Negroes was much less successful. This work was relegated to Edward White's "Harlem Division," which sought to reach Negroes not only in Manhattan but all over the country. Ten days after Bishop Hobson's inaugural address, Bell and White initiated this campaign with a statement of the Committee's civil rights policy which was mailed to Negro civic leaders and appeared in a few Negro newspapers in the Northeast:

> This Committee is in sympathy with all honest efforts in the interest of freedom, as we know it, regardless of race, color or creed, and therefore takes due cognizance of the problems confronting the Negro in America today.
>
> We believe it more important, however, that we—all Ameri-

63. *Ibid.*, June 28 and October 24, 1941.

64. Wayne S. Cole, *America First: The Battle Against Intervention, 1940–1941* (Madison, Wisc., 1953), pp. 76–78. He notes that the more liberal "Keep America Out of War Congress" and the "National Council for the Prevention of War" had better relations with some labor leaders than America First.

cans—should SAVE AMERICA FIRST with the determination that our internal or individual differences will be adjusted satisfactorily and in due time; for indeed if America falls, we all fall.[65]

Throughout the spring and earlier summer, most of the "Negro effort" was concentrated in the New York area, and even this was not of great scope. The Fight For Freedom enrolled a few well-known Negroes, such as the Reverend Adam Clayton Powell, Sr., and A. Philip Randolph; and it sponsored two or three rallies and a baseball outing.[66] But funds were limited because, unlike most Fight For Freedom chapters and divisions, the Harlem Division was not self-supporting. Partly to save money and partly to demonstrate Fight For Freedom disregard of color lines, the Division moved downtown into the national headquarters office in Rockefeller Center in August. (However, interventionism in the South remained a segregated affair, since the Warhawks were unwilling to challenge the prevailing social customs in an area where war fever was strong among whites.)[67]

Because of the financial limitations, the Fight for Freedom decided that it would generally eschew expensive direct advertising and mail appeals to the Negro public and instead seek the support of the molders of Negro opinion—editors, civil rights and civic leaders. Thus, beginning in August the Harlem Division sent letters to Negro editors, politicians, civil rights leaders and businessmen, inviting them to make statements or write editorials on "the Negro and the present crisis, national and international." [68] Subsequent dispatches flayed America First's stand on Negro rights. In one communique Robert Spivack characterized the isolationists' attitude as, "I am for me. Nothing else matters." America First, Spivack observed, demonstrates "the same calloused indifference to the problems of the Negroes in America that it has for the suffering of Czechs, Poles, Greeks or

65. Form letter from Cusick and Edward White, April 29, 1941, FFF MSS.

66. FFF news release, June 7, 1941, FFF MSS.

67. FFF news release, August 2, 1941, FFF MSS.

68. "Dear Editor," circular letter, August 21, 1941; "Dear Sir," circular letter, August 16, 1941; Edward White to Herbert L. Brice, November 11, 1941, FFF MSS.

any other minority living under Hitler's heel."[69] Edward White emphasized that Hitler regarded the Negroes as subhumans: "We must recognize that with Hitler victorious there is no future for the Negro here or anywhere else. We cannot afford the luxury of indifference. Hitler hates us more than the Russians or the British or the Jews. We have no place in his so-called New Order."[70]

Influential Negroes' attitudes toward intervention in World War II were not unlike the opinions of Negro leaders on involvement in Vietnam in 1968. Some declared their determination to resist a foreign aggressor (particularly a racist one), while he was still at arm's length. Some saw it as a "tactical advantage" in their struggle for equality at home for Negroes "to assume leadership in support of the President's foreign policy." But many believed in 1941, as in 1968, that the United States ought not expend its best energies on "foreign adventures" but should, instead, concentrate on solving its domestic problem of race relations. Thus, Eustace Gay of the *Philadelphia Tribune* wrote, "Many Negroes feel that Hitler can not be worse than what they are undergoing now," while P. B. Young of the *Norfolk Journal and Guide* declared, "So many Negroes are busy fighting Hitlerism here at home that they have not had much time to think about Hitlerism as a menace abroad."[71]

Negro leaders were ambivalent toward involvement in the war. Furthermore, Negroes in general were politically unaware and inarticulate, and they were conditioned by white society to accepting decisions rather than participating in them. The Negro contribution to intervention, therefore (despite the efforts of a few individuals like White and Randolph), amounted to little.

Foreign-language-speaking minorities were also subjected to some "special interest" appeals by the Fight for Freedom. From British Information Service materials, foreign embassy releases and refugee organization circulars as well as the regular news media, the national headquarters selected propaganda and

69. FFF news release, September 26, 1941, and November 4, 1941, FFF MSS.

70. FFF News release, November 29, 1941; Hans Habe, "The Nazi Plan for Negroes," pamphlet, FFF MSS.

71. Eustace Gay to Edward White, November 4, 1941; P. B. Young to Edward White, November 6, 1941, FFF MSS.

news about life in France, Italy, Poland, Norway, and Germany under the Axis. These were translated by the Fight For Freedom "Foreign Language Service" into the appropriate mother tongue and distributed to ethnic newspapers in New York and other eastern cities. Designed to appeal to the two loyalties of the reader—his patriotism for his adopted country, America, and his ties to his European homeland—the effects of such material were probably quite limited. In general the Fight For Freedom left the mobilization of hyphenate sentiment largely to already established refugee organizations or traditional ethnic associations with which it cooperated, keeping in constant touch with them by telephone or in person.[72]

The Warhawks were, however, particularly concerned about the plight of loyal German-Americans. Since the Nazis "claimed the loyalty of every man and woman of 'German blood,' wherever they may live," they observed, ". . . public opinion is more and more inclined to identify all people of German extraction with the Nazis." In keeping with their announced respect for justice at home, the Fight For Freedom leaders recalled the indignities suffered by many Americans of German extraction in the First World War and reasoned: "It would be dangerous not to be on guard against everyone connected with the totalitarian countries. Yet it would be disasterous to insult the great body of Americans of German descent by such suspicions and thus repeal their tremendous actual and potential contributions to the democratic way of life." [73]

Despite the existence of Reinhold Niebuhr's American Friends of German Freedom (with which they communicated and cooperated), the Fight For Freedom leaders instigated and provided some funds for an adjunct called the Loyal Americans of German Descent. Its president was Christian Gauss, Dean of the College, Princeton University; and its officers included Karl Brandt, economist; George Shuster, President of Hunter College in New York City; and Robert F. Wagner, Jr., New York State

72. See voluminious materials from British and Soviet information services, refugee organizations, and the multilingual news releases of the FFF Foreign Language Service, FFF MSS.

73. Loyal American of German Descent, "Statement of Aims," April 7, 1941, FFF MSS.

Assemblyman. These men helped to publicize the contributions German-Americans had made to their adopted country, and their organization participated in the campaigns of the Fight For Freedom.[74] Although never very large, the Loyal Americans of German Descent offered another outlet of expression for Americans of German background who were willing to fight in defense of the United States and for the overthrow of Hitler.

Efforts to convince other special interest groups were either continuations of the programs begun by the Century Group or were so skeletal in form when war intervened as to warrant only passing comment. The work with Roman Catholics begun earlier by William Agar and his associates, now focused especially upon the issue of aid to Russia, which will be discussed in the ninth chapter. The Women's Committee for Action, which had first cooperated closely with the Century Group and later with the Fight For Freedom, was superseded in the last week of November by a Women's Division of the Fight For Freedom. Attempts to erect a Small Businessmen's Division (based on the New York garment industry) and an attorneys' group also were barely begun when Japan struck at Pearl Harbor.[75]

The interventionist appeal to youth was carried on by eleven different bodies, some of them independent. Others, like the Fight For Freedom's "First-to-Fight" Division, or the Student Defenders of Democracy (sponsored by the Women's Committee for Action), were appendages of adult groups. They coordinated their efforts on an informal basis until November when, after persistent efforts by the Fight for Freedom Executive Committee, they merged into one organization—American Youth for Freedom—and rented office space in the same building as the Fight for Freedom. With opposition to the war so strong among undergraduates and others of draft age and because of their own relative disorganization until late in the game, the young Warhawks were unable to win majority support on college campuses.

74. *Ibid.*, Loyal Americans of German Descent, news release, July 4, 1941, FFF MSS.

75. FFF News release, November 29, 1941; "To Members of the Coat and Suit Industry" from Hobson, *et al.*, November 19, 1941; Willkie to Dulles, December 1, 1941; FFF news release, December 1, 1941, FFF MSS; Author's telephone conversation with Mrs. Henry G. Leach, May 3, 1965.

At best they demonstrated to the public at large that not *all* young people were opposed to United States participation in the war.[76]

* * * * * *

The Warhawks laid the foundation for their new organization with care. Because of their acquaintance with a wide and varied body of influential individuals, they were able to provide the Fight For Freedom with a list of sponsors which equaled in stature the "celebrities" on the other contending committees. At the same time, however, they kept the national leadership almost entirely in the hands of Century Group veterans. They succeeded in attracting the support of a number of Committee to Defend America chapters which were willing to take an "all-out" position and in establishing a working relationship with others and with the CDA's national leaders. In great part because of large contributions from Anglo-Saxon and Jewish sources, they were able to undertake an expansive advertising, mailing, and speaking program and to operate "in the black." The Fight For Freedom's speakers used national and regional radio facilities and large and small public rallies effectively. Interventionist speakers saturated the airwaves with daily interviews, addresses, and debates. There is no question that their case received a full hearing.

By December 7 the flow of requests for Fight For Freedom chapter charters had slowed to a trickle. The Committee's policy-makers sought to take up the organizational slack by a proliferation of special interest divisions or adjuncts formed along vocational, religious, ethnic, or generational lines. Often they duplicated the efforts of organizations with which the Fight For Freedom was cooperating. Sometimes their claims of speaking for their particular segment of society were exaggerated. However, the Fight For Freedom did achieve outstanding success with at least one important special interest group—organized

76. "Program—American Youth for Freedom Action Rally," November 11, 1941; The American Youth Institute, "Outline Plan of Foundation for Pro-Democracy Youth Organization," May 1, 1941; Marybelle Mason (ed., *The Cornwellian*) to Anthony Bliss, December 2, 1941; Albert S. Goldman (Local Advertising Manager, *The Dartmouth*) to Fight For Freedom, October 30, 1941, FFF MSS; Bliss to author, December 22, 1964.

labor. National and local labor leaders enlisted *en masse* in the interventionist organization. Large numbers of union executives, shop stewards, and labor newspaper editors participated actively in all the interventionist activities of the summer and fall.

Like some of the special interest appeals, the quality and usefulness of many of the Fight For Freedom's local chapters were open to question. On the evidence of correspondence in national headquarters files and local newspaper coverage, many of the 372 chapters exerted themselves only fitfully for their announced cause. Often, especially in isolationist strongholds, they seem to have been almost entirely unsuccessful in attracting public attention, much less widespread support. A chapter which made the local gazette only two or three times in six months—and there were many—could hardly be considered an effective force for intervention.[77] Of course, there presumably were many somnolent Committee to Defend America and America First chapters, too. And the major urban Fight For Freedom committees—in New York, Philadelphia, New Orleans, Denver, and even Chicago—did raise persistent voices for their cause. The results of the Fight For Freedom's organizing efforts were, therefore, uneven. To some objective observers, the large number of chapters and the proliferation of special adjuncts must have seemed less the outgrowth of a massive spontaneous demand for war than a carefully cultivated attempt by a determined minority to give the impression of size and spontaneity.

77. See regional "clipping books," FFF MSS.

VIII. Fighting for Freedom: Tactics

To attract attention to itself and stimulate support for war, the Fight For Freedom employed methods already tried by the Century Group, as well as new tactics designed for a nationwide organization seeking members *en masse* or dictated by the belief that the crisis was worsening. Petitions and public letters signed by select groups continued, and the vilification of isolationists expanded. At the same time the Warhawks now worked to promote their own organizational image as the bearer of the best American traditions of patriotism, civil liberties, and brotherhood. To get the public's attention they employed a variety of symbols, slogans, and shows.

In order to understand the Warhawks' choice of tactics during their period of nationwide organization, it is important to recall the world situation and the direction of United States governmental action and American public opinion from April to December, 1941.

The Fight For Freedom agitated for war in a context of gradually increasing American involvement and continuing public opposition to outright intervention. In April, before the new organization was publicly announced, President Roosevelt extended the Western hemisphere neutrality zone eastward to include Greenland, thereby forestalling possible German infiltration or invasion. With the British victories over the Italians in Eritrea and Ethiopia, he declared that the Red Sea was no longer a war zone and opened it to United States shipping. This permitted delivery of American Lend-Lease shipments directly to British forces fighting the Nazis in North Africa. Less than a week after Hobson's inaugural address, Roosevelt secretly instructed United States naval units to trail and report Axis submarines in the western Atlantic to the British and to attack any raiders which approached within twenty-five miles of British possessions in the Western hemisphere in which the United States had bases. Although he rejected for the moment the idea of American escort for British shipping in the Atlantic, the President worked quietly to defeat Senator Charles W. Tobey's Congressional resolution against convoys.[1]

The American government cooperated increasingly closely with the British. With the passage of Lend-Lease in March, the President dispatched W. Averell Harriman, international businessman and former chairman of his Business Advisory Council, to London. Harriman served not only as "expediter" of Lend-Lease supplies but also as a discreet means of communication between President and Prime Minister on political and military matters. On Harriman's suggestion, American civilian experts were soon overseeing vehicle and airplane maintenance and repair stations in the back areas of British North Africa. Also in March, British and Canadian staff officers in mufti conferred in Washington with their American counterparts on what to do in the event of United States-German hostilities. The following month, American, British, and Dutch staff officers met in Singapore to discuss military operations contingent on a Japanese-American war. British warships, battered in the eastern Mediterranean or off the coast of West Africa, soon were limping across the Atlantic to United States shipyards

1. William L. Langer and S. Everett Gleason, *The Undeclared War* (New York, 1953), pp. 422–46; Winston S. Churchill, *The Second World War: The Grand Alliance* (Boston, 1950), pp. 136–46; Henry L. Stimson and McGeorge Bundy, *On Active Service in Peace and War* (New York, 1948), pp. 367–70.

instead of running the sub and bomber gauntlet to drydocks in the British Isles.[2]

By late May, Britain's situation was as critical as it had been the previous summer. To be sure, German involvement in eastern Europe made invasion of the home islands less imminent than eight months before. But supplies of food and fuel were dwindling to the danger point, and British armed forces were suffering severely on the battlefield. In the Atlantic, Nazi submarines and surface raiders were sinking British ships two or three times faster than they could be built, thereby threatening to sever supply lines to the British Isles entirely. In the Balkans, the *Wehrmacht* had overrun Yugoslavia and Greece and was driving the remnants of the British defenders out of Crete, thereby making the eastern Mediterranean untenable for the Royal Navy. In the Middle East, Vichy's Syrian protectorate was falling increasingly under German control, and a pro-Axis uprising in Iraq had nearly overwhelmed the British garrison. In North Africa, Rommel's *Afrika Korps* was driving Wavell out of Libya and threatening to force British abandonment of Egypt and the Suez Canal. Furthermore, Spain appeared about to cast her lot with the Axis and—by closing the Straits of Gibraltar—deny the British access to the Mediterranean from the West.[3]

With Britain, America's "best immediate defense," under such great stress, on May 27 Franklin Roosevelt made his first major policy address since the "Arsenal of Democracy" speech. In forceful if unspecific phrases (based on another Sherwood-Rosenman draft), Roosevelt declared that Nazi control of "islands of the Atlantic" would jeopardize America's safety and that the United States must prevent the Axis from controlling the Atlantic and "gaining a foothold" in the New World. The United States would take "all additional measures necessary to deliver" Lend-Lease goods to the British, he declared, and therefore must speed up and increase her shipbuilding program and "help to cut down the losses on the high seas." [4] However, he avoided specific

2. Working Files 1–3, Harriman Papers; Mark S. Watson, *Chief of Staff: Prewar Plans and Preparations* (Washington, 1950) pp. 367–410.

3. Churchill, *The Grand Alliance,* pp. 197–304; Working File 1, Harriman Papers.

4. *New York Times,* May 28, 1941.

discussion either of American naval action against Axis war vessels or of intervention, despite the fact that at least four cabinet members (Stimson, Knox, Morgenthau, and Ickes) and the President's "specialists" on Britain (Hopkins and Harriman) believed that one or both of these steps was not merely inevitable but immediately necessary.[5] Six weeks later, Britain's rising losses in the Atlantic and the increased strain of convoy duty from England to northern Russia upon the Royal Navy called for further steps; and in early July, Roosevelt announced that American troops would replace British troops occupying Iceland, and American ships would be convoyed to that point. There Lend-Lease supplies could be transshipped to England in British bottoms under British escort. By the time of the Atlantic Conference in mid-August, the shipping situation was so critical that Roosevelt agreed to having British merchantmen join American convoys to Iceland, thence proceeding without time-consuming cargo transfers to Britain under Royal Navy protection.[6]

Confrontations between American naval and commercial vessels and Axis warships occurred periodically. In April, the destroyer USS *Niblack* became the first American vessel to fire depth charges at a German submarine. A little more than a month later an unarmed American freighter, SS *Robin Moor*, carrying no contraband, was sunk in the South Atlantic after her crew and passengers were put in lifeboats. After an uneasy lull in incidents through the summer, in the first week of September, Nazi bombs sunk a United States freighter in the Red Sea, and a U-boat unsuccessfully attacked the destroyer USS *Greer* in the North Atlantic. Despite the fact that the *Greer* had trailed and reported on the submarine to the British for several hours, Roosevelt made this incident the basis of an indignant radio address in which he enunciated the "shoot-on-sight" policy in the Atlantic some of his advisors had long advocated. The "very presence" of such raiders "in any waters which America deems vital to its

5. Stimson and Bundy, *On Active Service*, p. 367; John Morton Blum, *From the Morgenthau Diaries: Years of Urgency, 1938–1941* (Boston, 1965), p. 251; Harold L. Ickes, *The Secret Diary of Harold L. Ickes: The Lowering Clouds, 1939–1941* (New York, 1954), p. 485; Working File 1, Harriman Papers.

6. Langer and Gleason, *The Undeclared War*, pp. 575–80, 665.

defense constitutes an attack," he said. The United States Navy would no longer wait for Axis submarines to strike first but would "protect all merchant ships—not only American ships but ships of any flag"—by attacking any raiders it encountered. Thereafter, an undeclared state of war existed in the Atlantic between Germany and the United States, a condition belatedly recognized by congressional revision of the Neutrality Act in November.[7]

Two other aspects of American foreign relations also changed significantly during the summer and fall of 1941. On June 22 Hitler invaded Russia. This took some of the immediate pressure off the British as a Nazi cross-channel invasion now became unlikely. Heretofore, a vigorous enemy of communism, Churchill recognized the saving nature of Soviet involvement and immediately announced Britain's willingness to extend all possible assistance to the Soviets. Roosevelt, despite concern about public repugnance for the Bolsheviks, followed suit. In early July he sent Harry Hopkins to Moscow to find out how long Stalin could hold out. Hopkins returned convinced that the Soviets would not cave in before the winter and that they were, therefore, a worthwhile risk. At the Atlantic Conference in August, Churchill and Roosevelt made general plans to provide assistance to Russia and dispatched Harriman and Lord Beaverbrook, the British Minister of Supply, to Moscow to ascertain what supplies the Soviets needed. The Lend-Lease Protocol they initialed in Moscow in early October signified the Anglo-American commitment to the Soviet war effort, and was a further, explicit demonstration of the United States government's ever-deepening involvement in the struggle against Hitler.[8]

While circumstance drove Washington and Moscow closer together, the breach between Tokyo and Washington—opened by the Manchurian affair and widened by the Japanese invasion of China in 1937—threatened to bring war to the Pa-

7. Samuel Eliot Morison, *History of the United States Naval Operations in World War II*, Vol. I, *Battle of the Atlantic* (Boston, 1947), pp. 63–80; *New York Times*, September 12, 1941.

8. Churchill, *The Grand Alliance*, pp. 371–73; 451–76; Robert E. Sherwood, *Roosevelt and Hopkins: An Intimate History* (New York, 1948), p. 323–48; Working Files 6–8, Harriman Papers.

cific. The Japanese, after spending much wealth and many lives on the war with China, were determined either to crush Chinese resistance or obtain a victor's position of control through a negotiated settlement. They hoped that the American's would mediate—but not moderate—such a settlement. The United States government, a traditional defender of the Open Door and Chinese territorial integrity, viewed Japanese presence on the mainland as an act of aggression and denounced Japanese infiltration of French Indo-China and Thailand. Although reluctant to fight for China, Washington was also unwilling to be party to what Secretary Hull regarded as an immorally expedient compromise at China's expense. In the spring of 1941, while Japanese and American officials exchanged generally unconstructive proposals and counter-proposals, the United States government dispatched Lend-Lease shipments to the Chinese and made it easy for American aviators to join General Claire Chennault's American Volunteer Group, "the Flying Tigers."

Japanese designs on Southeast Asia quickly became the critical issue in relations between the two countries. Taking advantage of the European situation which demanded the greater part of Anglo-American attention, the Japanese occupied the southern part of French Indo-China in July and threatened seizure of neighboring Thailand. The United States government retaliated in early August by freezing all Japanese credits and assets in the United States and placing an embargo on aviation-grade petroleum and selected industrial products and raw materials. This, State Department officials presumed, would have the effect of forcing the issue. The Japanese now either had to compromise or seek these critical materials by invading the rubber- and mineral-rich Dutch East Indies.

Tokyo chose the latter course. As the Japanese deployed troops in larger numbers in Indo-China in the autumn, suggesting future movement into Thailand and the Dutch East Indies (and on the way, possibly, the Philippines), the American government planned to resist such expansion. By the first week in November, the President was seriously considering going to war with Japan if she attacked British or Dutch territory or if her troops advanced beyond 100° east and 10° north in Thailand.

After a series of government changes in Tokyo, decision-making lay largely in the hands of the military, which thought war with the United States overdue. Japanese newspapers made increasingly virulent attacks on the United States, and American intelligence learned from intercepted messages of Nipponese preparations for war. As a consequence, conversations which continued in Washington and Tokyo became increasingly irrelevant, and by the first week in December, President Roosevelt knew that war with Japan was probably only a few days away.[9]

For the interventionists in government and in the Fight For Freedom, American public opinion was moving—but too gradually—in their direction. Throughout 1941, the American people seemed overwhelmingly resistant to outright belligerency. According to a January poll, 88 per cent of those citizens expressing opinions opposed immediate hostilities. By May the figure had dropped to 79 under the pressure of the reverses the British suffered in the spring. There it remained, regardless of the increase in clashes in the Atlantic, Roosevelt's enunciation of shoot-on-sight orders, and Neutrality Act revision. At no time, however, did any reputable poll show that more than 21 per cent of the public desired a declaration of war on Germany.[10]

Despite this, the polls revealed that most Americans—85 per cent by May—expected their country would eventually become involved. Over 60 per cent thought Hitler would not stop until he had conquered the Americas and that beating him was more important than staying out of war.[11] And on the issues of occupation of Iceland (61 to 17 in favor), convoying war materials (52 to 39 per cent in favor), aid to the Soviet Union (73 to 14 in favor), arming American merchantmen (61 to 31 in favor), the President acted with the support of a decisive majority of those citizens who had an opinion. However, on the matter of Selective Service extension—a subject which suggested to the

9. Samuel Flagg Bemis, *A Diplomatic History of the United States* (4th ed.; New York, 1955), pp. 863–75; Langer and Gleason, *The Undeclared War,* pp. 3–48, 290–319, 464–88, 625–54, 836–61. Also see U.S. Congress, *Pearl Harbor Hearings Before the Joint Committee on the Investigation of the Pearl Harbor Attack* (Washington, D.C., 1946).

10. "Gallup and Fortune Polls," *Public Opinion Quarterly,* VI (Spring, 1942) pp. 149–64.

11. This figure rose to 68 per cent in November and December.

public mind American armies fighting another hideous trench and gas war—his margin (51 to 45 in favor) was much slimmer.[12]

For the interventionists, the poll results were disheartening. They were relieved by the public's understanding of the importance of Britain's survival and its acceptance of Roosevelt's slow escalation of United States involvement. But they were dismayed by the fact that interventionist sentiment crept up to 21 per cent in the polls and then no farther. The Fight For Freedom's frustration with its apparent inability to persuade a larger percentage of the public was one of the reasons that it resorted to such tactics as oversimplification and near-slanderous personal attacks.

* * * * * *

Some of the techniques used by the Fight For Freedom were carried over from the Century Group period. Its efforts at the time of Roosevelt's "Unlimited National Emergency" speech in May, for instance, were strikingly similar to the Century Group's activities before the "Arsenal of Democracy" in December. In early May at the behest of Francis Miller, Governor James H. Price presented President Roosevelt with a petition signed by Virginians at the dedication of a Woodrow Wilson Memorial in Staunton, Virginia. It asked that he formulate a policy which would assure the delivery of goods to Britain, and it asserted that "only the full and immediate use of all American resources can prevent the Nazi occupation of the West Coast of Africa and the British Isles." [13]

On May 11, Bell sent Secretaries Hull, Stimson, and Knox a private, confidential letter and a memorandum "worked out by a group of your friends," listing steps "which if taken by the Axis will make it evident" that the President must declare "a state of emergency." Among these were serious impairment of British shipping, Axis absorption of Spain or Portugal, German infiltration of Vichy North Africa, and Fascist subversion of Latin

12. "Gallup and Fortune Polls," *Public Opinion Quarterly,* VI (Spring, 1942) pp. 49–64.

13. "Petition to the President of the United States," May 4, 1941, FFF MSS.

American nations to a degree which would jeopardize the security of the Panama Canal.[14]

On May 13, fifty eminent members of the Fight For Freedom sent a telegram to the White House. They declared, "We are willing to pay whatever price our President finds necessary. We are the large majority. We are not afraid or disunited. We pledge ourselves to stand behind you. . . ." [15] On May 21, another public telegram, this time from Bishop Hobson, discussed the question of "whether or not the time has come for this country to enter the war as a belligerent." Hobson asked Roosevelt to consider whether Hitler could be defeated without our military assistance and assured the President that "the overwhelming majority of the American people would be behind you once these questions were authoritatively answered." [16] The day before the President was to speak, Dr. Van Dusen headed a group of Protestant leaders who issued a statement insisting "that there are evils greater than war and that among them are submission to or acquiescence in tyranny. Only the strength of the British Commonwealth and the Americas can prevent the extension of this tyranny over the whole of mankind." The signers closed by voicing the hope that their message was "a measure of support and assistance to you, Mr. President, in your forthcoming address to the nation tomorrow evening." [17]

After the speech similar efforts continued. When Roosevelt sent a note to James Warburg thanking him for a telegram praising the speech, Warburg took the opportunity to respond with a long and warm personal letter. In describing the "feeling among your supporters," he told the President that he and other Warhawks feared the British will to resist might "collapse" if American progress toward belligerency did not continue. He declared that public opinion was "far more ready for action" than either the President or the Congress seemed to believe. Although expressing his recognition "of the fearful responsibility which rests upon a President who puts himself in the position of having taken the country into war," he proposed to Roosevelt

14. Bell to Hull, Stimson, Frank Knox, May 11, 1941, FFF MSS.
15. Hobson *et al.* to Roosevelt, telegram, May 13, 1941, FFF MSS.
16. FFF news release, May 22, 1941, FFF MSS.
17. FFF news release, May 26, 1941, FFF MSS.

that he take new steps such as authorizing a joint British-American seizure of the Azore, Cape Verde, and Canary Islands without seeking prior congressional approval. (A month later Roosevelt used a similar technique in sending United States troops to Iceland.)[18]

The use of influential personal acquaintances to deal with the President, and the combination of confidential policy suggestions and exhortative public statements by groups of eminent citizens were methods identical with those used by the Century Group in connection with destroyer-bases, the Hoover food plan, and the President's December speech.

Like the Century Group, the Fight For Freedom recognized in Roosevelt a natural, if hesitant, ally, However slowly, he was moving the nation in the direction of increased involvement. Thus, the Fight For Freedom, like its predecessor, employed the technique of publicly stressing its solidarity with Roosevelt on foreign policy issues while simultaneously urging or even demanding that he take quicker steps along the road he had already begun to travel. To break with Roosevelt, however much he delayed or temporized, was unthinkable, for he was the only figure on the national scene who might possibly be persuasive enough to change America's mind about belligerency.

Typical of the combination of praise for past actions and demand for future ones was Bishop Hobson's statement on the announcement in August of the meeting in Argentia Bay and the Atlantic Charter:

> The world's two greatest leaders have issued a stirring summons. The eight points are our victory code. We urge that they immediately be implemented by forthright action. . . .
>
> Mr. Roosevelt and Mr. Churchill reveal a very basic understanding of the one thing that has thus far been lacking in this war. It never has been enough to fight for the *status quo* nor even for the end of Hitlerism. The people have wanted something new, decent and high-minded to fight for—now they have it.[19]

Hobson first praised the Charter and adopted it as the Fight For Freedom's "victory code" and then urged "action" to accomplish

18. Warburg to Roosevelt, June 6, 1941, UB MSS.
19. FFF news release, undated, FFF MSS.

the stated principles. Similarly, occupation of Iceland was greeted with an FFF statement of commendation and a request for the occupation of the Azores and ports in West Africa. At the same time that one Fight For Freedom newspaper advertisement rejoiced "The President Shows the Way!" others intoned "What are we waiting for, Mr. President? . . . Every Day Counts, Mr. President." When Roosevelt convoyed American ships in the Western Atlantic, froze Japanese assets, and embargoed critical materials headed for Japan in July and August, the Fight For Freedom lauded these moves. But it also clamored for enactment of its four-point "action" program: shoot-on-sight orders, repeal of the Neutrality Act, occupation of *all* strategic Atlantic islands, and severance of diplomatic relations with the Axis powers.[20]

Beneath the level of public awareness, there was in fact an extensive relationship between the White House and the Fight For Freedom. Most of it remains unrecorded in written records or contemporary newspaper accounts because it was carried on by telephone or through unofficial and informal channels. Peter Cusick recalls that the FFF's New York office spoke by phone with Steve Early and "Pa" Watson "at least once or twice a day." The Warhawks kept the White House informed (through Sherwood as well as Early and Watson) of the Committee's plans, the attitudes of their friends in the press, and the news they had received through Morgan and Wheeler-Bennett.[21]

On occasion they provided help on a particular issue, such as in May when Lowell Mellett, a Roosevelt aide, wrote Bell asking him to arrange to have Major Alexander de Seversky write a syndicated newspaper piece refuting the claims of Lindbergh and others that the *Luftwaffe* was invincible.[22] Also in May, Roosevelt himself directed Mellett to ask Bell to advise newly appointed Director of Civilian Defense, Fiorello LaGuardia, "in regard to the whole subject of effective publicity to offset the propaganda of the Wheelers, Nyes, Lindberghs, etc." In response to this request, Cusick rather than Bell spent several weeks in Washington in May and June working with LaGuardia.[23]

20. *New York Times,* June 26, June 28, October 4, 1941; FFF news release, July 21, 1941, FFF MSS.
21. Author's interview with Cusick.
22. Mellett to Bell, May 7, 1941, UB MSS.
23. Roosevelt to Mellett, May 19, 1941; copy in UB MSS.

The White House willingly assisted the Fight For Freedom. Early would sometimes read the verbatim record of the President's off-the-record press conferences to Bell over the phone so that the Warhawks would have a more precise idea of what the President was thinking. Early, Mellett, and David K. Niles suggested people to fill key positions on the Committee's staff and administration officials to speak at its rallies. In May, Wayne Johnson, who, as treasurer of the Democratic National Committee, had frequent and easy access to Roosevelt, passed the word that the President was annoyed by the inaction of some of his cabinet and would be glad to have the interventionist organization ask them to speak.[24]

Most administrationists solicited by the Warhawks took positions of open encouragement and even assistance—without joining the Fight For Freedom. Vice President Wallace invited Ulric Bell to take part in informal, private discussions he was conducting on war aims and spoke under FFF auspices. At the Fight For Freedom's behest, Secretary of Agriculture Wickard issued a refutation of Hoover's food plan. Mrs. Roosevelt, Secretary Knox, William Knudsen, and Sidney Hillman (the last two of the Office of Production Management) spoke for the Warhawks but did not join the Committee. Averell Harriman felt his government job precluded membership but encouraged his wife to participate. Colonel Donovan, Admiral Standley, and President Conant did actually become members and sponsors despite their involvement in intelligence, diplomacy, and "the wizard war," but, with his formal appointment as head of United States intelligence operations, Donovan resigned.[25]

Harold L. Ickes, Secretary of the Interior, worked closely with the Fight For Freedom, even attending an Executive Com-

24. "Conference—Friday AM;" Bell to Eleanor Roosevelt November 11, 1941, UB MSS; author's interview with Cusick.

25. Spivack to Tris Coffin, October 21, 1941; Spivack to Eleanor Roosevelt, December 9, 1941, FFF MSS; Sherwood to Steve Early, June 16, 1941; President's Personal File 7356, Roosevelt Papers; Harriman to Cheney, May 22, 1941. The collected papers of Stimson and Morgenthau reveal almost no direct personal correspondence with the Warhawks after the founding of the FFF. There are five or six pieces of correspondence between Bell and Knox about speaking dates (Knox had to postpone an FFF engagement.) and free advertising space in Knox's newspaper for the Chicago chapter.

mittee meeting on April 30, but he did not join the Committee because he thought his position in the government barred him from membership. At that meeting he declared regretfully that Roosevelt was continuing to postpone formation of a Federal propaganda agency. He broadly suggested that since the President was shirking the responsibility for arousing support for intervention, the Fight For Freedom had to assume it.[26] Ickes' statement was typical of his cantankerous independence. But, the evidence suggests that some of the men around the President —Early, Watson, Mellett, Niles, and Sherwood—also treated the FFF as an unofficial propaganda instrument for the administration. The easy and informal relationship between these officials and Fight For Freedom leaders and the give-and-take by telephone of confidential requests, suggestions, and information tends to substantiate this.

Furthermore, there were at least four instances during 1941 in which the White House "instructed" the Warhawks to take specific actions. The first, while the FFF was in the formative stage, was when several White House aides suggested the timing and character of the Warhawk's response to the "peace offensive."[27] The second occurred in April when both the Committee to Defend America and the Warhawks were asked to deemphasize their calls for convoying of lend-lease supplies to Britain because of congressional hostility.[28] The third, in September, was when the White House asked the FFF to postpone its call for a declaration of war because it might harm the chances for congressional repeal of the Neutrality Act.[29] The last was the

26. Ickes, *Secret Diary*, pp. 497–500. A propaganda agency called the Foreign Information Service was set up in New York shortly before Pearl Harbor under the auspices of Colonel Donovan's Office of The Coordinator of Information. However, it was not the *domestic* propaganda outlet to which Ickes had alluded. Rather, it was responsible for the dissemination of information *abroad*. Sherwood was its head, Warburg was in charge of formulating political warfare plans, and Douglas Miller and Edmund Taylor, two FFF speakers, were on the staff. Only after Pearl Harbor was the Office of War Information established (under the direction of former Century Group member Elmer Davis) to deal with both overseas and domestic propaganda. See James P. Warburg, *The Long Road Home* (Garden City, N.Y., 1964), pp. 189–91, Sherwood, *Roosevelt and Hopkins*, p. 943.

27. See p. 144.

28. See p. 234.

29. See pp. 259–60.

dictation by Sherwood on Roosevelt's behalf of a Fight For Freedom statement the day after Pearl Harbor.[30]

The President's direct participation in these activities was limited.[31] His "instructions" were nearly always passed through intermediaries. He did not appear publicly under the auspices of the Fight For Freedom, and, as one FFF leader recalls, we "had sense enough to know that the President could not even be *asked* to come." Sometimes he sent messages to be read at rallies, but he did this only when the meeting was of special importance and the speakers were of the first magnitude—Willkie, Knox, Wallace, or Mrs. Roosevelt. Otherwise, he instructed Early to refuse the request on the grounds that "the President can't single out one rally for special recognition." However, even some of the refusals could be interpreted as encouragement. In September Early informed Bell that the President had decided he could not "cut in" by telephone during a forthcoming Madison Square Garden rally. "His reaction," Early wrote, "was sympathetic but not favorable, and I think you know what I mean."[32]

Roosevelt's restraint in publicly cooperating with the

30. See pp. 264–66.

31. For evidence that Roosevelt received information about FFF activities through his aides; see, Edwin M. Watson to Douglas, February 13 and September 5, 1941, President's Personal File 1914; George Field to Watson, September 16, 1941, Official File 4054; Ross McIntyre to Lowell Mellett, October 25, 1941, Official File 4461; see copies of *Eyewitness;* "Wanted for Murder: Adolf Hitler," other FFF literature in Official File 4461, Roosevelt Papers.

According to Hyde Park records, Lewis Douglas saw Roosevelt in February, and he and Bishop Hobson had another appointment in September which was postponed and never took place. Wayne Johnson saw him in June. Marshall Field saw Roosevelt once in September, and President and Mrs. Roosevelt publicly received several Fight For Freedom delegations for picture-taking ceremonies in the summer and fall of 1941. Aside from public appeals directed at him by the Committee, Roosevelt received some personal letters. See Watson to Douglas, February 13 and September 5, 1941, President's Personal File 1914; Johnson to Watson, June 2, 1941, President's Personal File 7233; Field to Watson, September 16, 1941, Official File 4054; Watson to Bell, September 25, 1941, President's Personal File 2409; Roosevelt to Clark, July 7, 1941, President's Personal File 1956; Warburg to Roosevelt, June 6, 1941, President's Personal File 540; Pierre Jay to Roosevelt, April 20, 1941, President's Personal File 619, Roosevelt Papers.

32. Early to Bell, August 14, 1941, FFF MSS; Early to Bell, September 29, 1941, UB MSS; author's interview with Cusick.

Warhawks was undoubtedly due to the fact that he knew that open intimacy would provide his isolationist opponents with potent ammunition. At times he was also probably irritated by some of the Warhawks' strident demands upon him. Possibly, because he was trying to convince the public gradually of the need to fight and at the same time was adopting semi-belligerent policies which might well sidestep the United States into war via an "incident," he regarded close affiliation with the Fight For Freedom as a liability.

However, two episodes suggest that, whatever public posture FDR thought he had to adopt, he appreciated the usefulness of the Committee's "demands" upon him. On one occasion during the summer when the Fight For Freedom was about to publish a particularly sharp denunciation of administration tergiversation, Ulric Bell, concerned lest his group go too far, brought the text to the White House. Roosevelt read it, and then —cocking his cigarette holder at a jaunty angle—turned to Bell. "If you're going to give me hell," he said, "why not use some really strong language? You know, 'pusilanimous' isn't such a bad word." [33]

The second and overt demonstration of the Chief Executive's understanding of the Warhawks' role came after Pearl Harbor. On the occasion of a testimonial dinner for Bell in January, 1942, Roosevelt wired his congratulations for ". . . the fine work you have done during the past year and a half. Yours was not an easy task; but the vision and discretion which you brought to the work achieved very constructive results. I feel that what you and your loyal associates did made a contribution to the national security and national defense which is incalculable." [34] Despite Roosevelt's own reluctance to become too closely identified with the Warhawks, the appearance of other administration leaders as Fight For Freedom members or speakers conveyed the impression that the administration and the Committee held many views in common.

The Fight for Freedom's tactic of cooperating with Roose-

33. As told by Warburg, *The Long Road Home,* p. 187.

34. Roosevelt to Bell, January 5, 1942, President Personal File 2409, Roosevelt Papers. Secretary Hull sent a similar letter; Hull to Bell, January 2, 1942, UB MSS.

velt while urging more advanced steps than he was prepared to take probably had several results. Warhawk advertisements, news releases, and speeches probably acclimated the public to possible future policies in the same way that the Committee to Defend America had stimulated acceptance of the destroyer transfer before the actual event. While Roosevelt and his advisors privately considered convoying, occupation of some Atlantic islands, and "clearing the Atlantic of raiders," the Fight For Freedom and the Committee to Defend America were conditioning the America public to the reasonableness of such action. And, when Roosevelt decided to adopt and explain such policies, he found an audience already favorably "educated" to the issues involved. He could, therefore, attract majority support for *his* new position relatively easily.

On the other hand, the poll results seemed to indicate that public opinion was more responsive to presidential statements and events on or across the seas than to Warhawk propaganda. Also, the Warhawks' profession of solidarity with presidential policy seemed to reinforce the isolationists' contention that Roosevelt was intent on taking the nation to war. If the Warhawks advocated certain intermediate steps toward an ultimate goal of belligerency and asserted their loyalty to Roosevelt, and if the President took each of those intermediate steps one after another —what other proof was necessary?

* * * * * *

Some of the tactics of the Fight For Freedom amounted to adopting Century Group tactics to a nationwide effort. The Warhawk petitions, letters, and statements in 1940 had usually been signed by a few dozen "influentials." Now, on important issues such as convoying (in the spring) and Neutrality Act repeal (in the fall), the interventionists undertook petition-signing campaigns aimed at quantity rather than quality. The discreet requests by Century Group members to their eminent acquaintances asking for private letters to friends in the White House or State Department now became public exhortations for floods of letters to the President or to Congress on the subjects of convoys, Selective Service extension, and Neutrality repeal. The dignified signed statements opposing food for Europe, or supporting

Lend-Lease, which were so often relegated to the back pages of newspapers, were now largely superseded by full- or half-page paid advertisements complete with bold letters, cartoons, and simple, emotional slogans. They urged support for aid to Russia, de Gaulle's Free French, or a shoot-on-sight policy. They were certain to attract most readers' attention, and—for those who sympathized—they usually included a coupon for membership and contribution to the Fight For Freedom. The idea of all this was to involve great numbers of people in the interventionist movement and to give the impression that more than a dedicated minority favored war. The Fight For Freedom was trying to prove—or give the appearance of proving—that an overwhelming majority of Americans would support the war.[35]

The number of interventionist letters to congressmen which the FFF inspired can never be known, since few of the people who wrote to Washington announced their allegiance to one of the contending committees. For example, only 7 of the 126 letters on Neutrality repeal in the correspondence of Senator Charles McNary were clearly identifiable as FFF, Committee to Defend America, or America First—although most of the 126 voiced sentiments expressed by one or another of the committees. How many who took a pro-war or pro-administration position had been convinced wholly or partly by FFF propaganda? How many had been moved by the news from Europe or by words from the White House? None can say. One can state with reasonable certainty only that more people wrote letters to Congress than would have if FFF appeals had not occurred.

Evidence on petitions is also only fragmentary. The most sustained Warhawk petition drive centered on repeal of the Neutrality laws. The FFF national headquarters had received twenty-five thousand petition signatures before Congress acted, and FFF records suggest that as many as a quarter of a million others were sent directly from the chapters to the Capitol. This was a demonstration of considerable magnitude, but (as is shown in the next chapter) it was hardly the only factor influencing the vote in Congress.

35. For example, see "Neutrality Repeal" folder; Convoy petition, April 1, 1941; "What's Happening in the Fight For Freedom," August 12, 1941, FFF MSS.

It is probable that the petition and letter-writing campaigns did demonstrate to the peoples' representatives the existence of a sizeable, organized body of opinion favorable to firmer defense policies. The Congressmen could, of course, have learned much the same thing from public opinion polls—but the Warhawks were right in assuming that personal letters and petitions from home carry more weight with some legislators than poll results, especially if the polls show a fairly close division of sentiment. On the question of outright intervention, however, all the letters the Fight For Freedom could muster could not overcome the impact of consistent poll counts of four to one against immediate war.

Because of the increasingly critical situation overseas and because they were "going public," the Warhawks felt an increased need to draw a clear line between the "good guys" and the "bad guys." A small group of sophisticated men may find it possible to see different shades of gray in situations or admit their opponents' honest motivation and still act with unity and vigor. A national organization seeking public support, however, must pose a clear choice between itself and its opponents. If it considers that the issue with which it is concerned is extremely critical, it often finds itself driven to stating alternatives in simplistic terms. It projects up on its opponents all the attributes of Lucifer, while assuming for itself most of the heavenly virtues. So it was with the Fight For Freedom. Knowing that most Americans—even those opposed to war—despised Hitler and Mussolini, the Warhawks worked assiduously to pin upon each of the major isolationist figures the image of a Nazi, a Fascist sympathizer, or a dupe of the Axis. And, owing largely to the indiscretions of their targets, they frequently succeeded.

Chief among the targets of the Fight For Freedom was Colonel Lindbergh. The "Lone Eagle" came from Swedish-American stock and was an heir to the same midwestern Populist-Progressive tradition as Senators Wheeler and Nye. He had retained much of the popular appeal he had won with his flight fourteen years earlier and was using it in the cause of a form of extreme isolationism which appeared pro-Nazi to the Warhawks. He had spent considerable time in Germany as recently as 1938 and had even received a medal from Hermann Goering. During his sojourns in Germany Lindbergh had been so impressed by German industry and air power as to become convinced that the West could not stand against the Nazis. He also apparently absorbed some of the eugenic theories of "Aryan" racial superiority expounded by the Nazis. In 1940 and 1941 he addressed numerous America First gatherings and advocated absolute neutrality in the war and total abstention from all European affairs.[36]

The Fight For Freedom seized upon the Goering medal as a good issue and pointed out that although Lindbergh had resigned his United States Army commission in order to campaign against the war, he had never returned the Nazi medal. The Committee distributed cardboard replicas of the medal bearing the inscription, "For Services Rendered to the Third Reich."

Typical of the Fight For Freedom attacks on Lindbergh were a handbill distributed at a noontime rally on New York's Wall Street and a radio talk by mystery writer Rex Stout. The handbill quoted several recent statements by Adolf Hitler and Colonel Lindbergh and asked, "Did Lindbergh see the advance copy of the Hitler interview and take his cue from that? Or did Hitler see an advance copy of Lindbergh's speech?"[37] Stout, an FFF sponsor, predicted that Lindbergh might well become collaborationist President of the United States if Germany conquered the New World. "If I am accused," he continued, "of smearing Colonel Lindbergh in proposing him . . . to collaborate with the Nazis, I vehemently deny the charge. Consider his position. It is a fact that every fascist and pro-Nazi in America, without exception, applauds him and approves of him. . . . It is a fact that dozens of times in the past year he has been enthusiastically quoted in the newspapers of Germany and Italy and Japan."[38]

36. See Lindbergh's father's 1917 book reprinted as Charles A. Lindbergh, Sr., *Your Country at War and What Happens to You After a War* (Philadelphia, 1934); also, George Waller, *Kidnap* (London, 1965). The Fight For Freedom leaders were particularly well informed about Lindbergh since their friend and confidant, Aubrey Morgan of the British Information Service, was married to a Morrow daughter (as was Lindbergh). Morrow family get-togethers during that period were occasionally punctuated by heated exchanges between the two men.

37. "Another Funny Coincidence," undated handbill, FFF MSS.

38. "Talk by Rex Stout on WMCA," April 24, 1941, reprints, FFF MSS.

The clearest statement of the Fight For Freedom attitude toward isolationists in general and the tactics it was using to discredit Lindbergh (among others) came from the lips of Alexander Woollcott, who told his radio audience on May 27:

> Whether they [the isolationists] admit it or not, whether they like it or not, whether indeed, that is any part of their purpose, they are working for Hitler. Have you any doubt—any doubt at *all*—that Hitler would have been glad to pay Lindbergh an immense amount—millions for the work he has done in the past year? . . .
>
> Now don't get me wrong about this. I doubt that Lindbergh has taken or would take German money. . . . That does not alter the fact that [he is] working for him. For [he], like all the rest of us, [is] trapped in a tragic irony. In this world today there is no such thing as neutrality. You are either for Hitler or against him. You either fight him or you help him.[39]

Lindbergh's speech in Des Moines on September 11 opened to full the floodgates of Warhawk criticism. "The three most important groups," he said, "who have been pressing this country toward war are the British, the Jewish, and the Roosevelt administration." Although professing to understand how "the persecution they suffered in Germany would be sufficient to make bitter enemies of any race," he stated that

> Instead of agitating for war the Jewish groups in this country should be opposing it in every possible way, for they will be among the first to feel its consequences. Tolerance is a virtue that depends on peace and strength. History shows that it cannot survive war and devastation. A few farsighted Jewish people realize this and stand opposed to intervention. But the majority still do not. The greatest danger to this country lies in their large ownership and influence in our motion pictures, our press, our radio, and our government.[40]

Although many influential Jews *were* interventionists, Lindbergh's veiled threat to American Jews and his unsubtle use of the stratagem of making the obvious victim appear the aggressor

39. Alexander Woollcott, "A Voice From the Cracker Barrel," May 25, 1941, FFF MSS.

40. As quoted in Wayne S. Cole, *America First: The Battle Against Intervention, 1940–1941* (Madison, Wisc., 1953), p. 144.

laid him open more than ever to charges of sympathizing with the anti-Semitic Nazis.

The Warhawks pounced upon him. Peter Cusick called Lindbergh a "barefaced" anti-Semite and claimed that his extremism was repelling so many people that he was the interventionists' "most active recruiting agent." Bishop Hobson telegraphed General Wood to pronounce Lindbergh's words "foreign to the American character" and to demand that America First face up to the problem of anti-Semitism in its ranks. Hobson also sent fellow-interventionist Wendell Willkie a public telegram decrying "the ugly spectacle of Nazi anti-Semitism being made a plank in the platform of the America First Committee," and Willkie responded by calling the speech "the most unAmerican talk made in my time by any person of national reputation." The initial outburst was followed by a pamphlet created by L. M. Birkhead's Friends of Democracy and distributed by the Fight For Freedom, which described Lindbergh's cordial relationship with the leaders of the Third Reich.

The Warhawks were not alone in denouncing the Des Moines speech. As Wayne Cole noted in his history of America First, many new voices joined the outcry. Almost all the newspapers and magazines which commented—even the anti-interventionist Hearst chain—criticized the speech. Although the America First leadership decided not to censure Lindbergh, many influential isolationists, including General Hugh Johnson and John T. Flynn, protested to national headquarters. Occurring simultaneously with the *Greer* incident and Roosevelt's shoot-on-sight speech, Lindbergh's indiscretion helped put America First very much on the defensive. As Cole concluded: "Lindbergh's Des Moines speech was an extremely serious political blunder and dealt the America First Committee a staggering blow. It complicated the problem of preventing anti-Semites and pro-fascists from working through the Committee. It gave the interventionists their best opportunity to discredit America First." [41]

41. FFF news release, September 12, 1941; Waymack to Cusick, September 16, 1941; Hobson to Willkie, telegram, September 23, 1941; "Hitler and Lindbergh Are Spiritual Brothers Under the Skin"; "Is Lindbergh a Nazi?", pamphlets, FFF MSS; Cole, *America First*, pp. 145–54.

The Fight For Freedom used a more tangible approach in attempting to undermine another arch-foe, Colonel Robert R. McCormick, owner of the *Chicago Tribune*. In the late spring, while denouncing the *Tribune* for its "pro-Nazism" and McCormick himself ("Hitler likes him"), the Warhawks planned to create a new Chicago morning paper to "end the unAmerican monopoly" of the *Tribune*. Marshall Field declared that he would publish the newspaper if he was assured 175,000 pre-subscribers. Cusick told him to make preparations.

Field recruited the financial support and journalist skills of Silliman Evans of the *Nashville Tennessean* and Turner Catledge of *The New York Times*. Meanwhile, Cusick and Chicago Warhawks Courtney Barber, Jr., Albert Parry, and Anita Blaine McCormick (a cousin of the publisher) arranged a series of subscription-raising rallies at Chicago's Orchestra Hall and elsewhere in the area. Wendell Willkie headed the list of speakers, which included Adlai E. Stevenson, Paul H. Douglas, and Edmond Taylor, a former *Tribune* correspondent, whose booklet, *You Can't Do Business with Hitler*, was widely distributed by the Fight For Freedom.[42]

By September the subscription goal was met, and Marshall Field followed the announcement that the new *Chicago Sun* was about to be published with a visit to the White House, where the venture received the personal blessing of the President. The first edition of the *Sun* appeared on December 4, providing Chicagoans with a competent alternative for their early morning reading.

The Warhawks applied the "dupe-sympathizer-agent" technique to the two most outspoken senatorial isolationists, Burton K. Wheeler and Gerald P. Nye. Wheeler had drawn fire from the Century Group for his Lend-Lease statement about "plowing under every fourth American boy" and for raising the illusion of "a negotiated peace." In July the Fight For Freedom and the Committee to Defend America assailed him again, first for suggesting that the Senate impeach Secretary Knox for advocating use of the United States Navy to clear the Atlantic of Nazi

42. Author's interview with Cusick; Chicago *FFF Bulletin*, September 29, 1941, UB MSS; *New York Times*, September 18, 1941; *Time*, August 11, 1941.

raiders, and then for revealing plans for the American occupation of Iceland before it took place. Wheeler, the Fight For Freedom declared, was a "Twentieth Century Benedict Arnold [who] stands now in the same position as Quisling and Laval did before their countries became involved in a 'shooting' war." A cartoon was circulated depicting Wheeler, seated in front of a swastika, broadcasting American secrets to the world. "Hello, World," ran the caption, "They are about to leave for Iceland." The implication that the Montanan was a traitor could hardly be missed.[43]

The Warhawks found no need to overstate their case—not only against Wheeler but also against Nye and Congressmen Hamilton Fish, Stephen Day, Jacob Thorkelson, and George Tinkham—on the subject of franking privilege abuses. The Fight For Freedom leaders took notice in late May when the publisher of the "Report of Direct Mail Advertising" (who, of course, had a vested interest in limiting use of the frank) disclosed that American Fascists Donald Shea and Joe McWilliams were using Wheeler's frank to distribute their literature. Robert S. Allen kept the Fight For Freedom supplied with "inside" information on Wheeler and urged Bell "to hammer on this thing with all you've got." [44] When the Warhawks received photostats of the franked literature substantiating the allegations, they attacked.[45] This, they declared, was a criminal offense, since the postal statutes prohibited the lending or use of the frank "by any person for the benefit or use of any committee, organization, or association." The Fight For Freedom sent letters to Vice President Wallace, Speaker Rayburn, and the Postmaster General's office requesting definition and limitation of the franking privilege.[46]

Wheeler denounced the charges that "McWilliams or any

43. FFF news release, July 2, 4, 8, 11, 26, 1941, reprint from *New York Post,* July 11, 1941, FFF MSS; *New York Times,* July 4, 8, 1941.

44. Henry Hoke news release, July 24, 1941; FFF news release, July 12, 1941; Burton Wheeler to A. H. Becker, copy, July 7, 1941; Robert Allen to Bell, June 24, 1941; FFF MSS.

45. Available in FFF MSS.

46. FFF news release, June 28, 1941; Christian Gauss *et al.* to the Vice President of the United States, June 12, 1941; Chayes to Ramsey S. Black (of Postmaster General's Office), September 18 and November 17, 1941, FFF MSS.

other anti-Semitic organizations" had used his frank as "false" and "vicious libel." "If repeated," he said, "I will be forced to take action." He claimed that he had no way of keeping track of who received material under his frank, but that he himself had never sent out anything other than his own speeches under it. Furthermore, he charged, "some two million pieces of mail" had been sent out under congressional frank on behalf of the interventionists.[47] Wheeler's first assertion, about sending out his own speeches only, had some validity; the subversives who had obtained use of his frank circulated Wheeler's own words when these words coincided with their own purposes. His second statement was probably groundless. Legislators of interventionist views undoubtedly circulated their own thoughts on foreign affairs under their franks, but there is no evidence among Fight For Freedom documents that the Committee ever distributed materials under congressional franks.

On July 21, despite Wheeler's threat of legal action, Bell wired: "We are repeating publicly the fact that anti-Semitic, pro-Nazi and pro-German outfits have sent out mail on your frank. We note your threat to take action and invite you to do so immediately without hiding under the cloak of Congressional immunity."[48] Wheeler never did make his threatened legal response.

Shortly thereafter another news story revealed that Senator Nye's frank, too, was being used by a pro-Nazi unit of the Steuben Society of America, and that Representative Day's anti-British speeches were being mimeographed and distributed by George Sylvester Viereck, a registered agent of Nazi Germany.[49]

The final and most sensational disclosure came on August 26 when the Fight For Freedom accused Hamilton Fish of permitting William Pelley of the Silver Shirts to distribute under Fish's frank the "Protocols of the Elders of Zion," an anti-Semitic tract of "White" Russian origin.[50] In the same manner, the Com-

47. Burton Wheeler to Becker, copy, July 7, 1941, FFF MSS.

48. Bell to Burton Wheeler, telegram, July 21, 1941, FFF MSS.

49. Spivack to Leo J. Margolis, July 14, 1941, reprint of "Washington Merry-Go-Round," August 3, 1941, FFF MSS. John Roy Carlson, *Undercover: My Four Years in the Nazi Underground of America* (New York, 1943), pp. 414–16.

50. FFF news release, August 26, 1941, FFF MSS.

mittee said, Pelley had sent out envelopes calling the Fight For Freedom "The Fight For Jewdom." [51] Again, the Warhawks substantiated each charge with photographs of the original mailings. In its press release, the Fight For Freedom claimed that Fish, when contacted by telephone, had declared that he had not specifically granted this usage, but added, ". . . It doesn't bother me any. . . . There's been too much Jewism going around anyway." [52] Investigation by Allen and by federal officials soon revealed much more. Fish's office had been serving as the center of a ring of Nazi sympathizers who had made wholesale use of his frank. After an inquiry, a federal grand jury indicted George Hill, Fish's secretary, for perjury in answering questions regarding his relationship and financial arrangements with Nazi agents Viereck and Prescott Dennett.[53]

When Fish was ordered to appear before the grand jury on November 10, he pleaded congressional immunity and stated he was awaiting a House Judiciary Committee ruling on whether the jury's subpoena infringed his congressional privilege. "If Mr. Fish is innocent," Ulric Bell publicly declared, "the strong, bright light of the Grand Jury should do no harm. If he is not innocent, it will be a healthy thing to remove the stigma of a Quisling from our Congressional midst." Fish, however, remained silent. Despite this adverse publicity he retained his congressional seat until he was defeated in the 1944 elections.[54]

The franking controversy served the interventionist purpose excellently. By providing documentary proof of links between congressional advocates of America First and domestic Fascists or Nazi agents, the Warhawks cast a shadow on the patriotism and integrity of several of the foremost isolationists.

Like the franking issue, a Senate investigation of interventionist propaganda in the movies afforded the FFF a chance to

51. See originals in FFF MSS.

52. FFF news release, August 26, 1941, FFF MSS.

53. Hill was convicted of perjury, and Viereck was convicted for failing to reveal all of his activities as a registered agent, *New York Times,* February 7 and March 19, 1942. Testimony at the trials implicated Congressman Day and Sweeney, Senators Holt, Lundeen, and Fish.

54. FFF news releases, November 1, 11, 12, 1941; Bell to congressmen, circular letter, October 31, 1941, FFF MSS; *New York Times,* November 11, 1944.

accuse their congressional foes of Nazi-like anti-Semitism and disregard for law. Hollywood society at the time was composed primarily of first and second generation citizens of southeastern European and Jewish lineage, mixed with a number of individuals of Anglo-Saxon background. Together they had strong personal reasons for wanting an all-out American effort to aid the British and liberate the enslaved and persecuted nationalities of Europe. Hollywood figures were, therefore, deeply involved in the Fight For Freedom. Douglas Fairbanks, Jr., Helen Hayes, and Burgess Meredith, for instance, were among the FFF's most publicized speakers and fund-raisers. Samuel Goldwyn, Spyros Skouras, Darryl Zanuck, Walter Wanger, and Jack Warner were heavy contributors, and their influence was largely responsible for the outpouring of money and membership applications from Southern California, as well as the flow of motion pictures with pro-British or anti-Nazi themes.

Fearing the eventual effect of these films, the isolationists attacked. On July 31 Senator Wheeler charged on the floor of the Senate that various Hollywood studios were forcing their employees to attend a National Unity Rally sponsored by interventionists.[55] The following day Senator Nye told a national radio audience that the movie companies "have been operating as war propaganda machines almost as if they were being directed from a single central bureau. . . . The silver screen has been flooded," he asserted, "with picture after picture designed to rouse us to a state of war hysteria; pictures glorifying the war; telling about the grandeur and justice of the British Empire . . . while all the peoples who are opposed to her, including even courageous little Finland now, are drawn as coarse, bestial, brutal scoundrels." [56] Then he listed the movie moguls responsible for this. Noting the eastern European or Jewish background of most, he declared: ". . . In this era of world upset, when national and racial emotions run ariot and reason is pushed from her throne, this mighty engine of propaganda is in the hands of men who are, quite naturally, susceptible to these emotions."

Drawing on venerable Populist mythology, Nye told his

55. Darryl Zanuck to Bell, July 31, 1941, FFF MSS.

56. "Senator Gerald T. Nye over Columbia Broadcasting System," transcript, August 1, 1941, FFF MSS.

audience that behind the movie propaganda was the ever-present hand of the Wall Street conspiracy:

> Why do they want to push us into war? Well, they have interests, but here is one I can give you. One of the leading Wall Street investment houses made a study of these movie industries only a few months ago. It told its buyers that if Britain loses, seven of the eight leading companies will be wiped out. That report revealed that the quarters and half-dollars of the American movie patrons barely pays for the cost of producing these gigantic movie spectacles. The profits depend on the sales in the foreign market, which is now reduced to England and her dominions.[57]

Shortly thereafter, the Senate passed a resolution submitted by Wheeler and D. Worth Clark instituting a subcommittee investigation of the movies. As Chairman of the Interstate Commerce Committee, Wheeler appointed the subcommittee, and he selected Senators Clark, Bone, Tobey, and C. Wayland Brooks—all known isolationists—as well as Ernest McFarland. Hearings were scheduled to begin on September 9.[58]

Earlier, when faced with a congressional investigation of communism in Hollywood, the film industry had meekly submitted. This time, however, the movie-makers decided to fight, and, on the advice of Fight For Freedom leaders, they asked Wendell Willkie to represent them as counsel. Ulric Bell outlined the tactics for this issue. The movie industry and the FFF would go "fightingly on the offensive," striking "with bare knuckles" at the issue of anti-Semitism, the fact that the investigating subcommittee was "packed," and the fact that Bundist and Fascist support was being received by America First and its friends in Congress.[59]

To implement this plan, the Fight For Freedom publicized a communiqué signed by nearly a hundred prominent individuals. The introductory passage said the investigation had ". . . the most sinister implications. It will be a device whereby

57. *Ibid.*

58. *Washington Post*, September 8, 1940.

59. Robert Allen to Merle Miller, August 9, 1941, FFF MSS; "In appearing before the Inter-State Commerce Sub-Committee . . . ," UB MSS.

the whole interventionist cause will be hauled recklessly over the coals. It will enable the isolationists to raise subtly or otherwise the religious issue. . . . This attack should be met head on before it starts." The text of the protest, in the form of an open letter to Congress, called the inquiry "the most barefaced attempt at censorship and racial persecution which has ever been tried in this country" and condemned the "mockery" of justice which would occur if "a subcommittee [were to sit] in solemn judgment on charges drawn by itself." [60]

In a private letter to Merle Miller, Robert S. Allen denounced the investigation even more unsparingly:

> The whole movie affair is part of a deliberate anti-Semitic campaign. I heard on the Hill yesterday that this was deliberately cooked up for the double purpose of terrorizing the Jews on one hand to keep them from active participation in the anti-isolationist fight and on the other to arouse public prejudice against the interventionist cause on the Jew angle. This is one of the most sinister and vicious schemes yet undertaken by the isolationists. . . .[61]

As the hearings opened the Warhawks continued their attack. Their releases asked why the senators denounced pro-British films from Hollywood but made no objection to the distribution of Nazi propaganda films like "Sieg im Westen." Peter Cusick declared, "The current inquisition, we must conclude, is an attempt to blackmail the movie industry—to make it tell lies in the name of 'impartiality' and 'peace.'" The Executive Committee assailed Senator Nye as "the individual most directly responsible for the injection of religious issues into the debate on foreign policy." [62]

Hearings occurred intermittently during September, and the most exciting episode was probably Errol Flynn's brawl with Hollywood gossip columnist Jimmy Fidler after Fidler had testified to the presence of an interventionist conspiracy in the major Hollywood studios. The subcommittee could find no incriminating evidence, and by the beginning of October the continuation

60. FFF form letter, August 29, 1941, FFF MSS.
61. Robert Allen to Merle Miller, August 9, 1941, FFF MSS.
62. FFF news releases, September 12, 13, 18, 30, 1941, FFF MSS.

and purpose of the investigation was being attacked by subcommittee member McFarland, the Veterans of Foreign Wars, and even some moderate isolationists, such as Dr. Norman Vincent Peale. Rumors circulated that Senate critics of the investigation wanted to examine the subcommittee's expenditures. Under these circumstances Clark and his associates quietly discontinued the proceedings, and the Fight For Freedom, content with the ammunition the affair had already provided and claiming vindication of its Hollywood allies, turned its attention elsewhere.[63]

Sometimes the attempts to tag the "Axis sympathizer" agent on the other isolationists were ill-chosen or too extreme. For instance, the attack on Generoso Pope, New York construction executive, Tammany Hall leader, and publisher of the popular Italian language newspaper, *Il Progresso Italo-Americano,* was out of proportion to Pope's behavior. In the 1930's Pope (like many observers—including Winston Churchill) admired Mussolini for the domestic improvements he had wrought. He had even been photographed giving the Fascist salute at *Il Duce's* side. When Roosevelt declared the Italian invasion of France in June, 1940, a "stab in the back," Pope—like many other Italian-Americans—interpreted this not as a condemnation of the Fascists alone but as a slur on *all* Italians. "Americans of Italian origin," he proclaimed, "cannot stretch their profound devotion to their adopted fatherland to the point of tolerating systematic insolences against their original fatherland." [64] In the ensuing election Pope straddled the fence; his newspapers supported Willkie, while he preserved his local power by personally remaining within the Tammany tepee.

Shortly after the Fight For Freedom was founded, Pope applied for membership and made a large contribution. The Warhawks interpreted Pope's behavior not as a change of heart

63. *New York Times,* September 15, 22, 27, 1941; October 11, 1941. The Beards suggest that administration pressure on the movie industry dating from the naval expansion bill of 1938 was responsible for the anti-Fascist, anti-pacifist, and interventionist trend in pre-war motion pictures, Charles A. and Mary R. Beard, *America in Mid-Passage* (New York, 1939), pp. 597–602. However, the enthusiastic correspondence in FFF MSS between motion picture executives or actors and the Warhawk leaders refutes this hypothesis.

64. Quoted in Bell to Robert H. Jackson, May 27, 1941, FFF MSS. See also Louis L. Gerson, *The Hyphenate in American Politics and Diplomacy* (Lawrence, Kansas, 1964), p. 126.

but as another attempt to play on two teams at once. Bell denounced him on behalf of the Fight For Freedom as a "pro-Fascist" trying to "jump on the bandwagon" and a "political bigamist." His membership and gift were publicly spurned.[65] A verbal duel between the Fight For Freedom and Pope continued throughout a good part of the summer, with the Committee seeking, unsuccessfully, to have the Attorney General revoke his citizenship on the grounds that he had not fulfilled the oath of citizenship by "absolutely and entirely renounc[ing] and abjur[ing] all allegiance and fidelity to any foreign . . . power."[66]

Refusing the contribution and even publicly denouncing Pope's duplicity were undoubtedly reasonable and appropriate responses. However, to demand revocation of Pope's citizenship at a time when many *native* Americans advocated a policy of "accommodation" toward the Axis was to overstep the bounds of free debate.

An even more graphic illustration was the series of slurs directed at General Robert E. Wood, the head of America First. A graduate of West Point, Wood had seen duty in the Philippines and Panama before becoming Acting Quartermaster General during the First World War. After the war he became vice president of Montgomery Ward and Company, then vice president, president, and chairman of the board of Sears, Roebuck and Company. During the 1930's he had been a member of the Committee of the Nation (later the Committee for Constitutional Government), whose executive secretary, Dr. Edward A. Rumely, had been convicted as a German agent during World War I. The Committee, composed largely of conservative big-businessmen, like James H. Rand, Jr., and Frank Gannett of the Gannett newspapers, had opposed Roosevelt's fiscal policies and court-packing scheme. However, after Wood became head of America First, he made strenuous if unsuccessful efforts to keep

65. Robert Spivack to Lee Margolin, June 15, 1941; FFF news release, May 27, 1941, FFF MSS.

66. Bell to Robert H. Jackson, May 27, 1941, FFF MSS. Despite Pope's opposition to pre-war foreign policy, Roosevelt found it expedient during 1944 to seek a reconciliation with Pope and invited him to the White House on Columbus Day, 1944, Gerson, *The Hyphenate in American Politics,* p. 127.

his own organization free of questionable supporters. He also tried, fruitlessly, to keep the public debate between the contending committees on a high plane.[67] Despite this, the Fight For Freedom sought to apply the "dupe-sympathizer" tag to him.

In October, 1940, Wood stated that he would cease his opposition to the war if Congress declared war or if the United States actually became involved in hostilities. After Roosevelt's "unlimited emergency" speech on May 27, 1941, Ulric Bell telegraphed Wood to ask if the latter condition had been met. Wood replied that his statement did not apply to current circumstances. Later, after shoot-on-sight orders had been issued and United States Navy vessels actually torpedoed, the Fight For Freedom posed the issue again. Wood, apparently torn between loyalty to his organization and friends and his earlier promise, lapsed into silence.[68]

In the meantime the Warhawks attacked him in language only slightly more restrained than that employed on Fish, Nye, and Lindbergh. An advertisement in the *New York Times* on June 27 said: ". . . In his proclamation of attack on Russia Hitler singled out for quotation the words of one private citizen in all the world—the words of [America First's] Chairman, General Wood." [69] In August, Bell told the press:

> We are now convinced that the America First Committee and its chairman, General Robert E. Wood, do not take orders from Berlin. They merely think the same thoughts at the same time:
>
> 1. General Robert E. Wood said in Chicago today, "It would seem that the English Prime Minister has suffered a diplomatic rebuff. This statement is evidence that Roosevelt realizes he must listen more carefully to the American people than to Winston Churchill."
>
> 2. An authorized spokesman from Berlin said this: "The United States President and the British Prime Minister both suffered a catastrophic political defeat and flopped disastrously with their own people. It is in such a position that we hope to see them long remain."

67. Cole, *America First,* pp. 72–73, 116–20; Arthur M. Schlesinger, Jr., *The Age of Roosevelt: The Coming of the New Deal* (Boston, 1958) p. 198; Carlson, *Undercover,* p. 473–80.

68. FFF news release, June 12, 1941; Wood to Bell, June 6, 1941; FFF news release, October 21, 1941, FFF MSS.

69. *New York Times,* June 27, 1941.

"Grcat minds, it would seem, run in similar channels," Bell added.[70]

Although Wood was one of the more moderate spokesmen of America First, as its chairman he was the titular head of isolationism. Therefore, he had to be felled with whatever weapon was most effective. The insinuations and innuendoes the Warhawks used against him may have repelled some objective listeners. But they probably left an enduring impression on others which helped discredit isolationism in general.

The Warhawks themselves were frequently subjected to the same tactics of smear and insinuation by their opponents. For instance, Lindbergh repeatedly charged that the Warhawks were acting as agents of the British and (together with the President) were dragging the American people into a war they neither wanted nor needed to fight. After the Soviet Union was attacked, America Firsters sometimes tried to pin the Communist label on interventionism. The Wisconsin America First chairman, for example, placed a column-long advertisement in the *Milwaukee Journal* declaring, "WAR and then COMMUNISM: Dr. Albert Parry formerly with the Committee to Defend America and now Chicago Chairman of the Fight For Freedom Committee is a COMMUNIST." To document this allegation the ad quoted out of context a humorous article Dr. Parry had written ten years before. On an even lower level, *The Pink Reporter* of Three Forks, Montana, described the FFF as "that phony Jewish set up . . . [of] rat Comrades."[71]

The efficacy of the "dupe-sympathizer-agent" weapon as a

70. FFF news release, August 15, 1941, FFF MSS. Aside from Wheeler, Nye, Lindbergh, and Wood, Colonel McCormick of the *Chicago Tribune* ("Hitler's Sweetheart") and Senator Robert Reynolds, Chairman of the Military Affairs Committee and head of "The Vindicators," a North Carolina organization for white, Christian nationalists ("sinister clown"), were particular FFF targets.

71. Reprints of both in FFF MSS. The FFF asked the FBI to investigate *The Pink Reporter* for possible Axis connections. As the Century Group did earlier, the FFF seems to have maintained a working relationship with J. Edgar Hoover with respect to the discovery and investigation of pro-Axis fronts. See Spivack to FBI, July 30, 1941; Bell to Hull, October 22; November 3, 4, 1941; J. Edgar Hoover to Bell, June 6 and July 28, 1941, FFF MSS.

means of arousing public reaction depended in part on the evidence available to prove the allegations. Because of their own oversights or blunders, the isolationists tended to be more vulnerable to such thrusts than the interventionists. Also, since the overwhelming majority of the public sympathized with the British, an isolationist charge of "Anglophile" or "British agent" simply did not carry as much emotional force as an interventionist allegation of "Axis dupe" or "Nazi agent"—regardless of the supporting evidence.

If magnifying and stigmatizing their opponents' shortcomings were one side of the Fight For Freedom coin, then the other side was projecting the Warhawk image as a shining composite of fairness, morality, and inspiration. The Warhawks claimed American intervention was the last hope of Western civilization—partly because they believed the issue was indeed *that* critical and partly to simplify the situation for public consumption. As Conyers Read told a luncheon meeting of the Philadelphia chapter in May, "The issue is larger than the fate of the British Empire. It is even larger than the fate of America. It is the issue of civilization as we know it, of Christianity as we know it. It is the issue of the dignity of man and the dignity of truth."[72] Similarly, James Warburg outlined the tasks confronting Americans to the graduating class at Juilliard School of Music:

> . . . If we choose peace, we must do three things:
>
> We must fight and fight now with every resource at our command—no matter how ready or unready we may be. We must fight, and go on fighting, until this foul beast which has launched itself upon the world is slain.
>
> And when the beast lies dead, we must assume our full share of the burden of creating and maintaining a world order in which brute force may never again rear its ugly head—a world order so permeated with justice that the majority of men will not again be moved to violence.
>
> And finally, we must build here at home—and help others, who may want help, to build abroad—a social and economic order in which we apply the same ethical principles of justice and equality

72. Conyers Read, "The Fight For Freedom," an address at luncheon meeting of Philadelphia FFF Chapter, May 29, 1941, FFF MSS.

which we have long recognized and fairly successfully applied in our political order.[73]

Warburg's suggestion that American assumption of international responsibility in the postwar world would solve most problems was unrealistically optimistic. The pacifist A. J. Muste, for instance, was more foresighted when he predicted that a United States-Soviet conflict would inevitably follow a war against Germany. But if the Warhawks had any private doubts about the postwar world, they submerged them in floods of rhetoric about the great new world America could build in the peace that would follow Hitler's downfall. The necessity of rallying the public on the first issue—war—prohibited a reasoned discussion of the problems of a postwar settlement. Also, it is entirely possible that the Warhawks themselves could not bear the thought of another conflict to follow the one for which they were now preparing.

A combination of the tactical needs of the moment and their own personal convictions also governed the Fight For Freedom leaders' attitude toward domestic issues of human rights or civil liberties. Most of the Warhawks believed strongly in academic freedom, freedom of speech and religion, and equality of opportunity. But, in the context of the continuing public debate, belief was not enough. The Fight For Freedom sought to demonstrate its commitments to these ideals actively and at the same time tried to tie those who disregarded them to nazism or America First. Thus, when Governor Eugene Talmadge of Georgia fired two college administrators because of their association with the Julius Rosenwald Fund (which financed higher education for southern Negroes), Herbert Agar declared Talmadge "guilty of lynching academic freedom in Georgia." A Committee release said that the two were "now being crucified to satisfy the totalitarian appetites of Governor Talmadge and his Hitlerites," and demanded their reinstatement.[74]

Similarly, the Fight For Freedom dramatized the case of

73. James P. Warburg, "Commencement Address," The Juilliard School of Music, May 28, 1941, FFF MSS.

74. FFF news releases, July 16 and 18, 1941, FFF MSS.

Richard Scammon, a young employee of the University of Chicago, who had been forced to resign after he had challenged General Wood to a debate on the question of the occupation of Iceland. Wood and other midwestern isolationists were apparently heavy contributors to the university and its president, Robert Hutchins, opposed American intervention. Ulric Bell charged that Scammon had been fired not because of his work but because his views clashed with those of the university administration and its sources of income.[75]

While demanding freedom of speech for its own adherents, the Committee insisted on the same right for its opponents. When, at the end of May, a speech by leftist Congressman Vito Marcantonio over the National Broadcasting Company brought demands by some Hawks for "action" against N.B.C., Bishop Hobson dissented. He agreed that Marcantonio's speech was "an outrageous performance—unpatriotic, and generally just about what might be expected of one whose course has cheered America's enemies. But," he insisted, "we believe in free speech under the Constitution, no matter how much we disagree with what is said."[76]

Similarly, in July, when Senator Wheeler was denied access to the municipal auditorium in Atlanta, Peter Cusick declared that the Senator "must be defended in his right to speak in Atlanta, Georgia, or anywhere else that he chooses." This was so, Cusick observed, despite the fact that Wheeler himself sought to censor free speech by using "his influence to ban Walter Winchell's broadcasts from three leading Montana radio stations at Helena, Butte, and Boseman."[77] At other times the Fight For Freedom also spoke out against the muzzling of isolationist clergy.[78]

75. FFF news release, July 22, 1941, FFF MSS. Scammon was later to become Director of the U.S. Census.

76. FFF news release, May 31, 1941, FFF MSS.

77. FFF news release, July 19, 1941, FFF MSS.

78. In November a news story was circulated that the local Army commander in Denver, Colorado had placed "out of bounds" to servicemen certain churches whose pacifist-isolationist pastors were preaching American non-involvement in the war. Bishop Hobson issued a statement (FFF news release, November 7, 1941, FFF MSS) saying that he hoped the story was

The Fight For Freedom's stand on domestic human rights and civil liberties was tactically useful in getting attention for the organization through issues not directly related to foreign affairs. It certainly helped project a reputable image and may even have attracted to the banner of interventionism a few people who were primarily interested in domestic social justice and lawfulness and who became enthusiastic over the Fight For Freedom's expressed liberalism. The "domestic fight for freedom," however, was not merely a tactic. It was a constant precept of the Warhawks—a fact substantiated by the activities of the FFF's successor, Freedom House. A quarter of a century after Pearl Harbor, Freedom House continues to be not only an advocate of militant resistance to totalitarian aggression abroad but also a defender of libertarianism at home.[79]

In order to appeal not only to liberals and the highly educated but also to the mass of relatively unsophisticated citizens, the Warhawks used simple, repetitive slogans or symbols as well as stunts and "circuses." These techniques aimed directly at arousing mass emotions to a war fever. During the summer and fall both the Fight For Freedom and the Committee to Defend America focused their promotion efforts on the slogan "Stop Hitler Now!" and the "V" symbol popularized by Churchill and used as a calling card by the European undergrounds.

Beginning on July 24 both Committees sponsored "V for Victory" parades, and "V" rallies for Americans born in captive nations were organized all over the country. Powers models with "V" necklines promenaded down Broadway, and volunteers dis-

---

untrue. 'Such action," he said, "would be both foolish and dangerous. The men in this nation's democratic army are able to balance the facts of the present situation and determine the truth for themselves. . . . All of us know of the intemperance and frequent genuine dishonesty of certain isolationist leaders. But an American army must and will fight as a democratic army, not an opinion-controlled group of robots.

We of Fight For Freedom are confident that the men in this country's armed forces, as well as Americans generally, see the danger with which this country is confronted, and no loud shouting in Denver, Colorado, Washington, D.C., or Berlin, Germany, will mislead them."

79. See William Agar and Aaron Levenstein, *Freedom's Advocate: A Twenty-Five Year Chronicle* (New York, 1965); also see Freedom House statements supporting administration policy in Viet Nam, *New York Times*, December 1, 1965 and November 30, 1966.

tributed "V dot-dot-dot-dash" pins in the lobbies of motion picture theaters showing the film "Sergeant York." Airplanes flew over cities dropping "V" balloons, and local chapters asked symphony orchestras to play Beethoven's Fifth Symphony, with its recurrent theme—bom-bom-bom-BOOM. Buttons, car stickers, and wall placards bearing various interpretations of the "V" symbol were sold in stores and dispensed in factories, settlement houses, and youth groups. Concurrently with all the hoopla, newspaper ads bearing the "V" ensign depicted on-marching stormtroopers and bore the plea: "DON'T wait for the whites of their eyes, Mr. Congressman." [80] In speeches on the "Victory" theme, Wendell Willkie called to his countrymen, "We cannot achieve that goal [world peace and plenty] with words. We can achieve it only by *action* . . ." [81] Rex Stout declared, "Our country is going to fight a war. That is horrible. Will it be more or less horrible? More or less disastrous? More or less costly? More or less bloody? That depends on the speed and decision with which our country acts. We are the country. It is up to us." [82]

The Warhawks presented their reasons for "stopping Hitler now" in handbills or pamphlets entitled "Adolf Hitler versus the United States" or "Hitler Speaks about the USA." By citing pertinent passages from his speeches or writings, these sought to illustrate Hitler's interest in the Western hemisphere and his desire to conquer the United States. Most of the "Stop Hitler Now" material, however, concentrated simply on stimulating an emotional response—anger, indignation, or hatred. A series of pictorial advertisements cried, "Rise Up, America—Smash Hitler!" These showed Hitler forcing American submission ("Repeat after me, Yank: Adolf Hitler Hallowed be Thy Name . . .") or deriding American life ("American Women are No Good!"). Some pamphlets told in unsparing detail the story of the Ge-

80. FFF news releases, July 23, 24, 28, 30, 1941, and August 4, 1941; 'V-Campaign: Designation of Responsibility"; Bell to Elmer Davis, July 30, 1941; Roger Kellogg, "Magical V," sheet music; Reprint from *New York Post*, July, 1941, FFF MSS.

81. 'Talk by Wendell Willkie at Mass Meeting by All-Southern California Committee at Hollywood Bowl," July 23, 1941, reprint, FFF MSS.

82. Rex Stout, "Radio Address over WMCA," August 1, 1941, FFF MSS.

stapo, "the Nazi scourge in Germany, the conquered countries and the United States." Others, even more grisly, bore actual photographs of the hangings and firing squads which had followed the Nazi wave across Europe.

As the Nazis forced the Soviets back before Moscow and the British eastward across North Africa, leading Warhawk speakers hammered away at the need to act *now* to stop Hitler.[83] Ernest Hopkins, for instance, asked a rally in Darien, Connecticut, "Shall we carry the war to Hitler or shall we wait upon Hitler's convenience as to where and how he shall bring the war to us?"[84]

Recognizing that the human mind is capable of only a limited amount of unrelieved seriousness, the Warhawks made attempts to lighten their fare. A former warden of Sing Sing prison declared Hitler "a criminal type" in a nationwide broadcast, and the Fight For Freedom printed "Wanted Dead or Alive" handbills bearing the description, record, and photographs of the Nazi leader. At World Series time the Fight For Freedom distributed scorecards with the "Berlin Lineup"—"Fats" Goering, "Spider" Goebbels, "Lefty" Laval, "Heel" Hitler. The fan was asked if he wanted this team to win. If not, he was enjoined to "Beat the Hell out of Hitler."[85]

The Warhawks also used the "show" or "convention" to obtain publicity, raise funds, and increase membership. In August the Fight For Freedom organized a Theater, Radio, and Arts Division under the leadership of Mac Kriendler, Helen Hayes, and Burgess Meredith. This unit set to work immediately on the format of a road show designed to display as many popular interventionist entertainers as possible, and, of course, attract attention to the issue of American belligerency. On October 5 they presented the "Fun to Be Free" show to an audience of seventeen thousand in New York's Madison Square Garden.

83. "Adolf Hitler versus the United States of America"; "Hitler Speaks about the U.S.A."; "Rise Up America" folder; FFF news release, November 1, 1941; "Wanted for Murder: Adolf Hitler"; 'The Berlin Bullies," FFF MSS.

84. Ernest M. Hopkins, "Address at Darien, Connecticut Rally of the Fight For Freedom," November 18, 1941, FFF MSS.

85. "The Berlin Line-up," FFF MSS.

Later the show traveled to Washington, St. Louis, and Philadelphia.[86]

The performance opened with a patriotic musical revue written by Irving Berlin and narrated by Lynn Fontanne. After welcoming statements by Chairmen Meredith and Hayes came a "pageant" written by Ben Hecht and Charles MacArthur, with music by Kurt Weill. Narrated by Meredith, Tallulah Bankhead, and Claude Rains, it consisted of dialogue between America's war leaders from Patrick Henry and George Washington to Woodrow Wilson and Franklin Roosevelt, and culminated in a mock Axis invasion of the arena by hundreds of toy parachutists dropped from the catwalks high above. After an intermission, Billy Rose presented Jack Benny, Eddy Duchin, Bill Robinson, and others in a variety show; and the honored guests—Willkie, La Guardia, William Knudsen, and Herbert Agar—spoke briefly. At the end of four hours the audience departed with a souvenir brochure including Walt Disney cartoons and a Fight For Freedom statement demanding an immediate declaration of war on Germany.[87]

Also in the fall, the Warhawks believed their regional organization had progressed to the point that a national convention would be worthwhile. This convention took the form of a Fight For Freedom "Continental Congress" held in Washington on October 9 and 10. This gathering was intended less to entertain or raise money than to attract nationwide publicity, coordinate the efforts of local FFF chapters, and exert pressure on Congress. On the first morning all the female delegates walked the two blocks from their hotel to the White House where, by previous arrangement, Mrs. Roosevelt received them in a brief ceremony. In the afternoon and evening the delegates listened to the oratory of Bishop Hobson, Herbert Agar, Allen Dulles, Senators Carter Glass and Lister Hill, and others.

The following morning the delegates descended upon the offices of their senators and congressmen to urge repeal of the Neutrality Act—a subject on which Roosevelt had sent the Congress a special message the previous day. At noon all gathered in

86. FFF news release, August 21, 1941; Michael Straight to Bell, September 18, 1941, FFF MSS; *New York Times*, October 6, 1941.

87. "Fun to Be Free Program," October 5, 1941, FFF MSS.

Constitutional Plaza in front of the Capitol to pay symbolic tribute to the Goddess of Freedom atop the dome and listen to the words of Dr. Frank Kingdon of the New York FFF-CDA and Max Singer, National Commander of the Veterans of Foreign Wars.[88] The cascade of verbiage ended in the afternoon with a nationwide radio speech by Agar and the unanimous adoption of several resolutions including this one:

"LET IT BE THE SENSE OF THIS CONGRESS THAT WE DECLARE WAR ON NAZI GERMANY." [89]

* * * * * *

The tactics of the Fight For Freedom were in part the techniques of the Century Group applied to a larger organization. Attempts to reach administration officials through influential friends and private suggestions on policy continued, although on a diminished scale. Petitions and letter-writing campaigns were now based on mass public appeals rather than discreet personal solicitations from the Group members to a few of their friends. The Fight For Freedom leaders retained the Group's technique of emphasizing loyalty to the President while constantly insisting on more action from him, but they enlarged it for use on a number of new issues and dramatized it by buying numerous newspaper ads and sponsoring administration speakers.

More significant, because they seem indicative of the Warhawks' response to the special circumstances of 1941, were the techniques that were new or greatly transformed. These circumstances were the Warhawks' own conversion into a nationwide public organization, the gradual deterioration of the world situation (relieved only temporarily by the German attack on Russia), increasing United States involvement, and the American public's continued resistance to going to war. The need to engage support on a national scale and among diverse classes of people impelled the Warhawks to simplify their appeals, sloganize issues, and portray the differences between themselves and

88. "Continental Congress List"; "Program—Continental Congress for Freedom," October 9–10, 1941; Bell to Eleanor Roosevelt, telegram, September 30, 1941; FFF news releases, October 3, 8, 1941, FFF MSS.

89. "Resolutions"; "Minutes," October 10, 1941, FFF MSS.

the isolationists as matters of white and black. Because they were now a national pressure group urging action on an issue which affected every citizen, they felt a need to claim majority support —not just for the intermediate steps on which favorable public attitudes existed but on the paramount issue of war as well. (See following chapter on the issues.)

Taken together, the heightened world crisis and the inflexibility of public opinion on the issue of outright belligerency were a source of great frustration to the Warhawks. They were driven to the conclusion that sophisticated discussions of American geopolitical interests and even appeals to the American sense of mission and to religious convictions were not capable of quickly moving public attitudes any further. Hence they turned to tactics which, for men raised to the Establishment standards of fair play and common decency, were a last resort—personal vilification of opponents and arousing the baser emotions of fear, anger, and hatred. The new tone was quite removed from the discreet and gentlemanly manner in which the Century Group had begun a year before.

IX. Fighting for Freedom: Issues

The Fight For Freedom's main purposes dictated its positions on the major foreign policy issues of 1941. The Committee interpreted each major event or incident as a further reason for an immediate declaration of war or, at the very least, as proof of the need for ever-increasing gradual participation. The Fight For Freedom and the Committee to Defend America (which was moving closer to interventionism) urged government action and public support for all steps which would assist those who fought Hitler, and the FFF seized every opportunity to simplify the global situation for public comprehension by characterizing each national leader or government as hero or villain. In 1941 the Warhawks confronted a series of important issues: (1) the war in the Atlantic, (2) aid to Russia, (3) relations with the "satellite" Axis powers—Finland, Vichy, and Japan, and (4) declaring war on Germany.[1] We will attempt some estimates of the War-

1. Omitted here is the FFF's peripheral interest in military training and Selective Service extension. When a half dozen letters from draftees complaining about bad conditions and morale in training camps reached FFF headquarters in June and July, the FFF quickly forwarded them to Stimson and Mrs. Roosevelt. Robert Allen saw Stimson and suggested that the Secretary send Warhawk speakers to the camps to explain the war and

hawks' influence on official policies and public attitudes toward these issues.

At the same time the Fight For Freedom was coming into being, the Roosevelt administration was adopting new policies in the Atlantic. In March the President promised all aid necessary for a British victory, and in April he placed Greenland and all the waters west of 26° West longitude under the protection of United States naval patrol. Unknown to the public, he directed naval vessels to trail any Axis units they encountered and report their positions to the British. Because of their preoccupation with their new project, the Warhawks, though confidentially informed of these decisions, played no part in them.[2]

The question of convoying Lend-Lease supplies to Britain —on either American or British ships—also came to a head at this time. Throughout the Lend-Lease debate congressional anti-interventionists had protested that the next step after lending supplies would be seeing that those supplies were safely delivered. This, they argued, would quickly involve American merchantmen or escort vessels in armed clashes and, thereby, the

raise morale—an idea adopted, but only after Pearl Harbor. In August the Committee attacked publicly the "scenario" for National Guard war games for glorifying the role of the fascistic "Almat aggressor" army. However, for the most part the FFF felt that military training matters were best left to the acknowledged expert in the field, Grenville Clark, who, although an FFF sponsor, channeled most of his ideas through the Military Training Camps Association and through an intensive private correspondence with Stimson.

The Committee did rouse itself to slightly greater exertions when the question of extending the term of service of soldiers drafted under the 1940 Selective Service Law came before Congress in early August. The issue was an important one since, if service were not extended, the fledgling army would have been disbanded; but passage did not seem in doubt until a few days before the House vote. *The Washington Post,* for instance, predicted passage by a two-to-one margin in the Senate. Therefore, the FFF contented itself with a low-key letter-writing campaign (it claimed something over 10,000 letters), a clergymen's petition, and several ads in Washington papers announcing, "Mr. Congressman, this is from the folks back home," and insisting that the new army not be dismantled. When the Senate passed extension by 40 to 35 and the House by only 202 to 201, there must have been some recriminations (unrecorded, unfortunately) among the Warhawks about the Committee's relative lack of attention to this issue.

2. William L. Langer and S. Everett Gleason, *The Undeclared War* (New York, 1953), pp. 425–46; author's interview with Cusick.

United States in the war. Immediately after the passage of Lend-Lease, the Committee to Defend America, impressed by the worsening British shipping losses in the North Atlantic, announced its support for convoys. Although in the midst of organizing the Fight For Freedom, the Century Group began circulating a petition (among ordinary citizens as well as "influentials") which demanded the use of American merchant vessels, protected by American naval vessels, both manned by American crews. By March 31 a list of several hundred names had accumulated, and the petition was released to the press.[3]

The pro-convoy activity created a stir—but the wrong kind. Senator Tobey and Congressman Harry Sauthoff of Wisconsin introduced a joint resolution in Congress prohibiting the use of both American merchantmen and American naval vessels in supply convoys. Anti-interventionists in Congress rallied to Tobey and Sauthoff. The President, who had been discussing the possibility of convoys with his advisors, dreaded just such a resolution. He knew that the polls showed that the public still opposed (50 per cent to 41 per cent) convoying, and he feared that a congressional wrangle might crystallize attitudes and hinder eventual acceptance of convoys. Through Thomas Lamont he passed word to Eichelberger "not to wave the red flag of immediate convoy," and someone else, possibly Robert Sherwood or Steve Early, relayed this information to the embryo Fight For Freedom.[4]

The upshot of all this was that the Tobey resolution kept Roosevelt from convoying for the moment. Roosevelt successfully prevented the resolution's passage, and the Committee to Defend America and the Fight For Freedom de-emphasized their demands for convoys until early July. Then a change in the polls and the involvement of Hitler in Russia seemed to make convoys a "safer" issue. Even then, however, convoying failed to reassume a central position in interventionist statements about the Atlantic.

The de-emphasis of agitation about the Atlantic war

3. *Ibid.*, pp. 259–84; "Convoy Petition List," March 30, 1941; "Petition to Congress," April 1, 1941, FFF MSS.

4. Thomas Lamont to Eichelberger, April 8, 1941, President's Secretary's File 81, Roosevelt Papers.

ended with the Nazi invasion of Russia and the sinking in the South Atlantic of the S.S. *Robin Moor,* an unarmed American freighter with a non-contraband cargo. The *Robin Moor* attack served the Fight For Freedom as a springboard for three new demands which became its "summer program": (1) shooting on sight, (2) repeal of the Neutrality Act, and (3) occupation of *all* the strategic islands in the Atlantic. Its spokesmen emphasized that the attack on an "innocent cargo ship" demonstrated the "futility" of the Neutrality laws and the need to protect and arm American merchant ships. They cited the place of the attack as evidence that the Axis might be operating out of Dakar or preparing for a move on the Azores or Cape Verde Islands.[5]

The attack on Russia, aside from raising the troublesome issue of aiding the Reds, seemed to the Atlantic-oriented Warhawks to be an unusual opportunity. Within four days of news of the Nazi move east, the Fight For Freedom and the Committee to Defend America were urging the President to "clear the Atlantic" of Nazi raiders by employing all American naval and air forces available. On June 26 the national FFF Committee ran a full-page ad in the *New York Herald Tribune* declaring:

> EVERY DAY COUNTS, MR. PRESIDENT
>
> No one knows how long Russian resistance may last. But we do know that while it lasts we have our great opportunity. No one knows how long Hitler's back will be turned on the West. But we do know that every moment in which he is preoccupied with fighting his former fellow-gangster is a precious moment for us.
>
> Now is the time to clean up the Atlantic and to establish ourselves in the strategic positions from which we can keep control of the Atlantic no matter what may later happen in Europe.
>
> Now is the time to throw the full weight of our Navy and Air Force into the battle.[6]

A week later the Committee to Defend America took a similar ad in the *Herald Tribune* and other papers to say: "Okay, Mr. President. Go Ahead, Clear the Atlantic," and to urge shooting

5. FFF news release, July 7, 1941, FFF MSS.
6. *New York Herald Tribune,* June 26, 1941.

on sight, occupying "necessary" bases in the Atlantic and Pacific, and convoying. Consistent with the Warhawk intent to get America into the war, both organizations claimed that the *Robin Moor* sinking was ample motivation and the Russian invasion a favorable opportunity for the United States to begin active hostilities.[7]

Throughout the summer, interventionist speeches, ads, and news releases pleaded for convoys, shooting-on-sight, occupation of strategic islands, and repeal of the Neutrality Act. A cursory reading of the events from July through September suggests that they very largely got their way. In early July American troops assumed responsibility for the occupation of Iceland. By the end of August the United States Navy was convoying American and British ships as far as Iceland. Two weeks later Roosevelt had not only announced adoption of a shoot-on-sight policy, but his intention to seek repeal or revision of the Neutrality Act was also widely reported in the press.[8]

While many of the things the Warhawks wanted to see happen did in fact occur, their agitation was hardly the immediate reason for the changes. The occupation of *Iceland* was not the subject of intensive Fight For Freedom and Committee to Defend America campaigns but was mentioned only occasionally prior to its actual occurrence. It was of co-equal importance in the Warhawk demands with establishing control over the Canaries, Azores, Cape Verdes, St. Pierre, and Miquelon. Also, the Iceland expedition was *not* a response to favorable opinion poll results, since the first sampling on the subject was taken *after* the event. Rather, it was the result of Churchill's plea to Roosevelt that the British occupation troops in Iceland were needed desperately elsewhere. While it is true the Warhawks celebrated this step as a "bold, forthrightly action" which clarified the issues, nothing in their literature, private papers, or recollections suggests that they had a special part in the episode. The administration's consideration and rejection (for political reasons) of operations against Spain's Canaries, Portugal's Azores and Cape

7. *Ibid.*, July 3, 1941.

8. Langer and Gleason, *The Undeclared War,* pp. 575–80, 665; *New York Times,* September 12, 1941.

Verdes, and Vichy's St. Pierre and Miquelon further emphasized the Warhawks' lack of influence on "occupation" policy.[9]

Similarly, many factors unrelated to the Warhawks' exertions contributed to Roosevelt's decision in August to convoy all ships to Iceland and then (after Neutrality repeal) to Britain. Not the least among them was his personal desire—probably since December, 1940—to do so. By the summer of 1941 his most trusted advisors—Hopkins, Stimson, Knox, Morgenthau, and Harriman—had been vigorously urging such action for several months. The British Prime Minister had pleaded for increased American naval assistance during the Battle of the Atlantic in the spring and insisted during the summer that the new responsibility of convoying Lend-Lease supplies to northern Russia was straining his naval and shipping resources beyond their limit.[10]

Most probably the decisive factor was the shift in public opinion reflected in polls taken after the failure of the Tobey resolution. By mid-June the 41 per cent in favor of convoys had jumped to 55; and the 50 per cent against had fallen to 38. This change should not be attributed directly to Warhawk agitation, since they had steered away from the convoying issue after the warning from the White House. Attitudes were probably galvanized by continuing British reverses in the Middle East, the attention the *Bismarck* drama focused on British problems in the Atlantic, anger at the *Robin Moor* attack, and Roosevelt's enunciation of an "unlimited national emergency." The Warhawks exerted an impact only in a limited and indirect way. Their speeches and rallies contributed to the attention these events were receiving through the regular news media and to the general impression of public willingness to take new steps.[11]

9. "Gallup and Fortune Polls," *Public Opinion Quarterly*, V (Winter, 1941), 686; Langer and Gleason, *The Undeclared War*, pp. 587–89; FFF news releases, June 13 and 14, 1941, FFF MSS.

10. John Morton Blum, *From the Morgenthau Diaries: Years of Urgency, 1938–1941* (Boston, 1965), p. 251; Robert E. Sherwood, *Roosevelt and Hopkins: An Intimate History* (New York, 1948), pp. 276–77; Working File 1, Harriman Papers.

11. "Gallup and Fortune Polls, "*Public Opinion Quarterly*, V (Fall, 1941), 485; Winston S. Churchill, *The Second World War: The Grand Alliance* (Boston, 1950), pp. 253–332.

Unlike convoying, shooting-on-sight was a key proposal of the "summer program" advocated by the Fight For Freedom and the Committee to Defend America. The Fight For Freedom widely quoted Senator Glass' assertion that "we ought to . . . shoot hell out of every U-boat," and the Committee to Defend America explained in more restrained tones that supplying meant delivering supplies, delivering supplies meant escorting, and escorting meant shooting. Speakers, handbills, and news releases cited each clash between American and Axis vessels as further justification for a "shooting" policy, and they viewed each U-boat attack, whatever the circumstances, as part of Hitler's plan to "try to start something" or "test how far he can push us." [12]

It is debatable how much all of this effort actually affected the President's decision to adopt a shoot-on-sight policy. Certainly he was aware of the Warhawks' demands for shooting-on-sight, since Bell and Eichelberger sent copies of most of their ads and releases to White House aides. But the Warhawk agitation became irrelevant once Roosevelt had opted for convoy escorting. Then, a shooting policy—whether *de jure* or *de facto*—became unavoidable. Although the *Greer* was not actually escorting a convoy when attacked, a similar incident was probably inevitable once the United States Navy began shepherding British cargo ships. Roosevelt's wily interpretation of the *Greer* incident as "deliberate"—and not the Warhawks' summer-long demands—undoubtedly galvanized public opinion on shooting. Nevertheless, the Warhawks, through their prior agitation, surely provided much of the advance publicity for Roosevelt's September 11 speech; they "warmed up" the audience. The tactic they used in interpreting earlier isolated and probably unauthorized attacks as "deliberate" provocations dictated from Berlin, perhaps suggested to Roosevelt (by example only, however) the way to explain the *Greer* incident to the public.

Of all the issues involved in the Atlantic war, removing the Neutrality Act prohibitions on arming merchantmen and sailing to war zone ports received the most systematic and concentrated attention from the Warhawks. In part this was so

12. "What's Happening in the Fight For Freedom," August 12, 1941, FFF MSS; CDA news letters, July–September, 1941, Walter Batterson Papers, Sterling Library, Yale University.

because repeal or revision of a law depended on a decision by Congress, which was more susceptible to direct pressure from "back home" than were the men at State, War, Navy—or even the White House. Furthermore, by mid-September the Warhawks probably sensed that the coming Neutrality fight might well be the isolationists' last stand.

The campaign actually began well before, in July, at a time when the most recent authoritative polls showed only 30 per cent support for repeal. Desultory Fight For Freedom news releases echoed Senator Glass's statement that the Act had been "passed because a lot of people were afraid of Hitler" and that it was time to "tell him now that we are not afraid." Handbills depicting sinking ships and drowning American sailors proclaimed, "THE NAVY IS READY . . . take off our 'handcuffs' . . . give us a fighting chance." [13]

In late September, after the *Greer* and Roosevelt's shoot-on-sight speech, when the Chief Executive's intention to seek revision became well known, the Warhawk drive became more intensive. Bishop Hobson claimed that Lend-Lease had in fact already ended American neutrality, and he declared his Committee's aim to secure ten million signatures in favor of repeal. Fight For Freedom national headquarters mailed petitions to every member of the organization urging solicitation of at least ten signatures. Actually, by demanding out-right repeal the Warhawks (with their usual insistence on "clarifying" issues) were urging not only more than the administration thought politically possible but also more than the President probably wanted. He recognized that certain portions of the legislation (governing soliciting and collecting funds, munitions export control, and financial transactions) were desirable as they stood. This point was either lost on the Fight For Freedom or disregarded because it might complicate its appeals. Instead, the FFF repeatedly called for "complete repeal of our suicidal Neutrality Act." [14]

13. FFF news release, July 15; "Our Pals Were Killed . . ." FFF MSS. Partly because of financial and organization problems, the CDA was later and less vigorous in its drive for Neutrality repeal, CDA news letters, July–October, 1941, Batterson Papers.

14. Langer and Gleason, *The Undeclared War,* pp. 750–56; FFF news release, September 24, 1941, FFF MSS.

The results of this campaign seem relatively impressive. Sixteen hundred union executives and shop stewards pledged their support for repeal. Although the ten million petitions to Congress which Hobson predicted did not materialize, more than twenty-five thousand had been received at FFF headquarters by the time the House of Representatives voted on October 17. The reports of Fight For Freedom chapter heads on their local petition drives indicate that at least several hundred thousand signatures were sent directly to senators and congressmen. Of course, a simultaneous campaign by the America First Committee and other "keep-out-of-war" bodies (which declared Roosevelt was "asking Congress to issue an engraved drowning license to American seamen") may have had a neutralizing effect on the flood of repeal petitions.[15]

The Warhawks also worked to engage long-established organizations in the Neutrality battle. Through his own position in the American Legion, Ulric Bell cultivated the support of such key Legionnaires as Max Singer, the National Commander, and in mid-September the Legion's national convention adopted a resolution advocating Neutrality repeal and United States participation in the war.[16] Local FFF leaders also had considerable

15. "News of the Fight For Freedom," II, 7 (November, 1941); "Chapters" file, FFF MSS; Wayne S. Cole, *America First: The Battle Against Intervention, 1940–1941* (Madison, Wisc., 1953), pp. 162–66.

16. The annual national convention of the American Legion was held in Milwaukee, a center of pro-German and isolationist sentiment. Although individual Legion officials had been active for intervention early in 1941, Legion policy had traditionally opposed involvement in "another foreign adventure." In an effort to plumb the effect of the surroundings on the attitudes of the Legionnaires and to see if there had been a change in the policy of this influential organization, the Fight For Freedom employed Market Analysts, Inc.

The findings of their survey were taken by the Warhawks as proof that interventionism was growing among the common people of the United States and were publicized heavily in the newspapers of the Midwest. Of those queried 40.8 per cent felt the "United States ought to get into this war now," a figure nearly double that of contemporary Gallup polls; 74.7 per cent were sure "the United States will get into the fighting war before it is over"; and 67.8 per cent favored breaking off diplomatic relations with Germany and Italy.

A Milwaukee America First rally timed to coincide with the convention was notable for the general absence of visiting Legionnaires, and the Legion convention responded warmly to speeches of such Roosevelt supporters and interventionists as Secretary Knox, Mayor La Guardia, Louis

success in inducing chapters of the League of Women Voters, the Veterans of Foreign Wars, and the Farm Bureau Federation to take public positions in favor of revision or repeal and to apply pressure to their elected representatives.[17] Although the Warhawk petition campaign never approached the number of signatures its leaders had projected, the pressure the FFF and its allies applied upon doubtful congressmen—if not counterbalanced by equal isolationist efforts—probably had some effect.

There is no question that congressional and public attitudes toward the Neutrality Act changed during the Warhawks' drive. In September polls showed that the public was narrowly in favor of revision (46 per cent for, 40 per cent against, with 14 per cent undecided). By the time revision passed in early November, nearly two out of three citizens (61 to 31, with 8 per cent undecided) favored revision. Similarly, congressional attitudes changed from early October, when an informal poll of senators revealed only thirty-five in favor of arming merchantmen, to November 7, when fifty voted against thirty-seven to pass revisions permitting not only the arming of merchantmen but also the entry of American cargo vessels into war zones.[18]

Realism demands that we note once again that the change of views was not attributable to the Fight For Freedom and its allies alone—although their efforts probably influenced this more than any other "Atlantic" decision. First of all, revision was an "administration bill," and Roosevelt and his legislative lieutenants supported it with all their talents for cajolery and timing. Secondly, after shooting-on-sight began, changes in the Neutrality Law seemed even to some hitherto isolationists to be a natural and obvious self-defensive step. Finally, events in the Atlantic helped to change some minds. The fact that the destroyer U.S.S. *Kearny* was torpedoed with loss of life on the night of October

---

Johnson, and Paul McNutt. Furthermore, the convention adopted resolutions declaring "the defeat of Hitler and all he stands for" as the main national objective. "We insist," the Legionnaires concluded, "upon being prepared to do the fighting outside the United States."

17. See "Veterans of Foreign Wars" folder, "LWV" folder, "American Farm Bureau Federation" folder, FFF MSS; also see the correspondence from chapters of these groups in McNary Papers.

18. "Gallup and Fortune Polls," *Public Opinion Quarterly,* VI (Spring, 1942), 161. Langer and Gleason, *The Undeclared War,* p. 753.

16–17 undoubtedly contributed to the unexpectedly large majority by which revision passed in the House of Representatives the following day.[19] Similarly, the sinking of the destroyer U.S.S. *Reuben James* on October 30 with the loss of one hundred lives could not help but arouse sentiments which influenced the senators' votes on November 7. However hard the Warhawks worked and however much they propagandized such incidents, probably the events themselves—much more than propaganda—were responsible for the changes of attitude in the public and in Congress.

* * * * * *

Just as the Warhawks began their summer drive for action in the Atlantic a new and perplexing issue suddenly confronted them. On Sunday afternoon, June 22, Herbert Agar, Robert Sherwood, Dorothy Parker, and the Reverend Adam Clayton Powell, Sr., addressed a Harlem Fight For Freedom rally at the Golden Gate Ballroom, Lenox Avenue and 142nd Street. As they approached the hall, pickets bearing Communist-inspired placards denouncing "imperialist warmongering" berated them. However, after the meeting was over, Herbert Agar noticed that the demonstrators, who usually remained to accost the crowd as it left, were nowhere in sight. While the rally was in progress, word had reached the picketers that Hitler had attacked Russia.[20]

The invasion of the Soviet Union complicated considerably the black-and-white distinctions the Warhawks had been trying so hard to draw between the United States' adversaries and her friends. Russia was the land of atheism, purges, collectivization, and the OGPU. She was the despoiler of Finland, Poland, Lithuania, Latvia, and Estonia. Moscow remained the font of left-wing subversion and revolution throughout the world

19. Indicative of the temporary but significant impact of the *Kearny* attack was the fact that the House vote on the Senate-House compromise on repeal on November 13 was only 212 to 194, while the October 17 vote had been 259 to 138; Langer and Gleason, *The Undeclared War,* pp. 756–58.

20. FFF news release, June 22, 1941, FFF MSS.

—including the United States. Many Christians—especially Catholics—had long regarded communism as their traditional foe. Four months after the Russians were forced into the anti-Hitler coalition, two out of every three Americans still regarded the Soviet government as "equally as bad" or only "slightly better" than the Nazi regime. Despite this, at the outbreak of hostilities in Russia, polls indicated that most Americans (74 per cent of Protestants and 65 per cent of Catholics) recognized Germany to be the greater danger and desired a Russian victory. At the same time more than twice as many expected a Nazi victory as believed the Red Army would triumph. What should be the United States' policy toward Stalin now? Here, indeed, was a dilemma for an organization committed not only to the destruction of nazism but opposed to repression and totalitarianism in general.[21]

The Fight For Freedom leadership immediately recognized the danger of the new situation for their organization. They themselves had long capitalized on the fact that Fascists and Communists had identified themselves with America First. Now, it appeared, the Fight For Freedom, too, would have unwelcomed and disreputable allies. Therefore, on the day the Germans moved east, Robert Spivack, the Fight For Freedom publicity director, urged Ulric Bell to make an immediate "statement for the record to the effect that we repudiate in advance any Communist support for the Fight For Freedom."[22] Bell agreed and on the morning of June 23 issued a press release which said:

In order to spike at the outset any whispering campaign which might be started by the America First Committee or other appeasement groups, Fight For Freedom, Inc. desires to make clear its attitude regarding the Communists and the Communist Party of the United States. We repudiate here and now any support which comes from members of the Communist party or their sympathizers.

. . . When we have succeeded in crushing Hitler's Germany

21. "Gallup and Fortune Polls," *Public Opinion Quarterly,* V (Winter, 1941), 675; VI (Spring, 1942), 152.

22. Robert Spivack to Bell, undated memorandum, FFF MSS.

we do not expect the new world order to be patterned upon the models of the Nazi Reich or Soviet Russia. This is a war to extend democracy, not to limit it.[23]

Accepting the general assumption that Soviet resistance would only last a matter of weeks, the leaders of both the Fight For Freedom and the Committee to Defend America adopted the position that the opportunity had come to strike Hitler at a time when his attention was elsewhere. Therefore, they immediately implored the government to act in the period before Russian resistance was broken by "clearing the Atlantic" of U-boats. On the day after the Nazis crossed the Russian frontier the national FFF Committee ran an advertisement in *The New York Times,* the substance of which was reprinted in ads sponsored by local committees in St. Louis, New Orleans, Chicago, San Francisco, and elsewhere. The new Nazi action was "our supreme danger and our supreme opportunity," the *Times* ad declared:

> The danger is that the Quislings and Nazi stooges in this country will now try to lull us with the bedtime story that Hitler is saving the world from Communism, which all Americans abhor. The danger is that we may delay while Hitler secures his rear for the final assault upon Great Britain and the Western Hemisphere. . . .
>
> But the Russo-German conflict also presents a supreme opportunity. While Russian resistance lasts, Japan, vulnerable as she is to attack from Siberian bases, will scarcely cast her lot with the Axis.
>
> Our hands are freer than they have been since the war started to use our naval strength in the Atlantic.
>
> Now is the time for us to act in clearing the Atlantic Ocean of Nazi raiders where they might secure possible jumping-off places for attack on this Hemisphere.[24]

Their position received favorable comment in the internationalist press. Columnists who frequently shared the Warhawk viewpoint—Dorothy Thompson, Frank Kent (a "Summons" signer), Walter Lippmann, and Mark Sullivan—advocated immediate naval action in the Atlantic. And the Warhawks' position was also adopted by such influential papers as *The New*

23. FFF news release, June 23, 1941, FFF MSS.
24. *New York Times,* June 23, 1941.

York Times, Christian Science Monitor, Richmond Times-Dispatch, and *Omaha Evening World Herald.*[25]

However, within a few hours after the news of the German invasion of Russia, matters grew more complicated for the Warhawks. Their friends at the British Information Service asked Bell and Cusick to be present in their office when they received an important telephone call from London. The caller informed them that Churchill would announce his support for and alliance with the Soviets the following day. Bell passed this information on to Robert Sherwood at the White House, and when Roosevelt spoke on June 24, he followed Churchill's lead, telling the press that the United States was "going to give all the aid we possibly can to Russia." [26]

The Warhawks saw the danger in this issue. Advocacy of aid to the Soviet Union would inevitably draw the Fight For Freedom closer to the American Communists and might repel some present or potential adherents. Some interventionists would see material assistance to the Soviets as compromising the morality of their cause. Others would argue that any arms the United States gave Stalin would end up in Hitler's hands when the Russians were crushed or when Moscow, as in 1939, made another cynical bargain with Berlin.

The national leaders of the Fight For Freedom decided that their body had to support the President on this issue, regardless of the side-effects on their organization. They accepted as their own Roosevelt's logic that the greater danger must be met first and that "any rallying of the forces opposing Hitlerism, from whatever source these forces may spring, will hasten the eventual downfall of the present German leaders, and will therefore redound to the benefit of our own security." Although Fight For Freedom speakers tended to refer to *Russia* rather than the Soviet Union or the Union of Soviet Socialist Republics, they engaged in no whitewash of Stalin's regime. Typical of Warhawk utterances on the subject was the speech of Frederick Umhey, executive secretary of the International Ladies Garment Workers Union, at a New York rally on July 17:

25. Langer and Gleason, *The Undeclared War,* pp. 543–44.
26. *New York Times,* June 24, 1941; author's interview with Cusick.

> The destruction of Hitlerism is and will continue to be the cause to which we dedicate ourselves. This aim can best be served by extending unlimited aid to all the forces now allied together in fighting the Nazi hordes. The extension of aid to Russia while she is engaged in this struggle does not mean that we accept the Communist philosophy any more than our aid to Britain implies the endorsement of her colonial policy. Nor does it mean that we must make allowances [alliances?] with the American Communists. They are far too nimble line-changers to trust them to lead the fight for democracy.[27]

It soon became clear that most interventionist leaders were quite uncomfortable with the Russian aid issue. The Committee to Defend America preferred at all times to stress the "clearing of the Atlantic" more than the "aid" theme, and Fight For Freedom national headquarters, after establishing its position in support of the President, relegated the "aid" issue to the shadows in early August. Furthermore, the FFF's clipping albums show that most of its local chapters gave relatively little attention to this unpalatable matter in their advertisements and news releases.

The interventionists worked assiduously to disassociate themselves from Communist efforts to arouse sympathy and support for Moscow through "front" organizations. On July 1 the New York chapters of the Fight For Freedom and the Committee to Defend America joined with the Friends of Democracy, and the Legion for American Unity to denounce such a front—the American Council on Soviet Relations—as "the voice of Stalin in America. We are disgusted," their joint declaration said, "with the performance of American Communists, who change their line again and again, whenever the foreign policy of the Soviet Government requires a new line. . . . We are NOT for Stalin—we are against Hitler."[28] When Bell was approached by representatives of a suspiciously new "Committee for Action to Smash Hitler," he replied sharply: "Unfortunately, since your Committee did not awaken to the realization of the Hitler threat until

27. Langer and Gleason, *The Undeclared War,* p. 541; Frederick F. Umhey, "Address Delivered at 'Stop Hitler' Rally, Manhattan Center," July 17, 1941, FFF MSS.

28. FFF news release July 1, 1941, FFF MSS.

June 29, we can hardly rely on your sincerity. Therefore, there will be no endorsement from Fight For Freedom, Inc., nor any delegate attending your meeting. . . ."[29] Similarly, Courtenay Barber, Jr., the head of Fight For Freedom in Chicago, denounced "an all-Chicago anti-Hitler" conference because the woman who organized it had been a member of the communistic American Peace Mobilization until June 22.[30]

It was probably inevitable that, despite their efforts to keep a clean house, the Warhawks would be attacked by isolationists as "Communist-infiltrated"—and that some of the allegations would be true. The apparently baseless attack on the Chicago FFF's Albert Parry has already been mentioned. Some instances of left-wing infiltration, however, are indicated by the correspondence of the Fight For Freedom itself. In September Wayne Johnson informed Bell that the secretary of the District of Columbia chapter was "an out and out Red." In October Spivack warned that the Boston chapter was using members of the American Student Union, a Marxist body, for picketing. Although the Boston problem was solved, the Washington situation apparently was not, for on December 6 another aide wrote Bell that "the Washington chapter of FFF is fast acquiring the reputation of being CP controlled."[31]

The Russian aid issue again came to the forefront in October, when Averell Harriman and Lord Beaverbrook went to Moscow to negotiate a Lend-Lease agreement with the Soviets, and the administration asked Congress to increase Lend-Lease appropriations preparatory to supplying Russia.[32] Regardless of its distaste for Bolshevism, the public was willing to work with

29. Bell to Paul Allen, August 13, 1941, FFF MSS.

30. Chicago FFF news release, August 7, 1941, FFF MSS. It is interesting to note that fifteen years later membership in or employment by the Fight for Freedom *before* June 22, 1941, was still regarded by the Federal Bureau of Investigation as a favorable recommendation for security clearance; author's interview with Cusick.

31. Wayne Johnson to Bell, September 3, 1941; Spivack to Liddon Graham, October 28, 1941; Rosenfield to Bell, December 6, 1941, FFF MSS.

32. Both steps resulted from Hopkins' trip to Moscow in July during which he became convinced that the Russians could hold out at least until winter and were, therefore, a good risk; Sherwood, *Roosevelt and Hopkins,* pp. 333–45.

Russia to defeat Hitler. A *Fortune* magazine poll in October showed that 21.9 per cent of people were willing to accept Russia as "a full partner . . . in the fight against Hitler" and another 51.4 per cent favored "giving her some help if we think it will help beat Hitler." The most outspoken opponents of aid were a decreasing minority of congressional isolationists, the America First Committee, and some important individuals of the Roman Catholic faith, including Senator David I. Walsh of Massachusetts and Archbishop Francis Bookman of Dubuque.[33]

The Fight For Freedom leaders noted that earlier polls had revealed that Catholic attitudes "lagged" some 10 per cent behind the rest of the public with respect to the Soviet Union. Aware that nearly three of every four Americans accepted the idea of aiding Russia, and hoping to minimize the criticism they might receive as "pro-Communistic," the Warhawks restricted their renewed appeals for Russian aid to Americans of the Catholic faith.[34]

The very nature and timing of this effort is notable, since most of it occurred too late to have any effect on the congressional decision on aid to Russia. The battle for Catholic public opinion had been going on throughout the summer into the fall.[35] But, with the exception of circulating speeches by Supreme Court Justice Frank Murphy and Dr. Francis E. McMahon of Notre Dame and two articles by William Agar and Michael Williams, the Fight For Freedom contributed relatively little to it.[36] Only in the last week of October did the Warhawks seriously begin to mobilize—with the intention of demonstrating widespread Catholic lay and clerical approval of two "pro-aid" statements. These were Archbishop (of Cincinnati) John T. Nicholas' pastoral letter differentiating between aid to Russia and collaboration with communism, and Bishop Joseph P. Henley's rebuttal

33. Raymond H. Dawson, *The Decision to Aid Russia, 1941* (Chapel Hill, N.C., 1959), pp. 230–34.

34. "Gallup and Fortune Polls," *Public Opinion Quarterly*, V, 675.

35. Dawson, *The Decision to Aid Russia*, pp. 185–94, 231–38, 258–69.

36. Reprints of "Don't Let Hitler Confuse You!" *Catholic Review*, June 27, 1941; William Agar article in *Louisville Courier-Journal*, October 7, 1941; "Dr. Francis E. McMahon, Address Delivered over Station WBYN, Brooklyn, New York," August 28, 1941, FFF MSS.

of the Catholic Laymen's Committee for Peace's claim that "Catholics are more than 90 per cent opposed to war." The Fight For Freedom issued its first releases on both subjects on October 30.

Actually, an amendment to the new Lend-Lease bill barring aid to Russia had been defeated in the House of Representatives by 162 to 21 on October 10, and by October 23 the bill itself had passed both Houses of Congress by better than 4-to-1 margins. Although the President did not formally declare the U.S.S.R. eligible for aid until five days after the FFF releases, they had little effect on his action, for Roosevelt had made up his mind in the first week of October.[37]

The Fight For Freedom's impact on public and official attitudes toward the Soviet Union was, therefore, uneven. Its immediate and forthright insistence on the necessity of "working with" the new opponent of the Nazis, without accommodating or apologizing for communism, established a position to which most internationalists quickly rallied. The FFF's early statements on this issue may have had some favorable effect on public opinion in certain areas, thereby making it a little easier for some congressmen to later vote for aid to Russia. The Committee's *direct* influence on the legislative decision to assist Russia, however, was comparatively inconsequential. Because the Warhawks were uncomfortable with the aid-to-Russia issue, once they had established a pro-aid stance they tended to turn away from the matter. Their efforts to demonstrate Catholic support for Russian Lend-Lease were mostly too late and too limited to significantly affect official deliberations.

* * * * * *

Russian belligerency compromised the "purity" of the anti-Hitler coalition. No longer could the Warhawks proclaim their cause to be an unblemished crusade. Despite this, they continued to insist on clear delineation between the forces of good and the forces of evil in their statements on United States relations with France, Japan, and Finland.

The Fight For Freedom Committee differed sharply with

37. Dawson, *The Decision to Aid Russia*, pp. 231–32, 267–89.

the administration's French policy. Throughout 1941 the government maintained diplomatic relations with Vichy and applied pressure for limited objectives by promising food and other supplies and by threatening retribution for Axis collaboration. The Warhawks blamed this "wishy-washy" attitude on the "appeasers" and "defeatists" in the State Department. They pointed out that, by supplying the Nazis with food and parachute silk, the Vichy government had chosen its side. It should, therefore, be treated as an enemy.

During the summer especially, the Fight For Freedom publicly demanded that the United States cease provisioning France and North Africa, withdraw recognition of Vichy, and recognize Charles de Gaulle's Free French government-in-exile. To advance these views, it formed a "French Advisory Committee" which included dramatist Henri Bernstein, Eve Curie (journalist and daughter of the Nobel Prize winner), editor Phillipe Barrés and Catholic writer Jacques Maritain. This Committee took the lead on all "French" issues, denouncing Pétain's "betrayal" of France and France's allies and echoing the Gaullist thesis that Pétain, Laval, and Darlan did not speak for the French people. On such special occasions as Bastille Day and Lafayette's birthday, the Fight For Freedom and its advisory committee appealed not only for recognition of the Free French but also for occupation of Vichy-held Martinique and St. Pierre and Miquelon. Fight For Freedom advertisements in eastern newspapers periodically insisted on recognition of de Gaulle and implored, "Let's Recognize Freedom *Now,* Mr. President." [38]

The Warhawks were aware of the dangers of some of the steps they advocated. They realized an American gesture at Martinique or Dakar might serve as the pretext for German occupation of French North Africa. They understood that if the United States cut off supplies or recognized de Gaulle, Vichy, out of pique or because of German pressure, might turn over the remnants of the French fleet to the Nazis. They believed, how-

38. "Just an Idea, Mr. President," in *The New York Times,* July 11, 1941; FFF news releases, July 1 and 14, 1941; "Lafayette, the Marne, and De Gaulle"; "Bastille Day Radio Program with Wendell Willkie and Helen Hayes," July 14, 1941, reprint from *The New York Times,* August 19, 1941, FFF MSS.

ever, that Vichy was so tainted by its Axis connections that any relationship with it (and the implied acceptance such contact connoted) would be an impermissible moral compromise. Their critics pointed out, of course, that this unbending attitude was inconsistent with the Fight For Freedom's acceptance of Russia. But the Warhawks persisted, secure in the knowledge that the polls showed that 58 per cent of the public thought Vichy was helping Hitler and that only 13 per cent regarded the Pétain-Laval government as truly neutral.[39]

For the President and the Secretary of State, however, the advantages of keeping France neutral overrode their moral repugnance. Not only did they continue to recognize the Pétain government and abjure occupying French territory in the Western hemisphere, but they also proceeded with limited provisioning of unoccupied France and French North Africa, using this activity as a means of insinuating American observers and establishing communications with French opponents to Vichy.[40]

The Warhawks' attitude toward the Finnish government differed only in degree. Intent on securing as much of a buffer as he could against Hitler, Stalin had attacked Finland in late November, 1939. The stout Finnish resistance aroused sympathetic admiration in the United States but little practical assistance. After inflicting heavy losses on the Soviets (on which pessimistic estimates of Russian ability to resist the Nazis in 1941 were largely to be based), the Finns fell back. When their Mannerheim defense line was breached, they sued for peace in March, 1940. The settlement gave the Russians the Finnish city of Viborg, a naval base at Hangoë, and over 16,000 square miles of Finnish land. In the summer of 1941, however, the Finns utilized the opportunity presented by the Russo-German conflict not only to regain the territory lost earlier but also to drive across the Soviet frontier.[41]

The reactions of the Warhawks and the administration

39. Spivack to Warburg, August 15, 1941; FFF news releases, August 6 and 13, 1941, FFF MSS; author's interview with Francis P. Miller.

40. Robert Murphy, *Diplomat Among Warriors* (Garden City, N.Y., 1964), pp. 49–95.

41. Langer and Gleason, *The Undeclared War*, pp. 547–51. Hostilities actually began with the Soviet bombing of Helsinki in retaliation for alleged use of Finnish airfields by the *Luftwaffe*.

were nearly identical. The position of both revealed that they were willing to follow with harsh logic their judgment that defeating Hitler overrode all other considerations. Minimizing Finland's well-founded fears of future Soviet behavior, the administration and the Fight For Freedom demanded that the Finns desist. Both took the view that Finland's continued belligerency was sapping Soviet capacity to halt Hitler, and that the defeat of nazism took precedence over all other considerations. While Secretary of State Hull privately warned the Finnish minister that his country now risked being considered an Axis enemy, Bishop Hobson publicly assailed the Finnish government "for leading their people into slavery" by signing "the duplicitous anti-Comintern pact." The Fight For Freedom claimed their letters to contributors to and sponsors of Finnish relief organizations induced many to withdraw their support of the Baltic nation, and Bishop Hobson sent personal messages of protest to Finnish President Risto Ryti and Minister Hjalmar Procopé. Hull's diplomatic pressures and the limited public appeal by the Warhawks had little effect on the Finnish government, and, on the day before Pearl Harbor, the British honored their alliance to Russia by declaring war on Finland.[42]

Partly because events in the Pacific intervened and partly because considerable public sympathy for Finland lingered on, the Warhawks did not attempt to arouse mass interest in the issue. As in the instance of Russian aid, most local Fight For Freedom committees avoided the matter, and whatever was said on this subject originated from the national headquarters. The Warhawks had to be careful of their own members' sensibilities; West Coast FFF organizer H. B. Elliston spoke for many when he declared, "My heart and my head are in conflict over Finland."[43]

The Warhawk attitude toward the Japanese was, perhaps, more remarkable considering the fact that it was from Japan that

42. FFF news releases, November 7 and 25, 1941; Bell to "Fifty Americans Who Are Friends of the Finnish People," November 6, 1941; "Persons Connected with Finnish Relief"; Hjalmar Procopé to FFF, November 21, 1941, FFF MSS.

43. Bell to A. Henry Mosle, December 2, 1941; H. B. Elliston to Spivack, November 5, 1941, FFF MSS; Langer and Gleason, *The Undeclared War,* pp. 826–35.

the war they wanted eventually came. The Committee to Defend America had commented in its "house organs" on Japanese behavior since the late spring and even made resistance to further Japanese expansion one of its principles for the summer and fall. However, Japan occupied a very secondary place in the activities of the Century Group and the Fight For Freedom until November, 1941. They despised the Japanese government as a member of the Axis but paid it little attention.[44]

This was partly because of the fact that the leaders of the Group and the Fight For Freedom—the Agars, Miller, Bell, and Hobson—were largely men of the Eastern Establishment. Their ties were with Britain and Europe, not Asia, and it was natural for them to look eastward across the Atlantic rather than westward to the Pacific. While isolationists were inclined to view America as not vitally related to either Asia or Europe, the Warhawks considered the United States and Europe organically linked. But they, too, tended to consider Asians too distant, alien, and backward to threaten directly America's security.

More important than their Eastern-ness was their implicit classification of Japan as a "second class" power, a conclusion rooted in their appraisal of the relative military strengths of the Axis partners. The Warhawks knew that Japan was a small over-populated island nation dependent on tenuous sea lanes not only for war material but also for the minimum resources for survival. Her modern but limited navy would be unable to protect those supply lines from a sustained Anglo-American attack. Her air force and army had demonstrated their limitations by their failure to destroy an ill-equipped and inefficient Chinese army. Furthermore, her industries and population were heavily concentrated and therefore most vulnerable to aerial bombardment.

By contrast, Germany, the primary threat, could draw upon the resources of an entire highly industrialized continent, and her lightning conquest of that continent testified to her military proficiency. Her brilliant scientists possessed the potential for creating new weapons of awesome range and destructiveness if given the time to do so. Furthermore, as the Warhawks

44. CDA news letters, FFF MSS; and Batterson Papers.

saw it, Germany represented not only a more serious military problem but also an insidious ideological danger. While the Japanese proposed the limited and transparent ideal of Asian "co-prosperity," the Nazis offered a fully articulated ideology of main force. The attractiveness of this ideology to many beyond the borders of the Third Reich—carefully cultivated by agents of Berlin—enhanced Nazi power.[45]

Because of these considerations the Warhawks publicly mentioned Japan quite infrequently—and when they did, they tended to view Japanese activities in an "Atlantic perspective." They frequently characterized Japanese expansionism as intended primarily to relieve the pressure on Germany. In July, when the Japanese moved into Indo-China, Bishop Hobson termed their action "Hitler's attempt to create a diversion in the Pacific while his Nazi raiders continue their efforts to take over the Atlantic sea lanes. . . ." In October John Balderston wrote a Fight For Freedom wire story which discussed the effects of Japanese naval control of Asian waters. Japanese hegemony, he declared, was hindering the European war effort by restricting American Lend-Lease shipments to Russia via Vladivostok.[46]

Indicative of the Fight For Freedom's lack of emphasis on the Pacific threat was the infrequency with which the Japanese were mentioned in its official organs. The Labor News Service discussed the Japanese only twice—once in June, referring to the "appeasement" implicit in permitting Japan to continue to obtain oil in the United States, and again in October, with a brief article on the Japanese use of forced Chinese labor. The news letter to chapters, published bi-weekly, mentioned the Japanese only once —when they invaded Indo-China in July, and the weekly "Main Street" clip sheet never did.[47]

All this is not to say that the Warhawks entirely ignored Asian affairs. The Fight For Freedom regularly received the

45. See, for example, Helen Hill Miller and Herbert Agar, *Beyond German Victory* (New York, 1940).

46. FFF news release, July 24, 1941; Balderston to Fight For Freedom, telegram, October 23, 1941, FFF MSS. The *Washington Post* ran a daily column at this time entitled "Hitler Rules Japan."

47. Labor News Service, June 20, 1941, and October 31, 1941; "What's Happening in the Fight For Freedom," news letter, July 26, 1941, FFF MSS.

communiqués of Chiang Kai-shek's Trans-Pacific News Service as well as the more incisive periodic appraisals of Robert Aura Smith, an independent Asian specialist. When some issue related to Japan became particularly inflamed, the Committee took a public position. For example, in June it denounced continued trade in vital materials with Japan and demanded an embargo on the export of oil and other strategic resources. Bishop Hobson said:

> During the last two or three weeks millions of barrels of oil have gone to Japan from Los Angeles and other West Coast ports—this in face of the fact that oil is needed in this country. Some of it has gone in American ships, which are desperately needed for our own national defense.
>
> It seems that . . . an embargo is necessary because certain oil companies take the attitude that they refuse to face the situation until the Government has acted. Several oil companies, be it said in their honor, have recognized the danger and refused to ship oil to Japan with tremendous losses financially to themselves. A government embargo seems at present to be the only way to control those companies which are shipping oil at the present moment, with a very dangerous threat to this country as a result.[48]

He was joined in this appeal by members of the Committee to Defend America, the Clearing House for Youth Groups, and other pro-democracy bodies.[49]

A month later, when the President ordered Japanese assets frozen (in effect ending all trade with Japan) in retaliation for their encroachment on Indo-China, Peter Cusick said, "This marks the end of ten years of appeasement, we hope." He continued in a belligerent tone: "The Japanese are tempting and taunting us while their ships move toward Indo-China. Since they're asking for it, we ought to let them have it. Our answer should be an order to the U.S. Navy to shoot the Japanese destroyers full of holes and keep the Pacific free." Shifting his focus, Cusick attacked those in the State Department whom he believed were advocating appeasement:

48. FFF news release, June 17, 1941, FFF MSS.

49. CDA news release, June 18, 1941; Clearing House news release, June 30, 1941, FFF MSS.

That clique in our State Department which seemed to think we could continue to send Japan war materials even though we were committed to a program of aid to democratic China has been clearly repudiated by this week's events in the Pacific.

It was argued that by feeding Japan's war machine, we prevented her from moving in the Far East. Her action in Indo-China shows that it is as futile to attempt to bargain with Asiatic Fascism as it is to try "negotiating" a peace with the European dictators.[50]

Cusick's statement was exemplary FFF style. He uncompromisingly caricatured the Japanese as the Fascists of the Orient—thereby making them more comprehensible to those Easterners like himself, who focused their attention primarily on European affairs. He was ready to fight every enemy immediately—despite the fact that most naval authorities regarded war in both the Pacific and Atlantic as beyond their capabilities at the time. And he sought to simplify the issue and arouse emotions by blandly labeling Chiang Kai-shek's regime "democratic China."

In mid-October, when the relatively moderate Konoye government was replaced by the jingoistic Tojo cabinet, the Committee felt it was time to comment again, and Ulric Bell requested quotable statements for a news release from several dozen interventionists. Those quotes used revealed the FFF's hardening attitude—rooted in the belief (as Edward Mead Earle put it) that "a determined stand may well deter Japanese extremists." Most outspoken of the quotations used in the release was Ward Cheney's. Cheney combatively declared: "A Japanese navy spokesman said today that Japan's fleet was 'itching for action.' If that's the way they feel about it, certainly we don't want to frustrate them. Let's start the shooting now."[51]

As the confidential Washington talks between Secretary Hull and Japanese diplomats Nomura and Kurusu continued from October through November into December, the Warhawks grew fretful. Although the FFF leaders were familiar with certain confidential elements of the situation (such as the British promise to go to war with Japan if war between Japan and America occurred), they were completely unaware of the actual

50. FFF news release, July 26, 1941, FFF MSS.
51. FFF news release, October 16, 1941, FFF MSS.

state of United States—Japanese negotiations and of how close and inevitable war with Japan was. Some Warhawks reiterated their distrust of the "State Department clique" as rumors circulated about a proposed *modus vivendi* to buy time in the Pacific. On November 25 Christopher Emmet wrote Ulric Bell:

> The Wilfred Fleischer story on Japan in this morning's Tribune shows that appeasement is still brewing in the State Department. Of course any temporary settlement will be dressed up as a victory, but Japan's promises are utterly meaningless. And even if they evacuate Indo-China their threat will remain as long as they occupy bases on the China coast or in Manchucho. [*sic*]
>
> With the Caucasian oil almost cut off from the rest of Russia and with no means of getting aid to Russia except through Vladivostok, a Japanese attack might produce a Russian collapse even in Asia by next Spring or Summer. . . . War with Japan would have the same effect in increasing American unity and production as war with Hitler, as this is all one war.
>
> The Gallop Poll shows the public is with us on this if the committees, commentators and newspapers on our side stop neglecting Japan and get busy. Major Elliot [*sic*] has carried the ball almost alone. The others have shown a beautiful but rather naive faith in the State Department's handling of the negotiations.[52]

The next day Emmet warned a radio audience that a detente with the Japanese aggressors might be near and that ". . . Secretary Hull and his advisors, who for years have proved wrong in the Far East, seem about to repeat their old mistakes. . . . The mere fact," he asserted, "that negotiations in Washington are taking place while Japan is collaborating with the Axis in Berlin is demoralizing."[53] Underestimating the administration's determination in dealing with the Japanese and the advantages which would accrue to the Allies if Pacific hostilities were postponed, the FFF began distributing reprints of Samuel Grafton's

52. Emmet to Bell, November 25, 1941, FFF MSS.

53. Christopher Emmet, Jr., "Broadcast on China and the Kurusu Negotiations—Station WEVD,"November 26, 1961, FFF MSS. Hull says that he decided on the same day against offering the Japanese a *modus vivendi*. He cites "domestic pressures" as one reason for the administration's tougher attitude, Cordell Hull, *The Memoirs of Cordell Hull* (New York, 1948), pp. 180–87.

December 3 column. "How many dead Chinamen," Grafton asked, "are canceled out by one frown from Mr. Sumner Welles? . . . We do not balance the scales for the rape of . . . Nanking by refusing to sell clay pipes and dog biscuits to the Tokyo trade." [54]

Also during the first week in December, Bell and Robert Spivack drafted an advertisement which suggests that either their British friends or sympathetic American officials had alerted them to the possibility of joint Anglo-American action in Southeast Asia. Churchill and the British Ambassador, Lord Halifax, had for several weeks been urging upon Roosevelt a mutual commitment to resist by armed force further Japanese encroachments in that area. Their offer received the support of General Marshall, Admiral Stark, and the interventionists in the cabinet. But Roosevelt feared that going to war to save Thailand, Malaya, or the Netherlands East Indies, although strategically sound, would leave the American people badly divided. On Saturday, December 6, he was still pondering the issue.[55]

By remarkable coincidence, on the same day Bell and Robert Spivack completed work on an FFF advertisement which declared, "Stay Out of Thailand or We Fight!" Spivack had shown the ad to "brain-truster" Benjamin V. Cohen who professed no special knowledge of the subject but said that its publication would be useful. The *New York Times* accepted it for appearance in the Monday morning edition, but the events of the intervening day made it superfluous.[56]

By the beginning of December resistance to Japan had become the only remaining objective—aside from a declaration of war on Germany—for which the Warhawks could agitate. And the Fight For Freedom attacked this hitherto secondary issue, with the militancy, truculence, and over-simplification which had become its hallmark. American public opinion had long before crystallized in favor of halting further Japanese expansion and resisting a direct attack, the administration had

54. Samuel Grafton, "I'd Rather Be Right," reprint from *New York Post,* December 3, 1941, FFF MSS.

55. Langer and Gleason, *The Undeclared War,* pp. 911–21.

56. "Stay Out of Thailand or We Fight!" (draft), FFF MSS; author's conversations with Spivack and Cohen.

already settled on a policy of firmness, and the Japanese had by now decided on war. The last-minute furor of the Warhawks, therefore, had relatively little effect on the outcome of the United States-Japanese impasse.[57]

* * * * * *

The ultimate objective of all the Warhawk exertions was the direct involvement of the United States in the war against Nazi Germany. Since the Warhawks regarded Hitler as the one real threat to United States security and Western civilization, they considered continued American abstention from the war both unrealistic and morally irresponsible. Nevertheless, although they founded the Fight For Freedom as a frankly interventionist organization, at an early Executive Committee meeting they decided to postpone another direct call for intervention. They would constantly allude to "the need to fight this war" and would not discourage individual Fight For Freedom speakers from suggesting a war declaration. But they would refrain from launching an intensive drive for an immediate declaration until membership was sufficiently expanded to give such a demand real impact. They anticipated that their own efforts and the worsening international situation in ensuing days would prepare the public for acceptance of outright belligerency.[58]

By late August the Fight For Freedom leaders felt that their own organization and public attitudes had progressed enough to allow a war drive some chance of success. They polled their nationwide Policy Committee and obtained a favorable response (although some members thought a declaration of war was an out-of-date technicality). When the Committee to Defend America expressed its willingness to cooperate, the Fight For Freedom leaders prepared to launch the "declare war" campaign in early September.

However, when they were informed that the President was about to announce his intention to seek revision of the Neutrality Act and shoot U-boats on sight, the Warhawks—not wishing to embarrass him as he side-stepped toward belligerency

57. See footnote 53, this chapter.
58. "Dinner Meeting," Century Club, April 22, 1941, FFF MSS.

—postponed their new drive.[59] Although Roosevelt declared a shooting policy, not until October 9 did he actually present his Neutrality proposals to Congress, and by the end of September the Warhawks felt they had waited long enough. They decided to go ahead with their campaign for a declaration of war "based on the fact that the White House was told of their intention and did not suggest that they *not* do it." [60]

The Warhawks made the Madison Square Garden show on October 5 and the Continental Congress on the ninth and tenth the occasions to announce their new demand. At its conclusion the delegates to the Continental Congress unanimously adopted a brief and unequivocal resolution demanding that "we declare war on Nazi Germany." The statement in the brochure of the "Fun to Be Free" show set forth at greater length the rationale for such action. Once again the Warhawks reiterated their belief that the global conflict was a revolution against the value for which America stood. The United States could not abstain from the fight without accepting defeat. The United States Navy was already strong enough to provide great assistance to Britain in Atlantic waters and to hold the Japanese at bay in the Pacific. In a year or two an American air force would exist which could destroy Hitler's war machine—if the United States replaced the peacetime approach with wartime industrial policies. "We believe," the statement concluded, "that all minor problems—such as 'wildcat' strikes and 'business-as-usual' psychology—will be easy to solve when war is accepted. . . . The 'short of war' approach to the world revolution fosters disunity at home, while leading inevitably to a growing hopelessness abroad. For these reasons, we are for WAR." [61]

The Fight For Freedom news releases on the Washington convention headlined the war resolution, and Warhawk speeches stressed more than ever the need for all kinds of direct involvement—not just naval or even aerial, but the engagement of

59. Hobson to Henry B. Cabot, August 26, 1941, FFF MSS. The CDA apparently never did advocate an immediate declaration of war, but it did support the FFF by stressing that war would soon be necessary and was inevitable.

60. Author's interview with Cusick.

61. "It's Fun to be Free," brochure, October 5, 1941, FFF MSS.

ground forces as well. As before, but ever more imploringly, Fight For Freedom spokesmen intoned that America *was* the world's best hope, and that *this* was America's last chance. Herbert Agar set the crusading tone when he addressed himself to the question, "Why We Ought to Go to War?" "'All men' has been the great American phrase," he said. And it is the equal rights of "all men" which the Nazis hate and deny with "their silly racial doctrines [and] belief in a superior people who must run the world and have other people work for them as slaves. The Nazis are [therefore] the perfect and the foreordained enemy of the American idea. . . ." "America," he continued,

> if America ever dared to live up to her own greatness, is the culmination of the civilization of our Western World. The revolution against the civilization of our Western World has got to come to grips with America.
>
> Hitler himself said that, only six months ago, in a speech which for some reason so many of us seem to forget. He said that there are two worlds facing each other today, and that one of them must be destroyed. . . . If America joins the free peoples, our world will win. If America doesn't, our world will lose.
>
> The hour of decision is at hand.[62]

For the Fight For Freedom each new incident on the high seas—the *Kearny,* the *Reuben James*—were "compelling reasons" for declaring war. All of the already well-worn images—of America an island in a Fascist sea or America raped by invading Nazi hordes—were brought to bear again in the quest for the ultimate goal.

The effect of this agitation is uncertain. The last important public opinion poll on intervention was taken on October 4, before the "declare war" drive began. It showed only 21 per cent in favor of an immediate declaration—the same figure as in May. Probably, under the influence not only of Warhawk propaganda but also of the increasingly bloody incidents in the Atlantic, more Americans did convert to outright interventionism in the two months before Pearl Harbor. But it is almost certain that

62. Herbert Agar, "Why We Ought to Go to War," pamphlet, FFF MSS.

interventionism did *not* achieve a majority before December 7. If it had, Roosevelt might well have joined with the interventionists in Congress to force a vote on a declaration of war.[63] The absence of any serious effort by the President or by congressional interventionists to obtain such a declaration in the weeks before Pearl Harbor testifies to the Warhawks' failure to gain their original and ultimate goal of majority support for war. Only when directly and devastatingly attacked did America decide to fight.

63. From his knowledge of intercepted Japanese telegrams Roosevelt was aware that war in the Pacific was close. He might, therefore, have waited to let the Japanese strike first. However, he could not be sure that the *casus belli* which the Japanese would present would be provocative enough to arouse Americans to a fever pitch. The Japanese might have only moved further into Southeast Asia. Therefore, had majority support for war existed, Roosevelt probably would have asked for a congressional declaration.

X. An End and a Beginning

At 3:42 A.M. (Honolulu time) Sunday, December 7, the minesweeper U.S.S. *Condor* sighted a submarine periscope off Pearl Harbor in an area in which American submarines were restricted from submerged operations. Three hours later the destroyer U.S.S. *Ward* depth-charged and sank a small, unidentified submarine in waters nearby. In view of the recent numerous "sub scares" and the *Ward's* success in dealing with this seemingly isolated incursion, the local Navy Commandant relayed the news to his superior, Admiral H. H. Kimmel, through normal channels. His report reached Kimmel just before 7:40 A.M. Fifteen minutes later the first wave of Japanese dive bombers appeared over "Battleship Row." The greatest naval disaster in American history had begun.[1]

Bishop Henry Hobson had just completed a confirmation service in Athens, Ohio, and was driving to nearby Logan to speak for the Fight For Freedom, when news of the attack came over the car radio. His first reaction was shock and astonishment.

1. U.S. Congress, *Pearl Harbor: Hearings before the Joint Committee on the Investigation of the Pearl Harbor Attack* (Washington, D.C., 1946), pp. 58, 138.

He was not surprised that the Japanese had tried a sneak attack, but he was appalled that so vital a base had been completely unprepared to resist. During the past year he had argued for American intervention in the war against the Axis in the certainty that the United States fleet in the Pacific was sufficient to cope with the Japanese. Now, with a great part of that fleet smoldering and capsized at Oahu, his premise was thrown into the gravest doubt. The sense of relief and even elation he had expected to feel when the United States finally went to war was eradicated by the immense tragedy in Hawaii.[2]

Like Hobson, Francis Miller was traveling when the news reached him. Miller's train from Charlottesville to Washington was at the scene of the first battle of another great struggle—Manassas Junction, Virginia—when someone came aboard with the news that Pearl Harbor was under attack. At first the question in Miller's mind was, *who* was attacking Pearl Harbor? Like many of the Warhawks he was concentrating so much of his attention on European events and on Hitler that a *Japanese* attack came as a surprise. But by the time his wife Helen and their two small boys met him at the station, the first fragmentary reports had been superseded by more detailed ones. Miller now knew the aggressor and the enormity of the damage. As he recalled years later, "It was a moment when you were shaken to your very roots and wondered about the future of your country." American involvement, the interventionists knew, was now assured—but at a horrible price.[3]

Word of the attack reached Bell, Cusick and Madeline Sherwood in the national headquarters by telephone. Bob Sherwood called[4] to relate the shocking news and to make a request. There was something the Fight For Freedom *had* to do for the President, he said.

2. Hobson to author, January 14, 1965.

3. Author's interview with Francis P. Miller.

4. Mrs. Sherwood recalls that he telephoned from William Donovan's information office in New York. Cusick and Herbert Agar (who came to the office later in the afternoon) think Sherwood called from the White House. However, White House records for the seventh show no such call; author's conversation with Cusick and Mrs. Sherwood; Herbert Agar to author, January 30, 1968.

Roosevelt for some time had feared that if war came first in the Pacific, the country might direct all its attention toward Japan. Americans might lose sight of the fact that the Nazis were the more dangerous aggressor and that we were their next target.[5] There was a real possibility that Hitler and Mussolini might not honor their Tripartite Pact promise to assist Japan "with all political, economic and military means" in the event of hostilities between Japan and the United States. The President, Sherwood observed, could not say all this to the American people himself without calling for a declaration of war against Germany and Italy. Hopefully they would declare war first, but something had to be done to prepare the public in the event that Hitler and Mussolini did not act.

Would the Warhawks publish a statement urging the American people to demand a declaration of war against Germany and Italy? The Committee leaders agreed, and Sherwood dictated over the telephone a statement which appeared in newspaper advertisements across the country on December 8:

DECLARE WAR ON GERMANY AND ITALY!

Japan's treacherous attack on the United States was only an incident in the all-out world-wide war against liberty. . . .

What is happening in the Pacific today is inseparable from the entire Axis Strategy of War, the battle for civilization that goes on in Libya, on the Russian front, in every corner of the globe . . .

Those who have been misled in the past, advising us to appease our enemies, may now say that this nation must concentrate all its energies in the Far East, that we must forget the war in Europe.

That is what the Nazis want us to believe. This is the way of Hitler. That is the familiar Axis rule of "Divide and Conquer."

We will not be divided. We will not be conquered. We recognize that only an IMMEDIATE DECLARATION OF WAR ON ALL OUR AXIS ENEMIES WILL WIN THE FIGHT FOR FREEDOM.

Only if we declare war on Germany and Italy now can the battle against our enemies be won. Only in that way can complete

5. The Navy and War Departments relegated Japan to secondary importance in their contingency war plans, Mark S. Watson, *Chief of Staff: Prewar Plans and Preparations* (Washington, 1950), p. 373.

unity and effort on every front be achieved—with Great Britain, with Russia, with China, with every nation and every people battling against the barbaric hordes of the Axis. . . .[6]

The President and the Warhawks were relieved of the problem of arousing public and congressional support for a declaration of war against Germany and Italy when, two days later, Hitler and Mussolini chose to honor their Tripartite commitment and declared war on the United States.[7]

* * * * * *

After Pearl Harbor the Fight For Freedom leaders first considered and then rejected the idea of keeping the organization intact. In meetings on December 8 and 9 (before Germany and Italy declared war on the United States), the national leaders decided to continue the FFF's work. They would focus on getting war declared against Hitler and Mussolini, defining the democracies' war aims, sustaining domestic morale, and eradicating any "obstructionism" arising from the possible renaissance of America First.[8] On the eighth Bishop Hobson wired his chapter leaders and released to the news media a statement declaring the Committee "will continue . . . with greater energy than ever before."[9] As late as January 16 Hobson, while on the one hand preparing to "make the final adjustments, so that our meeting records will be complete," was, on the other, working on a four-point statement of war aims to be circulated by Fight For Freedom chapters.[10]

6. "Declare War on German and Italy," reprint of advertisement, December 8, 1941; Barber to William Agar, January 3, 1941, FFF MSS.

7. William L. Langer and S. Everett Gleason, *The Undeclared War* (New York, 1953), pp. 937–41.

8. Havell to FFF Speakers, December 9, 1941; Vance O. Smith to Bell, telegram, December 10, 1941, FFF MSS.

9. As quoted in Havell to FFF Speakers, December 9, 1941, FFF MSS.

10. Hobson to William Agar, January 16, 1942, FFF MSS.

The four-point program was:

"To fight for the maintenance of the free way of life in our own country.

"To win an all-out victory against the Axis powers.

"To insist upon the making of a righteous peace.

"To insure American particpation in world affairs after the war."

However, practical and policy considerations already weighed against the transformation of the Fight For Freedom into a wartime morale-building body. Many of the most important chapters had already dissolved or gone on "stand-by" status. On the day after Pearl Harbor, Courtenay Barber wrote from Chicago that members of his executive committee were proposing "we hibernate and do nothing for a period of sixty days." He noted that his local financial sources, always meager, were already drying up. Los Angeles executive committee chairman William B. Miller advised, "War disorganized Committee here, resulting [in] postponement [of] most activities until January." San Francisco's Archibald MacPhail reported that his chapter's work was drawing to a finish and that he feared its leaders would have to personally underwrite the deficit. By December 19 the committee in Maryland had decided "to discontinue operations . . . the main objectives of the F.F.F. having been obtained." [11] Chapter leaders reported that many of their younger members were rushing off to fight the war they had called for; older Warhawks hurried to take positions of responsibility in the mobilization program or to devote their full energies to putting their own commercial and industrial interests on a war footing.[12]

In the week after war began against Germany and Italy, the national leadership decided that the Committee had served its purpose and should be gradually disbanded. Francis Miller wrote to Hobson on the eleventh expressing the majority view:

11. Barber to Bell, December 8, 1941; William B. Miller to Bell, telegram, December 10, 1941; Archibald MacPhail to Cusick, December 17, 1941; George B. Simmons to William Agar, January 10, 1942, FFF MSS.

12. References are made to members' departures for the armed services in Frederick Hardisty to William Agar, December 19, 1941; William B. Miller to Bell, telegram, December 10, 1941; and Simmons to William Agar, January 2, 1942, FFF MSS. The federal government recruited extensively among the leading Warhawks. Archibald MacLeish enlisted Bell and Cusick for the United States Office of Facts and Figures in the week after Pearl Harbor, Hobson to Hans Kohn, March 10, 1942, HWH MSS. (Cusick soon enlisted in the Army as a private.) Within a short time Francis Miller joined Sherwood, Warburg, Douglas Miller, and Edmund Taylor in the Foreign Information Service, while Harold Guinzburg went to work for Elmer Davis' Office of War Information. Wayne Johnson took charge of petroleum matters for the War Production Board. Herbert Agar, a Navy Reservist, and Robert S. Allen, an Army Reservist, were activated with the ranks of Lieutenant Commander and Major, respectively.

"In view of the fact that we are now at war on all fronts the Fight For Freedom Committee ought, in my judgment, immediately to terminate its campaign of public propaganda. I feel very strongly that for the time being restraint in talk and argument is an urgent public duty." Miller regarded the danger of a wartime regeneration of America First as slight.[13]

In a meeting on the seventeenth, the Executive Committee formally decided to deactivate the Fight For Freedom. The Warhawks informed their chapter heads that the Committee was being put "on ice."[14] As others departed for wartime duty, William Agar was left in charge of national operations. When Frederick Hardisty of the St. Louis chapter asked for instructions, Agar replied:

> As you know the Fight For Freedom has restricted its operations for the time being. Most of our active executives will now be connected with Freedom House which will carry on the educational part of our program. Fight For Freedom continues to exist with me as director and I, also, will move over into Freedom House as soon as that is ready. When and if the propaganda side of our activities is again necessary we shall be prepared to enlarge and get busy.
>
> For these reasons there is nothing anyone can do to build up chapters at the present time. We do hope, though, that existing chapters will hold together.[15]

The "Freedom House" to which Agar referred had been founded on October 30 under the auspices of the Fight For Freedom and some members of the Committee to Defend America as a symbolic antithesis to the Nazi *Braunhaus* of Munich. This building at 32 East 51st Street in New York was (as Herbert Agar said when it was founded) to ". . . serve as an international center for all groups, exiled governments and individuals concerned with the defeat of Nazism and the re-establishment of world democracy. It is intended to become a world symbol of the fight against tyranny, not only the fight on the field of battle

13. Miller to Hobson, December 11, 1941, UB MSS.
14. Minutes, Executive Committee Meeting, December 17, 1941, UB MSS.
15. William Agar to Hardisty, December 23, 1941, FFF MSS.

but the fight in our own hearts. . . ."[16] As such it expressed the loftiest aims and aspirations of the leading liberal interventionists.

* * * * * *

What, then, was the nature of the interventionist movement and its leaders? What motivated them? How effective were they in achieving their ultimate objective and their intermediate ones? What influence did their rhetoric and aspirations have on American attitudes during and after the war?

The Warhawks were driven to action partly, at least, by their ethnic and cultural identification with Great Britain. The members of the original Century Group were largely Anglo-Saxon in background. Many had been educated in British schools, and some had served in Commonwealth armed forces or had spent significant portions of their adult lives in Britain. All were keenly aware that their country's culture, law, language, and government derived primarily from English antecedents.

The Warhawks were also inheritors of an internationalism rooted partly in the realism of Admiral Mahan and Theodore Roosevelt and partly in the idealism of Woodrow Wilson. Their own careers in foreign relations, in international business and law, and in letters seemed to reaffirm the interrelationship of North America and the rest of the world—particularly Europe.

The Warhawks' conviction that the United States had to intervene as soon as possible in the European war partly stemmed from their personal ties and sympathies. But that conviction was also based on their objective analysis of America's future in a world dominated by Hitler.

That analysis was almost certainly correct. Hitler's defeat *was* in the United States' interest, and he and his allies probably could not have been beaten without direct American involvement. Furthermore, the United States probably *should* have intervened as quickly as possible. There is little question that Hitler would have attempted to control at least parts of the Western hemisphere when he had the means to do so. Britain

16. FFF news release, October 30, 1941, FFF MSS. For the subsequent history of Freedom House, see William Agar and Aaron Levenstein, *Freedom's Advocate: A Twenty-five Year Chronicle* (New York, 1965).

and (later) Russia might have been able to overcome the Nazis eventually without American participation, but only after many years of fighting. In the meantime German science might have fashioned and turned upon them the global weapons of the fifties and sixties. These weapons Hitler might have also used against the industrial complexes and population centers of the eastern United States.[17]

However sound the Warhawks' assumptions, the practicality of their untemporizing, direct call for war is open to question. Their stridency provided ammunition for their opponents. It also frightened away some citizens who (while willing to give all-out aid to Britain and adopt other semi-belligerent policies) were repelled by the huge armies, heavy casualties, and domestic controls total war would mean. By announcing their ultimate goal—United States intervention—in June, 1940, and then reiterating it continuously throughout 1941, the Warhawks may sometimes have embarrassed Roosevelt, the very man they sought to support and influence. If they had espoused only one step at a time (as the William Allen White Committee tended to do), they might have helped to stimulate favorable opinion on the immediate issues—which were bringing belligerency ever closer—without voluntarily raising the spectre of all-out war. However, because they continued to press for war while also urging convoying, occupation of Atlantic islands, Neutrality repeal, and the like, they provided the isolationists with telling material. Isolationists could compare the Warhawks' entire program with what Roosevelt had already done and demonstrate, thereby, that by conspiracy or coincidence the President was taking the country along the same path and toward the same goal which the Warhawks were advocating.[18]

17. For an interesting account of German successes and failures in developing modern weaponry, see Samuel A. Goudsmit, *Alsos* (New York, 1947). Goudsmit demonstrates that Nazi wartime efforts to develop atomic weapons were far behind Anglo-American ones but that the Germans did have a substantial lead in rocket and jet propulsion development.

18. The best examples of this were the 1941 speeches of Colonel Lindbergh and Senator Nye. The FFF's "crank" file is replete with letters and postcards from extreme isolationists, denouncing the Warhawks and Roosevelt in one voice. The editorials of the *Chicago Tribune* and Father Coughlin's *Social Justice* hammered at the conspiracy theme throughout 1940 and 1941.

Regardless of the harmful side effects, the Warhawks generally operated on the assumption that forthrightness was necessary. Although after the "Summons to Speak Out" they temporarily subordinated outright interventionism to the immediate goals —a destroyer transfer, denying food to Hitler's Europe, and Lend-Lease, they grew increasingly convinced that direct public discussion of the need to fight was the only way to get the United States to go to war. They always considered time too short to wait for a gradual shift in public opinion and official policy (which might take years). They felt that the President and the other pro-Allies organizations were educating the country to its interests and the realities of the world situation too slowly. They believed that someone had to dare to take the advanced position —to "break the ice"—so that the administration and the public could follow. Their advocacy of the administration's current actions, plus "further steps," may have fulfilled this function. And, although their extremism may have sometimes embarrassed Roosevelt, it probably also helped free him to decide issues more in accord with his own judgment by neutralizing similar outbursts from the isolationists.

The effectiveness of the interventionist movement remains debatable. The Warhawks failed in their main purpose of persuading the United States to go to war voluntarily at a time and in a manner which would best serve American interests and security. Also, the war they advocated did not establish the world system of justice and rule of law to which they frequently alluded. Yet they did effectively contribute to America's eventual participation in the conflict.

Their achievements derived from the fact that they did not limit themselves to publicly demanding American intervention. At various stages the Warhawks provided manipulative, educative, and demonstrative services which helped to bring the United States closer to war. The Warhawks accomplished their most successful manipulations during the summer of 1940, when, as the informal and discreet Century Group, they relayed the British Ambassador's position regarding destroyers and bases to the American press and persuaded General Pershing to speak out in support of a transfer. They also helped convince administration officials of the desirability and method of sending destroyers to Britain and influenced Wendell Willkie not to attack the subsequent executive agreement. The Warhawks' maneuverings were a major and possibly indispensable contribution to the destroyer-bases deal, and that transaction is regarded by some authorities as the United States' first unneutral act.

Cut off from Roosevelt and Willkie by their repeated anti-war pronouncements and increasingly convinced of the need for public enlightenment, the Warhawks in the autumn of 1940 concentrated more on "awakening the American people" and less on manipulating men in power. Instead of dealing in confidence with the White House or the Republican nominee, they began organizing signed statements, circulating editorial reprints, and pondering other methods of reaching a wider audience with the rationale of interventionism. Only after Election Day, by which time the Warhawks' new course had been firmly set, were they able to re-establish discreet channels of cooperation with Roosevelt and develop a close relationship with Willkie.

The Warhawks' conviction that the public had to be educated to the need to fight this war and their belief that public support for steps leading to war had to be organized and graphically "demonstrated" to the policy-makers led them to found the Fight For Freedom. It is, of course, impossible to prove that the Committee or all the pro-democracy organizations together were decisive in developing favorable public opinion on any one of the actions the United States government took in approaching belligerency in 1941. Their appeals were never the sole influence on the public mind. Allied setbacks or successes as reported in the news media, presidential statements, and the pronouncements of columnists, commentators, and other "influentials" who advocated intervention without actually participating in the Warhawks' organization all had their effect.

Nevertheless, the Warhawks' speeches, statements, and advertisements probably did help undermine the isolationist assumptions upon which popular attitudes toward the "old world" were based. The aspersions they cast on the motivation and loyalty of leading America Firsters may well have served to raise doubts about the isolationists' credibility. The Fight For Freedom's advance promotion of convoying, occupying Atlantic islands, clearing the Atlantic, and repeal of the Neutrality Act almost certainly contributed to popular familiarity with and acceptance of these actions. When the President finally decided to announce such steps, he found an audience more "educated" on the issues and more amenable than it would have been without the Warhawks' groundwork. Similarly, the propaganda of the Fight For Freedom and the other pro-democracy organizations undoubtedly contributed to the growing public awareness of danger, thereby helping to prepare the American people for the shock of war when it finally came.

Directly related to the Fight For Freedom's "educative" work was the Committee's "demonstrative" function. The public opinion polls of 1941 reveal that no more than one in five Americans was convinced of the desirability of immediate belligerency. Yet the Fight For Freedom worked assiduously to show to the administration and the Congress and to the public itself that the American people would approve of all steps short of actual belligerency and would even accept war. To poll results showing that an overwhelming majority favored war if that was the only way to beat Hitler, they added their own estimation that it *was* the only way and came up with their "proof" that the American people were actually for war.

To reinforce their point they sought to demonstrate that each special interest group in the United States supported war—or the steps leading to it. They were particularly effective in galvanizing and channeling the activities of organized labor, veterans, and the entertainment world on behalf of the actions Roosevelt had already taken and the "further steps" the Fight For Freedom urged. They were relatively less effective in rallying women, young people, Negroes, and Catholics to intervention. But despite their lack of success among some groups, the Warhawks sought to create the impression that all of them either wanted war or accepted it as inevitable. Such efforts probably helped to neutralize the contrasting impression which the isolationist groups were trying to register. The Warhawk campaigns created a source of organized, vocal "evidence" to reinforce the poll results showing popular support for an increasingly firm diplomatic and military posture.

The *tactics* which the Warhawks employed in presenting

their case to the country in 1941 also require some conclusive comments. As the leaders of an organization appealing for mass support of a minority viewpoint, they had to make their message simple enough and emotional enough to attract the attention of all kinds of people—not just the elite. To a great degree they discarded their own gentility and sophistication in order to develop the broadest appeal possible. They attracted attention through stunts, shows, and sensational advertising. They sought to pose every issue, foreign or domestic, simple or complex, in black-and-white terms. They attempted to characterize each of their opponents as a dupe, a sympathizer, or an agent of Berlin. While they appealed to their countrymen's sense of brotherhood, liberty, and national mission, they also tried to arouse their fear, hatred, and rage.

The Warhawks' resort to extremes was in part the shrewd decision of leaders who understood that in public affairs one must often demand a whole loaf in order to get half of one. But it was also partly motivated by frustration. They were utterly convinced that intervention was crucial and yet they sensed that they were not persuading the public quickly enough. Therefore they employed any strategem which would win new adherents or disparage their antagonists. This was probably inevitable. On an issue as vital as war or peace, any group espousing a minority view will probably feel compelled to use every possible device to make its point. Thus, because they considered theirs to be the only path to national survival, these educated, experienced men of the Establishment—whose upbringing and social position seemed to dictate restraint, sophistication, and fair play—willingly descended to manipulation of facts, character assassination, and sensationalism. Any condemnation of their extremism must, however, include awareness of the flagrant behavior of opponents such as Lindbergh, Nye, Fish, and Wheeler.

The role the Warhawks played in propelling the United States toward the war (which it almost inevitably would have had to fight) is, however, only part of their significance. For years after their work together in the Century Group and Fight For Freedom, many of these men played vital roles in the formulation and enunciation of American foreign policy. Indeed, the history of American diplomacy and propaganda in the war and postwar years is in great part the story of the subsequent efforts of the individual Warhawks. One need only list such names as Robert Sherwood, Elmer Davis, Lewis Douglas, Will Clayton, James Conant, Dean Acheson, and Allen Dulles to substantiate this point.

Not only did the Warhawks contribute personnel, but their pre-war propaganda also helped to provide the rationale for fighting the war and making the peace. Some of these assumptions and slogans have complicated the realistic conduct of foreign relations. Others have probably been beneficial. On the one hand, the oversimplification of issues through the use of such phrases as "democratic, free China" or "the Free World" helped create popular legends which even today hinder the readjustment of national policy to realities. Similarly, rhetorical insistence on the overriding importance of "beating the hell out of Hitler" probably contributed to the uncritical popular (and official) acceptance of all members of the anti-Nazi coalition as "good guys." This attitude required painful reconsideration after Yalta and Potsdam.

On the other hand, wartime public acceptance of the internationalistic assumptions which the Warhawks militantly advocated has been primarily beneficent. Popular appreciation that events occurring outside the Western hemisphere can vitally affect United States security has been instrumental in the evolution of wartime and postwar policies. These policies have coincided more closely with the realities of America's self-interest and international position than had the policies of the 1930's. National agreement on the desirability of a leading role for the United States in a worldwide system of cooperation and security helped to assure—even before the battles were over—that the United States would not withdraw unto itself as in 1919 but would participate actively in the United Nations. Similarly, general recognition of Europe's paramount importance to the United States led not only to the Europe-first strategy of World War II, but also to the Marshall Plan and North Atlantic Treaty.

It must be noted that one fundamental Warhawk idea has probably been rendered obsolete by the development of nuclear weapons. This is the policy of total war to completely destroy the major enemy. In the world of 1941 America was in fact capable of waging such a war without placing its own national existence in danger. One of the war aims on which the Warhawks (and, indeed, the three major Allied nations) agreed was the total destruction of nazism. In 1968, however, *total* response to anything short of a direct nuclear attack on the United States or her allies seems nearly unthinkable. No matter how antagonistic the enemy's ideology, how aggressive his announced intentions, and how provocative his posturing, few responsible "Hawks" now advocate a declaration of war and all-out hostilities as a solution. Total war might annihilate the enemy, but its cost would probably be national suicide, or at least national mutilation. Because of the bomb, *limited* war for limited defensive objectives has probably become the most militant course open to the United States under present circumstances.

In retrospect one can see that all of these things, from the wartime adoption of internationalistic slogans and rationale to the obsolescence of the concept of total war, were largely unrelated to what the Warhawks did or did not do. Other internationalists, particularly President Roosevelt and his chief spokesmen, were also responsible for the general conversion to internationalism. Advancements in military technology and events beyond the control of any small group of men undoubtedly dictated some of the changes in domestic attitudes and new trends in American foreign relations. Although the Warhawks may have suggested or presaged the wartime oversimplification of issues and the concentration on destroying rather than circumscribing German powers, the intense pressures generated by war itself made such consequences almost inevitable. Similarly, it was not Warhawk exertions as much as fear of a third recurrence of German expansionism and the presence of a new aggressor on the Eurasian land mass which obligated the United States to participate in the postwar reconstruction and security system of western Europe. It was general awareness of America's global power and the challenge presented by the Soviet Union, more than the verbiage of internationalism, which thrust the United States permanently onto the world stage. The United States' postwar internationalism owes more to events, therefore, than to the foresight of the Warhawks.

This leads us back to what is probably the central theme

of this book—that there was *no* successful band of Establishment conspirators who got America into the war. It is true that, in the months from Dunkirk to Pearl Harbor, the Warhawks provided some services which helped to make it easier for the administration to take increasingly belligerent action. It is true that they had some successes in vocalizing support for or educating the public to accept more warlike behavior. It is even true that the Warhawks probably had a clearer vision of America's interests and future place in the world than most of their fellow countrymen. But neither the Century Group nor the Fight For Freedom were the prime movers in the United States' progression toward internationalism and belligerency. It was the crush of events which forced the nation to recognize its inevitable involvement in the world, the danger of continued isolation, and, finally, the necessity of war with the Axis.

Appendix

A Summons to Speak Out

The United States has now undertaken to meet the formidable challenge of Nazi Germany. Our program of national defense has been touched off by the invasion of the Netherlands, Belgium and France, and it is designed to repel any German attack on our territory or any invasion of our vital interests.

Belgium once acted in the same way to defend herself. Then, four weeks ago, the fact that she had erected forts on her eastern frontier with guns pointing toward Germany was officially cited by the German government as a justification for invading and subjugating her.

In the German view, the American defense program means that the United States has already joined with Great Britain and France in opposing the Nazi drive for world dominion—in the American view, Nazi Germany is the mortal enemy of our ideals, our institutions and our way of life.

These hard-won possessions of ours are not for sale. They are not for surrender.

If the British navy is destroyed or taken over, if the French army is defeated in final action, we shall have to face our job alone. We shall have to aid South America single-handed, in the presence of triumphant and hungry aggressors operating across both oceans.

What we have, what we are and what we hope to be can now be most effectively defended on the line in France held by General Weygand. The frontier of our national interest is now on the Somme.

Therefore, all disposable air, naval, military and material resources of the United States should be made available at once to help maintain our common front.

But such resources cannot be made available fast enough to hold the German army in check on the European continent or to prepare for the eventual attack on American interests so long as the United States remains legally neutral—nation-wide endorsement of the defense program shows that the American people has ceased to be neutral in any other sense.

For this reason alone, and irrespective of specific uses of our resources thereafter, the United States should immediately give official recognition to the fact and to the logic of the situation—by declaring that a state of war exists between this country and Germany. Only in this constitutional manner can the energies be massed which are indispensable to the successful prosecution of a program of defense.

National unity must rise out of disunity. Individual sacrifice and dedication must stand in the place of individual self-interest. Above all, the representatives of the people must be made aware that they have only a short breathing-spell left within which to prove their capacity to organize a united initiative. For, unless they act diligently and wholly in the national interest, forgetting themselves and their political ambitions, they will presently find themselves washed out—and our institutions with them—by the waters that are rising over the whole world.

The undersigned, as individuals, invite those citizens of the United States who share these views to express them publicly through the free democratic institution of the American press.

Bibliography

Manuscript Collections

BALDERSTON, JOHN L. Library of Congress, Washington, D.C.

The Balderston Collection is particularly helpful on the relationship between the Warhawks and William Allen White. Balderston's unabashed Anglophilism is reflected in his correspondence with White and with Clarence Streit, leader of the "Union Now" movement. Balderston's correspondence to Room 2940 from California in the winter of 1940–1941 was the main source of information for the Warhawks on the anti-interventionist activities of Ambassador Joseph P. Kennedy.

BATTERSON, WALTER. Sterling Library, Yale University, New Haven, Connecticut.

The Batterson Collection is a useful source on the activities of the Committee to Defend America in the New York and Connecticut areas.

BELL, ULRIC. Privately held.

Ulric Bell's papers, although small in volume were a most useful source, including several documents shedding light on the FFF's relationship to the White House, which were apparently not available elsewhere. In addition, in his papers was an outline of a book Bell himself had intended to write about the 1940–41 period. It served as a useful checklist for the author's own research.

CLAPPER, RAYMOND. Library of Congress.

CREEL, GEORGE F. Library of Congress.

DANIELS, JOSEPHUS. Library of Congress.

FIGHT FOR FREEDOM COMMITTEE. Firestone Library, Princeton University, Princeton, New Jersey.

This large and entirely unorganized collection was the single most important source on the Warhawks. Two decades after its acquisition by Princeton, the Fight For Freedom Papers remain a mixed mass of correspondence, office memos, newspaper clippings, mimeographed propaganda sheets and promotional materials of all kinds. This collection includes not only the papers of the Fight For Freedom but also considerable material on the Century Group, the Committee to Defend America, the Council for Democracy, and other pro-Allies bodies. However, its size and disorganization make it a forbiddingly time-consuming source unless the researcher is centrally concerned with the Fight For Freedom Committee.

HARRIMAN, FLORENCE JAFFRAY. Library of Congress.

HARRIMAN, W. AVERELL. Privately held.

HOBSON, HENRY W. Privately held.

HOPKINS, HARRY L. Franklin D. Roosevelt Library, Hyde Park, New York.

HULL, CORDELL. Library of Congress.

The Hull Collection, like those of President Roosevelt and of other cabinet members, was useful primarily in substantiating the fact that the Warhawks had less direct, personal contact after the fall of 1940 with the men who made American foreign policy. However the papers of Roosevelt, Hull, Knox, and Stimson also show that, despite a diminution of personal contact, the Warhawks did keep the administration informed of their activities and policies by sending a steady flow of their statements, declarations, and news releases to the White House and to the Secretaries of State, War and Navy.

KNOX, FRANK. Library of Congress.

MC NARY, CHARLES. Library of Congress.

MILLER, FRANCIS PICKENS. Privately held.

These papers were of particular importance with respect to the Century Group's activities from July to October, 1940.

MOFFAT, JAY PIERREPONT. Houghton Library, Harvard University, Cambridge, Massachusetts.

NATIONAL POLICY COMMITTEE. Library of Congress.

The NPC Papers illustrate the attitudes of the internationalists prior to Dunkirk and shed some light on the activities of the Millers, Van Dusen, and their friends during June and July, 1940.

PERSHING, JOHN J. Library of Congress.

PITTMAN, KEY. Library of Congress.

ROOSEVELT, FRANKLIN D. Franklin D. Roosevelt Library.

SHEPARDSON, WHITNEY H. Privately held.

The Shepardson papers were a valuable source of information on the nomination as Ambassador to Canada of J. Pierrepont Moffat, the "Summons to Speak Out," and the founding of the Century Group.

STIMSON, HENRY L. Sterling Library, Yale University.

VAN DUSEN, HENRY P. Privately held.

Henry P. Van Dusen's papers shed light on the relationship between the Warhawks and the British Embassy during the fall of 1940—particularly with regard to Herbert Hoover's food plan.

WHITE, WILLIAM ALLEN. Library of Congress.

Books and Pamphlets

ACHESON, DEAN G. *Morning and Noon: A Memoir.* Boston: 1965.

ADLER, SELIG. *The Isolationist Impulse: Its Twentieth Century Reaction.* New York: 1961.

This book analyzes the various ethnic, regional, intellectual, and religious factors influencing both isolationism and internationalism. Adler demonstrates well that isolationism at various times attracted the support of imperialists and militarists as well as pacifists.

AGAR, HERBERT. *A Time for Greatness.* Boston: 1942.

———. *The City of Man: A Declaration on World Democracy issued by H. Agar, F. Aydelotte, G. A. Borgese.* New York: 1940.

———. *The People's Choice from Washington to Harding. A Study in Democracy.* Boston: 1933.

AGAR, WILLIAM AND LEVENSTEIN, AARON. *Freedom's Advocate: A Twenty-Five Year Chronicle.* New York: 1965.

Freedom's Advocate is the sympathetic but solid institutional history of Freedom House, the successor organization to the Fight For Freedom.

ALSOP, JOSEPH W. AND KINTNER, ROBERT. *American White Paper.* New York: 1940.

AMERICAN ACADEMY OF POLITICAL AND SOCIAL SCIENCE. *Defending America's Future.* Philadelphia: 1941.

AMERICAN COUNCIL ON EDUCATION. *American Isolation Reconsidered: Education and the National Defense.* Washington: 1941.

ANGELL, SIR NORMAN. *America's Dilemma: Alone or Allied?* New York: 1940.

BAILEY, THOMAS A. *The Man in the Street: The Impact of American Public Opinion on Foreign Policy.* New York: 1948.

BALTZELL, E. DIGBY. *The Protestant Establishment: Aristocracy and Caste in America.* New York: 1964.

Baltzell has written what is probably the foremost serious study of the American WASP establishment. He sees the establishment saved from ossification and irrelevance by the outstanding individuals it has recently contributed to American political life and by its increased flexibility in assimilating individuals of talent and achievement whose only "failing" is their lack of WASP antecedents.

BARNES, HARRY ELMER. *Perpetual War for Perpetual Peace: A Critical Examination of the Foreign Policy of F.D.R. and Its Aftermath.* Caldwell, Idaho: 1953.

Barnes, Charles A. Beard, William H. Chamberlin, George Morgenstern, and Charles C. Tansill are leading figures in one "revisionist" school of historians of World War II. Although there are differences of opinion among them, generally speaking, these revisionists contend that Roosevelt planned American intervention long before Pearl Harbor and that he was in collusion with the British and with various Warhawk organizations to bring it about. They argue that Roosevelt welcomed the attack on Pearl Harbor, that his diplomacy had forced the Japanese into it, and that his neglect or complicity contributed importantly to the success or the Japanese attack. They hold that the primary results of American participation in the Second World War were not a world of peace and justice but rather the expansion of Soviet communism and the adherence of the United States to a policy of internationalism which commits it to global responsibilities which sap its strength without contributing much to its national interest.

BARNES, JOSEPH L. *Willkie.* New York: 1952.

BEAL, JOHN ROBINSON. *John Foster Dulles: A Biography.* New York: 1957.

BEARD, CHARLES A. *American Foreign Policy in the Making. 1932–1940.* New York: 1948.

——— and MARY. *America in Mid-Passage.* New York: 1939.

———. *A Foreign Policy for America.* New York: 1940.

———. *President Roosevelt and the Coming of the War, 1941.* New Haven: 1948.

BECKER, STEPHEN. *Marshall Field III: A Biography.* New York: 1964.

BEMIS, SAMUEL FLAGG. *A Diplomatic History of the United States.* 4th ed. New York: 1955.

BLANSHARD, PAUL. *The Irish and Catholic Power: An American Interpretation.* Boston: 1953.

BLUM, JOHN MORTON. *From the Morgenthau Diaries: Years of Urgency, 1938–1941.* Boston: 1965.

BOORSTIN, DANIEL. *The Americans: The National Experience.* New York: 1965.

BREBNER, JOHN BARTLETT. *The North Atlantic Triangle: The Interplay of Canada, the United States and Great Britain.* New Haven: 1945.

Brebner's book is the outstanding history of the interaction between the three English-speaking North Atlantic powers.

BROWDER, EARL R. *Fighting for Peace.* New York: 1939.

A leading American Communist, Browder wrote before the Nazi invasion of the Soviet Union. His books are prime examples of the anti-interventionism of the extreme left—prior to June, 1941.

———. *Second Imperialist War.* New York: 1940.

BURNS, JAMES MAC GREGOR. *Roosevelt: The Lion and the Fox.* New York: 1956.

BUTLER, J. R. M. *Lord Lothian.* London: 1960.

This authorized biography is pedestrian and rather unrevealing.

CAMPBELL, A. E. *Great Britain and the United States, 1895–1903.* London: 1960.

In the conclusion of his comparatively brief study, Campbell contends that the British have tended to regard Anglo-Americanism as a racial matter; both the British and the Americans were Anglo-Saxons. The Americans, he says, have interpreted Anglo-Americanism ideologically, in terms of shared political and legal institutions and similar attitudes toward the individual, the community, and the world.

CANTRIL, HADLEY (ed.). *Public Opinion, 1935–1946.* Princeton: 1951.

CARLSON, JOHN ROY. *Undercover: My Four Years in the Nazi Underground of America.* New York: 1943.

CHAMBERLIN, WILLIAM H. *America's 2nd Crusade.* Chicago: 1950.

CHURCHILL, SIR WINSTON S. *Blood, Sweat, and Tears.* New York: 1941.

———. *The Second World War: Their Finest Hour.* Boston: 1949.

———. *The Second World War: The Grand Alliance.* Boston: 1950.

COFFIN, HENRY SLOANE. *God's Turn.* New York: 1934.

COLE, WAYNE S. *America First: The Battle Against Intervention, 1940–41.* Madison, Wisconsin: 1953.

America First is the outstanding monograph on organized anti-interventionism in 1940–1941. Cole carefully documents the policies and organizational history of the America First Committee. He shows how it declined in the autumn of 1941 when the approach of war and the indiscretions of some of its leaders weakened its appeal.

———. *Senator Gerald P. Nye and American Foreign Relations.* Minneapolis: 1962.

CONN, STETSON and FAIRCHILD, BYRON. *The Framework of Hemisphere Defense.* Washington: 1960.

COUNCIL ON FOREIGN RELATIONS. *The United States in World Affairs, 1939.* New York: 1940.

———. *The United States in World Affairs, 1940.* New York: 1941.

CURRENT, RICHARD N. *Secretary Stimson: A Study in Statecraft.* New Brunswick, New Jersey: 1954.

DAVIS, FORREST. *The Atlantic System.* Cornwall, New York: 1941.

——— and LINDLEY, ERNEST K. *How War Came: An American White Paper.* New York: 1942.

DAWSON, RAYMOND H. *The Decision to Aid Russia, 1941: Foreign Policy and Domestic Politics.* Chapel Hill: 1959.

DAY, STEPHEN A. *We Must Save The Republic.* Scotch Plains, New Jersey: 1941.

DIVINE, ROBERT A. *The Reluctant Belligerent: American Entry in World War II.* New York: 1965.

DOUGLAS, LEWIS WILLIAM. *The Liberal Tradition: A Free People and a Free Economy.* New York: 1935.

DULLES, ALLEN W. and ARMSTRONG, HAMILTON F. *Can America Stay Neutral?* New York: 1939.

———. *Can We Be Neutral?* New York: 1936.

DZIUBAN, STANLEY W. *Military Relations Between the United States and Canada, 1939–1945.* Washington: 1959.

ELIOT, GEORGE FIELDING. *The Ramparts We Watch.* New York: 1938.

———. *Defending America.* New York: 1939.

———. *If War Comes.* New York: 1937.

FEIS, HERBERT. *The Road to Pearl Harbor: The Coming of the War between the U.S. and Japan.* Princeton: 1950.

This is probably still the best scholarly study of the deterioration of relations between Japan and the United States which led to Pearl Harbor.

FOREIGN POLICY ASSOCIATION. *Ten Years of the Foreign Policy Association: 1918–1928.* New York: 1928.

FREEDOM HOUSE. *This Is Freedom House.* New York: 1963.

GANZ, RUDOLPH. *Jew and Irish: Historical Group Relations and Immigration.* New York: 1966.

GELBER, LIONEL. *Anglo-American Friendship: A Study in World Politics, 1889–1906.* London: 1938.

Gelber documented at length the halting steps by which a "community of interest" developed between the United States and Great Britain at the end of the nineteenth century. He placed particular emphasis on the Spanish-American War, the Open Door policy, the Alaska boundary dispute, and the Panama Canal.

GERHART, EUGENE C. *America's Advocate: Robert H. Jackson.* Indianapolis: 1958.

GERSON, LOUIS L. *The Hyphenate in American Politics and Diplomacy.* Lawrence, Kansas: 1964.

GOODHART, PHILIP L. *Fifty Ships That Saved the World.* Garden City, New York: 1965.

Although unevenly written, this book by a member of

the British Parliament is a useful and sometimes humorous account of the destroyer-bases agreement. It is particularly strong on the British aspects of the negotiations and on the actual transfer of the vessels.

GOUDSMIT, SAMUEL. *Alsos.* New York: 1947.

Alsos is a true-life thriller about the efforts of the American Army to capture leading German rocket and atomic scientists in the closing days of the Second World War. It shows how far the Germans were from solving the problems of the atom and how advanced was their missile technology.

GRANT, MADISON. *The Passing of the Great Race.* New York: 1916.

GREAT BRITAIN, ADMIRALTY. *The Town Class Destroyers: The Story of the "Four-Stackers."* London: 1949.

This illustrated volume was probably prepared as a keepsake for VIPs and for veterans of the "four-stackers" which were transferred to the Royal Navy under the destroyer-bases agreement. It includes the combat histories of the fifty destroyers, each of which was rechristened by the British for a town existing in both Britain and the United States.

GREW, JOSEPH C. *Ten Years in Japan.* New York: 1944.

HALL, H. DUNCAN. *North American Supply.* London: 1955.

HECKSHER, AUGUST (ed.). *The Politics of Woodrow Wilson: Selections from his Speeches and Writings.* New York: 1956.

HIGHAM, JOHN. *Strangers in the Land.* New Brunswick, N.J.: 1955.

HILL (MILLER), HELEN and AGAR, HERBERT. *Beyond German Victory.* New York: 1940.

HOFSTADTER, RICHARD. *The Age of Reform: From Bryan to F.D.R.* New York: 1955.

HOOKER, NANCY HARVISON (ed.). *The Moffat Papers.* Cambridge, Massachusetts: 1956.

HOOVER, HERBERT C. *Shall We Send Our Youth To War?* New York: 1939.

HOWARD, GRAEME K. *America and a New World Order.* New York: 1940.

HULL, CORDELL. *The Memoirs of Cordell Hull.* New York: 1948.

HUTCHISON, BRUCE. *The Incredible Canadian: MacKenzie King.* Toronto: 1956.

ICKES, HAROLD L. *The Secret Diary of Harold L. Ickes: The Lowering Clouds, 1939–1941.* New York: 1954.

The Secret Diary tells of Ickes relations with the Warhawks, his own interventionist attitudes, and the hesitancy and confusion with which the American government moved toward military involvement.

JOHNSON, DONALD BRUCE. *The Republican Party and Wendell Willkie.* Urbana, Illinois: 1960.

This book includes a useful account of the interaction between the Republican nominee and the isolationist and internationalist elements within his party.

JOHNSON, HUGH S. *Hell-bent for War.* New York: 1941.

JOHNSON, WALTER. *The Battle Against Isolation.* Chicago: 1944.

William Allen White's biographer wrote this history of the Committee to Defend America by Aiding the Allies. It is informative and intelligent for the period of White's Chairmanship of the Committee but deteriorates badly thereafter.

KEYNES, JOHN MAYNARD. *The Economic Consequences of the Peace.* New York: 1920.

LANGER, WILLIAM L. and GLEASON, S. EVERETT. *The Challenge to Isolation, 1937–40.* New York: 1952.

Langer and Gleason wrote the foremost history of United States foreign relations from 1937 to 1941. These two volumes remain an indispensable reference for any serious student of the period.

———. *The Undeclared War, 1940–1941.* New York: 1953.

LANGER, WILLIAM L. *Our Vichy Gamble.* New York: 1947.

LEIGHTON, RICHARD M. and COAKLEY, ROBERT W. *Global Logistics and Strategy, 1940–1943.* Washington: 1955.

LEUCHTENBURG, WILLIAM E. *Franklin D. Roosevelt and the New Deal.* New York: 1963.

———. *The Perils of Prosperity: 1914–1932.* Chicago: 1958.

LUBELL, SAMUEL. *Revolt of the Moderates.* New York: 1956.

LUCE, HENRY R. *American Century.* New York: 1941

MAHAN, ALFRED THAYER. *The Interest of America in Seapower, Present and Future.* Boston: 1897.

MAYO-SMITH, RICHMOND. *Emigration and Immigration: A Study in Social Science.* New York: 1904.

MEYER, DONALD B. *The Protestant Search for Political Realism.* Berkeley: 1961.

MILLER, FRANCIS PICKENS and HELEN HILL. *The Giant of the Western World: America and Europe in a North Atlantic Civilization.* New York: 1930.

MILLER, FRANCIS PICKENS (ed.). *Some Regional Views of Our Foreign Policy.* New York: 1939.

MILLER, PERRY (ed.). *The American Puritans: Their Prose and Poetry.* Garden City, New York: 1953.

MILLIS, WALTER. *The Faith of An American.* New York: 1941.

———. *Road to War: America, 1914–1917.* Boston: 1935.

———. *Why Europe Fights.* New York: 1940.

——— and DUFFIELD, E. S. (eds.). *The Forrestal Diaries.* New York: 1951.

MORGENSTERN, GEORGE. *Pearl Harbor: The Story of the Secret War.* New York: 1947.

MORISON, ELTING E. *Turmoil and Tradition, A Study of the Life and Times of Henry L. Stimson.* Boston: 1960.

MORISON, SAMUEL E. *History of the United States Naval Operations in World War II.* Vol. 1, *Battle of the Atlantic.* Boston: 1947.

MUMFORD, LEWIS. *Men Must Act.* New York: 1939.

MURPHY, ROBERT. *Diplomat Among Warriors.* New York: 1964.

NEVINS, ALLAN. *America in World Affairs.* New York: 1941.

NOYES, MORGAN PHELPS. *Henry Sloane Coffin: The Man and his Ministry.* New York: 1964.

OSGOOD, ROBERT E. *Ideals and Self Interest in America's Foreign Relations: The Great Transformation of the Twentieth Century.* Chicago: 1953.

Osgood showed how the over-emphasis on America's idealistic reasons for intervening in the First World War and the frustration of those ideals at Versailles and thereafter caused an emotional revulsion from internationalistic policies during the twenties and thirties. He contended that it took the obvious and immediate dangers of 1940 and 1941 and the presence of a new postwar threat to permanently correct that attitude.

PRINGLE, HENRY F. *Why—Preparedness.* New York: 1941.

RAUCH, BASIL. *Roosevelt: From Munich to Pearl Harbor.* New York: 1950.

ROOSEVELT, ELLIOTT. *As He Saw It.* New York: 1946.

——— (ed.). *F.D.R.: His Personal Letters.* New York: 1950.

ROOSEVELT, FRANKLIN D. *The Public Papers and Addresses of Franklin D. Roosevelt,* 1937–1941 Volumes. New York: 1941 and 1950.

ROVERE, RICHARD. *The American Establishment and Other Reports, Opinions and Speculations.* New York: 1946.

This volume includes a light but suggestive article on the nature of the American Establishment.

SAYERS, MICHAEL and KAHN, ALBERT E. *Sabotage: The Secret War Against America.* New York: 1942.

SCHLESINGER, ARTHUR M., JR. *The Age of Roosevelt: The Coming of the New Deal.* Boston: 1958.

———. *The Age of Roosevelt: The Crisis of the Old Order, 1919–1933.* Boston: 1957.

SHEPARDSON, WHITNEY H. *The Interests of the United States as a World Power.* Claremont, California: 1942.

SHERWOOD, ROBERT E. *Roosevelt and Hopkins.* New York: 1948.

SOLOMON, BARBARA. *Ancestors and Immigrants: A Changing New England Tradition.* Cambridge, Massachusetts: 1956.

STANDLEY, WILLIAM H. and AGETON, ARTHUR A. *Admiral Ambassador to Russia.* Chicago: 1955.

STETINIUS, EDWARD R., JR. *Lend-lease: Weapon for Victory* New York: 1944.

STIMSON, HENRY L. and BUNDY, MC GEORGE. *On Active Service in Peace and War.* New York: 1948.

This classic biography-memoir recorded the words and actions of the foremost interventionist-in-government in 1940 and 1941.

STREIT, CLARENCE K. *On Freedom and Union Now.* New York: 1940.

———. *Union Now with Britain.* New York: 1941.

TANSILL, CHARLES C. *America Goes to War.* Boston: 1938.

———. *Back Door to War: Roosevelt Foreign Policy, 1933–1941.* Chicago: 1952.

THOMAS, NORMAN M. and WOLFE, BERTRAM D. *Keep America Out of War.* New York: 1939.

TULL, CHARLES J. *Father Coughlin and the New Deal.* Syracuse: 1965.

U.S. CONGRESS. *A Decade of American Foreign Policy Basic Documents, 1941–49.* Washington: 1950.

———. *Pearl Harbor Attack: Hearings Before the Joint Committee on the Investigation of the Pearl Harbor Attack.* Washington: 1946.

U.S. PRESIDENT. *Report to Congress on Lend-lease.* Washington: 1941.

U.S. DEPARTMENT OF STATE. *Peace and War: United States Foreign Policy, 1931–1941.* Washington: 1942.

VAN DUSEN, HENRY P. *Church and State in the Modern World.* New York and London: 1937.

WARBURG, JAMES P. *Isolationist Illusion and World Peace.* New York: 1941.
———. *The Long Road Home: The Autobiography of a Maverick.* Garden City, New York: 1964.
———. *Peace in Our Time?* New York: 1940.
———. *Unwritten Treaty.* New York: 1946.
WHALEN, RICHARD. *The Founding Father.* New York: 1965.
This is a sound, objective and sometimes unattractive portrait of Joseph P. Kennedy. It describes and analyzes the Ambassador's views regarding England's chances for survival and the need to "accommodate" Hitler and Mussolini.
WHITE. WILLIAM ALLEN. *The Autobiography of William Allen White.* New York: 1946.

Articles and Periodicals

Atlanta Constitution. June, 1940.
Baltimore Sun. June, 1940.
BEMIS, SAMUEL FLAGG. "Washington's Farewell Address: A Foreign Policy of Independence," *American Historical Review,* XXXIX (January, 1934), 250.
BILLINGTON, RAY A. "The Origins of Midwestern Isolationism," *Political Science Quarterly,* IX (March, 1945), 44–64.
BORCHARD, EDWIN. "The Attorney General's Opinion on the Exchange of Destroyers for Naval Bases," *American Journal of International Law,* XXXIV (October, 1940), 690–97.
Borchard questioned the legality of the destroyer-bases agreement and saw in it the danger that the expanding scope of executive agreements might erode the constitutional treaty-making process.
BORG, DOROTHY. "Notes on Roosevelt's Quarantine Speech," *Political Science Quarterly,* LXXII (September, 1957), 405–33.
Borg showed that the adverse reaction of certain portions of the press to Roosevelt's speech did not in itself end the administration's tentative efforts to find a way to assist the Europeans in reaching some understanding with Hitler.
Boston Globe. June, 1940.
BRIGGS, HERBERT W. "Neglected Aspects of the Destroyer Deal," *American Journal of International Law,* XXXIV (October, 1940), 669–79.
Briggs found the "deal" to violate both the Walsh Amendment and international law.

Chicago Daily News. January–June, 1940.
Chicago Tribune. June, 1940–August, 1941.
Cincinnati Enquirer. June, 1940.
Daily Worker. June, 1940.
DAVENPORT, RUSSELL W. "The Ordeal of Wendell Willkie," *Atlantic Monthly,* CLXXVI (November, 1945), 67–73.
Written by a leading Willkie supporter and advocate of a destroyer transfer, this article described Willkie's difficulties in trying to lead his predominantly isolationist party to victory on a moderately internationalist platform.
Denver Post. July–September, 1941.
Detroit Free Press. June, 1940.
Emporia Gazette. June, 1940.
HIGHAM, JOHN. "Antisemitism in the Gilded Age: A Reinterpretation," *Mississippi Valley Historical Review,* XXXXIII (March, 1957), 559–78.
HUTCHINS, ROBERT M. Speech in New York, February 19, 1941, *Vital Speeches of the Day,* VII (March, 1941), 9–14.
Los Angeles Times. June, 1940.
Louisville Courier-Journal. June, 1940–November, 1941.
MASLAND, JOHN W. "Missionary Influence Upon American Far Eastern Policy, 1937–1941," *Pacific Historical Review,* XI (1942), 281–99.
MILLER, FRANCIS PICKENS. "Atlantic Area," *Foreign Affairs,* XIX (July, 1941), 727–28.
MILLER, HELEN HILL. "Planning the War for Peace," *Virginia Quarterly Review,* XVIII (January, 1942), 72–83.
MILLIS, WALTER. "This is not 1914," *Reader's Digest,* XXXVI (January, 1940), 97–101.
New Orleans Times-Picayune. June, 1940, and July–December, 1941.
New York Herald Tribune. 1938–January, 1942.
New York Times. 1937–January, 1942.
New York World-Telegram. January, 1941.
Philadelphia Evening Bulletin. June, 1940.
Public Opinion Quarterly. IV–VI (1940–1942).
Richmond Times Dispatch. June, 1940.
ROOSEVELT, FRANKLIN D. "Our Foreign Policy: A Democratic View," *Foreign Affairs,* VI (July, 1928), 573–93.
St. Louis Post-Dispatch. June, September, 1940, and July–December, 1941.
San Francisco Examiner. June, 1941.
Social Justice. May, 1940–December, 1941.

STROMBERG, ROLAND N. "American Business and the Approach of War," *Journal of Economic History,* XIII (1953), 58–78.
Stromberg documented businessmen's confusion and their concern for the economic disruption and political consequences which American involvement in the war might cause.
Time. May–October, 1940.
VAN DUSEN, HENRY P. "What is the Church?" *Journal of Religion,* XVII (October, 1937), 410–27.
WALKER, FRANCIS A. "Immigration and Degradation," *Forum,* XI (August, 1891).
Washington Evening Star. June, 1940.
Washington Post. September, 1937, and May, 1940–December, 1941.
WRIGHT, QUINCY. "Repeal of the Neutrality Act," *American Journal of International Law,* XXXVI (January, 1942), 8–23.
———. "The Transfer of Destroyers to Great Britain," *American Journal of International Law,* XXXIV (October, 1940), 680–89.
Wright argued that the transfer did not violate international law. The United States, he said, was not a neutral but rather "a supporting state." Since Germany had violated international agreements, to which it was a party, Wright argued, the United States was not bound to honor those agreements in her relations with Germany.

Unpublished Reports and Essays

CHADWIN, MARK LINCOLN. "The Destroyer-Bases Agreement of 1940." Unpublished Masters Essay, Department of History, Columbia University, 1962.
CIVILIAN PRODUCTION AGENCY. "Industrial Mobilization in the Defense Period." Unpublished Manuscript, National Archives.
DRUMMOND, DONALD F. "From Peace to War: Neutrality and Non-belligerency of the United States, 1937–1941." Unpublished Doctoral Dissertation, Department of History, University of Michigan, 1949.
KNOBLOCH, EVELYN. "The Nazi Bund Movement in Metropolitan New York." Unpublished Masters Essay, Department of History, Columbia University, 1961.
SECRETARY OF WAR, Office of the. "The National Emergency, Part I: July, 1940–December, 1941." Unpublished Report, Stimson Papers, Sterling Library, Yale University.

Index

Acheson, Dean G., biographical data, 58–59; legal opinion on destroyers, 97; leaves Group, 113, 114; open letter to Congress, 150; mentioned, 60, 66, 107
Adams, James Truslow, 122
Advertisements, attacking Wood, 221; in "V" campaign, 227; in "Stop Hitler Now" campaign, 228; on Atlantic war, 235–36; on German invasion of Russia, 244; on France, 250; after Pearl Harbor, 265–66; mentioned, 274
Agar, Herbert, signs "Summons," 37; recruits Alsop, 81; sees Roosevelt on destroyers, 86–87; at Hay-Adams, 105; on awakening American people, 110–11; enunciates Group's new direction, 111–12; attacks Ford, 125; organizes food plan statement, 139; on Catholic appeasement, 146–47; wants national organization, 161; as FFF speaker, 179; on aid to Russia, 188; on academic freedom, 224; gives logic for war declaration, 261; in World War II, 267n; on Freedom House, 268–69; mentioned, 38, 43, 48, 51–53 *passim*, 66, 70, 124, 133, 144, 156, 165, 169, 170, 174, 178, 229, 242, 253
Agar, William, biographical data, 61; and work with Catholics, 111, 112, 147–48; writes pamphlet, 122; on Hoover food plan, 137; seeks Irish bases for British, 148; left in charge, 268; mentioned, 60, 70, 153, 248, 253
Aid to the Allies, internationalist support for, 19; Roosevelt early acts of, 28–30 *passim*
Allen, Robert S., joins Group, 114; investigates use of Fish's frank, 215; on film investigation, 218; in World War II, 267n; mentioned, 168, 232n
Alsop, Joseph, biographical data, 56; recruited for Group work, 81; reports on British defenses, 81–84; helps draft Standley speech, 92; leaves Group, 113; mentioned, 54, 89, 99, 102
Altschul, Frank, 89
America First Committee, geographic distribution of leaders, 66; friends in Congress, 67n; brief history of, 118–20; policy views of, 119; contends against Century Group, 120–23; characterized as "Nazi transmission belt," 121; popularity among students, 123; assailed as "anti-labor," 183; fails to attract labor, 184; letters to Congress, 207; fails to censure Lindbergh, 211; tied to Nazis by franking controversy, 215; and Neutrality Act revision, 240; opposes aid to Russia, 248; mentioned, vii, 16, 62, 66, 68, 109, 169, 179, 190, 217, 220–22, 243, 266, 268, 273
American Communist party, 14
American Council on Soviet Relations, 247
American Expeditionary Force, 28, 62, 145, 150
American Friends of German Freedom, 162, 187
American Friends Service Committee, 136

American Legion, 240
American Peace Foundation, 17
American Peace Mobilization, 247
American Student Union, 247
American Volunteer Group, 56, 196
American Youth for Freedom, 188
American ships, to evacuate British children, 75
Amerika-Deutsche Volksbund, 10. *See also* Bund
Anderson, Admiral Walter S., 83–84
Anglo-Saxons, tendency to interventionism, 19–20; lack of self-identity, 19n; names of Group members, 70; funds from, 189; mentioned, 69. *See also* Establishment
Anglophilism, and interventionism, 19–20; regional factors influencing, 20; mentioned, 56, 71
Anglophobia, 11, 12, 147
Anti-Comintern Pact, 68n, 252
Anti-semitism, Nazi acts of, 10, 53; mentioned, 11, 20, 25, 147, 154, 211–18
Armstrong, Hamilton Fish, 60
"Arsenal of Democracy" speech, 149–51, 193, 200
Athlone, Earl of, 139
Atlantic Conference, 195, 200
Atlantic Ocean, U.S. weakness in, 65, 81; Luce fears clashes with Germany in, 76; under British control, 150; developments in, 192–95; occupation of islands in, 206, 235–37, 270–73 *passim;* war in, 232–42; Nazi invasion of Russia affects, 244; Japan seen in perspective of, 254; mentioned, 4, 260
Attorneys, in Group, 58–60; in FFF, 188
Auhagen, Freidrich, 76–77
Austin, Senator Warren, 152
Axis, 22, 68n, 162, 232, 265–66

Bailey, Senator Josiah W., 15
Baker, Burke, 170
Balderston, John L., signs "Summons," 37; biographical data, 55–56; operates news service, 101–2; responds to personal attack, 115–18; reports on Kennedy, 126; on Japan, 254; mentioned, 54, 69, 100, 135n
Battle, George Gordon, 174
Bayless, Judge Wayne, 153
Barber, Courtney, Jr., 212, 247, 267
Barres, Phillipe, 250
Beard, Charles A., 4, 5, 153
Beaverbrook, 195, 247
Bell, Laird, 170
Bell, Ulric, biographical data, 51–52; and destroyer deal, 105; directs Room 2940, 113, 114; article on Nazi newsreels, 121; on Kennedy "menace," 128; sends questionnaires, 133; and British Information Service, 139; placates Hull on Vichy, 142; and Lend-Lease, 152–55 *passim;* favors national organization, 161; as chairman of Executive Committee, 170; contacts with newspapers, 172; and Committee to Defend America, 174–75; and San Francisco shipyard strike, 181–82; seeks "state of emergency," 198; relations with Roosevelt, 201–2, 204–5, 238; on franking abuses, 213–15; on film investigation, 217; and Wood, 221; on Scammon case, 225; rejects Communist help, 243–44; and Japan, 256, 258; and Pearl Harbor, 264–66; service in World War II, 267n; mentioned, 64, 77, 81, 112, 124, 133, 140, 144, 169, 174, 178, 184, 247, 253, 257
Bemis, Samuel Flagg, quoted, 16
Berlin, Irving, 229
Berlin, Mrs. Irving, 120–21, 153
Bernstein, Henri, 250
Bingham, Barry, and Hutchins, 128; pays Bell, Agar salaries, 178; mentioned, 51, 77, 81, 129
Birkhead, L. M., 22, 157, 162, 211
Bone, Senator Homer, 106, 217
Bookman, Archbishop Francis, 248
Boston, FFF chapter, 247
Brandeis, Louis D., 59
Britain, internationalists urge cooperation with, 17; encourages U.S. expansion, 18; U.S. efforts

to aid, 29, 75, 78, 279; U.S. ties to, 43, 47, 52, 53, 69–70; Group members educated in, 61; effect of fall of, 68; Group's familiarity with, 68–69; need to keep her fighting, 72; CDA asks credits for, 79; Britain's needs, 82–83, 100–1, 115, 117; Irish bases sought for, 148; Catholics and aid to, 147–48; Group's ties to, 269; mentioned, 52, 55, 59, 63, 253, 260. *See also* British, British fleet, British Information Service, Commonwealth

British, evacuation from Dunkirk, 3; cash-and-carry orders, 28; appeasement, 57; Embassy, 74; children, 78–79; situation in the air, 82; morale raised by destroyer deal, 107; refuse food plan, 135; Group relationship with, 139, 143; labor movement, 183; situation, April to December, 1941, 191–97; staff talks with U.S. and Canada, 192; warships repaired in U.S., 192–93; ships convoyed by U.S. Navy, 236; declare war on Finland, 252; promise war with Japan, 256; mentioned, 24, 75, 271. *See also* British fleet, British Information Service, Commonwealth

British fleet, U.S. dependence on, 18, 55, 79, 81, 92; need of destroyers, 82–83, 91; guarantee regarding, 41, 75–76, 85, 98–99, 105; mentioned, 4, 20, 43, 45, 77–88, 102–3, 148, 278

British Information Service, 139, 186, 245

Broadway, represented in Group, 64–65

Brooks, Senator C. Wayland, 217

Browder, Earl, quoted, 14

Bruce, Mrs. David K., 177

Bullitt, Ambassador William C., 38, 79

Bund, 10, 14, 217

Burke-Wadsworth bill, 93. *See also* Selective Service

Burlingham, Charles, 97

Businessmen, fear war disruption and controls, 13; support preparedness, 28n; in Group, 56–58; isolationism among, 123–28

Byrne, Chancellor James, 147

Cabinet, U.S., meeting of August 2, 1940, 88

Cabot, Henry B., 170

Canada, Moffat as minister to, 33–34; mentioned, 41, 64, 99, 103, 192

Carr, William, 147

Carroll, Vincent, quoted, 37

Cash-and-carry, 26–30 *passim*

Catholics, W. Agar, as specialist on, 61; in Group, 70; British, 94; and aid to Russia, 187, 243, 248–49; mentioned, 141, 273

Catholic Laymen's Committee for Peace, 249

Catledge, Turner, 56, 212

CDA (CDAAA). *See* Committee to Defend America by Aiding the Allies

Century Club, 66, 80, 88

Century Group, its name and membership, 44; early policy views, 44–45, 72–73; biographical data on, 45–70; expenses, 52, 113; attitudes on combat, 66; fears of German victory, 68; as Anglo-Saxon "ethnic" response, 69–71; as Establishment response, 69–71; reasons for wanting war, 72–73; operation of office, 76–78; second meeting of, 80–86; cooperation with CDA, 78–79, 85; seeks Roosevelt-Willkie cooperation, 85; campaign for destroyers, 87, 104; supports British needs, 101; personnel and functions change, 109–14; its adjuncts, 114; attacked by Senate isolationists, 115–18; and America First, 120–23; publishes pamphlets, 122; responds to isolationists, 129; welcomes Roosevelt victory, 131; objectives during winter 1940–41, 132; opposes Hoover food plan, 134–41, 143; seeks relaxation of British blockade, 137–39; relations with British, 139; reacts to peace offensive, 143–44; and Irish bases for Britain, 148–49; and "Ar-

senal of Democracy" speech, 149–50; and Lend-Lease, 151–56; inadequacies revealed, 156; dissatisfied with other pro-Allies bodies, 156–58; invites pro-Allies leaders to meetings, 162; FFF approach to Roosevelt similar to, 200; and convoys, 234; on Japan, 253; ties to Britain, 269; motivation and influence, 269–77; tactics, 273–74; mentioned, viii, 45, 48–54 *passim,* 70, 74, 99
Chiang Kai-shek, 255, 256
Chairman, of FFF, 165–66; honorary, 164–65
Chase, Mary Ellen, 170
Cheney, Ward, biographical data, 52–53; sees Roosevelt on destroyers, 86–87; at Hay-Adams, 105; and Group expenses, 113; seeks business support, 124; votes for Roosevelt, 131; asks war with Japan, 256; mentioned, 56, 68, 169, 174
Chennault, General Claire, 196
Chicago, center of isolationism, 10, 20, 129; FFF chapter, 267
Chicago Tribune, reacts to "Quarantine" speech, 25; on destroyer deal, 106; on Lend-Lease, 153; attacked by FFF, 212; mentioned, 153, 270n
China, Japanese invasion of, 195–96; mentioned, 196, 253–58, 275
Christian, anti-communism, 243; involvement in current affairs, 45, 62, 165–66
Christian Front, 11–12, 14, 120
Christiancy, George, 90
Churchill, Winston S., requests arms, 24, 30; informed of Warhawks, 41; requests destroyers, 41n, 75; and destroyer-bases agreement, 96–105 *passim;* seeks Irish bases, 148; and aid to Russia, 195, 245; and occupation of Iceland, 236; mentioned, 87, 125, 219, 221, 226
Clark, Senator Bennett Champ, 115
Clark, Senator D. Worth, and film industry, 217–19; mentioned, 153
Clark, Grenville, directs Military Training Camp Association, 19; at Group meeting, 80; signs letter, 149; mentioned, 18, 155, 168, 170, 233n
Clayton, Will, opposes "Summons," 36; biographical data, 56–57; visits St. Louis, 152; favors national body, 161; mentioned, 48, 68, 124
Clergymen, in Group, 61–62
Cleveland, Richard F., 32, 37, 80
Coffin, Henry Sloane, biographical data, 61–62; describes talk with Hull, 80; seeks relaxation of British blockade, 137–39; responds to Hoover, 140; mentioned, 49, 69, 95, 158
Cohen, Benjamin V., opinion on destroyer transfer, 89; shown FFF ad, 258; mentioned, 97
Cole, Wayne S., quoted, 119, 211
Commission to Negotiate the Peace, U.S., 57, 59, 65
Committee on Public Information, 55, 158
Committee to Defend America by Aiding the Allies, founded, 22; Group establishes relations with, 51; Sherwood's role in, 64; geographic distribution of leaders, 65–66; cooperation with Group, 78–79, 85; and news service, 101; helps create adjuncts, 114; attacked in Senate, 115–18; New York chapter, 156, 163; relations with FFF, 173–76; cooperates with FFF, 175, 179–80, 226, 232; chapters join FFF, 189; letters to Congress, 207; and Atlantic issues, 233–41; and shoot-on-sight, 238; and aid to Russia, 244, 246; denounces Communist front, 246; on Japan, 253, 255; on declaration of war, 259, 260n; and Freedom House, 268; mentioned, 48, 50, 60, 66, 68, 75, 112, 120, 159–63 *passim,* 169, 190, 203, 206, 270
Commonwealth, British, 41, 47, 68, 75. *See also* Britain, British
Communism, Warhawks accused of, 222
Communists, FFF problems with, 242–49; mentioned, 14

Conant James B., biographical data, 60; on Hoover food plan, 135n; open letter to Congress, 150; Conant-Douglas telegram, 149, 151; in FFF, 202; mentioned, 140, 153, 168, 170, 179
Congress, U.S., Group's friends in, 67; isolationists in, 67n, 98; open letter to, 150, Lend-Lease bill, 152–56; petitions to, 154–55, 206–8; Neutrality Act revision, 239–42; on aid to Russia, 249; mentioned, 78, 89, 176, 273
Conspiracy theory, of U.S. entry into World War II, 71n
"Continental Congress," and declaration of war, 260; described, 229–30
Continentalism, described, 4, 16; Acheson opposes, 59. *See also* Isolationism
Contributions, to FFF, 177–78
Convoys, British ships join U.S., 194; FFF and, 233–41; mentioned, 75, 192, 206, 270, 272
Coolidge, President Calvin, 16
Coolidge, Mrs. Calvin, 170
Couch, William T., quoted, 159–60
Coughlin, Father Charles, 11–12, 120, 147
Council for Democracy, helps create adjuncts, 114; limitations of, 157; mentioned, 22, 112, 162
Council on Foreign Relations, described, 17; mentioned, 32, 37, 47–48, 52, 57, 65, 89, 113, 170
Crum, Bartley, 182
Curie, Eve, 250
Curran, Father Edward Lodge, 147
Curran, Joseph, 153
Cusick, F. H. Peter, joins work in Room 2940, 114; contacts with British, 139; seeks Willkie support for FFF, 164; as executive secretary, 170; contacts with newspapers, 172; and finances, 176; on FFF relations with White House, 201; on film investigation, 208; calls Lindbergh "anti-semite," 211; seeks subscribers for *Chicago Sun,* 212; defends Wheeler's right to speak, 225; on appeasement in State Department, 255–56; and Pearl Harbor, 264–66; mentioned, 64, 168, 181

Dabney, Virginius, 95
Danaher, Senator, John, 115
Daniels, Jonathan, quoted, 35
Darlan, Admiral Jean F., 250
Davenport, Russell, reports Willkie's acquiescence, 105; mentioned, 89, 107
Davis, Elmer, biographical data, 56; leaves Group, 113; in World War II, 267n; mentioned, 54, 69
Day, Representative Stephen, 213, 214
"Death tags," 143–45, 156
DeGaulle, General Charles, 207, 250–51
Democratic party, 10, 11, 23
Dennett, Prescott, 215
Destroyers, Willkie support for transfer sought, 80; legal barrier to transfer of, 83–84; Luce urges *quid pro quo* for, 84–85; Group's rationale for transfer of, 86; discussed by news service, 102; mentioned, 44, 51, 75. *See also* Destroyer-bases agreement
Destroyer-bases agreement, 74–108; effect of, 107–8; mentioned, 143, 200, 270, 272
Dewey, Thomas E., 30
Domestic Fight For Freedom, 224–26
Donovan, Colonel William J., speaks on draft, 79, 92; resigns from FFF, 202; mentioned, 125, 168, 170, 179, 180, 203n, 264n
Douglas Lewis W., hosts first Group meeting, 43; biographical data, 50–51; works with CDA and Willkie, 75, 78–80; drafts memorandum, 75; and destroyer transfer, 89, 96; on Willkie's acquiescence, 105; on Group's future function, 110; more involved in CDA, 114; warns of British defeat, 123–24; opposes food plan, 135; drafts telegram to Roosevelt, 149; travels for Group, 152; asked to report on national organization, 161; gives assurances on CDA, 162–63;

mentioned, 56, 67, 68, 105, 144, 155
Douglas-Shepardson memorandum, 75–76
Douglas, Melvyn, 170
Douglas, Paul H., 212
Dow, Douglas, 36
Dubinsky, David, 149
Dulles, Allen W., biographical data, 59–60; leads study of production, 110; leaves Group, 113, 114; mentioned, 48, 58, 67, 169, 170, 229
Dulles, John Foster, 97n
"Dupe-sympathizer-agent" technique, 208–23, 274
Dunkirk, 3, 43, 47, 53, 72, 277

Earle, Edward Mead, 256
Early, Steve, on response to "Arsenal of Democracy" speech, 150; and FFF, 201–4; mentioned, 52, 144, 234
Educators, in the Group, 60–61; British, 94; mentioned, 141
Eichelberger, Clark, works for Neutrality repeal, 20–21; organizes CDA, 22; sees Roosevelt on destroyers, 86-87; attends Group meetings, 101; and FFF, 174; as head of CDA, 175; mentioned, 17, 78, 157, 160, 234, 238
Eliot, George Fielding, biographical data, 55, rejects negotiated peace, 143–44; mentioned, 54, 69, 257
Elliston, H. B., quoted, 252
Embargo, against Japan, 26–27, 255
Emmet, Christopher, quoted, 257
Entertainers, 273. *See also* "Fun to be Free" show
Establishment, Eastern, described, 69; Group as members of, 69–71; conspiracy theory about, 71n; FFF contributions from members of, 178; and the Japanese, 253; mentioned, 70, 274
Ethridge, Mark, quoted, 124; mentioned, 51
Europe, interdependence with North America, 46, 55, 69, 269; Eastern, 59; conditions in occupied, 134–41, 183; food for, 271; U.S. interest in, 275–79 *passim;* mentioned, 75
Evans, Silliman, 212
Everitt, Helen, 111, 112
Executive Committee of FFF, decides labor tactics, 180–81; seeks merger of youth groups, 188; decides to deactivate, 268
Extremist groups, 14–15

Facism, 12–13, 71, 125, 243. *See also* Italy, Mussolini, Spain
Fairbanks, Douglas, Jr., 216
Farrar, John, 162, 168
Federal propaganda agency, 158
FFF. *See* Fight For Freedom Committee
Fichte-bund, 10
Field, George, 78
Field, Marshall, signs telegram, 149; sees Roosevelt, 204n, 212; starts *Chichago Sun,* 212; mentioned, 169, 170, 174, 178
Fight For Freedom Committee, and Catholics, 61; the "domestic" 128n–29n, 224–26; founding of, 158–67; Declaration, 161–67 *passim;* inaugural address, 167–68; list of sponsors of, 168; structure of, 169–71; Executive Committee, 169; finances, 169, 176–78; Policy Committee, 170–71; local chapters organized, 170–73 *passim,* 176; regional strength of, 171; contacts with newspapers, 172; absorption of other groups, 173, 175–6; relations with CDA, 173–76; speakers bureau, 178–80; rallies, 179; attacked by isolationists, 179n, 222; quality of local chapters, 190; and "Unlimited Emergency" speech, 199; "Action" program, 201; relations with Roosevelt administration, 201–6; on issues of summer 1941, 201; petition and letter-writing, 206–8; attacks Lindbergh, 208–11; attacks McCormick and *Tribune,* 212; dispute with Pope, 219–20; attacks Wood, 220–22; policy positions, 232–62; and convoys, 233–41; summer program, 235; aid to

Russia, 242–49; denounces fronts, 246–47; on Finland, 251–52; and Japan, 252–59; seeks declaration of war, 259–62; plans after Pearl Harbor, 266; end of, 267–69; leaders' service in World War II, 267; conclusions about, 269–77; mentioned, viii, 52, 54, 60–64 *passim*, 77, 101, 151
Film industry, pro-Allies sentiment in, 65; investigated by Senators, 215–19
Finances, FFF, 176–78
Finland, 27, 232, 242, 249, 251–52
"First to Fight" division, FFF, 188
Fish, Representative Hamilton, constituents seem to oppose, 122; allows Pelley to use frank, 214–15; mentioned, 80, 213, 221, 274
Fisher, Walter T., 36
Fleischer, Wilfred, 257
Flynn, Errol, 218
Flynn, John T., 147, 211
Fontanne, Lynn, 229
Ford, Henry, Group attacks, 124–25; mentioned, 119, 123, 129
Foreign Policy Association, 17, 136
"Four Freedoms," 150–51
France, cooperation with urged, 17; planes for, 29; Group opposes supplies for, 141–42; mentioned, 27, 43, 45, 63, 68, 136, 166, 187, 249–51, 278–79. *See also* Free French, French
Frankfurter, Justice Felix, 97
Franking privilege controversy, 213–15
Freedom House, 226, 268–69
Free French, 207, 250–51
"Free World," 275
French, will to resist, 3–4; occupation of the Ruhr, 7; attempt to buy planes, 25–26; cash-and-carry orders, 28; appeasement, 57; Indo-China, 196; mentioned, 24. *See also* France, Free French
Friends of Democracy, Group circulates materials from, 121; limitations of, 157; mentioned, 22, 114, 162, 211, 246
"Fun to be Free" show, 178, 228–29, 274
Gallup Poll, 27, 30, 154, 177, 240n, 257
Gannett, Frank, quoted, 15
Gauss, Christian, 187
Gay, Eustace, quoted, 186
German, conquest of Europe, 3–4; invasion of Britain, 44, 78; Group fears effects of victory of, 68; businessmen, fate of, 121; reaction to Hoover food plan, 135; invasion of Russia, 193, 195; science, 270; fear of renewed aggression from, 276. *See also* Germany
German-Americans, isolationism among, 9–11, 20; Nazi efforts among, 10–11; mentioned, 70, 187–88
Germany, danger to U.S., 81, 278–79; conditions in, 183; invades Russia, 242–49; as primary threat, 253; mentioned, 60, 72, 75, 97n, 136, 187, 232, 243, 260, 261, 265–67 *passim*
Gerrard, James W., 153
Gibson, Ernest W., as head of CDA, 162, 163
Gillette, Senator Guy, 153
Glass, Senator Carter, as FFF honorary chairman, 164–65; on U-boats, 238; on Neutrality revision, 239; mentioned, 67, 229
Goldsmith, Arthur, 174
Grafton, Samuel, 127, 257–58
Graham, Frank, 127
Green, William, quoted, 140; mentioned, 127–28
USS *Greer,* 194, 211, 238, 239
Griffith, Richard M., 170
Grillo, Frank, 183
Guinzburg, Harold, biographical data, 63–64; and Willkie trip to Britain, 133; in World War II, 267n; mentioned, 70, 169, 170, 178

Hackworth, Green L., 105
Halifax, Lord, 258
Harbord, General James, 38, 90
Harding, President Warren G., 16
Hardisty, Frederick, 268
Hardman, J. B. S., 170
Harlem division, FFF, 184–86
Harriman, E. Roland, 149

Harriman, W. Averell, goes to Britain, 192; to Moscow, 195, 247; and FFF, 202; mentioned, 194 237
Havell, George, 178
Hawaii, 5, 264. *See also* Pearl Harbor
Hawks, definition of, vii. *See also* Century Group, Fight For Freedom Committee, or individual names
Hayes, Carlton J. H., 147
Hayes, Helen, 216, 228–29
Hearst, William Randolph, 23, 144
Hearst newspapers, react to "Quarantine" speech, 25; criticize Lindbergh, 211
Hecht, Ben, 229
Henley, Bishop Joseph P., 248
Henry, Patrick, 229
Hessler, William, 77
Hill, George, 215
Hill, George Watts, signs "Summons," 37; biographical data, 58; works with Couch, 160; mentioned, 48, 56, 80, 156
Hill-Couch Committee, 160, 173
Hill, Senator Lister, 229
Hillman, Sidney, 183, 202
Hitler, Adolf, aggression in Europe, 3–4, 24–26; trading with, 124; and Hoover food plan, 135–37; as anti-American, 146, 227–28; and Christianity, 147; Negroes and, 186; Lindbergh and, 209–10; "Stop Hitler Now" campaign, 227–28; and Atlantic, 234–35, 238; declares war on U.S., 266; Hawks fear domination of, 268–70; mentioned, 4, 13, 15, 20, 21, 24, 27, 43, 45, 57, 61, 72, 76, 118, 155, 162, 167, 172, 242–48 *passim,* 257–61 *passim,* 264, 265, 275
Hoare-Laval scheme, 24
Hobson, Bishop Henry W., signs "Sumons," 37; biographical data, 62; and Protestants, 111; responds to survey, 133; and blockade, 141; responds to Hoover, 141; accepts FFF chairmanship, 165; inaugural address, 167–68; telegram to Roosevelt, 199; on Atlantic Conference, 200; attacks Lindbergh, 211; defends Marcantonio's right to speak, 225; says Lend-Lease ends neutrality, 239; on Finland, 252; on Japan, 254, 255; hears of Pearl Harbor, 263–64; on future plans, 266; mentioned, 43, 61, 70, 158, 167, 169, 183, 184, 229, 253, 267
Hoffman, Ross, 147
Hoffman, Theodore, quoted, 10
Hollywood, represented in Group, 64–65
Holman, Senator Rufus, 155
Holt, Senator Rush D., attacks Group and news service, 115–18
Hoover, Herbert, plan to feed occupied Europe, 50, 134–41, 147, 156, 200; alleges opponents willing to compromise, 140–41
Hoover, J. Edgar, 77, 222n
Hopkins, Ernest M., biographical data, 60–61; responds to survey, 133; on "Stop Hitler Now," 228; mentioned, 125, 151, 194, 237
Hopkins, Harry, 64
House of Representatives, U.S., and Neutrality revision, 239–42; mentioned, 153, 183, 233n. *See also* Congress, U.S.
House Un-American Activities Committee, 14
Howard, Graeme, 121, 123
Howard, Roy, 145
Hull, Cordell, supports Stimson Doctrine, 24; Bell's friendship with, 51; approves Alsop work, 82; in Cabinet debate, 88; congratulates Pershing, 91; and destroyer negotiations, 96–97; and Group in fall, 1940, 113; opposes freezing Axis assets, 129; and French policy, 142, 251; and Irish bases, 148; and Finland, 252, talks to Japanese, 256–57; mentioned, 74, 81, 83, 107, 152, 198
Hutcheson, William L., 184
Hutchins, Robert M., Group attack on, 128–29, 225

Iceland, occupation of, 194, 236; mentioned, 33, 201
Ickes, Harold L., favors aid to Al-

lies, 29; in cabinet debate, 88–89; seeks Tobin membership in FFF, 182; works closely with FFF, 202–3; mentioned, 179, 180, 194
Indiana Defense Committee, 173
Ingersoll, Ralph, 127
Internationalism, description and history, 16–22; of Warhawks, 269; public acceptance of, 275–77
Internationalists, view British fleet as U.S. defense, 18; fear one-power control of Europe, 18; fear effects of isolated U.S., 21–22
Interventionists, defined, vii; fear Nazi invasion of Britain and Western Hemisphere, 33. *See also* Century Group, Fight For Freedom Committee
Irish-American, support of Coughlin, 11; Anglophobia, 11–12; isolationism, 11–12; mentioned, 70, 92, 146–49
Isolationism, description and history, 4–16; doubts of strength of democracy contribute to, 15; Republican, 24, 50, 80, 87, 103, 131; denounced by Lewis Douglas, 50–51; Hobson denounces, 62; among businessmen, 123–28; in Milwaukee, 240n; mentioned, 56
Isolationists, some support naval rearmament, 27–28; in Congress, 67n, 78; react to destroyer deal, 106; in Senate attack Group, 115–18; FFF controversies with, 208–23; in Senate investigate film industry, 215–19; attacks on Hawks by, 222; in Congress oppose aid to Russia, 248; see Hawk-Roosevelt conspiracy, 270; FFF neutralizes, 273. *See also* America First Committee
Italian-Americans, 12, 219
Italy, 72, 187, 265, 267. *See also* Mussolini, Benito

Jackson, C. D., 22
Jackson, Katherine Gauss, 111, 112, 114, 169
Jackson, Attorney General Robert H., opinion on torpedo boats, 87; on legality of destroyer transfer, 98, 104; in "National Unity" drive, 133
Jaffe, Louis I., quoted, 36
Japan, U.S.-Japanese relations, 26–27, 195–97, 252–59; as a secondary threat, 253; mentioned, 68, 232, 244, 249, 260, 263–65 *passim*
Jay, Pierre, 169, 170
Jews, opposed to Nazism, 20; in Germany, 25; in Century Group, 70; FFF contributions from, 178, 189; in Hollywood, 216–18; mentioned, 14, 63, 64, 126, 154. *See also* Anti-semitism
Johnson, Senator Hiram W., 4
Johnson, General High, 95, 211
Johnson, Louis, 240n–41n
Johnson, Wayne, active in forming FFF, 164; and FFF finances, 170, 176–78; seeks Tobin membership in FFF, 182; on communism in Washington, D.C., chapter, 247; in World War II, 207n; mentioned, 104, 204n
Jones, Jesse, 152

Kaufman, George S., 145, 168
Kaufman, Mrs. George S., 153, 178
USS *Kearny*, 241, 261
Kellogg-Briand treaty, 47
Kennedy, Ambassador Joseph P., opposes U.S. involvement, 12, 121; Group seeks his resignation, 125–28; warns Jews in Hollywood, 126; mentioned, 129, 147
Kent, Frank, 37, 244
Keynes, John Maynard, 5
Kimmel, Admiral H. H., 263
Kingdon, Frank, 174, 230
Kintner, Robert, 56
Knox, Frank, appointed to cabinet, 28–29; approves Alsop work, 82; in cabinet debate, 88; cooperates with FFF, 202; mentioned, 18, 81, 83, 84, 91, 98, 107, 194, 198, 204, 237, 240n
Knudsen, William, cooperates with FFF, 202; mentioned, 36, 229
Konoye, Fumimaro, 256
Knutson, Representative Harold, 106

Kriendler, Mac, 169, 178, 228
Krock, Arthur, 94–96
Kuhn, Fritz, 10, 11
Ku Klux Klan, 15, 120, 183
Kurusu, Saburu, 256

Labor, FFF appeal to, 180–84; FFF success with, 189–90; British, 94; mentioned, 112, 176, 273
LaFollette, Robert M., Sr., 7, 153
La Guardia, Fiorello, Cusick works with, 201; mentioned, 153, 229, 240n
Lamont, Thomas, 124, 234
Land, Admiral Emory S., 181–82
Landon, Alfred, 133
Latin America, 27, 47, 68, 75, 198–99
Laval, Pierre, 250, 251
Leach, Henry Goddard, 170
Legal obstructions to destroyer deal, ways around, 97–98
Legion for American Unity, 22, 246
Lehman, Governor Herbert H., 152, 153
Lend-Lease, America First opposes, 119; congressional and public debate, 151–56; Protocol, 195; China receives, 196; to Russia, 237, 247; as ending neutrality, 239; mentioned, 163, 192, 207, 212, 233–34, 254, 271
Lewis, Kathryn, 184
Lindbergh, Anne Morrow, 121
Lindbergh, Charles A., and peace offensive, 143; attacked by FFF, 208–11; charged with anti-semitism, 210–11; and conspiracy theory, 270n; mentioned, 119, 201, 221, 222, 274
Lippmann, Walter, 90, 244
Littauer, Lucius, 177
Logan Act, 100
London Economic Conference, 50
Lothian, Lord, tells Van Dusen need for destroyers, 41; tells Churchill of Hawks, 41; arranges British speakers, 94; writes memo of British needs, 100–1; cooperates with Group on food plan, 137–39; dies, 139; mentioned, 50, 75, 81, 96, 99
Louisville Courier-Journal, sponsors "Unity" rally, 133; mentioned, 38, 51, 53, 77, 121, 124, 128
Loyal Americans of German Descent, 187–88
Lubell, Samuel, cited, 10
Lubin, Isador, 181
Luce, Henry R., biographical data, 63; on Douglas-Shepardson memo, 76; talks with Hull and Roosevelt, 80–81; suggests *quid pro quo,* 84–85; leaves Group, 113, 114, 135n; mentioned, 49, 74
Lucey, Bishop Robert E., 147
Lundeen, Senator Ernest, 8

MacArthur, Charles, 229
McCormick, Colonel Robert R., attacked by FFF, 212; mentioned, 106, 144, 153
McFarland, Senator Ernest, 217, 219
MacKenzie King, W. L., 99, 103
MacLeish, Archibald, at Hay-Adams, 105; recruits Hawks for Office of Facts and Figures, 267n; mentioned, 89n
McMahon, Dr. Francis E., 248
McNary, Charles, 80, 131, 207
MacPhail, Archibald, 267
McWilliams, Joe, 14–15, 120, 213–14
Mahan, Admiral Alfred Thayer, 18, 269
"Main Street," 172, 254
Mallory, Walter, 89
Marcantonio, Vito, 225
Maritain, Jacques, 250
Marshall, General George C., 84, 104, 258
Marshall Plan, 275
Maryland, FFF chapter, 267
Mather, Cotton, quoted, 6
Maverick, Maury, joins Group, 114; denounces Hutchins, 128; responds to survey, 133; mentioned, 153, 179
May, Stacy, 32, 37
Mellett, Lowell, and FFF, 201–4; mentioned, 144
Meredith, Burgess, 174, 179, 216, 228–29

Mergers, of FFF and CDA chapters, 173–76
Military situation, April to December, 1941, 191–97
Military training, 19, 232n–33n
Miller, Douglas, 267n
Miller, Francis Pickens, hosts interventionists, 32; and Moffat appointment, 33–34; and "Summons," 34; biographical data, 45–48; leaves Group office, 52, 113; directs office, 75–78 *passim;* writes memo on second meeting, 84; on Krock, 95; and news service, 101; at Hay-Adams, 105; explains Group's function, 109; and Ross article, 115–16; addresses DAR, 145–46; wants national organization, 161; gets Glass as honorary chairman, 164; and Virginia petition to Roosevelt, 198; hears of Pearl Harbor, 264; on termination of FFF, 267–68; service in World War II, 267n; mentioned, 35, 38, 43, 49, 69, 70, 89–90, 112, 140, 144, 156, 158, 165, 169, 253
Miller, Helen Hill, signs "Summons," 37; opposes organized pressure group, 40–41; sees Lothian for Group, 100–1; writes pamphlet, 122; mentioned, 32, 45, 77
Miller, Merle, 218
Miller, William B., 267
Millikan, Robert S., 149
Millis, Walter, on World War I, 5; signs "Summons," 37; signs Conant-Douglas telegram, 149; mentioned, 38, 77, 168
Milton, George Fort, 77
Moffat, J. Pierrepont, 33–34
Moley, Raymond, 57
Molotov-Ribbentrop Pact, 14
Morgan, Aubrey, 139, 201
Morgenthau, Henry, Jr., and plane production and sale to French, 25; favors aid to Allies, 29; favors freezing Axis assets, 129; and aircraft for Britain, 130; mentioned, 151, 194, 202n, 237
Morrow, Mrs. Dwight, 155
Movie industry, lectured by Kennedy, 126; Senate investigation of, 215–19
Mumford, Lewis, 37, 162, 168, 179
Mundt, Representative Karl, 80
Murphy, Justice Frank, 248
Mussolini, Benito, declares war on U.S., 266; mentioned, 12, 13, 15, 24, 38, 154, 265
Muste, A. J., 224

National Committee on Food for the Five Small Democracies, 135. *See also* Hoover, Herbert
National Defense Advisory Commission, 28, 36, 129
National Policy Committee, function, 47–48; mentioned, 32, 40, 49, 58, 77
"National Unity" drive, 133–34
Naval Expansion Act of June 1940, 83–84
Navy, United States. *See* United States Navy
Nazis, conquest of Europe, 9, 13, 20, 21; in the U.S., 10–11; delude some Catholics, 147; aided by Vichy, 250; mentioned, 34, 62, 72, 254. *See also* German, Germany, Hitler
Negroes, and interventionism, 184–86; mentioned, 176, 224, 273
Neutrality Act, internationalists oppose, 17; revisions of November 1939, 26; repeal desired by Lothian, 101; Congress votes revision of, 235–42; revision mentioned, 29, 184, 195, 206, 259, 270, 273; repeal asked in FFF petitions, 207; mentioned, 76, 156
Neutrality zone, 26, 192
New Deal, 14, 50, 53, 61, 92, 146
Newsmen, in Group, 54–56
Newspapers, carrying "Summons," 38–39; FFF contact with, 172; ethnic, 187
New York City, center of interventionism, 20; street battles with isolationists in, 179n; ethnic newspapers in, 187; mentioned, 65, 156, 169, 170
New York Fight For Freedom Committee to Defend America, 156, 173–75

New York Herald Tribune, coverage of Pershing speech, 91; mentioned, 33–34, 54, 55, 77, 103
New York Times, coverage of Pershing speech, 91; accepts ad on Japan, 258; mentioned, 33–34, 38–39, 56, 77, 212, 244
USS *Niblack*, 194
Nicholas, Archbishop John T., 249
Niebuhr, Reinhold, 22, 158, 187
Niles, David K., suggests FFF labor head, 181; and FFF, 202–4; mentioned, 144
Nomura, Admiral, 256
Non-belligerency, desired by Lothian, 101
Nonpartisan Committee for Peace through Revision of the Neutrality Law, 20–21
Norris, Senator George W., 7
North Atlantic Treaty, 275
North Carolina Committee to Defend America Now, 160
Nuclear weapons, 22, 275–76
Nye, Senator Gerald P., investigations of munitions industry, 5; on destroyer deal, 106; on Lend-Lease, 152; and franking abuses, 214; attacks film industry, 216–18; and conspiracy, 270n; mentioned, 8, 67, 80, 115, 153, 201, 212, 213, 274

Ogdensburg Agreement, 99
O'Hara, Bishop Edwin V., 147
O'Neill, Eugene, 148n
Overlock, Dorothy, 128, 169, 170

Pacific Ocean, 26, 72, 236, 252–60 *passim*, 264–65
Pacifism, Protestant, 8–9, 225–26n; slows preparedness effort, 27; student, 9, 128; at Union Theological Seminary, 49; new magazine aimed at Christian, 158; mentioned, 64
Panama, Declaration of, 26
Parker, Dorothy, 179, 242
Parry, Albert, accused of communism, 222; mentioned, 212, 247
Parsons, Geoffrey, biographical data, 54–55; drafts part of Willkie speech, 103; leaves Group, 113, 114; mentioned, 67
Peabody, Endicott, 58
Peace offensive, 143–44, 212
Peale, Dr. Norman Vincent, 219
Pearl Harbor, FFF reaction to, 263–66; FFF plans after, 266–67; mentioned, 12, 135, 169, 177, 205, 226, 252, 277
Pecora, Judge Ferdinand, 22
Pelley, William Dudley, uses Fish's frank, 214–15; mentioned, 14, 120
Pepper, Representative Claude, 67
Pershing, General John J., speaks on destroyers, 86, 89–91; mentioned, 107, 271
Petain, Marshall Henri Philippe, 141, 251
Petitions, on convoys, 234; on Neutrality repeal, 239–40; mentioned, 206–8, 233n
Philadelphia, FFF show in, 229
Pickett, Clarence E., 136
Pittman amendment, 26
"Plattsburg movement," 19
Poe, Clarence, 35
Policy Committee, FFF, polled on war declaration, 259
Polk, Frank L., 58, 113
Pope, Generoso, dispute with FFF, 219–20
Populism, relationship to isolationism, 6–8; myth of conspiracy, 7–8, 216–17; Lindbergh heir to, 209
Potsdam Conference, 275
Powell, Reverend Adam Clayton, Sr., 9, 185, 242
Price, Governor James H., 152, 198
Pringle, Henry, joins Group, 114; writes pamphlet, 122; opposes supplies for France, 142
Procope, Hjalmar, 252
Propaganda, federal agency, 158, 203, 203n
"Protocols of the Elders of Zion," 214
Public opinion, as of March, 1940, 3; as of May, 1940, 4; on World War I, 5; in May, 1940, on outcome of war, 26–27; in June, 1940, on outcome and U.S. involvement, 30-31; attitudes in, July, 1940, 43; on destroyer transfer, 104; war would be sup-

ported by, 121–22; polls show Roosevelt leading, 130; changes on Hoover food plan, 141; on Lend-Lease, 154; on intervention, 197, 273; on shoot-on-sight, 197; on Neutrality revision, 197, 239, 241; on Iceland, 197, 235; on Russia, 197, 243, 248; on arming merchantmen, 197; on Selective Service extension, 197–98; effect on FFF, 198; on convoys, 234, 237; on France, 251; on declaration of war, 261–62; mentioned, 104
Publishers, in Century Group, 63–64

Questionnaires, 133–34

Radio, FFF use of, 179, 180
Rand, James H., Jr., 220
Randall, Clarence B., 170
Randolph, A. Phillip, 168, 183–86 *passim*
Rayburn, Speaker Sam, 213
Read, Conyers, active in forming FFF, 164; intervention as a last hope, 223; mentioned, 169, 170
USS *Reuben James,* 242, 261
Reynolds, Senator Robert, 154
SS *Robin Moor,* 194, 235, 237
Rockefeller, John D., 177
Rockefeller, Laurence D., 177
Rockefeller Center, Harlem Division in headquarters at, 185; mentioned, 169–70, 175
Roosevelt, Mrs. Eleanor, cooperates with FFF, 202; receives FFF delegations, 204n, 229; mentioned, 180, 232n
Roosevelt, President Franklin D., supports World Court membership, 16, 23; founds Wilson Foundation, 17; influenced by Mahan, 18; foreign policy views and actions 1920–39, 23–26; and League of Nations, 23–24; and Japanese, 24, 196–97, 255, 264–65; and Neutrality Act, 24, 26, 239, 241; "Quarantine" speech, 25; accelerates defense preparations, 25–28 *passim;* and Soviet Union, 27, 195, 245, 249; names National Defense Advisory Commission, 28; appoints Stimson and Knox, 28–29; seeks release of modern planes, 29; policy in 1940–41 conditioned by public opinion, 30–31; sees Herbert Agar, 54; prior relationship with Group members, 57–61 *passim;* has Sherwood draft speeches, 64; and destroyer-bases agreement, 84–89 *passim,* 97–99, 103–6 *passim;* relations with Group in fall 1940, 110, 113; and 1940 election, 126, 129–31; indecisiveness after election, 132, 134; sends Willkie to Britain, 133; rejects negotiated peace, 144; "Arsenal of Democracy" speech, 149–50; State of the Union Address, 150–51; and Lend-Lease, 151; FFF stresses solidarity with, 181; policy, April-December, 1941, 191–97; "Unlimited National Emergency" speech, May 27, 1941, 193–94, 199; and shoot-on-sight policy, 194, 198; petitioned by Virginians, 198; urged to seize Atlantic islands, 199–200; relationship with FFF, 201–6; and Italian-Americans, 219; on convoys, 234, 237; and Iceland, 236; on Vichy, 251; and war declaration, 259–60, 262; Sherwood requests ad on his behalf, 264–65; Hawks may have embarrassed, 270; and conversion to internationalism, 276; Roosevelt or his administration mentioned, vii, viii, 20, 38, 50, 51, 52, 53, 56, 58, 59, 60, 66, 74, 75, 85, 91, 95, 100, 106, 107, 125, 131, 147, 152, 155, 211, 221, 229, 233, 270n, 272. *See also* White House
Room 2940, operation of, 76–78; circulates materials, 121–22; material on Hoover food plan, 130; material on Irish bases, 148; mentioned, 101, 113, 114, 124
Roper, Elmo, 122
Ross, Charles, 115–18
Rosenfield, Abe, 181–82
Rosenman, Samuel, 64, 151
Rublee, George, 97

Rumely, Edward A., 220
Ryti, Risto, 252

Sachs, Alexander, 145
St. Louis, FFF show in, 229; FFF chapter, 268; mentioned, 170, 171, 244
St. Louis Post-Dispatch, editorial on "Summons," 39; article on interventionism, 115–18
Salaries, FFF, 177
Sanctions, against Japan and Italy, 17
Sandburg, Carl, 179
San Francisco, shipyard strike, 181–82; FFF chapter, 267; mentioned, 244
Scammon, Richard, 225
Schrembs, Archbishop Joseph, 147
Selective Service, bill, 93; extension, 206, 232n–33n
Senate, U.S., attack on Group in, 115–18; on Lend-Lease, 153, 155; investigation of film industry, 215–19; and Neutrality revision, 239–42; mentioned, 58, 76, 233n. *See also* Congress, U.S.
Seymour, Charles, 149
Shafer, Representative Paul W., 106
Shepardson, Whitney H., involved in Moffat appointment, 33–34; drafts and signs "Summons," 34, 37; biographical data, 57; drafts memo with Douglas, 75–76; leaves Group, 113, 114; and Ross article, 115; mentioned, 32, 43, 48, 56, 68
Sherwood, Robert E., publishes ad, 38; biographical data, 64; leaves Group, 113; on Hoover food plan, 136, 139; opposes supplies for France, 142; and "Arsenal of Democracy," 150; asks ad for Roosevelt, 264; in World War II, 267n; mentioned, 66, 69, 144, 145, 151, 152, 155, 201–4 *passim,* 234, 242, 245
Sherwood, Mrs. Robert E., 113, 178, 264
Shipstead, Senator Henrik, 8, 115
"Shoot-on-sight" policy, 194, 207, 211, 221, 235–41, 259
Short, Representative Dewey, 80
Shotwell, James, 20–21
Silver Shirts, 14, 120
Singer, Max, 230, 240
Skouras, Spyros, 170
Smith, Alfred E., 21
Smith, Paul C., 182
Smith, Robert Aura, 255
Smith "right-to-work" bill, 183
Social gospel, 8–9, 48–49
Social Justice, 11, 12, 270n
Soviet Union, U.S. policy toward, 26–27; invasion of, 95, 242, 244–46; British convoys to, 194; aid to, 207, 232, 242–49; threat from, 276; mentioned, 59, 172, 224, 251–52, 254, 257, 270
Spain, 24, 79, 198
Speakers bureau, of FFF, 178–20
Special interests appeals, 176, 189
Spence, Charles M., quoted, 36
Spivack, Robert, on Communist support, 243; drafts ad on Japan, 258; mentioned, 185, 247
Staff talks, involving U.S., Britain, Canada, Netherlands, 192
Stalin, Joseph, 13, 15, 27, 243–46 *passim,* 251. *See also* Soviet Union
Standley, Admiral William H., signs "Summons," 37; biographical data, 65; speaks on destroyers, 92; in FFF, 202; mentioned, 43, 48, 70, 168
Stark, Admiral Harold R., views on destroyer transfer, 83–84; approves deal, 104; mentioned, 258
Stassen, Governor Harold E., 152
State, Department of, and food plan, 135; and France, 250; assailed by FFF, 255–56, 257; mentioned, 59, 196
Sterling, Admiral Yates, Jr., 79
Stevenson, Adlai E., 212
Stimson, Henry L. supports Neutrality revision, 21; appointed to cabinet, 28–29; approves Alsop work, 82; in cabinet debate, 88; on legality of destroyer transfer, 98; mentioned, 38, 74, 81–84 *passim,* 107, 194, 198, 202n, 232n–33n, 237
"Stop Hitler Now" campaign, 226, 227–28

Stout, Rex, as FFF speaker, 179; assails Lindbergh, 209; in "V" campaign, 227; mentioned, 145, 168
Streit, Clarence, 20
Stuart, R. Douglas, Jr., 118
Student Defenders of Democracy, 114, 123, 157, 169, 188
Sullivan, Mark, 244
"Summons to Speak Out, A," draft, arrangements and response to, 34–38; impact of, 38–40; text of, 278–79; mentioned, vii, viii, 45, 49, 54, 57, 58, 59, 62, 65, 80, 92, 162, 164, 244, 271
Swope, Herbert B., 140, 162, 174, 175

Taft, Senator Robert A., 30
Talmadge, Governor Eugene, 183, 224
Taylor, Edmond, 179, 212, 267n
Thacher, Thomas, 97
Theater, Radio and Arts Divisions, FFF, 228–29
Third Reich, 76. *See also* Germany
Thompson, Dorothy, and Kennedy resignation, 127; attacks Lend-Lease opponents, 155; mentioned, 77, 145, 244
Thorkelson, Representative Jacob, 8, 213, 254
Tinkham, Representative George, 106, 213
Tobey, Senator Charles W., 192, 217
Tobey resolution, 234, 237
Tobin, Dan, 170, 179–82 *passim*
Tojo, General, 256
Total war, concept of, 275–76
Trail-and-report orders, 233
Tripartite Pact, 62n, 265, 266
Tucker, Henry St. George, 137–40 *passim*

Umhey, Frederick, quoted, 245–46
United States, foreign policy, 1933–39, 24–27; need for mobilization, 72–73; government actions April-December, 1941, 191–97; interest in German defeat, 278–79
United States Army, 28, 30
United States Army Air Corps, 28
United States Navy, assessment of strength of, 18, 260; expanded responsibilities of, 26, 95n; protection of Britain by, 29, 75, 92, 95; trails and reports subs, 192; action in the Atlantic, 194–95; convoys British ships, 236; hostilities sought in Pacific, 255; at Pearl Harbor, 263–64; mentioned, 28, 45, 56, 59, 60, 72, 82–84, 233
"Unlimited National Emergency" speech, FFF and, 198–99; mentioned, 221, 237
Union for Democratic Action, 22

"V" campaign, 226–27
Vandenberg, Senator Arthur H., 30
Van Dusen, Henry Pitt, urges sustained effort, 40; informs Lothian of Group, 41; biographical data, 48–50; suggests fleet guarantee, 85; arranges speeches by Britons, 94; liaison to Protestants, 111; on a "committee of national safety," 161; and "Unlimited Emergency" speech, 199; mentioned, 61, 69, 75, 158, 165, 169, 170–71
Versailles, treaty and conference, 4, 5, 21, 43, 57–59 *passim*
Vichy, 232. *See also* France
Viereck, George Sylvester, 214, 215

Wadsworth, Representative James, 152
Wallace, Vice President Henry A., 202, 204, 213
Waller, William, 80
Walsh, Senator David I., 12, 98, 115, 248
Walsh amendment, 83–84, 87, 98
Wanger, Walter, biographical data, 64–65; on Kennedy, 126; mentioned, 69, 70, 216
War, Roosevelt says no foreign, 130; undeclared, in the Atlantic, 195; declaration of, campaign for, 230, 232, 258, 259–62, 265; against Italy, 265; declaration of, mentioned, vii, 33, 43, 169, 171, 270, 279
Warburg, James P., biographical

data, 57–58; seeks business support, 121, 124; writes pamphlet, 122; talks to Roosevelt, 131; drafts letter to Congress, 150; drafts FFF Declaration, 161; on Atlantic islands, 199–200; on interventionism, 223–24; in World War II, 267n; mentioned, 56, 68, 70, 144, 165, 169
Warhawks, definition of, vii; biographical data, 45–71. *See also* Century Group, Fight For Freedom Committee
Warner, Edward P., 32
Washington, D.C., FFF show in, 229; FFF chapter, 247
Watson, General Edwin M. ("Pa"), 52, 201–4
Watson, T. J., 153
Waymack, W. W., 77, 134
Weeks, Edward M., 149
Weeks, Sinclair, 170, 171
Weems, Parson, quoted, 6
Weill, Kurt, 229
Welles, Sumner, 26, 27, 97, 258
Western Progressives, 7. *See also* Populism
Weygand, General, 279
Wheeler, Senator Burton K., and peace offensive, 143; on Lend-Lease, 152, 154; FFF attacks, 212–13; reveals Iceland plans, 212, 213; and franking abuse, 213–14; and film investigations, 216–17; right to speak defended, 225; mentioned, 8, 201, 274
Wheeler-Bennett, John, 139, 201
White House, and the Group, 66–67, 144, 152; welcomes Kennedy assistance, 126; relationship with FFF, 201–6; visited by FFF women, 229; told of war declaration drive, 260; mentioned, 52, 64, 105, 113, 176, 207, 238, 272
White, Edward, 184, 186
White, Walter, 171
White, William Allen, seeks Neutrality revision, 20–21; organizes CDA, 22; and draft, 79; and Roosevelt, 87, 89; policy differences with Group, 79, 156–57; surveyed, 133–34; resigns, 175; mentioned, 15, 78, 107, 163
William Allen White Committee. *See* Committee to Defend America by Aiding the Allies
William Allen White News Service, attacked by isolationists, 115–18; mentioned, 56, 85, 100–2
Wickard, Claude, 202
Willkie, Wendell L., favors aid short of war, 30; and destroyers, 51, 86–89 *passim*, 94–96, 106–7; acceptance speech, 55, 102–3; Group and, 67, 133; and Republican isolationism, 79–80; addresses Chicago rallies, 124, 212; in 1940 campaign, 130–31; supports Lend-Lease, 152, 153; and FFF, 164, 179; calls Lindbergh speech "unAmerican," 211; represents film industry, 217; on "V for Victory" theme, 227; mentioned, 50, 74, 75, 85, 114, 153, 180, 183, 204, 219, 229, 272
Williams, Michael, 114, 147–48, 248
Wilson, Charles E., 124
Wilson, M. L., 32
Wilson, Woodrow, quoted, 6–7; as internationalist hero, 16; mentioned, 5, 23, 45, 58, 229, 269
Wilson, Woodrow, Foundation, 17
Winchell, Walter, 225
Women, British, 94; mentioned, 141, 273
Women's Committee for Action, 114, 122–23, 152, 157, 188
Wood, General Robert E., preaches accommodation, 121; and peace offensive, 143; FFF attacks on, 220–22, 225; mentioned, 118, 153, 211
Woollcott, Alexander, 179, 210
World Court, 16–17
World War I, 46, 57, 60–63 *passim*, 65, 68, 93
Wriston, Henry, 33–34
Writers, 139, 141, 142

Yalta Conference, 275
Yarnell, Admiral Harry C., 79
York, Sergeant Alvin, 179
Young, P. B., quoted, 186
Youth, appeal to, 188–89, 273

Derso and Kelen
CANADA
CAPE VERDE
DAKAR
USA
CANAL
PANAMA
AZORES
MARTINIQUE
BRAZIL

U.S.A.
Derso and Kelen
FIGHT FOR FREEDOM RELEASE